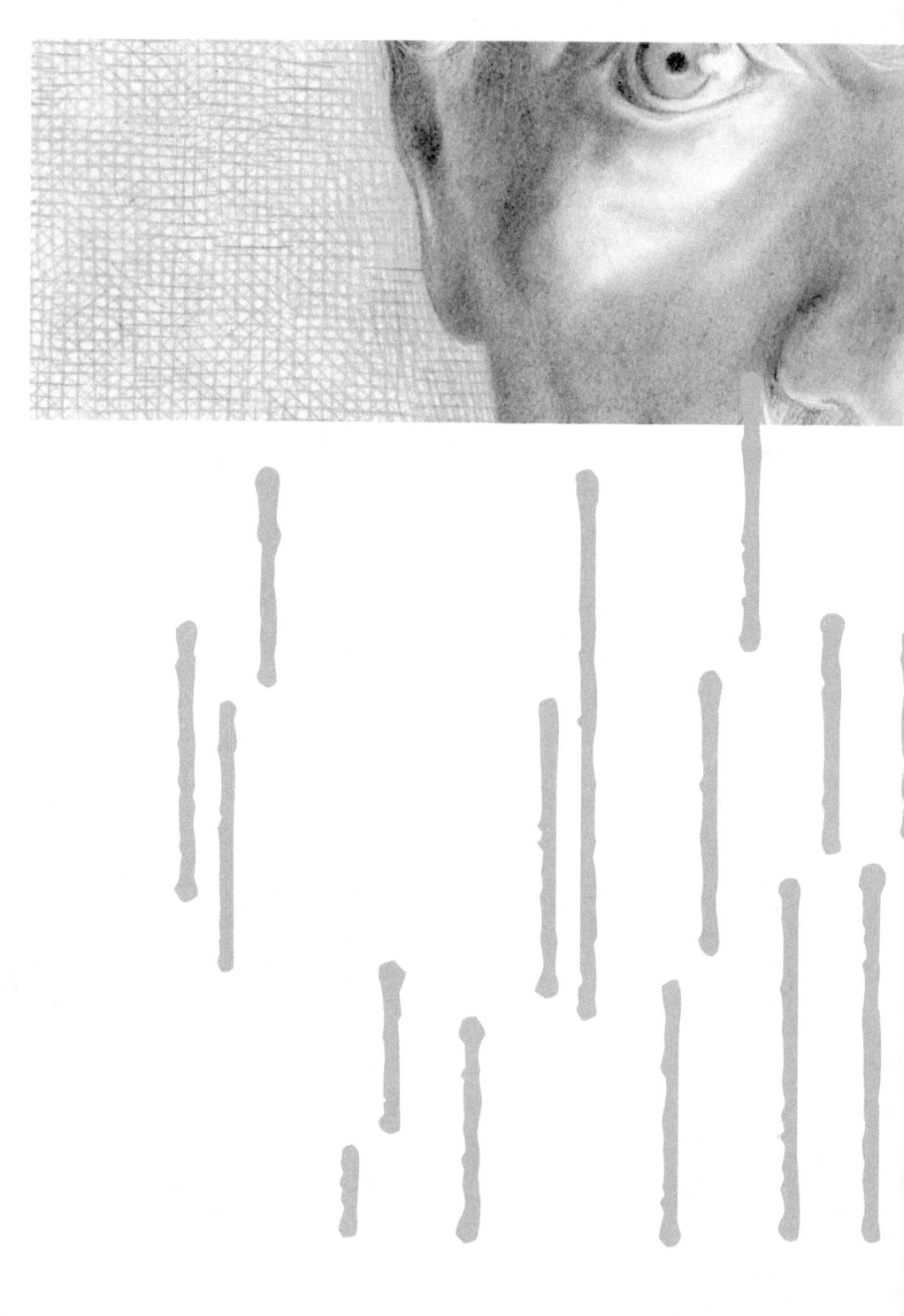

A CITY FULL OF VOICES

ESSAYS ON THE WORK OF ROBERT KELLY

Edited by Pierre Joris
with Peter Cockelbergh & Joel Newberger

Contra Mundum Press   New York · London · Melbourne

Preface © 2019 by Pierre Joris, Peter Cockelbergh, and Joel Newberger; essays © 2019 Contra Mundum Press and each individual contributor.

First Contra Mundum Press edition 2019.

All Rights Reserved under International & Pan-American Copyright Conventions. No part of this book may be reproduced in any form or by any electronic means, including information storage and retrieval systems, without permission in writing from the publisher, except by a reviewer who may quote brief passages in a review.

Library of Congress Cataloguing-in-Publication Data

A City Full of Voices: Essays on the Work of Robert Kelly / Pierre Joris, Peter Cockelbergh, Joel Newberger, eds and Preface.

—1st Contra Mundum Press Edition
626 pp., 6 x 9 in.

ISBN 9781940625348

I. Joris, Pierre; Cockelbergh, Peter; Newberger, Joel.
II. Title.
III. Preface.
IV. Joris, Pierre; Cockelbergh, Peter; Newberger, Joel.

2019952613

TABLE OF CONTENTS

0–VI	PREFACE
VII	FRONTISPIECE: Phong Bui
0	Gerrit Lansing	"Sombre Fulguration"

       THREADS 13: ROBERT SAYS   4

1. A BOOK OF IMAGES REVISITED

8	Charles Olson	Response to Robert Kelly's "Notes on the Poetry of the Deep Image"
9	Robert Creeley / Jerome Rothenberg	Exchange on Deep Image
16	Denise Levertov	An Argument. In Response to *Trobar* #2 Kelly's "Notes on the Poetry of the Deep Image"
19	David Ossman	Comments on Montage
22	Stan Brakhage	[Two letters]

       THREADS 14: ROBERT SAYS   32

2. A BOOK OF EARLY RESPONSES

36	Paul Blackburn	The American Duende
42	Kenneth Irby	On Her Body Against Time
47	A Letter and a Rattle from Jerome Rothenberg
52	Clayton Eshleman	On *Finding the Measure*
54	Diane Wakoski	On *Songs I—XXX*
57	P. Adams Sitney	My Debt to Robert Kelly

THREADS 15: ROBERT SAYS   72

3. A BOOK FROM VORT MAGAZINE

76	Guy Davenport | Kelly in Time
80	Jonathan Williams | Joyous Rodomontade & Instant Remoulade for the Flatbush Flash
82	Theodore Enslin | A Brief Take on R.K.'s *Mill of Particulars*
84	Norman Weinstein | On Robert Kelly's Work of the Morning

THREADS 16: ROBERT SAYS   90

4. A BOOK ON NARRATIVE

94	Christina Milletti | "Getting Word"; The Force of Language in Robert Kelly's Short Fictions
102	Sharon Mesmer | Unfinished Sentence → Unfinished Sentience. Revisiting my Essay "Ordering Emptiness: Robert Kelly's *The Scorpions*"
108	Steven Fama | A Truly Trippy Prose Poem. On *Cities*.
116	John Yau | A Map that Never Stays the Same. On *A Line of Sight*.

THREADS 17: ROBERT SAYS   128

5. A BOOK ON THE OCCULT / KNOWLEDGE

132	Charles Stein | Re: The Occult. Robert Kelly and The Esoteric Traditions
148	Tamas Panitz | A Note on Robert Kelly's *Calls*, and The Island Cycle
152	Sylvia Mae Gorelick | Kelly After Nietzsche: On "Her Voice In All These Years"
164	Alana Siegel | Thoughts on Thread

THREADS 18: ROBERT SAYS   168

6. A BOOK OF READINGS

172   Edward Schelb | Home Movies of the Angels: *Songs I—XXX* and Stan Brakhage's Cinematic Dance
191   Billie Chernicoff | Reading *The Loom*
219   Thomas Meyer | Hieroglyph of This Unfallen World. On *The Convections* (1978) and *The Book of Persephone* (1978)
225   G.E. Schwartz | Of Dromenons, Silences, Sentences, & Emptyings
235   Kimberly Lyons | Falling Flowers: Reading Robert Kelly Reading Li Shang-yin

THREADS 19: ROBERT SAYS   242

7. A BOOK ON LINE AND MEASURE

246   Ron Silliman | What *Measure* Measures: Robert Kelly in the Sixties
262   Jed Rasula | Flesh Dream Books
274   Allen Fisher | Robert Kelly: Facture and Reception in the Field

THREADS 20: ROBERT SAYS   292

8. A BOOK ON HOW TO READ

296   Pierre Joris | A Primer for the Gradual Understanding of Robert Kelly
314   Jennifer Moxley | Charlotte's Cardinal: Some Thoughts on Robert Kelly's Poetry
328   Peter Monaco | "We are all made of stars": the Demands of "Reading" Robert Kelly
349   Peter Cockelbergh | "Day by day. Make it new." On Searching for RK starting points and Teaching *Threads*

THREADS 21: ROBERT SAYS   362

9. A BOOK OF BIRD'S EYE OVERVIEWS

366   Jed Rasula | Ten Different Fruits on One Different Tree
408   Elizabeth Robinson | That Hollow Place Inside the World Just One Word Down
415   Mary Caponegro | Incessantly the Sum

THREADS 22: ROBERT SAYS   426

10. A BOOK OF SPECIFICS

430   Thomas Meyer | The Middle Voice
437   David Levi Strauss | 20 or 30 Things I've Learned From Reading Robert Kelly
442   Michael Ives | East of the Sun, West of the RK: Christic Sections / "Thread 31" Annotations
455   Joel Newberger | Kelly's Consistency
460   Charlotte Mandell | This Island Music

THREADS 23: ROBERT SAYS   466

11. A BOOK OF INTERROGATIONS

470   David Ossman | Interview for *The Sullen Art*
476   George Quasha & Charles Stein | *Ta'wil* or How to Read
509   Clayton Eshleman | 20 Questions for Robert Kelly

THREADS 24: ROBERT SAYS   526

12. A BOOK ON RECENT WRITINGS

530   Barbara Roether | The Island Cycle: Fire Exit, Uncertainties, The Hexagon, Heart Thread, Calls

537   Jordan Reynolds | The Place of Love: Say What We Do to Each Other Goes On

551   George Quasha | Uncertainties: Robert Kelly, *Ta'wil*, and the Poetics of Singularity

570   Billie Chernicoff | On Robert Kelly's *Seaspel*

574   Kush | "Nvame Dreams Ritual"

578   EDITORS

579   LIST OF CONTRIBUTORS

589   ALSO BY

PREFACE

THIS VOLUME is both a continuation of & a complement to *A Voice Full of Cities: The Collected Essays of Robert Kelly* (2014). Rather than sending the reader back to the introduction of that volume, we will pick up bits and pieces of it in the current preface as we go along. We started our companion introduction by suggesting that — unlike the more traditional or academic middle-of-the-road poets, and unlike some of the more recent avant-garde movements such as the Language poets — Robert Kelly belonged to a grouping (with Rothenberg, Antin, Wakoski, Eshleman etc.) for whom the writing of the poem was the central fact, even if, or especially because, these poets took it upon themselves to extend the possibilities of the poem into an (Olsonian, Duncanesque) field that enables it to include essayistic / critical / manifesto-ish modes & moves.

This unfortunately (?) also played itself out in terms of critical writing on these poets' work: though there were & are small or larger reviews of their new books in the so-called little magazines, these are by nature fleeting, disappearing events. More importantly, such little magazine reviews are also an activity these poets considered neither essential (as the career-obsessed middle-of-the-roaders seemed to consider them), nor even *poethical* in view of their claims & desires for an avant-garde experimental life in poetry that would set their practice apart from official verse culture. And so, those official registers have returned the compliment: neither Kelly nor his closest *compañeros & compañeras* have received public acknowledgment — or only very skimpily, "du bout des lèvres" as the French put it — of their work via reviews, essays, or monographs in either the journalistic middle ground of the official culture brokers (NYTBR, TLS, NYRB, LRB, LABR — to cite the most obvious of their acronymic instances), or in the more arcane academic reviews or presses.[1]

---

1. Not that that generation (Kelly, Rothenberg, Antin, Eshleman, Wakoski, Economou, etc.) are exceptions. The "Collected" volumes of poetry or essays by major non-mainstream poets such as Olson, Creeley, Duncan still await reviews in the likes of the magazines mentioned above, while a mass of middle-of-the-roaders with 5 or 6 slim volumes as their life work will take up whatever minimal space is left to poetry reviews just there.

This, however, does not alter the stance of the poets in question — or Robert Kelly's in this case. In fact, it may induce a reflection on the nature of the critical & journalistic enterprise of reviewing & evaluating poetry. Thus in the mid 70s RK himself announced a turn away from traditional "literary criticism" toward what he called the "deictic," which he defined as follows: an "act of criticism [that] means to represent a new possibility, not a Criticism but a Deicticism, deictic (Greek *deiknumi*, I demonstrate, rather than *krino*, I judge). This new or deictic possibility means to gesture towards, walk along beside, assert ontologies, abstain from evaluations, prestiges." An open gesture that shows & accompanies the work it reads. It seems to us that it is exactly toward this kind of deicticism that our contributors are moving, or developing the traditional review (as still present in the earliest responses to RK's work, which were indeed "book-reviews" in a more or less traditional sense)[2] with such a nonjudgmental consideration of the work in mind.

An underlying question to ask here is, of course, how such acts (i.e. of writing / reading) fare in the Heisenbergian universe of relativity in which the action of observing (i.e. reading) influences, changes, slants what is being observed (i.e. writing)? Or could the work of art be a mirror universe of the work of the real, where what is changed is not what is observed but rather the one who observes? One of us has for more than 50 years now remembered a comparison Robert Kelly spun out during a 1968 gathering of students, in which he rhetorically asked what the perfect cover for a pop or rock album would be. Baffled, we kept our silence, and Robert gave his answer: a mirror, he said, because what you look for in this music is a reflection of yourselves, a recognition, identity, sameness. (He used the example of the popular music of the time, but today it could also apply to the poetries coming from the mass of popular creative writing programs, as well as to the more critically esteemed official verse culture productions). And then Kelly went on to

---

2. If the editors decided to include an early Denise Levertov review, in which she is somewhat critical of Deep Image, it is to show just that — especially since the ensuing reactions, such as Paul Blackburn's, are all the more interesting in that they discuss precisely how the new is not easy to come through, requiring, as it does, a more open, i.e. nonjudgmental consideration.

PREFACE

say something along these lines: Art is the exact opposite of this self-recognition, this sameness. Engagement with art — be it poetry, music, whatever — is what changes you into something you were not, did not know you could be. Or as one of us would phrase it later in his classrooms, after retelling just this "Kelly story": "Art makes a difference — in you, & thus in the world. That is its *raison d'être*." It is this Heisenbergian mirror-effect that writing about (reading) transformative poetry needs to bring to the fore, & is, we believe what RK's "deictic" responses entail.

A slightly more "esoteric" (or maybe, in truth, "exoterising") shared reading practice is furthermore developed in several of the essays via the Sufi concept of *ta'wil* as "exegesis of the soul" first proposed by Henry Corbin, picked up by Olson & Duncan, & then deepened & expanded simultaneously by Charles Stein & George Quasha in their 1974 conversation with Robert Kelly on exactly "How to Read" the *Loom*. On the other hand, there are other, just as valuable approaches to Kelly's work as that demonstrated by one of us in his retelling of teaching Kelly's work to a class of Belgian high-schoolers. That oldest of complaints — "there's too much Kelly to know where to begin & how to start talking about the work" — is primarily an excuse: you can enter anywhere, open any of the (yes, 80+) books & get started. We hope that the very variety of the contributions gathered here is proof of exactly those possibilities. Maybe one could therefore detum RK's 2-liner from *Seaspel* — "Write more than you know / to know more than you write" — & make it say: "Read more than you know / to know more than you read."

*

As already indicated by the title and subtitle, this volume reflects a slightly aslant mirror structure of the first volume, both in terms of the 12 specific "books" that make up *A Voice Full of Cities* and in terms of the *THREADS* sections which are a direct continuation & link (hence the first THREAD in this volume is 13). In that sense, the editors of *A Voice Full of Cities* had carefully assembled 12 books that combined respect for a broad chronological focus with a concentration on key concepts derived from RK's poetry and poetics. The same holds for the present volume, for which the editors have also assembled 12 books that combine a broad chronological focus (in the first three books, and then in the final book, "Book 12: Recent Readings," especially), with one on key concepts that traverse both volumes (such as books 1, 4, 5, 7 and 10, dealing with, respectively, image, narrative, the occult / knowledge, line & measure, and "everything else," here interpreted as "specifics"). A third focus, however, constitutes a multiperspectivalist approach of RK's poetry and poetics itself: whether early responses (book 2), readings (book 6), how to read (book 8), or bird's eye readings (book 9), they are all, as said, open gestures that show & accompany the work they read.

Picking up our cue from the tantric weavings of *The Loom*, as well as from one of Kelly's syntactically experimental books of poems, *Threads*, we had woven 12 *THREADS* across the first volume of collected essays, *A Voice Full of Cities* — and have continued this weave in the companion volume of critical essays on RK's work. These new 12 sections of *THREADS* — in which "Robert says" — consist of various interview excerpts that directly, or indirectly, speak to the "books" they precede & to the other *THREADS* they are woven into. As in volume 1, the editors have used Kelly's words only.[3] In this way, both volumes together offer the reader not only a "collected" & "critical" essays, but also a *"SELECTED INTERVIEWS."* This holds for the present volume especially, as the editors have chosen to dedicate a single book — Book 11 — to three landmark interviews with Kelly in full, that also mark three different moments in time: 1963, 1974, & 2007.

The 24 *THREADS* furthermore signal one way in which *A Voice Full of Cities* & *A City Full of Voices* speak to each other, indeed,

---

3. For the *THREADS* of this volume, the editors made use of the following interviews: Joshua Stolle, "An Interview with Robert Kelly" (ca. 1970s); James Stalker, "Interview" (ca. 1980); Dennis Barone, "Nothing but Doors: An Interview with Robert Kelly" (early 1980s); Larry McCaffery, "A Rose to Look at: An Interview with Robert Kelly" (1988); Bradford Morrow, "Robert Kelly: *Conjunctions* Interview" (spring 1989); Bonnie Langston, "Interview with Robert Kelly for the Kingston *Freeman*" (July 13, 1994); Simone dos Anjos & Pietro Aman, "*The Modern Review* Interview" (2006); Mark Thwaite, "Robert Kelly *ReadySteadyBooks* Interview" (2006); Sam Lohmann, "*Peaches & Bats* Interview with Robert Kelly" (April 2007, published Winter 2008); Leonard Schwartz's *CrossCultural Poetics* "#93 Listening Hard" (2005), "#99 Red Actions" (2006), and "Path & Counterpath" (2009).

PREFACE

overlap & fold into one another — as indicated by their titles & internal structural organization as an assemblage of "books." A key topos in his poetry & poetics, Kelly's voice thus literally opens up on a myriad of cities the reader is invited to visit & explore.

The editors of this volume again wish to thank loudly and deeply a number of friends: first of all, the many RK *compañeras* & *compañeros* who have so generously contributed to this volume, and who have shown us great patience during the editing process. Secondly, to Alessandro Segalini for his typesetting efforts, and to Rainer J. Hanshe, for his support & precise understanding still, and for backing a second time a project of this scope. And finally, to Robert Kelly, for saying it all, for writing everyday… Un très grand merci to you all, as this book could not exist without you, and your generosity.

Brooklyn, Manhattan, & Lille, June 2019

GERRIT LANSING

SOMBRE FULGURATION

a poem occasioned by 2 lines of Olga Orozco's

for Robert Kelly

Reconocía en ellos distantes mensajeros
de un país abismado con el mundo bajo las altas sombras
  de mi frente.

I.

    compel an eerie recognition
                              it does
          half awake   in first sunlight
          memories of other beds

                      voices whispering

"sultry fulgurations" from "Esthetique du Mal"

    shadows slowly drifting on the coverlets

    winds rock the house

                  dispelling

        dark the messengers

from a land abysmed with the world under

                my head's high shadows

    ancient players of an ancient game

o

II.

we are how many

        underneath one's face

    low personages

        tumbling a destiny

we never guess to be one's own

    golden thread

        a threatening .

Were warned you were

    against the water   weird water

        black and green.

No passwords for opening the cave.

III.

Beholden

    the big invisible peach is here.

    makes you nervous,   proximity

    of stunning holes or clutches.

SOMBRE FULGURATION

Sand falling from the sky

    a sudden clangor disturbing the picnic.

No matter what   no matter what

    the loopy messengers deserve our welcome

    flying high and low   curious in curve.

THREADS 13: ROBERT SAYS

from: *The Will of Achilles*

25.
Can't thought get further?
Is an image an answer?

In India the wisest one
held up a flower. Smiled.

This happened so long ago
every century or so someone remembers

and writes it down
as if it had just happened. The sea

he thinks is not an image,
it is one long forgetting

wide deep chill and everything goes down.
If the sea were only one thing

what would it look like?
Patroclus lying dead at his feet?

*

You think of Olson as such a strong vocabularied man, and yet if you look at the opening words, Olson's lines almost always begin with "the," "a," "of," "to," the very, very weak beginning, and the lines then are really shooting up, each one shooting up, starting from zero and becoming. I'm not saying this is true in every case because I haven't ready every Olson poem this way, but I notice how different his is from Duncan's work, which begins strongly. Every line tends to have a very powerful beginning with a tendency for him even to bear a particular kind of word stress which you can hear from reading, not just in vocabulary, but in his actual articulation of it. So you can force a Duncan poem to sound like an unDuncan poem, just by shifting the word stress to the second word in the line. He's doing a sonnet now, made entirely of monosyllables, so that it begins with monosyllables. Cinematic seems to be a word that I could use to describe lots of "the's," and "a's," and "of's." You begin reading it pretty easily but the sixth or seventh line, and certainly by the whole sestet, it's no longer clear where the sentence stress should be. The words really occur almost in isolation, so that the reader's tendency toward a fluent articulation of them is baffled. I think that's interesting, because he's doing there with stress what I'm doing in the sentence with phrasing and syntax. But at any rate, this business of a weak line beginning or a strong line beginning seems to have a lot to do with the nature of that voice, the poet's identity. I think my tendency is to have a weak beginning of the line, which I then sometimes revise differently, but I notice in looking through my notebooks how many lines begin in that sense weakly, and that is the line as an uphill poem. I like to tell myself stories that people coming from a kind of Judeo-Christian-Puritan tradition always begin with a whole and rise from there. Trying to meet Christ at the end of history would be laying the Messiah at the end of the line. Whereas people with a more balanced or secular or less neurotic childhood would begin more strongly balanced, and the line will run this way. Duncan, I think, is a good example.

in conversation with James Stalker
[ca. 1980]

1.
A BOOK OF IMAGES REVISITED

> Both at the time of its birth and when it is in full flight, the image within us is the subject of the verb to imagine. It is not its direct object.
>
> Gaston Bachelard, *Air and Dreams*

CHARLES OLSON

RESPONSE TO ROBERT KELLY'S
"NOTES ON THE POETRY OF DEEP IMAGE"

not imageS but IMAGE

ROBERT CREELEY & JEROME ROTHENBERG:

EXCHANGE ON DEEP IMAGE

San Geronimo Miramar Patulul, Such.
Guatemala, CA. November 6, 1960

Dear Jerry,

Thank you very much for the copy of your book — which seems to me very handsome & clear. Thanks too for the copy of Robert Kelly's notes. As yourself, I find them interesting. I think, however, that this concept of "image" becomes very generalized, i.e., generalizes, pretty quickly. E.g., "The clothed percept is the image." This is too vague for me, since I feel that speaking, or writing, itself becomes a "percept" and in this guise a deep influence on the "thing said."

 More particularly, as a contrast, read Williams' notes on Zukofsky at the back of *A*, i.e., Williams speaks of his own sometimes bewilderment at Z/s intent, i.e., "The poems whatever else they are are grammatical units intent on making a meaning *unrelated* to a mere pictorial image." I know that Kelly has more in mind than that, i.e., "pictorial image," and yet I feel he consciously or not uses the "picture" as base term from which his sense of "image" derives. That is, I feel he means all to be shaped to the term of an "image" (picture), the "verbalized image" as he says. In my own sense, there is an "image" in a mode, in a *way* of statement as much "image" as any reference to pictorial element, e.g. the white night, the color of sorrow, etc. Pictorial image there relates of course as any other element, but to my mind not as importantly as rhythm, or the structure in which rhythm may operate freely — as a "poem" etc. Again as a parallel to these concerns, Zukofsky writes apropos some poems sent him: "[one is best] when the analysis comes thru the lyrical; the danger of *The Woman* and *The Plan* is that the analysis sometimes becomes melodramatic: on the other hand, getting an image by something like the privation of it or transformation of it thru the physiology of the sound & cadence counteracts it — the melodrama..." It is that Kelly describes all this question of mode too briefly, i.e., "The image is the measure of the line. The line is cut to fit it..." Of course, but in quite what sense?

Isn't then the image as much that cut, of line, as it is what that cut of a line makes, of a reference, pictorial or otherwise? That's where I tend to wander. I cannot agree to that which does not place great emphasis upon structure — in all possible reaches, certainly in Kelly's also — and so again feel the problem which something even as careful as this seems to lead to. For example, take the discussion of that line from your own poem, in which he drops the "No!" i.e., the first word in the line, in this case syllable, itself an exclamation, and so obviously of some inevitable weight in the whole term of said line.[4] I at least wondered, i.e., what is a "line" if you can drop such a word, and then calculate its measure. I don't follow that.

But I don't want to spend the whole letter with such apparent quibbling, i.e., you'll see simply enough wherein I am bothered — and why I can't quite agree.

The whole presence of this sense of image bothers me a little, in present work. I hope I understand what lacks, as Robert Bly might speak of them, are pointed out — but I don't honestly feel them as a lack, and/or believe poetry to encompass a great many manners and emphases, from "epic" to "lyric," and feel of course that in each a dominance will be aimed at for this or that aspect of the so-called whole. I think translation, dealt with too loosely, has not been able to surmount the problem of logopoeia, and this has made an accumulation of loosely structured poems exciting mainly for their "content," their reference as "pictures" of states of feeling etc. I'd hate to see that generalizing manner become dominant, no matter the great relief of having such information about what's being written in other countries etc. But I wouldn't back an inch off the need for as craftsmanlike poems as possible, not at all meaning "tidy" etc. We are too far along, in many grounds so-called, now, to back off, e.g., from Ginsberg in opening KADDISH sections, to Dorn's long line in THE AIR OF JUNE, to O'Hara's casual line, or Duncan's formal organization of "canto" structure in POEM BEGINNING WITH A LINE BY PINDAR — Olson's MAXIMUS and "field,"

---

4. From the poem, "Invincible Flowers" in *White Sun Black Sun*. The full line reads: "No! Give me plastic flowers, flowers in granite and ice ..." while Kelly in his essay reprints it with the 'No!' omitted.

Williams' late poems, etc. i.e., it seems a bad time to lose sight of those areas. It would make a poet like Corso if he might learn them. It makes Burroughs, in prose, singular in his ability. So ...

I am grateful to see the book, and very happy that you have it out — i.e., it's an interesting beginning in no sense "polite" (for me to say so), and you will take it from there, god knows. Anyhow, figure my worry as follows: that the "imagists" had in mind a sharp registration of an "objective" substance, be it tree or woman's mouth, an avoidance of general words etc. — and that proved dull once accomplished, i.e., the poems got awfully quick and then glib and finally banal in their laconic method — they left a lot out because they could only concentrate upon the "quick picture" etc. Now "image" becomes an involvement with the psychology of reference, what the preoccupation with structure tended to forget (and so became often dry in its lack of "content," simply a machine of manner, etc. — but I wonder if image can be isolated in this way, or if it will not tend to make sensational reference overvalued. This is the aspect of surrealism to me least interesting for example — the scarey parts (however interesting on first contact etc.). Anyhow that's what's on my mind.

All my best to you.

Bob

New York November 14, 1960

Dear Bob,

I appreciate greatly the concern in your last letter about the implications of our speaking of new ways into the poem through image, etc. Since I approach my own assumptions with unrest and deep-down doubts, for you to raise questions from out there will hardly appear as "quibbling" or "picking away." God knows, if we're to bother with anything like the "truth" of what we say — and make it (somehow) a place of meeting — we shouldn't resist the clear, hard statement of our differences, but determine where we now stand to later find each other. In picking up the thread, then, I want to avoid for now trying simply to fit my position to what I read as your attitudes, vocabulary, etc. (doesn't accommodation or equivocation for the sake of agreement only distort and alter what the real point is?) and to attempt rather to let the differences emerge.

You're right that "pictorial image" is not what's in mind (the imagists largely beside the point in this), but something else that may start there only to emerge as different in the poem — i.e. the movement (action) of the poem. I've used the term "deep image" to mark out the difference, and Kelly's revised Notes follow through on this. Definition makes me a little dizzy — feeling the danger, I mean, of being trapped in a (theoretical) limitation too easily arrived at. So, for myself, the method (as in *Floating World*)[5] has been to explain by example (in selection of the poems) and suggestion (in the appended prose-statements). If I try now, it's not as anything final, rather to make the leap and falter, hoping something of value will be reached in the end.

To speak quickly, I connect "deep image" with *perception as an instrument of vision*, i.e. a visionary consciousness opening through the senses, grasping the phenomenal world not only for its outward form (though this also, of necessity) but winning from a compassionate comprehension of that world a more acute, more agonizing view of reality than by rational interpretation, etc. ("Psychology of reference" seems to me to limit the possibilities implied here, which should be left free to develop beyond the closed subjective, etc.)

Even more closely put in "There Is No Natural Religion" and "All Religions are One."

Nor is the idea brand new: Blake (and Smart before him) having practiced something like it before the 19th century — the deep image suddenly there and (even stranger) emerging in open or free forms (not only long-line "biblical" either) — plus an awareness of what the problem was: "If the doors of perception were cleansed every thing would appear to man as it is, infinite. For man has closed himself up, till he sees all things thru' narrow chinks of his cavern."

5. *Poems from the Floating World*: magazine published by J.R. from 1959 to 1963.

And elsewhere:
"How do you know but every Bird
 that cuts the airy way
Is an immense world of delight,
 closed by your senses five?"

So there are really two things here, conceivable as two realities: 1) the empirical world of the naive realists, etc. (what Buber and the hasidim call "shell" or "husk"), and 2) the hidden (floating) world, yet to be discovered or brought into being: the "kernel" or "sparks." The first world both hides and leads into the second, so as Buber says: "one cannot reach the kernel of the fruit except thru the shell"; i.e. the phenomenal world is to be read by us: the perceived image is the key to the buried image: and the deep image is at once husk and kernel, perception and vision, and the poem is the movement between them.

(I don't mean to say, by the way, that there are no other ways of conceiving "the poem": enough to think here of what might be called "deep image poem" or "visionary poem.")

Form, then, must be considered here as emerging from the act of vision: completely organic. Olson too in Projective Verse (tho differently oriented) seems to say the same: why I find it surprising when other projectivists treat it almost as a closed system. But I don't want to get into that, at least not till I've put it in my own terms.

Form, to my mind, is the pattern of the movement from perception to vision: it arises as the poem arises and has no life outside the movement of the poem, i.e. outside the poem itself. (This implies too that the experience of the poet, unlike that of the mystic, is patterned and developmental, i.e. expressive; the mystic, so I'm told, may not even be said to be seeking a vision of reality, but absorption within it — silence rather than speech. But mystics are close to visionary consciousness and are often poets themselves.)

So, two things at least describe for me the "new" imagination beginning with Blake, Whitman, etc.: 1) the idea of perception as an instrument of vision, and 2) of form as organic (a pattern of total movement, inseparable from that movement). So, if you isolate Kelly's statement "the line is cut to fit the images," I would agree that it doesn't hold. No more than to say "the image is cut to fit the line." (But just before that he's said: "the image and the line structure cannot be chosen and built up independently," which makes me tend to read the words you quote differently.)

But I don't want either to simplify the problem of composition by reducing it to automatism, something beyond the poet's will. (What's called "automatic writing" reads to me like confused consciousness rather than any kind of penetration.) While the breakthrough, the real poem, seems often simply to occur ("in a flash of light," Yeats says), the condition of its occurrence, before and after, is that of real freedom, so the poet can control and create. (Imagination, too, must be free to overcome the merely rational order of perception and drive it toward vision.) Even beyond the first emergence, it seems to me possible to break the immediate structure for the sake of heightened vision, to force a deeper opening, etc. Anyway one isn't simply a prisoner of what comes first, since freedom in the poem is total and the exercise of freedom extends beyond the first sighting, etc. But a basic structure — where the poem has come well — seems to me to inhere from the beginning, and to change the patterns of line or sound arbitrarily (i.e. in disregard of vision) is to damage the totality. (Conversely any later re-casting of image would force a change in line, etc.)

To bring it together thus far, the following (roughly) would be the "principles" on which I stand:

> The poem is the record of a movement from perception to vision.
> Poetic form is the pattern of that movement through space and time.
> The deep image is the content of vision emerging in the poem.
> The vehicle of movement is imagination. The condition of movement is freedom.

Having reached here, I'm aware of many specific things still to be said, but feel that to push it much further would be to dam up the possibilities of new development, or open the way really for the imagist banality you spoke of. Huidobro (naming himself a "creationist") saw the genius of the new poetry in its power to create rather than imitate (each poem a new creation, not a copy of nature or of other poems), which seems to me to place a maximum value on the unique differences between poets, as all have different eyes and minds; i.e. the important thing is not to make a school, but to hope for a refocusing of concern toward a "deeper" view, a departure from the merely literal, from the imitation or simple description of experience, a breaking down of perceptual limitations, a sense of urgency and desperation in the assault on reality — all matters of spirit and energy, of inner direction. (I mean here that even beyond "deep image," etc., is the overriding force of Blake's "poetic genius" (daemon) or Lorca's "duende" — simply, perhaps, passion acting on things.)

Other things too I'd like to speak of, many suggested directly by your letter or earlier correspondence with Duncan, Snyder, etc., talks with Kelly, Schwerner, and others here: the role of imagination (the power to freely associate perceptions — probably the main link, or only link, with the surrealists that Bly makes so much of); the question of limiting vocabulary, etc. (I think in terms of an empirical language, not simply the concrete words of the imagists); the difference between deep image and Yeats' symbols. Jungian archetypes, etc.; the important question you raise about "mode" as image; the naming of origins (not only beginning with Blake, but back into ancient texts); etc. etc.

Well, having got started I now take a deep breath and put all else off for a 2nd letter, hoping I haven't taken liberties in writing so much now; only that the questions were real and the desire to get something off held back for too long a time. Write as you can, tho I can't hide that I look forward to more from you. I'll pick this up on my own in a few days, if all goes well.

    Best as ever,
    Jerry

DENISE LEVERTOV

AN ARGUMENT. IN RESPONSE TO *TROBAR* #2
KELLY'S "NOTES ON THE POETRY OF DEEP IMAGE"

An insistence on the need for "deep image" seems to me unnecessary because all real poetry must always contain deep images. When the deep image is consciously sought, the unconscious of the literate modern poet seems to throw to the surface images which pass for deep because they are not strictly bound by rational preconceptions and because they resemble in a vague atmospheric way a whole body of other images made familiar to us in a half-century's literature. But are they really so deep? I at least do not find in them the deep satisfaction, the nourishment, the material for inner development, that I find in the truly archetypal images in fairytales, folktales, and myths, or in the deep images of poets of the past who were not deliberately aiming for depth but rather for clarity and fidelity to their experience.

Many of the poems for which it is claimed that they are a new poetry of the deep image have a certain quality of impersonality; not the austere impersonality of archaic sculpture (for instance) but an impersonality that seems to arise from the poets sharing a conception of what is poem-stuff and what is not — a literary conception akin to what was once believed about "poetic diction." It is from a level of the unconscious very close to the surface that these images seem to have arisen; a level at which memories of other poems are stored; so that too often there is about them the triviality of second-hand impressions, even of clichés. While I may experience certain sensations while reading such poems, I am left at the end of them with only the vaguest feelings, and five minutes later it is hard to remember anything about them.

The attempt to write only on a certain level causes these poets to ignore whole areas of their lives. That gives strength to the poems of Creeley and Duncan, poets so different from each other but clearly head and shoulders above most of their contemporaries? Surely it is 1) their sense of form (especially Creeley) 2) their sense of musical structure (internal harmonics) (especially Duncan) and 3) the fact that their poems arise directly from their actual experiences, the happenings of their lives, and not of one chosen level of their lives but any level. Points 1) and 2) condition point 3) so that their poems are never mere quivering pieces of autobiographical raw material. Duncan and Creeley understand the use of the objective correlative. They each have a coordinating intelligence which correlates impressions. Phanopoeia and melopoeia are subsumed in logopoeia. But what makes their poems convincing is not only their craftsmanship but that sense one gets from them that these poets do not induce "poetic" experiences, and that in any of their poems the objective and the subjective as they experience them exist (as in all our lives they do) in dynamic interplay.

Another result of an exclusive concentration on the deep image is a neglect of form. Kelly's propositions on the rhythm of the movement of images, the rhythm of breath and line, the counterpointing of these images, the acoustics of spaces, etc., don't seem to be manifested in many of the poems he prints. Perhaps the flaw in his thesis — (with parts of which I feel myself in agreement) — lies mainly in these two sentences: "Plucking things from the street or from the unconscious is comparable to the digging of ore," and "Supplying the image in its fullest force is thus partially a function of language." On the one hand he over-estimates the value of this deliberate digging into the unconscious, and on the other he underestimates the function of language by assigning it thus a differentiated function as if the poem could if need be exist without it. *Poems are made with words.* All poets should reread Pound's *A.B.C. of Reading* and some of his essays at least once a year. Indeed, it would be most useful if someone with a press would produce wall-cards bearing key sentences from these works so that poets could hang them about their rooms as "God Bless Our Home" is hung in country kitchens. The poems of the deep image seekers are apt to *remain* prima materia, liquid protoplasm. And academic poems are completely static, petrified. But poems can, and I believe should, become definite bodies, as protoplasm becomes a living and solid creature, and move as such a creature will move in its living.

Kelly says that "only in the native linguistic patterns can the deep image communicate at full strength." But in shutting themselves within a convention, the deep image as they conceive it being regarded as the sole poetic image, these poets lose touch with those patterns and write in a literary idiom.

I believe that the truly deep image comes when it is not pursued. The primary requisite is that the poet have something to say — he should be driven not by the desire to create poems but by the need to create them. And the more that which he has to say relates to his whole self — his dreaming self, his domestic self, his demon-ridden self, his cheerful self, his bad-tempered self, his practical self, his social and his most secret selves, the whole gamut — the more value his poem will have to the reader. (And if the poet does not care whether his poem has meaning for anyone beside himself he has no business putting it into circulation.) Will one deny the deep image to Homer, Dante, and Shakespeare? It is when the whole man is engaged in the poem that poetry has its full power. I am not speaking of statement but of implication — full statement being humanly impossible. And I am the last person to deny the reality of the worlds of dream and vision — I believe that as Jung has said, "everything that acts is actual." But these worlds are parts of a whole, and the soul in its growing finds its illustrations, counterparts, obstacles, and doorways in all the parts.

One word more — is it necessary to "restore a poetry of desperation"? If a poet is desperate he will write desperate poems — or perhaps he will write poems of a ferocious gayety [sic]. But one cannot set out deliberately to restore a poetry of desperation. Where did this poetry formerly exist, by the way? Oh, in many times and places, no doubt — but spontaneously and of necessity.

The Floating Bear #11 (July 1961)

DAVID OSSMAN

COMMENTS ON MONTAGE

(For refs see Eisenstein's *Film Form*)

I.

Using the concept of cinematic montage as a poetic mechanics, it is possible to infer the following as suggested techniques:

1. Basic reconstruction of the event or action in montage fragments: both single words & more complex word / combination / images.
2. Final reconstruction by means of the collision of images and the conflict of their different and separate elements.
3. Determination of the basic images by "free accumulation of associative matter" (SE). That is, a controlled (edited) complex of ideas, words, images: none of which is particularly related to another, except in that *collision* is possible, thereby producing montage and the intellectual *whole* of the poem.

Chinese ideograms are formed from 2 or more "purely *depictive* hieroglyphs" (SE).

"A very important aspect of the poetic form was the way in which words were constructed by setting two separate images side by side, which together suggested a third." And: "In spite of the concreteness of the individual images, the total effect of the poetry is extremely abstract, removed from the particular accidents of time and place." Nicholson in *Firefly in the Night. A Study of Ancient Mexican Poetry and Symbolism.*

II.

Assuming that the poet is concerned with reconstructing (Kelly says "transforming" — there is a distinction) an event, personality, graphic image, aural experience, or any combination of these, he will "verbalize that consciousness (as distinct from his original experience of it) ... offer pictures to represent thoughts." (Ciardi)

The poet must obviously exercise the same control over the images that a film editor does over separate lengths of film, composing a sequence or scene. He must edit: select what comes automatically or subconsciously in reference to the subject at hand and arrange it in some hyper-conscious order. (The pure automatic poetry of the Surrealists is generally unacceptable as true creativity. The advantage to it, and to any cultivated sense of the automatic, is the vivid, startling imagery which often may result: but without adequate controls?)

If the poetic reconstruction is made with fragments from consciousness (indeed, sub-consciousness) and the fragments combined into a montage, the montage will gain complexity with each new "sequence" in collision with the last and the next, and the poem will be one purely of images. (Kelly makes somewhat the same point).

The poem resulting from this construction can be narrative or descriptive in form, or can be *only* a montage, one highly complex whole, as free from considerations of time and space as its images are.

III.

Direct verbalization of words and images evoked by the experience provoking the poem do not preclude *control*. Assuming the innate control when the poem is initially set down, the first revision controls the image material by line-construction, punctuation, etc. *Delineation and Structure of Lines:* the line is a complex image, not a single one. It can exist also as a single image, but that image must bounce off the preceding image (line) dynamically.

Punctuation: or the lack of it, plus the separation of lines into verses gives the poem certain linguistic properties and heightens the image materials. The poet's personal language characteristics should dictate not only the shape of the line-image but the tone (texture) of the punctuation.

Technical Devices: alliteration, assonance, consonance, rime etc. used as taste and intuition dictate.

Other Controls: intuition will offer better choices of words, simple images, will point out the necessity to expand or condense. It is the final governing control.

IV.

Kelly says "transformation" and I use the word "reconstruction" in much the same context. I believe that transformation is the *result* of the poem, obvious to the reader, but not the only consideration of the poet with his material.

That which caused the poem is fragmented in the mind into images. The fragments are reconstructed by means of a montage, thus effecting the transformation.

1. Cause ("inspiration," event etc.)
2. Fragmentation (over a period of time)
3. Reconstruction (with image-fragments)
4. Revision (of 1st draft and succeeding drafts)
5. Finished poem — new experience — transformation — new reality

The Floating Bear # 13 (September 1961)

STAN BRAKHAGE

TWO LETTERS [6]

1.

January 9, 1965

Ah, yes, dear Robert —

you shall hear much from me on THIS matter, postsumptuously... tho' perhaps not all NOW, herein — this being a day of coming down with cold, strapped throat pulling on my brain, etc.

Of all the dictionaries', I think I like Welsh: gwost: best, the clear sense of "a going out": but, as the mouth in its creation of hollow for air intake and THEN "o" expellation with "st" shut out, runs thru most pronunciations of that word, it implies an in AND out going form — "guest," mostly expellation, being perhaps truest Western sound sense at latest, as (D.H. Lawrence's intro to "Bottom Dogs"): "The savage American was conquered and subdued at the expense of the instinctive and intuitive sympathy of the human soul. The fight was too brutal...the heart was broken" ... and/or ... "Once the heart is broken, people become repulsive to one another secretly, and they develop social benevolence... The American senses other people by their sweat and their kitchens. By which he means, their repulsive effluvia. And this is basically true. Once the blood-sympathy breaks, and only the nerve-sympathy is left, human beings become secretly intensely repulsive to one another, physically, and sympathetic only mentally and spiritually." ... etc. And, viz "Western":;

---

6. What follows is the transcription of two letters from Brakhage to Kelly. The original typescripts are kept in the Brakhage Archives and may be found at this location: Robert Kelly Correspondence (1965—1980), Box 20, Folder 1, The Brakhage Archives, Norlin Library, University of Colorado, Boulder. Thanks to P. Adams Sitney for the photo reproductions, and to Marilyn Brakhage for permission to reprint the letters here.

"The deep psychic change which we call the breaking of the heart, the collapse of the flow of spontaneous warmth between a man and his fellows, happens of course now all over the world" (by which: "world": Lawrence meant "Western," knowing little, as nor do I, of The East).

Ah Robert, it is just that I <u>would</u> kindle warmth here, keeping this place by the sweat of its kitchen, ALL its rooms LIVING, nourish its in stincts, make it an into-it place, it is just THAT that makes me avoid "social benevolence" and/or forms of lonely "arabs," etcetera...I read the sense anyway, via fairy-tales (the sense of Western Grimness) that: "Guest COULD be messengers from God" and/or gods and goddesses themselves as of old test...could THUS be other, and not necessarily messengers of The World either. But there is no doubt in my mind that P. Adams brought much good into the house — sense, for instance in my very rejection of him, OF what I'm doing...and, for another instance, via his gift of THE GEOGRAPHICAL HISTORY OF AMERICA OR THE RELATION OF HUMAN NATURE TO THE HUMAN MIND (G. Stein), the SURE sense of heart break's begin again and/or a gain, viz:

"That is what makes politics and religion and propaganda and communism and individualism the saying yes and this is always the same that is because it is the human mind and all the human mind can do is to say yes. Now do you see why there is no relation between human nature & the human mind. Human nature can not say yes, how can human nature say yes, human nature does what it does but it cannot say yes. Of course human nature can not say yes. If it did it would not be human nature.

Saying yes is interesting but being human nature is not interesting it is just like being anything and being anything is not interesting even if you can say anything because the only that is interesting is saying yes. Poor America is it not saying yes, is it loosing the human mind to become human nature. Oh yeah."

The ROUND DANCES (& Trobar & Matter-of-Fact-Chart) arrived this morning's mail; and phrases thereof move immediately into my living — for instance, as of this letter: ALL atmospheres engendered by guests are (as your benevolence, my crabbiness) are dancing partners in the light of the TEMPERament):

> "The birds are in one tree now, neglect, neglect, how many
> > hours blind here in darkness,
> > > afraid to turn the light on,
> > > > not every augury, not any
> > augury worth enduring.

It is a large world you swing, Great Man, and one that has such tempers OF NECESSITY in it...but how CLEARLY you put it: "worth enduring" — beyond any of my a(u)rgur(y)ing. And then how you clarify the "my own" (dog, film, etc.) which has upped and set me these last several years, viz:

> "you are such eyes & in your letter to my wife you write of
> > your "own" self,
> alyssum . which takes its name, it is not madness
> <u>I would be large in commendation of this herb, were I but</u>
> > <u>eloquent</u>"

and then, and lending PURE distinction to those searches I was, phone-wise, making last night to you viz: eyes searching for name-sake among the stars <u>&</u> stars in the eyes (and ears) of The World, and then your:

> "It is your eyes that carry you, you must go with them"

<u>AND</u>:
> "The focusses surround the sight, the world dances
> > between our eyes."

And all of ROUND DANCE: THE ANIMAL (others I've only had time to take in phrases thereof) moves thru me in a dance with Stein's observations on dogs sleeping for distinctions between HUMAN NATURE & THE HUMAN MIND, viz, here:

> "There is no real reality to a really imagined life any more.
> "Nothing I like more than when a dog barks in his sleep.
> "That is a reality that can be known not by listening but by the dog who is asleep and feels like barking, he barks as if he barks and it is a bark

it really is a bark although he is only dreaming. How much does he know that he is barking.

"Human nature moves around and does the human mind move around."

I feel, by copying her here, some prime distinction of your rythmn — ah YES, it is the DIMENSION (as distinct from Stein's flat art)...and now on check that you ARE, yes, playing on my mind's rythmn centers distinctly in ROUND DANCES (as I found envisioning centers shifted one to another with clarity, as of eye shift, in *WEEKS*) these being more of (g)ear shift ((g) there to denote more total body movevolvement, as of rythmnwise) and these do BE, then, yes, CLEARLY DANCES ("Clear, or in the clear, among joiners and carpenters, is applied to the net distance between two bodies, where no other intervenes, or between their nearest surfaces" — Webster's)

Okay,,, this is the next day — cold manifesting itself in knee weakness... THAT tension between brains & pain. Ah, my dream comes suddenly to feelingmind now — the phrase "People, people everywhere/ and not a drop to drink" (memoirs of a disappointed vampire?)....a muggy grey people-moving atmosphere — deadly silent..silent? — NO: a hiss of escaping steam. What were all these people, what was I, doing? I cannot remember.

Last night we had guests: four people came up from Denver, with projector, asking to see films. I called my friend Angelo DiBenedetto over (thank God: One of the four was continually insulting. I showed films, extended graciousness, graySHUSHness, finally shutUPness, friend Angelo patient trying to explain something of 2000 years of western culture to the dissatisfied man with the projector, etcetcrerrrrrrrrrr. Suddenly a strange woman arrives, come searching for Angelo, natch — comes in out (angel sent, I say) of the night. Party breaks up; BUT frayend with projector searches me out (needles-needles every air and not a stitch in time) — I turn on his flapping mouth slooooowly (Actually feeling as if in slow motion) and say: "I'm WARNING you, I have NOT the patience of my friend Angelo to put UP with your kind." He turns white (Jane said even she was frightened to see my face), apologizes constantly for half an hour until I contrive to get him and friends AND projector OUT. Then I let Angelo read your letter; and he reads it aloud to his girl friend, and Jane and I. Somewhere in it he begins to cry; and we all sit around (THAT closeness) feeling deeply moved by the beauty of it, the giving benevolence of it; by I am also moved by the SURE sense that I must contrive, however crudely at first, some means, and meanness if necessary, whereby ONLY the godsent of ANY man can enter these environs, let alone this center (no that center may BE let alone, AS center of my working process need no imposition of morality or other because its environs are goodly, Godly), know the center of, say, this kitchen: that soup bowl: is NO place I care to manipulate a long spoon, that evil thrives on such fascinations, such lure to such tricks as contriving ways and means to eat with the devil, endless nutz and pee tricks, etcetera. This house will be [a?] place for those who come to do the good work, find each his pleasure in himself, a share of godliness with each other. And, ah, yes, we will take in wounded heroes, as I take P. Adams to be ("clean of Europe," yes, but NOT clean of what was given him, NOT chosen by him, to defend there) but in the, from NOW on, sense of: leave your rings at the door, no loaded closed systems allowed, and so forth — "to the end of the world"...which finds its end in each instant of any being right here, wherever any and all are, after all — as IS said and done... ah MEN!

And to help your "crabbiness" a little — bless you for uplift of mine into open clarity — DUENDE is in THIS house, ALL issues thereof, each of which we much look forward to receiving...I have also seen complete collection in Pocatello (you know where!) and three such complete collections in S.F., plus a full supply thereof at City Lights.

 Love,
 Stan

 Ah, God, I could go on for hours. Rythmn centers much differently than visions do in the mind. It seems to me, for instance that any approximation to wave of sound evokes most center sense of hearing but then TOO most inner penetration. A wave-like rythmn, then,

OUTside/inSIDE ultimate in hearing. A direct repetition seems more at surface, as drum, of ear: but a steady flow of variations plus some more middle ground of inner hearing. For instance:

"The birds are in one tree now"

pulls, as if, directly upon the brain cells for association, whereas:

" ,neglect, neglect,"

is a drum bridge at the ear(drum)'s surface TO, as if in answer to, the inner as sociate (that is: if it had been preceded by a wave-like rythmn the reach would have been in t'other direction, viz: OUT.) Taking the next, then, as one large hollow between wave crests ("many" and "darkness"):
"how many
hours blind here in darkness,"

falls (because of direction given by repeat beat TO inner and by hollow of wave, as always, made up of flow) to some innermost rythmn center to pluck at the borders of the subconscious.

Well, but there's a lot of strata I'm leaving out: and I'm leaving off of this, for now, only because I'm sure to start forcing some sense into where I've not entirely sensed. Anyway, you know your work is going a lively ROUND and about this house.

Love,
Stan

2.   December 4, 1979

Dear Robert,

    SENTENCE <u>maximum</u> <u>density</u> is the most thrilling new writ I've seen in a decade (save only Guy Davenport's "Tatlin" and "DaVinci's Bicycle" stories which equally meet my necessities as reader — my eye always out for some equivalent of the light-likeness or 'electrical' movement of mind...what else?); and I am very touched that you sent me this xerox preview, ghosts of fingers holding down the page for passage, that shadowy margin, and all...much thanks.

    "Star fact" or "Star contriving the fact" the secret title of this passage, Jane's formula taking equal numbers of first and last words which'll 'make sense' or "Jane chord" as it has come to be called by Hugh Kenner (who got it from Guy) and is thus known among critics these days as an analytical method — much to Jane's surprise...tho' not mine, as I've long known the importance of her off-the-shoulder commentaries: anyway, I thought you might enjoy trying the Jane-chord on your library.

    When I was living with Robert Duncan and Jess, trying very hard to be a writer ? (as film seemed expensively impossible), the only piece of writing I managed which interested Robert at all was a descriptive passage which used every verb for double energy, so that sentences enjammed and swung there upon 'the action', so to speak'. The effect was, indeed, very cinematic, as Robert recognized immediately — a "montage of language" as he wrote to James Broughton, whom I'd not yet met. I was disappointed in Robert's characterization at the time because it seemed a confirmation of myself as writer-of-movement/cinematographer; but as I came to accept that fate, this moment retrospectively seemed the 'turning point'. All writing since then was essentially devoted to cinema. "Metaphors on Vision" utilized something of this 'montage' technique but only to "X" thought, verbal thought. NOT certainly further it. Thus I'd wondered all these years about some uncertainly field-of-possibilities which I'd, perhaps, only stumbled onto some periphery of... (good place for a dangling, don't you think?) NOW then comes this, or some relative, 'field' in FULL flowering of more possibilities than I could EVER have imagined. It is not just that these words of yours carry multiple associations racking thought back and forth (as is a norm of poetry) but that the sentences MOVE multiply in consideration, thus all thought always thrusting forward, all past tensions moving also forward only and, thus, as superimpositions of MOVEMNT upon any/every instant of the act of reading. And all this with a beseeming effortlessness of unpunctuated language, a rythming which beguiles as song ought, and a 'story' that rivals the simplicity of Tolstoy at his best.

As I come across:
"there is a syntax of these trees "cathected"
"she said and my spirit overstood a law":
I am directed back into Sigmund Freud's "Project for a Scientific Psychology" where I've encountered "cathect" most of any reading I've ever done; and I find there principles of thought process which directly apply to your grammar — that the particularities of any 'bind' of impulse, that the law of affect for memory, "is for certain mammals always true"...that you have spelled it out. (I have set myself the task of reading the complete Freud, Strachey translations, over the next couple years — the "Project" is to be found in Vol. 1).

The Vedas have light coming from sound (The Bible, too, tho' most tend to overlook: "God said"). Certainly there's no more beautiful descript hatching images of light-likeness since *The Cantos* than in this maximum density of yours.

"... a rover for the shining
perschute invisibly glissando on the air"

and then:
"to prise the metaphor right off the wall"
couldn't help but remind me of that portrait I made of you, first of the "15 Song Traits" — still the best 'take' given to me on the creative process.

How more perfectly entertain ""cathected" she said" than with "this conspiracy of light"; and yet as "conspiracy" attaches to the movement of "immortal day" and, of that necessity, to "I give of this," thus also "my peace" distantly echoing "the world," "<u>of light</u>" (my underline) naturally breaks off, from all that previous weight, to "of light to know my mind." It is wondrous. It IS cathexis.

At the very beginning of "Four," at the very instant I'm (of habit) wanting 2nd lines "know" to be "known" you give me the "n" and an, also, "o(h!)" for "o better word to say so." It is miraculous: Your incredible memory, which has always awed me (and often led you into assumptions of reference I couldn't possibly follow) now, herein SENTENCE, put to the task of juggling multiplicity of movement, the most <u>simply</u> thing/ that of ALL thought, the physiological reception and constantly shifting reflexion of and 'reflection' upon all affect.

Is SENTENCE a larger poem, from which this "maximum density" is taken? And what is "Centaur 12"? I mean, whatever it IS, I want ALL of it. Tho' there's no hurry, as I'll be working this thru me for some time to come…perhaps forever.

THREADS 14: ROBERT SAYS

It's not until I read the poem aloud, in the presence of strangers, that I really begin to see what it is and how it works. Reading aloud, even to a private party but all the more so in public, is the best engine of revision I know. So it's important for me, in the act and aftermath of composition. If I were a filmmaker, I would call public reading the 'post-production' phase of the work. I learn so much as I read, alert (after all these years of experience) to the mood of the audience, the look on that one face, whoever it might be, I tend to stare at frequently as I read, taking his or her reaction as fiduciary, a sea-mark for my journey.

in conversation with Simone dos Anjos and Pietro Aman (2006)

Now, at the same time there was the Blue Yak poetry collective and bookstores and other kinds of reading enterprises. There was a whole combine of operations and many little magazines flourishing. All of it was very local, but since it was local in the great city its local had a different kind of importance. Everything must be local to begin with, because it cant begin by being general anywhere. It has to be somewhere and by being local to the great city at its great moment, defining the language and defining the poetic task, the things that people were involved in focused. Some focused through the Black Mountain or the Ashbery and so on. I wanted to stay clear of that. I was continually revivifying myself, I though with the primitive, with the barbaric, with that which comes from outside the culture and every now and then brings life to it again. This is a model that becomes more and more familiar the more history you look at. Everything, then, was local, local and exciting.

It had to do with America. *It had to understand* America *as a single place, a village of ultimate reference, internal reference, so that no reference had to be made. We were all singing to one another. You know, the famous nest of singing birds and since we were all on the same block it wasn't necessary to identify who was on the roof, who was behind the car taking off the hub cap. It was not necessary to identify those people. It wasn't necessary to sing the fact of the condition into presence. I think that's where Sorrentino's* Neon, *Kelly's* Trobar, *Rothenberg's* Floating World *might have some agreements. There are really no relations amongst those other than a kind of shared conviction that* this *is the* place and that what goes on here has to be sung in the place.

When I moved up here [Annandale-on-Hudson, NY] in '61, naturally my connections with those locations in the specific neighborhood sense were broken. Gradually I saw myself and Rothenberg and the rest of them dwindling away from a public center and very much growing into their own work. By that time I was ready to get into my own work and if I wanted to lay down a law it would be that young poets from the time they're 18 till they're 25 should be busy publishing other peoples' work. In every age there are going to be neglected poets. When we came along Zukofsky was immensely neglected, a great poet to whom nobody had ever paid any attention. It was necessary to pay attention.

in conversation with Dennis Barone
[Early 1980s]

2.
A BOOK OF EARLY RESPONSES

PAUL BLACKBURN

THE AMERICAN *DUENDE*

At first, I had intended this as a simple review of Robert Kelly's first book ("Armed Descent," Hawk's Well Press, 1961), but there is so much more material than that available (still) over these two-and-a-half years (1960–62) that I do not think I can limit my discussion to that book alone.

Let me be clear about this from the beginning, so that I shall not have to lead up to it: I know a number of poets under 30 whose works hold intimations of future greatness: no one of these, save Kelly, has already written great poems. And if the evidence of craft in his work to date by the stretch of anyone's critical imagination be called immature, please God may we all live to enjoy the maturing of it.

Touching the organization of the longer poems, it looks at first as if he swallowed Olson's *Projective Verse* like a butter cookie: Pound also very much in evidence. He can handle a short line with an ear approaching Creeley's for truth, but his diction is always very much his own. For instance:

OXHERDING POEM
Ten-pai-nam-k'a, twenty-first of
the twenty-five disciples of
Padmasambhava, tamed wild yaks
of the northern desert.

It is horned.
It moves in snows
and rocks. It
does not run.

By the tail, by
its fringe of hair,
you can't take it.
It is horned.

Ring a bell. The
sound will follow
in snows, over
rocks. Ding ding.

To tame it: not
to catch it. They
come to the bell.
Have a handful

of salts. Its tongue
is very black. It
will take salt, it
also is hungry.

They come. Ding.
The sun shines
six hours a day.
It is horned.

The animals walk through his poems with a distinctness that becomes almost emblematic, the yak, the bear, the lamb, the pig, bats, owls, wildcats, horses, deer, fish and the human animal too, in his relationships, his complexities, disappointments, frustrations. The costs of love, rebirth, compassion, discovery are there, reading the surface or reading under the surface, it is still explicit:

The alchemist
(twenty years over the alembic)
his left hand fisted, snotrag on cheekbone,
who shall weep
       and wake up in the morning
selling flowers in the veins of his arms
crying down the streets jonquils jonquils
the needle stuck in his brain
inventing true north

and toward the end of that poem which is about failure, love, compassion, and waste, the direction or directness comes again:

>   where the streets run north
> roughly but Broadway to the true north
> and asked
>   what corners is he on today with his music?
> He was here yesterday and
> sold daffodils
>   NAME IS LOVE
> movements somewhere in time
> since our own eyes are not still
>
> in the sleepless dark
> to travel with made light
> holds his hand to his face & weeps for the lost struggle

To quote Miss Levertov (in *Floating Bear* on "such poetry"): "While I may experience certain sensations while reading such poems, I am left at the end of them only with the vaguest feelings, and five minutes later it is hard to remember anything about them." What she is backing away from by such an admission is, I think, the very real hallucination possible (call that poetic if you want to) if you read Kelly closely and openly enough to admit the world of the poem. The disparate materials cohere in a way that they must have cohered for the poet at the moment of writing, the organization is so sound that you will float on that lake wherever that storm was to come and believe that:

> [...] a god will come to smell the hairy grass
> and stitch us together
> a perfectly empty blue sky

or in the simple invocation (Spel V of "Thor's Thrush"):

> now the meadow drinks
> now drink I
>
> cup, good cup be full

A kind of mystique of the earth and the things of earth, which we use or waste, and so tie us to ourselves or make us alien to our own lives, persists throughout all of Kelly's work. And perhaps a man's helplessness faced with either. The same image, in fact, used in different poems proves for me at least the validity and clarity of his vision & compassion in this respect: from the poem *Armed Descent* (strangely not included in the book):

> Later I walked under a tree,
> and over the pouring road time
> came back roaring from the sky.
> In summer, there are no bears
> passing empty-pawed in the woods,
> quietly rooting the hollowness
> of things.
>   A winged seed
> of a tree flew to my shoulder
> and I could not give it birth
> or feeding in my flesh. I came
> to all that was left of a farm,
> a stone farmhouse behind the church-
> yard. The lime of its stonework
> burned in the sky.

And from "Sun of the Center":

> the drying leaf the wooden stalk
> hardening from within, brittle
> which stand up out of earth and are wasted
> brown at the edges the color of earth but the impulse
> wasted, the somersault of the seed ended in mid-air
> no ground to fall back to perishing in air
>
> into the hot wind
> that plays over the grains of soil
> and lies down in hot sunlight and is called dog
> and falls over itself in the mountains and is called river
> and spreads out over the earth and is very close to being alive

> but let only him whose body is of earth exist and sing
> the shape of a man proceeds from all sides to center
> and he is the star whose body is called movement
> and in his hands the sun puts out branches
> leaves and petals break out of silver
> the corn is eaten, the animal howls, the sun flowers.

One finds the mind constantly at work and pitch in these poems, but the intellect is far from being the sole recording instrument, and what it works at is form and structure, which would seem to belie statements on "deep image" made both by Kelly and Rothenberg. Kelly's perception is constantly forced by his receiving the world, and it seems not a matter ever of his "reaching for the deep image." Images crowd him as though he were St. Francis and the images birds. It has to be a matter of choosing, or at worst of allowing himself to be forced by them. Presuming some balance between the two. Those images come because, perhaps, they are bidden, because he is gifted with poetry. That much of his theme is helplessness and waste, and how to control our lives and the lives of others without useless destruction (see the "Oxherding Poem" or "The Boar") and with care for the thing-in-itself, seems only to reinforce this view of his method. Like Olson at his most hot, he is barely in control of what assails him. But, in the long poems especially, the pace is slow, so that you can see with what care he clarifies his poem and brings it to you. Don't read it with impatience or it will turn back into itself and go away.

> By the tail, by
> its fringe of hair,
> you can't take it.
> It is horned.

For that objective sense of "the other" let me close this with three more quotes. Does this seem to be getting to be a goddamned anthology? From part II. of "The Exchanges":

> To protect you from the secret, she said,
> that vowels & consonants fuck each other into speech
> which you could not bear
> for not knowing the efficient question

and from a short poem "Outwords" printed also in *Origin 5*, second series:

> Inside the sense of the thing
> the heat of it
> like a picture I have never seen
> rides her white bicycle through tall grass
> at the edge of sight
>
> the heat makes that tremble
> against the clouds
> if she stood in front of my window & raised her arms
> there would be no sky
>
> I am lost in her sense of it
> her hands closing

and from "After Love":

> There it is . watch it with
> its own eyes

Because that interpenetration between poem and reader must take place, I imagine that the many people who perhaps must at first refuse the hallucinating clarity of it will be put down by this poetry. They will find themselves standing about it like so many sentinels locked in themselves like a cloak of darkness, handing out policy slips, and there in the center is this great large world in all its sun and shadow, spreading.

Kulchur #7 (autumn 1962)

KENNETH IRBY

ON *HER BODY AGAINST TIME*

In a conversation with Eckermann on January 29, 1826, Goethe said of the poet:

> as long as he expresses only these few subjective sentences, he can not yet be called a poet, but as soon as he knows how to appropriate the world for himself, and to express it, he is a poet. Then he is inexhaustible, and can be ever "new"...

It is that movement into the world that is so strong a breath out of this book that I don't know finally how to separate the poems and the earth they mingle part of. As Sartre saw Faulkner's novels, like stones or trees, accepted simply because they are there, exist. But the passage of Kelly's book is not of objects, poems, given one by one across the pages — it is the flux, each goes on, comes out, but it is a process of change with the world, going beyond whatever we "accept" of stones, trees, or even angle of sight across the same field. Almost more than any book of poems I know, this is a *whole*, the poems are movements that only flow together: the *book* must be read and gone into, not a poem here, there. It is as if Kelly knew he could not force the flow of his perceptions each time into one poem, but let them come and go as they would, flow to the top, bubble, subside, so that by the end of the book they *are* all there, the facets in all their accurate multiplicity — but no single poem begins even to give them all.

I somehow always see Kelly up there on the Hudson, roaming his back yard, garden, plat of lawn, whatever, that merges, goes right on into the forest out back, somewhere turns down to the Hudson; cutting willow branches, mushrooming, gathering dandelion greens. After Louis Zukofsky, these are the most gratefully *peaceful* poems we have here — but peaceful in no blind or idiot fashion; peaceful as Pasternak is peaceful, because the certainty and affirmation come from what is in the objects of our existence, the *action*, the *flow* that is in them, we are in; and there is no *fight* with what is there.

You are gone into world.
You move in unvisited places & sun moves round you,
no alchemical earth but a
burst of food & flowers
bearing your own darkness,
spring up to sustain me

         ("The first beloved in her flesh")

As he wrote in *Nomad*, Autumn 1962:

> Since we are men, in the human scale of time & space relationships, the discovery is of ourselves through the visible, of the visible through ourselves. The gateway is the visible; but we must go in.

Not simply visible, but all by which we apprehend: toes, to ears, to hairs in the nostrils. Not sillily that there is some vast curtain that we *must* tear back each time if we are to see the *real* grass: but that we do not usually feel very far, not just depth, but sideways or whatever whichaway: be open when the sideways glance shows what had not been known before, then accept it, do not turn away. Where are we? Who are we? What can we do, that is an action, not simply a grate of possibilities? — how answer except to plunge, accept, come open into the real world, further and further, whether it is the old mown wheatfields in the mind or the sunlight clear out my window to the mountains east holding off the Llano Estacado from this valley.

 I mean to say that for Kelly the vastnesses of our persons is not simply something to talk of, as I speak here, but it is to be acted upon: the poem is the means *he* has to go in there:

> We cannot move in the space of God. In the process of discovery (not invention) we call poem, the hidden real must be "created" in the same instant it is found. I have in mind this instantaneousness when I speak of the poem happening, too, of the poet in his poem. (*Nomad*, Autumn 1962)

I do not believe with Paul Blackburn in his review of Kelly's work in *Kulchur* 7, that this quality of the world and his life that Kelly gives us, is one of *hallucination*, for that word to me is of the meaning Webster gives us: "perception of objects with no reality" — but that's to quibble and I don't want that, I mean, simply, to say that the poems are *very* real, open doors, swing them open, but the vista is not of dream or even the visions of mescaline and LSD. It is as Huizinga said of the people when they were "half a thousand years younger," that their view of the world still had the directness of child life. But Kelly is no child, and there is no innocence from ignorance in what he gives us. But I think Blackburn hits home when he says:

> A kind of mystique of the earth and the things of the earth, which we use or waste, and so tie us to ourselves or make us alien to our own lives, persists throughout all of Kelly's work.

And accurate, too, when he says that many people will simply not be willing to open themselves to the multiplicity and directness of the world these poems offer, God knows, they must be read slowly, carefully, this book of *Her Body Against Time* the more, or they will slip on away and maybe leave you damp a little, but hardly knowing whether it rained or not.

So. *Her Body Against Time* is the record, or better, the action itself, of a man living as closely as he can to the objects of earth around him, whether it is up at Bard-on-the-Hudson or where. But just because this book is off in those woods behind his house, it would be stupid to say Kelly is not aware of the tear and rupture socially, politically that goes on, on off beyond the fringe of those woods; I don't know of any more accurate and hard-hitting "social" poem going than "Third Avenue" in that same *Nomad*; or "The Spread" in *Sum* 2, that says more of Kennedy's assassination finally than any of the dozens others written "for the occasion." "Beauty," wrote Christopher Caudwell, "is the knowledge of oneself as a part of other selves in a real world, and reflects the growth in richness and complexity of their relations." We reflect what we can of the fight down this street, if we have ears or eyes at all, as we can, at least no turning the back and a wince; ignorance of what happens everyday to people, "innocence" of it, is the failure and sin — the more when innocence in our time comes to be that blindness that lets a 10-ton truck come barreling through the wall of the house and not even know it. Read "Third Avenue" and try to pretend it's not there.

It is finally to speak of the "craft" in this book — a question I honestly do not believe is there if one reads the book at all. It is as Ed Dorn speaks of Olson, that there is no trafficking possible with his means. The poems speak for themselves. As Kelly says (in *Nomad* again), "A poet's craft is his ability to orient himself by the use of words, his ability to allow a poem to be its own emergent form"; "a man's whole life of work is barely enough to come to a method." As he wrote me in a letter last summer:

> some people were put off by my apparent indifference to "craft" in those Notes. It was simple humility to avoid that particular matter (of the essence tho it is) in a time when, e.g. Olson, Zukofsky, Dorn, Creeley, Levertov (not to speak of EP & WCW) have been loud   right   heard ...

The poems, as I say, speak for themselves;

> The shade dissembles,
> you did not come here
>
> but everything wears your skin
> grass walks the way you move
> with your time
> down the field
>
> we did not meet inside,
> where shadow guards
> the administration of such music,
>
>   ("The dream does not come")

The distance from here in Albuquerque to Annandale-on-Hudson is a very short one — no further than the grass in my sight out the front window, than the trees that grass is under. The moon is full tonight; it shines there, too. And I reckon we all enter it, it enters us. Right down this street is no closer or further away than that. Our realm, even the dust in the driveway we might dance down kicking the dust with our heels, where everybody in the world comes in — so the closeness this book gives us is not just the objects of the world, but of ourselves, all of us,

how much more
will I see
or see again:

the problem
hurts, I have
no eyes to

see it, no
flesh or time
to see it

through. A day
walks from sun
to shadow

on grass wet
from a last
sweet rain, It

solves itself
outside me
in the air,

I am with
the old men
watching one

spring go out.

("The process")

Kulchur #14 (summer 1964)

JEROME ROTHENBERG

LETTER ON "DEEP IMAGE"[7]

16 August 65

...Your questions concerning "deep image" and your relation to that etc. seem valid, and I would certainly think you should go at it *your* way, since all any of us have ever tried to do was to stake out an area of concern or, by naming something we had sensed, to then close in on it as matter useful to our separate workings. All in all I wonder if it might not have been better to speak of, say, an *open* image rather than a *deep* one, since we were in effect trying to make possible again a situation prior to the closed thought inherent in metaphor, symbol, etc., all such usages no longer meaningful to us. We wanted freedom for the mind to move among words and things, to *invent* (in the twofold sense of *discovering* and *making*) relationships without finality. This fusion-like process has seemed to me a great and ancient power in the poem, though one always in danger of hardening into symbol or being disregarded in favour of a kind of descriptive image that too often boils down to a statement of how we *expect* the world to be. It is in this sense that reality first became the issue for us even if we had to lie half the time to keep at it — and that last is always the most difficult to get across, that we would be willing to trespass against the *common sense*.

OK. My only discomfort with "deep" at this point is that we may seem to be taking for granted a psychological origin (in the unconscious) and though it often feels that way, I wonder if it isn't finally beside the point, i.e.: that there's so much in any poem etc. that seems to come unmediated (what Kelly speaks of as "man making himself the instrumentality of vision") as if it were all arising *within* us. I believe certainly in making that vision possible, but whether this involves a quickening of conscious thought or a mining of the unconscious may simply be a question of how we choose to describe it. The main thing is to be always in pursuit.

---

7. Robert Kelly's accompanying letter, also published in *Eleventh Finger* #2, can be found in *A Voice Full of Cities*, "1. A Book of Images: Deep and Other."

About the bibliography etc., Kelly is probably right, though I think there's a special difficulty for him in that the major focus of his work has shifted toward that of Olson, and I imagine he now feels not at ease to be thought of as someone other. No matter — since we've all gone our different ways as we'd encouraged each other to do from the start....
Best, as ever   Jerry

Eleventh Finger #2 (1965)

A ROUND OF RATTLES, BY AND WITH ROBERT KELLY

Robert Kelly was a poet essential to my own formative years as a poet, a time of transformations now a half-century in the past. With him there was a brief time in which we struggled together with the dimensions of "deep image" as a strategy of composition developed by us along with a cohort of contemporaries in New York & elsewhere. In my own case this was the forerunner to that ethnopoetics to which I came on my own by the end of the 1960s, but looking back now I feel sure that it was Robert who was an early one, & possibly the first to point me in that direction. Rounding out his seventh decade now, he represents for me & for many others a poet of the greatest powers & with a devotion to our art & to the shared life from which it springs second to none in my memory.

With something of that in mind he wrote to me recently to recount a memory he had of readings of mine in which I used a Seneca Indian horn rattle to drive home my spoken performances. He enclosed with that a poem that spoke to those occasions, and I answered with a short group of prose poems that used his nouns in the manner of what Jackson Mac Low, another member of our cohort, called *nuclei* — a form of composition that I had used earlier in *The Lorca Variations* & other poems. What follows, then, is Robert's rattle poem, along with my poems in response to it. My admiration for his life & work is no less now than it was those many years ago, & my gratitude is even greater.

Jerry's Rattle

wakes the dead.

It quacks.

I translate rocks
he said, I say pebbles,
I know ground
I know leather things
because they say.

When the eagle comes by itself
let it settle or fly off
who know what it carries in its beak
my business is to watch

watch with my rattle
watch with my mouth

with the rattle of my rattle I see everything

and when it flaps away
leaves one feather after it
I try to pick it up
but it's only the eagle's shadow
I try to pick its shadow up
and it turns into my shadow

and this makes me fly.

My teachers said
Fly on your shadow only
leave the machines alone
fly on your shadow
it will never fall.

Who were the dead I was waking
and why were they dead
and what were they doing
packing their valises
and tying their colorful bundles
on the day 13-Death
the only day in the year they could go

where do they go
I don't have to know
I have to wake them
I have to let them go,
they're waiting for me
to rattle my rattle,

go, I murmur in my ordinary
language, go home
lovely spooks,
find your way home,
ride the ringing of my rattle all the way

a sound carries

the dead ride our music
the dead ride sounds
the way I ride shadows

nothing else counts
but making sounds
and finding the way home.

home is always somewhere else

that's why all the music we need
that's why I rattle my rattle

when I was little boy
the radio used to say every week
only the shadow knows

only a shadow is always at home

the sun thinking its way through the clouds
makes it happen
the firelight makes it happen

we invented fire
so we could have shadows at night

the sun is a rattle that sings shadows
I belong to everything when I make noise.

                                                Robert Kelly

Variations on a Round of Rattles
for Robert Kelly

1

The noise of pebbles in the mouth of someone dead is next to nothing. Underneath the sun a boy is wrestling with his shadow, & his shadow with another shadow. Home is always somewhere else, a rattle & an eagle feather all that's left. Daylight nearly over. Firelight foreshadowing the night.

2

Everything the night conceals from us is yet alive. Even the rocks are when they're stuffed into a rattle and the sound they make surrounds us as the shadow of a cloud might on the way to night. Here in our final home machines like living things cast shadows also, & the year ends with a lonely rattle sound. Spooks bearing bundles run from everything like shadows where we wait & dream.

3

The business of the dead is spinning shadows, banging leather rattles, faking a language not their own. How good to spend a week away from home, valises packed & ready for a day out in the sun. A rattle makes a sound we love to hear, another rattle leads us where the shadows beckon, and the shadows form a single shadow under which we hide.

4

13-Death calls out to us. His is a music darker than a radio, so far from home, so fraught with sounds the dead might make, our fallen teachers, eagles screaming through their beaks, who make the ground shake, where we sit around a fire. Is it a rattle or a distant ringing, or a rattle that the dead can hear and join us, shadows overhead & with a lonely rattle far from home?

Jerome Rothenberg

Poems & Poetics blog (2011)

CLAYTON ESHLEMAN

ON *Finding the Measure*

Kelly's work will ultimately be seen as a constellation, such as Blake's and Olson's rather than individual poems (Creeley, Burns etc.). Reading him now carries some of the mystery that reading Blake at the beginning of the short prophetic histories might have; his work draws grandly on his reading experience and while this experience is genuine (any reference anyone cares to check in a Kelly poem will turn out not only accurate but will also quite often turn reader on to a new area), — it comes into the poem un-steeped, that is, the referential is still at this point more evocative than the in-point to Kelly's own mind. A necessity almost to clear the house at every point (tho I must say here that often I do not check Kelly's references, I look at them as foreign words or as sound-walls, like an area of an abstract painting wch is part of the composition & shd be judged as such; therefore what he is clearing from his house, I mean my expression above, may mean nothing, for, Xrist, what really do we ever know of another man's processes if he is invading territory that we do not have instant emotional reality on?). In all of Kelly's work, in some especially of the weakest of it, is compassion and understanding, and willingness in the best Christian sense to sacrifice for others. The literariness that I personally object to (I mean I want to say that if Kelly would let the vulva out of the bag, ho! he would break, I mean, Break into chant and the metapedagogical physics would consume in the fire of direct utterance — I know this is absolutely horrible to say to Kelly as his fulcrum is the world of learning and one shd grant him the possibility that thru his chosen world he can drive out the chariot of his soul) I am aware has often as its intention the bringing of new material into the poem, and is, as such, K's responsibility to where he is. In *Finding the Measure,* wch interests me in terms of Kelly's own process (by wch I mean he has a good head so I am interested in reading anything he writes), there are also a half-dozen stunning poems, the best of wch is the last one in the book. Kelly's death preoccupation seems to worry more than enter; he also has a tendency to speak for others when as far as I'm concerned he is speaking for himself (vide "Last Night," a lovely piece, but wch Marie Benoit, a friend of mine, pulled apart on the basis that Kelly pulled her into an involvement and judgement that she did not feel). I mean (again), the "I" is a pillar of fire and "we" is a non-look. Kelly's sense of female drives me up the road to Carolee Schneemann's place where I find him preoccupied in the head of the poem with sexuality wch never seems to release. Or is that mine? Boy, what a Victorian thing a review is! I keep waiting for Kelly to pound me thru the wall with a poem and it's like a lovely creature I don't know and only partially embrace. I love his Picasso-like concern for all forms, their rape and revitalization. Given his stamina (vide *Axon Dendron Tree*) and knowing, we can expect everything of him, and he shd be pushed very hard for everything. As he would have his King, Robert Kelly, who is also my friend, keeps his cup full, and it is a large brass one, and the wine is hearty and good.

There is no end to it, until there is.

Caterpillar #5 (1968)

DIANE WAKOSKI

ON *SONGS I—XXX*

> But fashion teaches brevity
> and brevity, I'm sorry to tell you,
> is a lie.
> I must be longer with this music.

Kelly writes this in a poem called "New York." It is a sentiment that resonates for me, deeply, as a poet who admires, rather distantly, short small lyrics. Kelly, however, is an interesting phenomenon, for he seems to be able to work in either long or short lines with equal grace. His sparse lyrics are the mode for *Songs*.

> Now it is tired & the rain
>   speaks itself into the earth
> Now it is tired & cold
>   there is no rain, the earth
> is no woman to talk to, no mother
> of anyone we can easily be.
>
>   ("Song IV")

Yet he is a man who in 15 years of writing poetry (he is about 35) has probably averaged a thousand poems a year. In 10 years of publishing, he has published at least 20 books of poems that I know of, plus a novel and an anthology of contemporary poetry. This makes an obvious problem for the reader of Kelly, for assuming that you have the time and the devotion to find all the books, some of which have been offered in editions of as few as 100 copies, and the will to read them, you must still take it on faith that the best, the most interesting, of Kelly's work has been published.

    I have been to parts of the country where I hear Kelly spoken of, in spite of his youth, as one of the best poets of our time, and in other places where serious and good readers of poetry have never even heard of him, to say nothing of having read his work. This discrepancy between his production and his availability interests and troubles me as much as anything in the literary world today. I have always believed that it is to a young poet's advantage to publish with small or underground presses. I have also always felt that poets are the worst editors of their own work and therefore the best procedure as a young poet is to get all of your work in print and then let some editor who likes you put together what seems most interesting. Put this into collections which will have wider circulation and availability. However, where do you get an editor who can read through 15,000 poems and make books out of them? Well, obviously, the author of those 15,000 poems becomes the editor. Kelly is a various poet, a man of several modes but one voice, yet there is no collection of his which gives the uninitiated reader this sense at all.

Songs is a collection of what Kelly calls "experiments in the extended lyric." In the terminating notes to the book Kelly says: "These poems are parts of a continuous process of finding each day's song, not of a long poem or any such thing. Roots and manifestations recur: we walk the same streets day by day." *Songs* is definitely a true part of Kelly's work, but hardly a representative one. In a way, despite his prolific bulk as a writer, Kelly is a small and delicate writer. He says,

> I was not a tree,
> I hung in my bones like a man in a tree,
> the tree talked . I said nothing .
>
> ("Song XVII")

and it reinforces what I always feel when I hear Kelly reading his poems: that what he is saying is unimportant, but it is how he is saying it, and that in placing the emphasis there, he is making a kind of abstract music out of poetry. I do not mean music here as song. I mean that after days of reading bad poetry or attending to student work, when I begin to ask myself why in the world anyone would want to write poetry and forgetting the Lorca and Stevens that always restore my faith in art, I can turn on my tape recorder and listen to Robert Kelly reading his poems and relax, sure that the American language is a beautiful instrument, that, couched in the singing of polysyllabic words is the simple love of speaking. I listen to Kelly's poems not for overall meanings or ideas, nor for narrative content or arguments, all of which are my own primary interests in poetry, but rather for his words of wisdom which suddenly crop up in an amazing texture of language. There is a kind of contradiction between Kelly and his poetry, in that Kelly the man is extremely erudite, a reader of several languages, a lover of ancient wisdom, a ponderous heavy intellect suspicious of the unlearned, while his poetry, riddled with exotic words, ideas, ancient or bookish references, does not have the effect of serious talk at all; it is rather a man singing very softly to himself all the most beautiful words he can think of to calm himself, to make himself believe in life. I suspect Kelly sometimes of being a choirmaster writing a gigantic mass which would take 10 years of continuous singing to perform; the mass would be for people celebrating life as a religious event, and the fact that all the connections were abstract, and unless you sat attentively for the whole 10 years you would not see them, would not bother you. Stopping by to listen, you would always be moved by the beauty. When it is simplest, it is most beautiful. And probably that simplicity could not exist other than from such a complex mind. I do think Kelly is a beautiful poet, but I wish to heaven we could get a nice representative 700-page book of his poems one of these days, so that those of you who have not been listening to him for 10 years, as I have, could hear that various voice too.

Poetry (September 1971)

P. ADAMS SITNEY

MY DEBT TO ROBERT KELLY

I have lately learned of myself that I cannot long be away from the myths and still flourish. Never fully persuaded (faith sways), I erect the myths again, fill them with my life when I am strongest, that they may sustain me when I am not...

During the same conversation with Brakhage and Sitney where it became clear that I could write something about Maas, it became evident too that events within the time of life are susceptible of understanding most when they, in their forms and rhythms, reconstitute the mythical patterns we rediscover from earliest history...

All that is crucial is hidden in childhood, a childhood impressionistically reflective, now inaccessible to the normal, inevitable operations of my memory. I would not explore them if I could, fearing being trapped in memory...

Rest easy. My childhood and youth will never be here exposed. But I am thinking at this moment of an event in what I take to be my 15th year, an event that brought together, in some kind of focus, the radiations of that image, and cast them forward into my future, for a little while at least, an organized beam of light.

These discontinuous paragraphs come from an essay entitled "Geography of the Body" where "that image" refers to seeing the eponymous film of Willard Maas. I find myself walking along the path of those words today because an email conversation with Joel Newberger and a rereading of "Geography of the Body" after more than 50 years made it nearly clear that I could write something about Robert Kelly, if I allowed myself to fill, with a tangent of my life, the myth Wallace Stevens (following Plato) called "The Noble Rider," that is, the myth of The Poet.

Sometime in the Fall of 1963 I accepted an invitation from Stan Brakhage to ride with him on an afternoon visit to Robert Kelly. Brakhage's brother-in-law, the poet Jack Collom, whom I had met a few years earlier at the New Haven Poetry Society, drove us to Kelly's apartment, a glass box on the campus of Bard College where he taught English. I had never heard of Kelly. Brakhage, following a suggestion from Robert Duncan, had recently looked him up on one of his visits to New York City. Brakhage may have attended a reading Kelly had given in the city and leaped at the suggestion of showing his latest films at Bard. During the three-hour drive from Connecticut to Annandale-on-Hudson, Brakhage told us of the intense identification he had with Kelly, as if he were his *double*. They had the same first name, although Brakhage's adoptive parents had discarded the Robert. Long before he thought of making films he had imagined himself a poet. Like Kelly he adored Pound, Zukofsky, Olson, and Duncan. Above all, his reading of Kelly's "Sun of the Center" rhymed with his own major work-in-progress at that time, *Dog Star Man*. Later that week, when I read "Sun of the Center" in the copy of *Armed Descent* Kelly gave me, I thought I saw what he meant.

Despite the buildup of Kelly Brakhage gave us, I was not prepared for the man. He was Gargantuan: I had never encountered anyone as intelligent, as well-read, as prolific, as frank about his lusts, or as physically big as Kelly was then. In fact, he was so big that I soon realized I had seen him two years before in New York, as a member of a heartbreakingly small parade of protesters carrying signs decrying the imminent execution of Caryl Chessman, the murderer and rapist who had educated & reformed himself during his 16 years on death row in a California prison. Years later, I would witness Kelly's embarrassment and anger when an overjoyed redneck in an upstate New York town rushed to shake his hand as the fabled wrestler Haystacks Calhoun. The man persisted, not dissuaded by Kelly's denial or my intervention. We must have been a curious spectacle. At 18, I was the skinniest boy I knew. I struggled to maintain 100 pounds, and that included the considerable weight of my pimples.

But by that time Kelly had come to incarnate for me The Poet, and his work Poetry. I think I can pinpoint the moment in my mind when that Allegory possessed my appreciation of the man. It was hearing him read over several months a long poem as it emerged. The poem was *Weeks*, a masterpiece in 148 parts (that was so garbled by Mexican typesetters that Kelly cancelled the book's distribution). Hearing in stages the long exfoliation of that book-length poetic sequence permitted me to witness the emergence of words in rhythm from an apparently roiling source through the vatic instrument Kelly allowed himself to become. Although I had read of this phenomenon in Horace, Shelley, and Mallarmé, I did not grasp its startling truth until I could see it at work. The words that bubbled up into *Weeks* seemed to retain a capillary or magnetic connection to the Source itself, insuring the immediate or future eruption of surprising conjunctions. Shocking and delightful.

As he was writing *Weeks*, I visited as often as I could. Each time he read aloud the sections he had written since my previous visit. I was never alone during those sessions. At first Charles Stein was always there, often with his friend Josie Rosenfeld. Just as I was the editor of the mimeographed avantgarde film journal, Stein had *Aion*. Later two Bard students were constant visitors, Harvey Bialy and Timotha Doane, who would be his first wife. Sometimes Stein's high school friend, the prose writer and editor of yet another little magazine, *Io*, Richard Grossinger, came, often with his fiancée, Lindy Hough. Even Kelly had his own inexpensively produced journal, *Matter*.

I've never gotten over *Weeks*. Its fusion of elliptical lyrics and paragraphs of stylized didactic prose celebrated the names of days as our mythology, as "lissome ladies," along with ordinary American automobiles, and the extraordinary miracle of books amid smatterings of Provençal, Latin, Arabic, French, German, and Sanskrit. The sequence shimmers with sexual energy.

Section 7 is a good place to start (if we cannot have the whole poem):

> Friday & the need to touch
> in Rhinebeck
> hardpowder snow down merging
> going down
>
> This is the day of Venus
> not in mythology
> but in the word itself
> the days themselves
> among our language
>   the day of Frigga, Friya,
> Friya's day

now Frig was Wotan's woman
& knew like him such swoons of buggery
her heart took fire from
& burned all night for seven years

    a flaming tree
    in heaven

her name is *friction*. Friday is friction's day.
Frig. To masturbate or sometimes used, frig, in place of,
to stand for fuck, as euphemy, as the action does,
knowing no better, this music & not another. Frig.
    or where will the friction
    come from.

The day of the fractioning machine. The town.
They wait around. A girl drops her book
& crouches to get it, laughing, & is
instantly fucked all over, they're waiting,
driving, coming in the instant of her bend.
Cunt ass underarm open mouth under her chin
under the flesh of her thighs the knees
squeeze between the thighs between soft calves
between her knees between the soles of her
violent at her navel between her cheeks
in her tangle of public hair crushed
between her knees between the soles of her
feet in her dress flailed against her back
gripped in each of her clenched pulling
tearing rhythmic unknowing inkstained hands.

She stands up gingerly shaking loose the
rainpuddle drops from the wilting book.
Where will the friction come from. Knowing
nothing she drives off, they stand there,
giant ache of their energy, waiting, vigilant,
baffled. No tongue will cool it, no laughing

> throat swallow it down forever. How long can you
> ride without getting a hardon. Rhythm is not
> friction. They are waiting for an answer.
> It is getting dark on a Friday afternoon.

The lines contract with lyric tension and expand toward an epic narrative of the etiology of the common English name for the fifth day of the week. Not until section 10 does the long poem articulate its program:

> The agonies of weeks, to fit a season.
> How will they render meaning from solstice to equinox
> in terms of number, the weeks,
>   thirteen,
>   so the number
> of Sabbatarian weeks in a season, in a spring, is the
> number of lunar months in a year, the moons, weeks,
> turnings, *wicu*, turnabouts, the moon's weeks —
>
> & the French say, like the Latin model, hebdomadaire,
> built on seven days, built on the pediment of Saturn's
> throne,
>   for Saturn is the lord of weeks, & on that day
> shabbath, thou shalt rest, that day of the great star,
> Shabbathai, the far one; Saturn is the Lord of Weeks,
> Lord of Compromised Time, the Chopper that lights our
> days to bed & concludes the time.
> Sun we say, Moon, Tiu,
> Woden, Thor, Friya, but go to Saturn to end the week,
> go to source, the endless fountain of limitation.
>   But
> moon's week is an actual turning, a passage we can see
> from dark to full to dark,
>   & what is wrong with mythology
> is not its poetic, but that it is ungodly linked with
> civil calendars of dead states.
>   Out of the civil calendar
> the days come whittled to purposes beyond our meanings;

robbed of value our suns go down & come up each morning,
shrouded, their potency concealed in weekly names—
mythology is the civil calendar, the dark Father who
obsesses every actual sight taste touch or smell of what
is here passing only once through our lives,
                                                the calendar
that teaches us to dishonor what the day brings by bringing
the day to a simple matrix of seven, a turnabout that is
no turnabout but only the flip of a page of a cashbook,
we are stifling beneath the collapsed categories of ruined
republics, bones of dead heroes cluttering the time, paroxysms
of archive, denying us the clarity of what the sun is
day by day, the moon is night by night, & what they shine
on, or from what they withhold their light.

The Jeremiad against the banality of weekly time transmutes Kelly's muted Blakean fury at the *civil* calendar of the modern *polis* into the quest for another sort of Friday where the mythic resonances of a highschool girl retrieving a textbook from a puddle amid the lusting imaginations of a gaggle of young studs stands revealed. These highschoolers, all high-schoolers, are the prisoners of compulsory schooling by daily schedules, temporarily released every Friday afternoon to indulge the tortures of their erotic illusions.

In 20, for the first time in *Weeks* the breath-inflected lines slip into prose poems, only to rekindle as lyric cries:

Cars take us there
    glass
the dashboard & above it
glass
to all we come to

    the sun in trees
    & in the rearview
    darkened
        rushing
    from where we
    are

not back to where we were or could have been
an impossible town of fair women
fuller than colors
          — at Red Hook
dense in evening sun new girl in town
flexed like Love's bow on the corner,
for the bus —
          are or could be where we
are going, cars take us there, all
that is to be: one curve of glass

— the journey has no meaning. What should be the flight of flesh or spirit to its home becomes an endless series of starts & stops. The man who would go a journey is a squid in a net, taking his environment in him & spitting it out, for speed's sake, in spurts of motion that carry him, only so far as the next town. In reality these towns are the points of intersection in the network, that is, they are the net.

& town
is body
& hurls onward
who would
be in
touch with
it,
to the
next, the
next: Cars take us there & seem in our control. Actually it is another day, & speed the speedometer shows not the true speed. Allegro. Andante. Allegro. What is the true speed. Nets that are roads & streets & towns determine more than the rhythm. The melody. Each day of the week. Its own melody? Sunday Chrysler. Monday Oldsmobile. Tuesday Pontiac. Wednesday Mercury. Thursday Plymouth. Friday Chevy, Venus' car. Saturday Ford. Or Ford is Tuesday sometimes. The shift. The clutch. Going. Riding. Walking. Riding. This is the shift.

> The lights
> to which we move
> unclear, shapes hidden in the blaze of sun.
> Brightness, a body at the heart of it,
> at the end of every street, every knot
> in the net's toils,
>   where Love's arrow comes to rest.

After 26 years of lovingly trudging the streets of cities — Brooklyn, New York, Paris — Kelly learned to drive when he when to teach at Bard College. American cars, and their parts, entered the mythic network of his poems, as vehicular movement and voyeurism through shatterproof glass gradually replaced the rhythms of walking and sitting.

A long prose paragraph near the conclusion of 39 allows the didactic voice of the Orphic professor into the poem:

> We have not yet even after 500 years of easy printing come to understand what a book is. There are secret books — hidden in the putative hoards of white brotherhoods, sealed in providentially occluded caves, locked in cellars of the Vatican of Protestant imagination. But there are other books inherently secret: they can be printed & distributed as widely as the Archons like, yet remain secret. I am not speaking of books textually or intellectually difficult. *Finnegans Wake* is a hard book, but not a secret one. *A Midsummer Night's Dream* is as easy as you please, but remains secret. Again, I am not speaking of 'occult' traditions or gnostical or privileged interpretations. Though Steiner finds *Faust* an Eleusis of mysteries, the play is not secret. Occultists resort to endless pains to interpret received texts, only to the end of missing what is there: there are books, the secret books of which I speak, toward which the hermeneut must struggle *within himself.* The secrecy of which I speak has to do with the way a book, however subtly read, at times will veil its real purport from the mind of the reader not ready to make its concerns his own. It will hide it that critical moment in the true history of the world when the reader is ready to use what the book is. We say, go back to a book. That is like: go back to your lover, go back to your religion, go back home, go back & start again. What incredible

nonsense it is to say *re-read* (compare *re-eat*, *re-feel*, *re-come*) if we have no implicit sense of the delicate interconnections of text & time. The secret book opens when the reader is ready to use: not a moment before.

And I got up this morning to type this down after it had sat two days in my notebook, & a letter came from a friend, & in it, speaking of Zukofsky, I find: "somewhere he speaks — or quotes — to the effect that Aristotle, I think, that there are certain books that require one to have thought the thoughts in them in order to understand them."

> Because the book
> John ate on Patmos
>   or book a man wrote
> is not different from his life
>   in that it is less real:
> what a book is
> what we read

Years later, at a reading in New York City, Kelley would gloss the title of his latest book, *Flesh Dream Book* (1971) as the three things he most prized. The anaphora "go back to your lover, go back to your religion, go back home, go back & start again" now strikes me as the 'secret' motto of Kelly's whole œuvre, hidden in plain view.

And then I wonder if it is mere narcissism that makes me so fond of the play of meter and prose in 61 where I am the unnamed friend who brought him *The World of Elementary Particles*:

> Let it be pleased
> of body
>
>   parts barely
> that they are parts
> & sing,
>
>   song of parts,
> part song :

>   this all to make the whole being,
> part of song
>   & part,
>   to sing.
> Parts.

Can I write today that F. came to the house to show me her thighs? I wanted to say that to a friend, who spoke of the beautiful body of his woman. But then I was frightened of how ugly & dirty that sounded. She came to my house. Her parts. Yet how could I put into the sight a story purpose: she came to show me, she came She came, & much else. I saw amidst all the other articles & rhythms of life, her thighs. Words & gestures, attitudes towards poetry, attitudes towards the world. She spoke of *stance,* & my eyes filled mind with her sitting dance, moving the veils. And I thought of how I had told Brakhage that watching his my mind was at the mercy of my eyes, & went on to tell him that the glyph of *Matter* represented a man at the mercy of his means. All this brings clear light into left thighs held her secrets close, the background, but the problem remains. What kind of man is it sits in a house & watches the parts of women. Or, could say: she came to show me her thighs. Plainly I am fascinated with the image of a women displaying her parts. The parts of the song, parts of the body, part of fortune Today on the phone I asked a friend to bring me *The world of elementary particles,* & he thought it was a book about those incredible words in Greek, the particles from which the sense or color of an utterance reflects. Another friend brings me a clipping from a newspaper headed "New Theory of Matter Supports Idea of a Few basic Particles." This day of parts. Yet fascination is a process by which reeds are bundled together, an unbreakable whole is made, symbol of man's authority: wholeness. My fascination with parts leads to a whole I have struggled to discover: the body. How can I support, bear, bare, the idea of a few basic particles Parts bearing parts, a woman baring her parts. Me watching. God willing, parts of the world. What kind of man sits in his house watching the parts of the world.

            Those parts
            from which
            the color
            of the whole
            proceeds,
                              reflections of the part
on part,
            to make the whole,
                                  who told me
of parts,
            who brought
                        into the house,
                                      parts, to show
me or give
            the few
            basic
            particles
            we are.

108 remains the most satisfying 'political' poem I know; for in it what is "beneath the collapsed categories of ruined republics, the bones of dead heroes cluttering the time" shows through as tragic litter:

I suppose
Malcolm X
that rusty
sharpened
beercan of a
mind to have
been the first
uneasy witness
at the death
of the dream
of polis,
clear evidence
of what we have
used & tried to
discard.

But matter is indestructible,
matter is infinitely transformed,
we watched all fall the beercan at the side of the road
darken until the snow came
come out rusty in spring
turn red in the dry summer
crumble in the fall & snow come to bury it again
& by spring it was gone
into itself into earth again
released from form

I suppose Malcolm X
whose murder
we thera-
peutically contrived
as sole sure balm
for all his questions,
not answers,
to have noticed
how unfeeding our
uses & abuses both
become, how little
we can love

I suppose Malcolm X in his hatred for me
to have been the perfected instrument of clarity
that says cut out this
shit what is wrong here
is you are you & I
am me & nothing
you've ever thought up
yet brings us together,
die if you will not love me,
die if you will not talk,
      that says
      this gate
      is too low

     for me to
     enter
     upright
& I have crawled here far enough
         from that interesting predicament
you put me in
       to test my spirit
             my readiness
for your dialectic.
        I have no spirit I have hands & feet
& knees sick of this culture,
    I will not shield you
    from bare sun
    of your impoverished
    imagination, energy
    without vehicle, power
without art or grace to be art or wit to see
    this plain sun rise
    on the day of my death
in what was not
ever polis.

  The unfolding *Weeks* was my education in the sources of poetry. My debts to Kelly and his compulsive generosity were enormous. He wrote the brilliant and otherwise unknown essay on Willard Maas for my *Filmwise 5–6* issue devoted to Marie Menken and Maas — partially quoted at the head of this essay. For an issue of *Film Culture* I edited, he provided the astonishing essay "The Image of the Body" and allowed me to reprint it in *The Film Culture Reader*. (Kelly's love of human bodies, his expansive sense of magic, and his sublime disdain for conventional narrative made his rare writings on cinema perceptive and very original.) Decades later I read in Charles Olson's *Selected Letters* that Kelly had promoted my cause as film critic of Olson's *Niagra Frontier Review*. He wrote the text of the marriage ceremony of my first wedding: *Words in Service*. He got me my first fulltime teaching position, when Bard College started a film program in 1972. In 2006, he wrote "Adamagica: Magic and Iconolatry in Film" for a conference on Magic and Cinema I organized at Princeton University; only recently did I hear an interview with a researcher at Wagner College in which Kelly gave me more credit for the cohesion of the American avantgarde cinema than I could possibly have deserved. His unwillingness to flaunt such largess allows me to expect to discover others, periodically for the rest of my life.

In retrospect, his many gifts to me dwindle beside the foremost that was religious — a distinction, that is, between *poeisis* and *religio,* he probably wouldn't admit — namely, that he came from a working class Irish-American family and considered his early Catholicism a strength, not an embarrassment, seeded the ground for me to return to the practice of Roman Catholic rituals after an adolescent repudiation of The Church (in sympathetic identification with the brilliant Jews and professorial WASPS of my native New Haven); I had never met another Catholic like him.

One peculiarity of Kelly's genius is the synthetic nexus of religion, eros, sport, and poetry in his imagination. It issues in surprising combinations and discriminations. Even a casual remark he made in the Bard faculty dining room touched upon it. I must have complained to Bard's Rabelaisian sculptor, the late Jake Grossberg, of the acute pain of amorous rejection. With his usual exuberant humor, Jake corrected me: "Why, if you get one Yes out of three tries, you're batting 333; those are Hall of Fame statistics!" As if pondering Grossberg's remark, Kelly said he found the association of eros and sport fascinating: "I've always thought loving a new woman was like changing my religion." That was before I realized he was becoming a Buddhist.

THREADS 15: ROBERT SAYS

People have to find the materials or minds to do work on the world, for the world; the poet has at least the materials right there in the mouth. Words. Language, which is always there and common to all, so the poet is always walking through familiar places, holding familiar objects to display to those around about. Making them unfamiliar, so they can be seen. Language, no matter how arcane we become with it, language keeps us always with other people. Joyce's polysemous and difficult tongueplay in the late work comes out of his fierce determination to respond to the social fact, we dream in language and wake to speak. Language is always social. Language is the other — the other in our own mouths.

The poet is someone who has nothing to say except what language lets. And 'let' is an old, odd word in English, that means both permit (let the children play) and prohibit (let and hindrance). Language lets, poets listen, and that listening is their main responsibility, when coupled with what language lets them, makes them say, keeps them from saying.

Maybe the deepest responsibility of the poet is the simplest: Keep talking.

The enterprise that Shelley spoke of, despite his own voluminous political writing, I think is true because of the adjective. The more unacknow-ledged we are, the more effective legislators we are. Unacknowledged even by ourselves. Especially by ourselves.

Look, poetry works when it reveals & when it gives pleasure. Those are the two things I know it can do. It can also bore and preach and fulminate and be disagreeable, can murmur confessions best left in the leatherette diary with the little heart-shaped lock, can posture politically and be very, very self-important.

But when the poet is the legislator, the poet is not sounding off. The poet is sounding. Not what I think about the government, but what language lets me speak into the whirlwind around me.

in conversation with Simone dos Anjos and Pietro Aman

The Modern Review (2006)

3.
A BOOK FROM VORT MAGAZINE

"Can anyone out there imagine a line defined by three points going under the names Pound, Olson, and Kelly?"

Barry Alpert, editor of *Vort* magazine (1972–1976)
in *Vort* #5, the Robert Kelly issue

GUY DAVENPORT

KELLY IN TIME

After Methuselah, the deluge. Tribe of Ezra, sons of Olson, shaggy nephews of Doc Williams — they have been like the Mongol hordes camping in the ruins, milking their mares beside the temples, roasting their elk over the legs of imperial chairs, mistaking astrolabes for gods, confusing art with magic.

The first Visigoths in Rome wore their unshorn hair combed forward over their faces, tucked under their bronze-buckled cowhide belts awash around their knees. Their wide cheekbones held open a slit in this yak's coiffure through which they looked and breathed. And men descended from the Volsci and Gracchii married their oiled and comely daughters: opposites breed.

Olson was a kind of Goth — a man of awful energy and awful sloth. A philosopher's brain in a bear's body, Ruskin's eye, Rimbaud's ear — given a shot at metempsychosis, he would have wavered forever between choosing to be Plutarch (the most civilized man known to history) or the antlered and masked shaman of the Dordogne hunters of 30 millennia ago. Which is what Olson was: Plutarch crossbred with a shaman. It was the shaman who misunderstood Pound's ideograms and made signs and incoherent words of them; it was Plutarch who chose the subjects as vast and solid as the Great Wall of China. Pound's first apprentices were masters of the lute: Bunting and Zukofsky. One can name other schools, outposts; they are for the most part particularizers, specialists (Marianne Moore, Hilda Doolittle).

Olson released the true Gypsy eclecticism that Robert Kelly and his tribe embraced with a passion that has not been seen in American writing since the pagan Whitman walked barefoot into the library quiet of Transcendentalism. An index to American culture is our seesaw exchange of quiet and noise. Literature had gone into a Chinese hush when Whitman's robust voice made dust rise from the rug and canted the pictures on the wall, Emerson, Thoreau, and Emily Dickinson in a room would have made no more noise than Gandhi and a mouse in a box.

Whitman was steep of decibel; so was Pound, and both got quieter and quieter as they brought their work and lives to a close. The great boom of solid sound came next from Kelly and his generation (an indefinable area, but we know when we have got to the boundaries — Kelly made one map in *A Controversy of Poets*).

Whatever the characteristics of the tribe, Kelly is a phylarch, a master, a stylist who for all his eclecticism is always distinctly himself.

He is the one *Caterpillar* poet (if we can designate that magazine to indicate a school) for whom Olson's barbarian abandonment of logical syntax was an advantage rather than an obstruction. Kelly is too avaricious of keeping in sensual touch with reality to let sense flake into nonsense. His most elusive fragments have a sentence implied in them. The barbarism that Olson invented and encouraged is the mode our poetry has chosen; Europe is what barbarism made of the ruins of Greece and Rome.

Barbarism is energy, Kelly has written constantly without let or stint for an uninterrupted 20 years. Like Valéry, he fills volumes of notebooks. He has published a shelf of books. He gets a lifetime of work into a year. He has Picasso's energy and fertility of invention.

Barbarism is generosity: the barbaric sense of how to make a thing is the opposite of the classical. The Parthenon is a design achieved by eliminating everything but floor, roof, pillars, and the god inside. A Gothic cathedral was elaborated until the entire country had spent its last penny on stone, workmen, gold, lead, glass. There is no end to a Kelly poem, it is a cataract of energy.

Zukofsky spends three days choosing a word, hoping not to have to use it, after all. Kelly up-ends the dictionary daily; he has a use for every word, any word.

Barbarism is endless curiosity. One never asks seriously what a Kelly poem is about. First of all, as a Picasso is a Picasso whether it depict woman or jug, a Kelly poem is a Kelly poem. It dances in his way, sings in his intonations, insisting on its style. No American poet except perhaps Wallace Stevens has his sense of balance in a line. What Eliot and Pound slaved over Kelly seems to have an innate gift for balancing out. Most poets suffer agonies trying to hide the effort by which they achieved an effortless line. Kelly has nothing to hide: the untiltable balance is there to begin with.

Such skill frees his mind to meditate, to think, to play. And that's what's happening as a Kelly poem moves down the page. He turns a subject with grace and delicacy, as if he must be careful not to smash it with the lover's touch — paintings, flowers, a woman's voluptuousness, glass fruit, things that bruise, break, or withdraw if handled roughly.

And he prefers a multiple subject. He has the Chinese sense of bringing diverse things together into a stark symbol, and is happiest when he himself can't quite see the meaning of the sign he's made. Thus his poems are mysteries to be pondered, something to dream on rather than puzzle out. To understand in our times has sadly come to mean to dismiss; Kelly moves in the opposite direction. I should think that he would be interesting to the philosophers (had we any), for he seems to me to be a man determined to think deeply and carefully about Being itself (perhaps the one subject that pervades his poetry), a subject that philosophy has lost all talent for treating, and a subject which the vulgarities of our culture have coated with grime.

Kelly is a realist coming after an age of abstraction (IN an age of abstraction, rather, for neither the flesh, the spirit, nor tincture of iodine has the least reality for the rulers and regulators of our economic and political existence). Kelly's sense of the body, for instance, is prehistoric, utterly uncivilized. He would cheerfully vote for a Holstein cow to represent him in Congress. He would rather admire a head of cabbage than read *Das Kapital*.

The exquisite web of intellectual understanding that holds the elements of Eliot's and Pound's poetry together has, I suspect, too insubstantial and imaginary a reality for Kelly, who prefers eyebeams (like Donne), sympathies (like Smart), and analogies of strong vehicular articulateness.

You do not read a Kelly poem; you dance it. He is the most musical poet of our time except Zukofsky, from whom he must have learned that the language in a poem treads a measure as prime duty.

Generalizations about Kelly function only so far. His poems have a way of being particular. One cannot read over two poems at a sitting, for instance. He has written an Ohio River's length of poetry. Some sharp critic should first of all try to say where the divisions come, where the grand themes enter and leave. Then we need some close readings of individual poems, to demonstrate how deceptive the lyric gestures are and how meanings are laid into the poem several different ways at once, like the multiple systems at work in a living leaf. The sensitivity on the critic's part here will be comparable to the scientific nicety of measuring the weight of sunlight on a mosquito's wing. This has been done, but it will be harder to say how Kelly can run such power through so many fragile things and keep them from flying into atoms.

The power is new (that is, from outside, barbarian); what it flows through was perhaps about to crumble (as Olson knew: he saw the world principally as rubble); Kelly has performed an energetic, untroubled, endlessly inventive reconstruction. It will take awhile to get used to its newness, but you only need to read two lines together to see that it is alive.

Vort #5 (1974)

JONATHAN WILLIAMS

JOYOUS RODOMONTADE
& INSTANT REMOULADE FOR THE FLATBUSH FLASH

Robert Kelly, having identified me as "America's Largest Open-Air Museum," now gets his, with my very own "1974 Stately Pleasure Dome of American Poetry Award." It conveys to my mind a figure of Chestertonian girth and solemnity, yet with secret small clothes designed by Père Ubu.

Deo volente and *Vort* permitting, I wish to celebrate the man, as colleague and friend. The literary work I leave to others with a better capacity to take on this big mind in its big head.

First thing is the human amplitude. How I enjoy the bass notes Robert brings out of his gullet. A superb reader of poems — cello tone, rich and modulated, not strident. I appreciate the 20,000 calories a day he ingests, and the mountain of work he gestates in return. I like the giant, braided challas, the omelets by the half dozen, the milk cans full of one third sugar, one third milk, one third coffee — by the gallon. What pleasure to sit in a room with a man with such manners, such attentiveness, and such conversation. As I say, there are qualities I imagine in a Chesterton or an Elgar or a Ford Maddox Ford; especially, the marvelous capacity to befriend.

Then, there is the ear for music, plus the Jesuitical (almost bizarre) range of information. What two modern English composers did he want me to tell him about? Sorabji and Cyril Scott! Who knows a note by either these days. Kelly already knew about Havergal Brian and Lord Berners, of course. I would not be surprised to learn from Robert that Stephen Foster wrote six adequate symphonies, or that Scott Joplin studied with Chabrier in Anderson, South Carolina, in the 1890s. He seems to know the name of every opera yet composed, including the minor ones by Schreker, Dukas, César Franck, and Gustav Holst.

I wish I could read Kelly more often with the care he deserves. The size of the work scares me away, makes me think I'm ignorant, or lazy, or "not serious enough." He himself would never suggest such things, but the corpus remains daunting. I've had my troubles over the years with writers who let down the floodgates — Olson, Dahlberg, Patchen, Zukofsky, Goodman. You need lead in your pants and rocks in your head to take the dare with some poets. They come *at* you, and try to set up permanent housekeeping, and put NO VACANCY signs outside. Which, in fact, would not be Kelly's way. He knows there is appetite in each of us for more than One.

Finally, I both envy and respect his capacities: all those books I'll never read; his kindness to students; the discretion and personality he puts in his letters. To my knowledge, Guy Davenport is his only peer at these talents in the whole country — and god knows I look for such men. Who else do you know who can invent a work called *Argyrum Nitricum, or, A Dialogue on the Art of Light-Shadowing*, by "Enthusiastes Mancuniæ" (Salford, 1841), and then write it?

From the depths of a vile and hideous no-booze, no-fat, no-sugar diet in the blackness of the Yorkshire January, I summon all energies and declare general rejoicing that Robert Kelly lives at a time when we may know him.

Vort #5 (1974)

THEODORE ENSLIN

A BRIEF TAKE ON R.K.'S *MILL OF PARTICULARS*

What does one say? What is possible to say of the work of one who stays so close to me as man and poet that at places it is almost a foregone conclusion that whatever is said or written is of value — can be assimilated without the usual weighing and judging? I do not mean to say that everything of Kelly's has been of equal service to me, nor that I have thought every book successful in the same ways. His own list: *Armed Descent*, *Axon Dendron Tree*, *Finding the Measure*, *Songs I—XXX* (to which I would add *Round Dances*) and this one, *The Mill of Particulars*, is possibly the distilled best of it all. And if the very long poem, *The Loom*, were published, it might be asked, where can he go from here? The important thing to remember is that he can and will. The grace and the scholarship together. I once said to him that he had harmed other writers — something I'm sure hurt him. But, no, Robert, it isn't in any way your fault — merely that so spectacular an output, sheer volume, or show of knowledge — which is genuine — is a come on to some others who have no real strengths of their own. "Aha. This is the way it's done. If I hear about something tonight, I will be an authority at breakfast, and I will have written two volumes by the end of the month." This is nonsense. What is valuable for other writers in Kelly, or in anyone else of comparable stature, is not the individual method: that is Kelly, or whoever. The underlying enthusiasm together with the grace and knowledge, how to use it, the animus, are what is important. But what *does* one say? Of *The Mill of Particulars*? Suddenly there are places where individual poems sing out of the roots of poems we have known for a long time — other Kelly poems, other poems, poets, and times. Other lives. The themes, preoccupations: "Arnolfini's Wedding," "In Mahler's Sleep," "Juncture," with that marvelous two lines:

> Jeff stares out from the penny stamp
> like a man watching hailstones flatten his corn —

Minor and funny, perhaps. But haven't all of us wondered at that uneasy pain on a one-cent stamp? Is Thomas really concerned with the state of the nation, or his own hopelessly confused finances? No. His immediate crop is being ruined, and there's nothing he can do about it. And we won't forget it. This is as important a function of poetics as any of the so-called "deep" concerns. And we'd better be grateful. Such a beautiful poem as "The Sound." Crystalline, delicate, full and powerful. Or that little one:

> A MEASURE
> Some nights the moon straight overhead is not far
> it is a node in the spine, a woman
> could easily reach it combing her hair.

The point, if any is needed, is that it is more quickly recognizable in short takes like these than in more complex workings, just where a man has taken himself and his art. These reify/reaffirm what we know to be happening in the more weighty concerns with music or painting, or those special knowledges so stupidly labeled "occult." One comes to a whole man, and this is his book.

Vort #5 (1974)

NORMAN WEINSTEIN

ON ROBERT KELLY'S WORK OF THE MORNING

> "e deleitet se en trobar en caras rimas; per que las
> soas chanssos non son leus ad entendre ni ad aprendre"
> Arnaut Daniel

In this time of the dream of Kali's dance I move toward those poets who perfect in their art rhythms implicit in that Goddess's swift steps. For in the pulsing heart of the poem the Kalidance, the contracting/expanding breaths of an age & world body are recorded in their full splendor & horror. In the dance of the Poet's mind, in its particular turnings, hesitations, & beginnings, thru that most elusive veil called language, the rhythmic composition of the living universe is declared. Thru the voices haunting Mrs. Yeats on a train between Los Angeles & San Francisco, thru the voices that spoke to Charles Olson in a dream & dictated thru the shadow mask of Pound, "Let the song lie in the thing," thru the voices from Outer Space that haunted Jack Spicer, thru the alchemies of Robert Kelly, we hear the footfall, the pulsing green blood of the planet itself. Consider Jess's cover design for the first edition of Robert Duncan's *The Opening of the Field*: the round dance of the children in a place guarded (& continuously re-created) by the poet's imagination, defining the activities of the poet's mind as a watchful dancing. The playfulness of the poet's operations of mind, the nature of its mental transmutations, is at the center of my reading of Robert Kelly's work, & my concern with this element of his writing surfaces a memory of being his student many decades ago.

 I am sitting in a classroom at Bard College, 1969, my final few months before graduation. I had applied to Bard originally because of my feeling for Kelly's poetry and editing after reading the anthology *A Controversy of Poets* co-edited with Paris Leary. Selected poems culled from his early books (*Armed Descent, Lunes, Her Body Against Time*) included in that anthology were engaging, tho' not overwhelmingly so. The mark of his editing, in contrast to the largely conventional choices of poets selected by Leary, impressed. But what most deeply moved me, then & now, were the opening words of Kelly's concluding essay in the book:

> Because we cherish life, we cherish the poem as a life-sustaining force. Its strength is the strength of an object: a thing made, a thing present in the orders of our perception.

This stance, so close to my own that I had been stumbling to articulate clearly during adolescence, moved me to seek Kelly out as a key teacher on my first day at Bard. Thru courses with innocuous names, "Introduction to Poetry" and "American Poetry from Pound to the Present," Kelly's powers as poet and educator continued to inspire, energize, and usefully unsettle. My memory moves most vividly to the final course with him, an intensive study of the poetry of Pound, Carlos Williams, Duncan, & Zukofsky. Speaking of Pound's appreciation & luminous appropriation of Arnaut Daniel's lyrical voices, Kelly read — no! — really chanted, sang, an example of Daniel's poetry mimicking birdsong, sublime melopoeia, offered in Pound's *ABC of Reading*:

> L'aura amara
> Fals bruoills brancutz
> Clarzir
>   Quel doutz espeissa ab fuoills.
> Els Letz
> Becs
> Dels auzels ramencz

Kelly then contextualized Arnaut's genius by discussing a sweep of troubadour poetry, distinguishing between *Trobar Claire* — the immediate, lucid, easily comprehended mode of troubadour poetic expression, & *Trobar Clus* — the willfully puzzling & difficult verse. At that moment in the classroom he situated his own poem within that ancient domain of Trobar Clus, & so I heard Kelly's voice interlacing with that of Arnaut Daniel in a pivotal poem in Kelly's *Flesh Dream Book*:

> sought an engagement
> with the words would

> (rare rimes, words
> from the athanor)
> would not be easy
>
> I am Arnaut who loved the air   (but the air is L'Aura)
> & hunted hares on oxback
> & swam against the tide

"Words / from the athanor" reminds us that Kelly's mind, like Arnaut's, is a transforming fire, fire place defining a process that is a life moment-by-moment making meaning. Alchemy, Kelly's guiding metaphor for transformational poetry, is a daily work, misunderstood labor, outcomes denied by voices steeped in sentimental conservative conventions. Kelly's alchemical metaphors reflect daily acts of courage in/forming his capacious imagination & craft. In "The Alchemist" Kelly declares:

> & if we do not get up and destroy all the congressmen
> turn them into naked men & let the sun shine on them
> set them out in a desert & let them find their way out,
> north, by whatever sexual power is left in them, if we do not
> seize the president & take him out in daytime & show him
> the fire & energy of one at least immediate star, white star,
> hammer that down in his skull til he hears only that
> rhythm & goes & enters the dance or makes his own,
>
> we will walk forever down the hallways into mirrors &
> stagger & look to our left hand for support

Kelly's poetic vision gathers essential things of this earth in memorable patterns. He relishes a "thingy" vocabulary, as do alchemists in describing initial stages of their transformational operations. And these elementals — man, woman, flesh, dream, book, earth, sun, stars — are lenses making possible the materialization of a luminous path to follow, thru which Kelly makes a shaman-like passage in his poems, passing thru myriad visible-invisible worlds. Listen hard to his starkly spare word list: "man" "woman" "flesh" "dream" "book" "earth" "sun" "stars." Such debased words resounding despite centuries of misuse. Yet Kelly reanimates them to a renewed splendor thru syntactic play, through a rhythmic constitution of their primal energy, thru "Finding the Measure." As Kelly writes in the preface to his book of poems with that title:

> The organism
> of the macrocosm, the organism of language,
> the organism of I combine in ceaseless naturing
> to propagate a fourth,
>   the poem,
>   from their trinity.

then advances to:

>   Finding the Measure is finding the
> specific music of the hour,
>   the synchronous
> consequences of the motion of the whole world.

Kelly's still point in the turning world for most of his adult life — where I was fortunate to meet and study with him — is Bard College, nested adjacent to a pastoral tiny patch of a town, Annandale-on-Hudson, less than a 20 minute spirited hike from the banks of the Hudson River, midway between NYC & Albany, & 90 minutes north of Manhattan. Maybe a million miles, or one, a mere decade, or moment, or flash of a light-year from Black Mountain College. Who can count the miles? Kelly's poems in their alchemical flashing color showers can hardly be housed elsewhere it seems for long. Yet he came to Bard after a deeply-grounded memorable childhood in Brooklyn. Urban consciousness never has completely left him. He rocks in the stressed rhythms of his poems between his city past and his greenest of green (both literal and imaginary) Hudson Valley Bard College home:

> *what is not here*
> *is nowhere*
>
> men
> should live in cities
> shun

> those ghostly edens of twilight
> where all we have never been
> mocks what we are

But that is not the advice he ever took for himself for very long, scurrying back to Bard with all due haste after short-term teaching engagements in other locales. His poems startle with a sense of vivid immediacy reflecting the strange enchanted-kingdom-bohemian-happenings that are a regular feature of the Bard College landscape. I imagine Kelly often stirred by the utter strangeness of Bard's artistic atmosphere, lovingly notated in this Kelly poem celebrating a national holiday in Bard style:

> & so it is on July 4th the inhabitants of Annandale
> march up the road in cool sun
> a fife a drum a plastic kazoo
> a starter's pistol, a union Jack
> held by an elegant man, an American
> early American, flag, by a girl, flag,
> Ea the fife, Enki the drum, Enlil the flag
> of the western sky filled with dying stars
>   stars being born
> some returning to their places & the world begins again

So Kelly's mind moves from that most debased of national rituals, the showing of the colors on July 4th (that same holiday & its specific music that so moved composer Charles Ives), to images evoking Sumerian deities, all the way to words echoing those of occultist Aleister Crowley's "Every man and every woman is a STAR." The base composition of our everyday lives is transformed, redeemed, and rendered golden thru Kelly's poem. He forges a hard-won beauty in his poems, sustaining our lives during Kali's sway. And so let the poet have the last word:

> for all we see we know nothing,
> our utterance alone makes
>
> something of this death.
>
> Adam after hundreds of years
> laying him wantonly down to rest.

Vort #5 (1974)

THREADS 16: ROBERT SAYS

But I have to say their names. The great prose writers, most of them concerned with the Novel (novella = the news), but some of them with other varieties of the news. I set them down as I think of them, all mixed together the Ones who taught me how to tell, the Ones who taught me what kinds of things can be told, the Ones who taught me how to tell into an evolving structure. Some of them I still read, some I read intently once and likely not again in this lifetime. All of them I feel gratitude and reverence towards. I mean by that a feeling of warmth and affection and tenderness comes over me when I just hear their names: Joyce, Sterne, Swift, Melville, Herodotus, Thomas Browne, Malory, Kafka, Lucius Apuleius, Wolfram von Eschenbach, The Mabinogion, Thomas Mann, Rabelais, Dostoevsky, Rilke's fiction, Hoffmann, Novalis, Nietzsche — those are the first ones for me. And later along came Twain, Wodehouse, Johnson, Hesse, Stein, Flaubert, Musil, Wyndham Lewis, Perec, Heidegger, see how everything gets mixed together, Ruskin, Kleist, Beckett, Flann O'Brien, Tolstoy (but just War and Peace*), Hofmannsthal, Gide, Céline, Broch, Bulgakov, Saramago, Malaparte,* The Pilgrimage to the West *and its exact contemporary or almost its alter ego, Don Quixote, "The Twenty Five Zombies" (the great Sanskrit cycle mostly known through Zimmer's The King and the Corpse), Buber's Tales of the Hasidic Masters, Sebald, Benjamin's Arcades Project. And the great storytellers of our own language, Stevenson, Chesterton, Kipling, Buchan, Haggard, and their magical child Borges, and then those strange writers, mostly excluded from the canon (and therefore safe to go on rousing and renewing), who took fear and awe as their subject as other writers had taken love: Poe, Shiel, Lovecraft,*

Machen, M.R. James, and Charles Williams who balanced fear and love like some Thames-side sephirothic tree. Three I came to late: Henry James, whose work held me off for years because of its concerns, outer concerns at least, with property and propriety, until I could no longer resist the sensuous intelligence of his sentences, the sustained richness of his distinctions. John Cowper Powys, admirable, deplorable, lovable — a man who searched out the meaning of what it means to be a human male — not the job, not the role, but the male existence itself, the tender, yearning, hopeful, terror of a man. His A Glastonbury Romance *is a great novel, but he's a hard taste to acquire, it took me years, then suddenly he was for a while all I wanted to read, his flaws as wonderful as his successes. Finally, a shame to know how long before I read him all the way through,* Proust. The Remembrance *is one of the first books I ever bought, but I never did more than read* Swann's Way *and look for romance in* The Cities of the Plain. *Then finally, less than ten years ago, I read it straight through, and knew it at last for what it is, a single, immense book, not a series. The greatest of all novels, the perfection of the form and what the form can do, when the story stretches out over all the world a person ever has. I am still shivering from it, remembering, re-reading, reading here and there in French, reading Proust's other works, essays, pastiches, always coming back to the Magisterium of that one life work.*

in conversation with Simone dos Anjos
and Pietro Aman
The Modern Review (2006)

4.
A BOOK ON NARRATIVE

CHRISTINA MILLETTI

"GETTING WORD"; THE FORCE OF LANGUAGE IN
ROBERT KELLY'S SHORT FICTIONS

> Or you are a jar into which all the
> honey of time has been poured.
> When time ends, the jar will break,
> & there will be left only the honey
> you've gathered or restored.
>
> — "Injune," Robert Kelly

Kelly's Fiction and the Limits of Narrative

Given Robert Kelly's remarkable prolixity — over 50 collections of poetry, 4 collections of short fiction, 1 published novel (*The Scorpions*, 1967), and one unpublished (*Parsifal* at last count totaling approximately 2,000 pages) — it is truly astonishing that so little criticism has been written about his work. The difficulty is in part one of sheer volume. (Where, quite simply, should the critic *begin*?) Another is the range — across genres, among forms — in which Kelly works. After all, Kelly has not only earned great repute as a poet, but he also writes fiction in both short and long forms (*Parsifal* portends the encyclopedic), as well as a selection of "hybrid" & "collaborative" texts such as *The Loom*, *The Cruise of the Pnyx*, *The Garden of Distances*, and *Unquell the Dawn Now* that defy strict categorization. Kelly's "deep image" æsthetic, meanwhile, often embeds his work with an oracular tone — his work aspires to the "visionary" in many respects — and, to equal this task, the scope of his prose and poetry traverses, with omnivorous intensity, the realm of ancient and imaginary lands, current political and spiritual tensions, as well as the daily livery of domestic life. More than this, Kelly claims to make little apparent distinction between his projects. As he remarks in the "Afterword" to his first collection of short fiction, *A Transparent Tree* (1985): "My concern is for writing, and for me poetry and fiction and anything else are at times useful but scarcely necessary labels to identify momentary crest-forms in the idea of language writing and language saying."[8] It might be said, in other words,

---

8. Robert Kelly, *A Transparent Tree* (1985) 195.

that Kelly is predominantly interested in how language comes into being, how language takes shape, not the genres that organize their content. As such, the subject of his many varied works resides, I propose, in an ongoing elaboration of the force of language — its potential and its limits — in the daily life of its users. Fertile and rich, each of Kelly's worlds bears the infinite potential of this imaginative spirit. As Edward Schelb remarks, "For Kelly, there is no limit to narrative; the fecundity of words cannot be harnessed."[9] The key then to understanding Kelly's project, one might surmise, is an elaboration of the nature of the limits posed in and by his work: from what tensions they arise and to what purpose.

At first glance, Kelly himself appears to resist precisely this kind of examination. "If I were a critic," he suggests, "I would write a book of Endings ... The ending he [the writer] comes to doesn't end the story — it just reveals him, dusty-jowled, triumphant, self-revealed. If you want to find the writer, forget the autobiography and look at the last pages of the books."[10] Of course, this seems coy advice given the very *wealth* of endings Kelly offers his readers, mere pauses, as it were, in the volubility of his enterprise. It comes with very little surprise that, as Jed Rasula notes,[11] Kelly's declaration to "write everything" seeps into several of his poems, perhaps most notably in *The Loom*:

> ... Say it all
> over again
> but say it all.
> Write everything.
> In ten thousand years
> We have only scratched the surface.
> In another ten,
> the surface itself
> will be worn away.

---

9. Edward Schelb, "The Charred Heart of Polyphemus: Tantric Ecstasy and Shamanic Violence in Robert Kelly's *The Loom*," *Contemporary Literature* 36:2 (summer 1995) 341.

10. Op. cit., 200.

11. See Jed Rasula's "Robert Kelly: A Check List," in *Credences: A Journal of Twentieth Century Poetry and Poetics* 3, Nº 1 (1984 spring): 91–124.

> Will we get to
> the fruit we posit
> beneath the rind?[12]

For Kelly, writing is as often marked by the organic and mythic processes revealed in this brief excerpt, as it is by his interest in the power of language to describe the unspoken, the unremarked, the unimagined: the ability of language to articulate what we can't yet *think*.[13] The command "write everything" refers, in short, not just to what is known, but, just as significantly, to what is *unknown*: everything that language can bring into being.

In his essay "The Gaze of Orpheus," Maurice Blanchot offers insight into this power of language by attempting to examine its limits. As Blanchot reflects, it is Orpheus' desire that sends him to hell to save Eurydice, desire that makes him turn to see his desire, and desire which — by turning to see her — then makes him lose the object of his desire. Orpheus cannot *not* look, even though he knows that to look is to lose, because the success of *not* looking would in fact represent a paradoxical failure of the same desire that propelled him to search for his wife in the first place. Seen in this light, Eurydice comes to represent not just the limits of art, but, more precisely, the limits of the desire the artist tries to describe or reveal in language. "The act of writing," Blanchot concludes, "begins with Orpheus' gaze, and that gaze is the impulse of desire ... But Orpheus already needed the power of art in order to descend to that instant." Later, Blanchot puts it another way: "In order to write one must already be writing."[14] It is this moment, this movement in language, I propose, on which Kelly's prolixity draws, and which he illustrates

---

12. Robert Kelly, *The Loom* (1975) 209.
13. As Kelly remarked, paraphrasing Aristotle during his Plenary Lecture at "Inside Theory / Outside Practice," a Graduate Student Conference at the State University of New York at Albany, "Language allows us to say what we cannot think" (March 24, 2001). See: Pierre Joris & Peter Cockelbergh, *A Voice Full of Cities* (2014) 515 ff.
14. Maurice Blanchot, "The Gaze of Orpheus," *The Gaze of Orpheus* (1981) 104.

— again and again — through the multiple modalities of what he calls "language writing and saying." His short fictions are less interested in resolving the narratives they entertain, than in the expression of desire as language — desire as an act of language — of shaping language into perception. My aim in this brief examination, as a writer of fiction, is to think through the nature of Kelly's desirous language as it appears particularly in his four collections of short stories: *A Transparent Tree* (1985), *Doctor of Silence* (1988), *Cat Scratch Fever* (1990), and *Queen of Terrors* (1994).

Each as Everything

Kelly devotes the second movement of his poem, "Injune," to a short prose fable regarding the nature of narrative that might shed light on how he views his own short fictions. There, an angel informs a writer that narrative is not linear as is generally supposed, before going on to suggest a more complex model based on a network of actions that generate a multiplicity of effects:

> An angel came to me today & told me that my proud dislike of narrative reveals an unwillingness to be accountable for my own actions; I contended that narrative is mostly greediness for guilt. Storytellers fussily choose details. Let the selection be natural (I punned); let what happens happen. Let what happens reveal itself fully & truly in what happens next. If that were true (he smiled) I would have only one pair of wings. You are in the grip of a simplistic belief about causality, hence excuse yourself from natural act. You think this causes that; not so — these cause this. All these cause those.[15]

History too, the angel then goes on to suggest, works on just this model: "... it took many millions [of years]," it remarks, "for you to become the killers you are."[16] This image immediately calls to mind Walter Benjamin's

---

15. Robert Kelly, *Red Actions: Selected Poems 1960–1993* (1995) 101.
16. Ibid., 102.

"angel of history." Yet, whereas Benjamin's angel is faced toward the past, the wreckage of human catastrophe piled up before it as it is blown backward toward the future, Kelly's angel suggests that the present, past, and future are much less autonomous categories. They are in fact interwoven so that future events can be seen prefigured, even the root of, events in the past (inasmuch as the present). History, like narrative, in other words, is not a chain, but a variable network of associations — the branches for instance, of the "transparent tree" that gives Kelly's first collection its name. As Kelly writes:

> I think of fiction as a transparent tree, an intricate, unimpeded proliferation of branches from a common stem. The stories go on, each visible though all the other others, mutually exclusive only by logic (that woodcraft of Time), not in Vision. The shape of a story is the viability of its seed: how ungovernably it will ramify... the writer no more controls the ultimate fiction than the gardener controls the pears plucked by bold children at midnight from his artful espalier.... A story goes on and no branch obliterates another, however they may twist and stretch to share the nurturing light of the reader's after-imaginings, their only eternity.[17]

Over time, he suggests, his fictions go on to take various hues; they grow, become gnarly, alter in shade and density. Stories, in other words, are not isolate or rigid, but interconnected and always subject to change. Narrative is ungovernable; it reproduces in ways its author cannot predict. That is its power, its challenge, its hope.

Kelly's fundamental sense of narrative in part explains his contention in the "Afterword" of *A Transparent Tree* that his first book of short fictions isn't a collection of stories in any conventional sense, that in fact "the stories in this book are not very like one another... Each," he goes on to reflect, "is trying to be everything."[18] In other words, the stories in *A*

17. Op. cit., 199.
18. Ibid., 196.

Transparent Tree — much like Kelly's other collections of short fictions — are less bound by their characters or contents (conventional constituents of fictional *techne*) than their sense of narrative's capability. In result, his fictions are wide-ranging — offering glimpses into the discreet, often exotic worlds, of their inhabitants: from an Old Testament pagan, to the President of Prideful Oil, from a small town doctor to a futuristic scribe (even a drunk bridesmaid). Yet, each story is grounded by a common, powerful desire: the wish to reveal how the world of its protagonists is governed by the words they use to understand it. They are not stories bound by plot, so much as their inhabitants' perceptions of the world around them — and the language they use to make meaning of it for themselves.

For instance, the narrator of Kelly's very short fiction "Orange" (from the collection *Cat Scratch Fever*) showcases this phenomenon when he describes a habit he had as a child of wrapping "his salty old leather belt around his eyes. Through the little holes pierced in the belt for the buckle's tongue (they told him it was called, like the flap in his shoe or the floppy thing in his mouth they kept telling him to hold), he found he could see better."[19] The belt through which the child sees is not unlike the lens of language that colors the rest of Kelly's stories: it not only offers a way of seeing, but it alters the child's perspective as well. Our perceptions, Kelly suggests, are effects of language, not just representations that language communicates or describes. Indeed, as the story continues, the narrator considers questions of race — how racial issues are shaped in and by language — and how language has the ability to place its subjects in the world even as it can disenfranchise them from its fundamental power structures. For Kelly, language isn't just a representative medium: it is nothing less than thought itself.

This philosophical tenet underscores all of Kelly's fictions, and it is the bond that unifies the stories in each collection, and the four collections together as well. Kelly goes further in "The Book and Its Contents," a story from *Doctor of Silence*, in which language is revealed to be perilously material. There, a small town doctor discovers a book that not only composes itself, but whose words — a peacock, an elephant,

---

19. Robert Kelly, *Cat Scratch Fever* (1990) 24.

a small city, schoolgirls with baskets of flowers — each come into being as it is read. The doctor himself eventually disappears under mysterious circumstances, and his patient (the narrator of the story), sends the book to a Fortean Museum[20] where it is filed under the listing of "Conjurations and Spells, Bad Effects of" — a category which the narrator notes is "clearly nonsense, unless we choose to regard the whole panoply of human language as one interminable magic spell that long ago got utterly out of control."[21] Kelly is even more direct with this theme in "Russian Tales" — a series of 37 stories from *Cat Scratch Fever* that Kelly describes as "fairy tales" — in which he allows "language to tell its own stories" by transcribing Slavic morphemes from a grammar book (Townsend's *Continuing with Russian*) into their aural English counterparts.[22] The resulting stories are random, unplanned narratives which highlight that language, as Kelly puns, "is utterly able."

In keeping with this theme, the difference between the writer and the written is downplayed in Kelly's work. The result is a complex relation of the writer *in* and *with* language (as opposed to his expression *through* it). As Kelly implies, language is the substance of both. The "biblical calf" advises a worshipper as much in Kelly's story *The Calf of Gold*:

> Try to remember as much as you can, try not to forget what it felt like in you when you weren't sure whether my strength poured into you or yours into me. You will never be sure, there is no difference — remember the feel of it then, of not being sure, but of knowing the energy was moving, and you could not be sure of you or sure of me.[23]

Language, in short, is the thematic desire that connects Kelly's fables with stories that traverse lands, travel across books, through people

---

20. Charles Fort (1874—1932) was a writer and skeptic who researched "anomalous phenomena."
21. Robert Kelly, *Doctor of Silence* (1988) 53.
22. Robert Kelly, *Cat Scratch Fever* (1990) 47.
23. Op. cit., 10.

and history, the uncharted and unchartable lands in the mind, rifts in time, space, and logic. All of these terrains within the imagination are territories that Kelly negotiates with awe for how his characters (how we) continue to make connections, how we understand the world both *in* and *as* language. As he remarks, "I suppose that if my fiction has one pervasive theme, it is that people (my feckless heroes and heroines, my me) do not know what is happening to them. In the bewilderment of sensuous focus and inconstant intention they move, heroically enough, waiting for the world to decipher itself, or clue them in. Waiting for word in a strange town."[24] Kelly's narratives, in short, are about "getting word," about moving, not just forward but in all the directions that language permits: to make "transparent," as it were, that language itself is a "honey" (to return to the epigraph of this paper) for which the writer — created in and creating language — continually moves in an ongoing state of desire.

---

24. Op. cit., 198.

SHARON MESMER

UNFINISHED SENTENCE → UNFINISHED SENTIENCE
REVISITING MY ESSAY "ORDERING EMPTINESS: ROBERT KELLY'S *THE SCORPIONS*"

Looking back at my essay, written in I-can't-remember-when, I see all my preoccupations of that time, front-loaded and projected onto Robert's novel: silence (and its manifestations as sound), story, time, ordering/cataloging, ancient rituals in contemporary life, Ramanujan. Very interesting. (At least to me.)

I began the essay with Robert's "Afterword" to the second edition of *The Scorpions*:

> When I was a little boy, I had a favorite time. It was on the rare morning when I was home from school, sickness or religious holiday, and my parents were at work and I was alone. I would sit on the blue day-bed in the dining room, downstairs, the window shaded by the mulberry tree, and listen to the clock ticking ... Silence, deep silence, with one clock singing through it ... as if the very sound it made were the cloth that silence wore to let me see it.

Silence provided an entrée into the world of his novel, and I connected it with emptiness, and — my pet investigation of that time — story:

> "Story is the record of ourselves in the moment that proceeds out of one silence (or emptiness) and ends in another."

But is silence really so connected to emptiness that the terms are interchangeable? Isn't that like always deploying the "disorder" definition of chaos, when the word really suggests something more akin to "formlessness"? It's no surprise that human beings applied "chaotic" to mean "formlessness"; we did, after all, come up with the told-tales that ordered formlessness for us, making our quotidian groundlessness manageable. And isn't the ability to tell stories a distinct feature of our humanness? In my essay I noted:

How we have always ordered that moment in stories, plays, songs and poetry, mimics birth, living, and dying: arriving, lingering, leaving — a simple framework within which content is everything. And the content of the one moment is always the pure experience we create against the emptiness, to fill it. Perhaps the purpose of such ordering (and its ubiquitousness: even sitcoms are stories, after all) is reassurance: yes, you are still in the moment, still alive and moving through the passage. It's the song we sing back to ourselves through Time. Thus, if, as Kelly suggests, sound is the cloth that silence wears to be seen, then story is how we individualize the cloth, how we insinuate and mark our having been in the moment by the fabrics, patterns, the ceremonial or quotidian uses we ascribe to it. But there is always the silence, the emptiness, to contend with, and the cloth is no true protection. This, the narrator of *The Scorpions* knows, and seeks in every moment to fill and order the emptiness. In 188 pages, the word 'empty' and its related forms appear 38 times.

Thus my essay began on a misapprehension, despite my precision regarding other ideas (mostly my own), but a misapprehension not so far removed from the one at the heart of Robert's novel — I see this now, actually, and will get to it later. For now, I'm saying that my essay presented what seemed, at first (and maybe only to me), like a cogent case for the ordering of emptiness, just like Robert's novel builds a good case for the Scorpions being responsible for the cryptic and threatening messages that baffle the narrator. The narrator of the novel is, as Robert describes in the "Afterword": "... a genius of the apotropaic, a rhapsodic paranoid, and a bad man." "Bad"? I don't know about that. But he did contribute something to the composite narrator in my own short story, "Revenge," an excerpt of which was included in the recently-published anthology *I'll Drown My Book: Conceptual Writing by Women* from Les Figues (and originally published in my short fiction collection *In Ordinary Time*, Hanging Loose Press, 2005). In my essay I described Robert's narrator as:

> ... a mystically-inclined, rather libidinous shrink who is enticed (by his own sense of the significance of things) into a chase that culminates — unexpectedly, for both narrator and readers — in a

shocking murder. After he and one of his patients receive cryptic messages written in violet ink and signed 'Order of the Scorpions in the East,' he begins looking for clues as to who this group might be. Soon, he is followed while driving, and harassed.

In my short story "Revenge" he went from shrink to university professor (familiarity breeds contretemps?), and instead of being on the trail of the Order of the Scorpions, a mysterious, medieval seeming-mafia, he was on the trail of a beautiful, manipulative, lower-class termagant. (A further note: "Revenge" was written to seem, to all appearances, to have been written by the prof. about the termagant, but we see at the very end that the termagant has written it about the prof., and herself. But back to the connections at hand.) As I wrote in my essay:

> ... to find the Scorpions, we soon see, is not the point. The detailing, the observations, the measures and speculations, are. So that when nothing definitive turns up at the end, and the tale ends with an unfinished sentence, we are not disappointed, because we have seen our own ordering of emptiness sung back to us.

"Sung"? I might not have used that word had I written that essay today. But I was trying to bring everything around to the idea in Robert's "Afterword": "Silence, deep silence, with one clock singing through it ... as if the very sound it made were the cloth that silence wore to let me see it."

These days I'm not so interested in those notions of silence / emptiness. But I am interested, now, in the misapprehensions I created (if only for myself), following, perhaps, as I noted in my essay, the example of Robert's narrator, the libidinous shrink:

> One of the ways the narrator orders and measures emptiness is by obsessive listing. There appear to be (by my rough count) at least 15 discrete lists, and other kinds of orderings that may be thought of as lists. These first three are actual lists:

> "Then the fat envelope from the Humble Oil & Refining Company with my month's credit-card billings ... rubber-stamped with all the places I'd been. Natick, Mass. Essex, Mass. Street. Paramus, N.J. Easton, Pa. Ninety-sixth Street. Ninety-sixth Street. $78.41.

> Sally put a cigarette between my lips: Guess what it is. The dark papery taste elided fragrance, spoke of filter. Kent Belair Oasis Lark? No. Winston Salem Masterpiece Omega? No. Marlboro Tareyton pudding-n-pie. No. Galaxy? No. Parliament red Luckies Pall Mall gold? No. I give up. Go on... Paxton Carlton Montclair. No. I give up. L&M. No... Do you give up? I said so three times. Tempo. Time out? No, that's the cigarette: Tempo. The taste of time; empty, flat; spoiling the mouth; untaste."

(Note that punctuating this particular list is talk of Eros Proktikos: A Dissertation on Anal Erotism, by Anonymous, which the narrator discovers in an outhouse during the early stages of his quest, and which is blank except for a pencil-written narrative called 'Among the Eosites' — one of three stories-within-stories in the book — which itself contains possibly the most dizzying sets of lists:

> Colonel Eddebly read off a list of words ... Turkey soup. Whiffletree. Corpus luteum. Earwax. Tennyson. Guano. Cantilever. Excise tax. Spurious. Bludgeon. Widgeon. Pigeon. Whortleberry. Cloaca. Dog. Andrew Jackson. Sandcastle ...

Later, the narrator is perusing a book (one of many) for information on the Scorpions. Nothing gets turned up, but what he does find comprises this list-within-a-list:

> ... I encountered the Illuminati of Vaduz, the Wood-Masters of the Poconos (all safely behind bars now), the Underarmers (sobaquistes) of Port-au-Prince (who determine the soul's election to grace by the odor of the axillary regions, as tested by their Committee of Three), the curious Neo-Nasrany of Trucial Oman, who contend that Mohammed was an avatar of Jesus, and like him suffered crucifixion ... the Sons of Saint Fiacre, an Irish terrorist group whose stock-in-trade is the introduction of plant poison into English country gardens ... the Masters of the Hidden Howdah, a society of babus dedicated to the occupation and enslavement of the

> British Isles by the Indians, a goal at least numerically feasible; when their one-flight up Calcutta headquarters were raided, the police found their leader (known only as Ashoka XVII) flown and the premises empty except for a huge cabinet photograph of Ramanujan, three dozen Japanese tape recorders and many copies of *The Serpent Power*.

Digression: the mention of Ramanujan, the genius Indian mathematician, was of special interest to me. Ever since I'd read Robert Kanigel's *The Man Who Knew Infinity* in 1991, I was obsessed with the man to whom answers to complex math problems were provided by his family goddess, Namagiri. Both Ramanujan's mother and grandmother were devoted to Namagiri, and in fact the grandmother had a vision of the goddess warning her of "a bizarre murder plot involving teachers at a local school" — are there echoes of this in Robert's book? Of course, I wanted to think so, even if there weren't.

End of digression. In my essay, I wrote:

> The climax of the book should come when the narrator is kidnapped and brought to a ritual. We (and he) think the nature and purpose of the Scorpions will finally be revealed. But, appropriately, this doesn't happen. His presence at the ritual is as mere witness ... All the narrator's research and knowledge comes to naught — these aren't the Scorpions! They're just a bunch of flesh-worshippers — like himself! He continues on, and catches up with the group that harassed him at the beginning of the story. This encounter ends when he murders two of them, but no real conclusion is offered (were the kids really the Scorpions, or just rural pranksters?) He picks up the girl, Iris, who was their traveling companion. She seems nonplussed that both of the men are dead.

Thus: the misapprehensions at the heart of both Robert's novel, and my essay. Both narrators built their cases with lists, but in the end ... nothing is solved. Perhaps one difference is that, in my essay, no one died.

Robert's novel is a delight. Can I say that about my essay? Not so much.

One thing I can say is that, like Iris, I am "just a simple girl hitchhiking": Robert's novel ends with an incomplete sentence — "Right ahead of us was a soft dense patch of mist. We entered it and the boat" — and so does my essay:

> Does the narrator trouble to wonder whether he has misapprehended the clues? No. That he has come so far and come up empty? It doesn't seem so. He will go on with his rituals and his orderings and his measuring of Time, perhaps more so than ever. And what if I myself, as another kind of witness, have misapprehended the clues — as in Kafka's telling of the man who waits for the door to be opened, and then finds it has been open all the time, and is now about to be closed? That just may

Ramanujan said: "The death of a person can only occur in a certain space-time conjunction point."

Can the end of a story (or essay) be

STEVEN FAMA

A TRULY TRIPPY PROSE POEM

Robert Kelly's *Cities* is arguably not poetry. It's written in prose: a 65-page fictional travel memoir, of a kind, with elements of fantasy and sci-fi, all narrated in the first person by an imagined character named Selvage Immanuel Hodgkins.

It's also difficult to find, at least in its original edition, which has, as detailed below, an exceptionally fine cover design. There currently are only about a half-dozen used copies for sale on the internet's used book sites, ranging in price from 15 to 100 dollars. If you can afford to do so, get one, I advise, and quick. Otherwise, you can try to borrow a copy from a private collection (good luck) or from a library (it's only in about 100, all but a few associated with universities). It's also available in *A Transparent Tree* (2013), an omnibus collection of Kelly's fictions (note: I insist *Cities* is a prose poem!).

And yet despite, or maybe because of its ambiguous character given its prose, and somewhat occult status, *Cities* — a most fantastic work — ought to be celebrated as poetry, and more widely read. And thus the mission here today: to show and tell a bit about *Cities* and its prose poetry, and perhaps encourage some to go out and find it.

For my discovery of *Cities*, Larry Fagin, who circa 2005 included the book on his list of "poetry neglectorinos," must be credited. As must Ron Silliman, who published Fagin's list on his blog, thus bringing it, and Kelly's book, to my attention.

When Fagin listed Kelly's *Cities* as a poetry neglectorino, he remarked, and I think tellingly, "I know, it's prose, but...."

The key there is the "but." I don't exactly know what Fagin meant by that qualifier. However, by including the book on his list even while acknowledging its character as prose, it seems clear that Fagin considers *Cities* a kind of poem. I agree. Kelly's book is poetry, despite being a fictional first-person memoir told in sentences, paragraphs, and chapters/sections. More specifically, it's a prose poem, rich with heightened attention to and use of language, and passages that burn with imaginative energy.

The opening sentence of *Cities*, a question posed by the fictional narrator to himself and to the book's readers, reveals much about the narrator and the work's subject matter, but much more about the richness of Robert Kelly's imagination and the poetic-ness of the writing:

> Where shall I take myself with my ostrich luggage and peacock pride?

Well right away there's poetry, yes? I mean especially in those two adjectives — "ostrich" and "peacock." From those words, poetry — er, um — takes wing!

First there's the obvious relation between the two adjectives. Both drawn from the world of ground-dwelling birds, they thus connote moving across the earth, and thus directly relate to, and reinforce, the notion of moving across the earth, or travel, the (*voilà*!) underlying subject of both the first sentence and the poem itself.

The adjectives also provide detail and color. Via the birds, they also suggest not only movement across land or even actual flight (as in a plane), but via association and deeper connotations, imaginative flight.

There isn't another combination of adjectives that would have worked so well, and so poetically. I mean, it's just a perfect freaking opening. You, the reader, sit down with *Cities*. You open the book. You turn to the first page, and the first sentence. And there it is, that greeting in the form of a question, and just like that, in that question, and more important, in the eyes of your mind, the narrator's: W-o-w! Away we go! The "ostrich luggage and peacock pride" suggest it will be quite a trip. A journey both extravagant and outsized.

Yet notice how the first sentence plays, how the critical details are relayed by Kelly. It couldn't be more straightforward. They are extravagant and out-sized, yes, but the narrator is disarmingly open and direct about it all. In this way, it all comes off as totally believable.

That mix of specific, vivid detail and an "I'm just-telling-it-like-it-is" tone is what gives *Cities* its irresistible verve. Here's the narrator, on the second and third pages, introducing himself:

> I am 47 years old, in excellent physical condition, of more than moderate wealth, of rubicund and mesomorphic physique but Saturnine disposition. I own houses in New York, London, Paris & Calcutta; lodges in Scotland, New Mexico, the Côte d'Azur, Ceylon and Darjeeling; apartments in Moscow, Tokyo, San Francisco, Rio and Cairo. I own seven cars, a ranch in Argentina, 3000 acres of Maine timber, a palace in Iran, two yachts, four motor boats, a modest old Ford tri-motor, a houseboat on the Irrawaddy, a 37-foot limestone wall richly carved with Hindu fable, a moderately powerful radio station In Luristan, a controlling interest in three small cheese companies and a middling oil cartel. I own no pets. I own three cemetery plots outright, one acre's freehold in Westmorland, the largest dairy farm in Hokkaido, and one glass eye. Many monophthalmics own two or several glass eyes, fragile things that they are. But I unswervingly put my faith in the law of Unicity, which seems unlikely twice to rob one man of the same eye.

This is all "droll and explicit," to use a phrase Kelly puts in the narrative in the sentence that immediately follows the above-quoted text. But of course it is also fantastic. Chiefly and primarily fantastic. As in amazing, there is no way on earth this could be true.

And yet, there comes a point in the paragraph above — for me it was somewhere around the carved limestone wall and three cemetery plots — where the waves of imagination capsize all resistance. Disbelief drowns. There's no fucking way any of it could be real, yet it seems as if every last thing there actually is.

This tone — essential to the impact of *Cities* — results in large part from Kelly's use of (poetry alert) details. Many of the things discussed in the paragraph above are given specified quantities. Others are provided with adjectives ("middling" and "small" and "largest," for example), that make the modified items far less abstract. There is also spare but effective use of exotic and unfamiliar place names ("Irrawaddy" and "Luristan" for example (consult your atlas) and filigree (a wall "richly carved in Hindu fable"), mixed in with the well-known ("San Francisco") and more plain ("houses")). There are also vocabularic gems ("rubicund," "mesomorphic," "Saturnine," and "monophthalmics") scattered about, the kind of words that when as here used infrequently deserve the appellation poetic.

The paragraph quoted above also features a snap-to-attention rhythmic change. In about its middle, and in contrast to all the other sentences, which are compound, sometimes with multiple clauses, there is one super-short sentence, of four little words: "I own no pets." That one seems to me a deal-sealer. Amidst all the long sentences, the mind latches onto that one, and not just because it's a jab mixed in with a series of roundhouse sentence-punches. Kelly, I think, has a particular reason he uses the short sentence to grab your attention.

That the narrator owns no pets seems surprising, given all the possessions that have been just listed, and those that follow. But while surprising, it doesn't seem untruthful. Quite the contrary: it strikes one as honest. Truthful. This narrator doesn't have everything, and what's more, he admits it. The point is immediately reinforced, of course, by the detail involving the glass eye. These admissions of limits, of imperfections, seem admirably honest. This approach disarms skepticism. This here narrator is exceedingly incredible, but not totally so. Kelly, the poet, in this way calibrates his story-poem details so that it seems real, so that we accept that what is told is simply just the way it is, or was.

Kelly's convincing approach is essential because this travel memoir, while passing through or mentioning certain well-known places (e.g., Moscow, Paris, Rio) is not much concerned with them. Nor is it concerned with any place that you or, really, anybody, has ever visited, or even heard about. Instead, the prose poem provides, to use the narrator's words from a few pages in, "an account of some of the secret cities of the world."

Yes, "secret cities," with some of them quite hidden, as in existing at and in the same time and space, and thus parallel with, some other, better-known place. And thus away, away-away, we readers go, go, go.

4 · A BOOK ON NARRATIVE

In *Cities*, the reader = initiate, the poet-narrator = adept. To me, that's an enjoyable dynamic: poet, please show me the (a) way.

It'd be difficult to properly describe or even just list all the places visited by the narrator in *Cities*, or the various modes of transportation used, or customs and ideas encountered. Of course doing that would spoil the fun you'll have once you get hold of the book.

Suffice it to say that there's lots of great stuff. In one paragraph, for example, you'll read something related to nuclear fission that occurs in a particular city, and then just a few pages later there's a discussion of another secret city's published writings, which are never in prose but instead written in accord with a "rigidly observed metrical formulæ."

What, you doubt that everything in that city — its name, by the way, is "New Harappa" — is written in accord with strict principles of poetic form? Well, Kelly may well have anticipated your skepticism. Once again, Kelly buttons it all down with plenty of detail. In this regard, his narrator presents a schemata of the verse form used in New Harrapa, described as "a distich of double lines":

$$
\begin{array}{llll}
/\,x\,x & /\,x\,x & /\,x\,x\,x \mid & /\,x\,x^{a} \\
/\,x\,x^{a} \mid & /\,x\,x & /\,x\,x & /\,x\,x^{b} \\
/\,x\,x^{b} & /\,x\,x & /\,x\,x\,x \mid & /\,x\,x^{c}
\end{array}
$$

&c.

And this form is then explicated, via a description of other applicable rules, as follows:

> The words marked *a* must exemplify alliteration *and* assonance, or rime, with one another, but not both. In the third foot of the first line, and only there, may occur a free number of unstressed syllables. The *b* rime (or assonance or alliteration) links each distich to the next. Distichs are commonly endstopped (and always in the older huënëha, 'old man's lullaby,' an expanded simple narrative form

involving "lays" or strophes of 50 distichs), and cæsura never follows the second *b* rime — hence the *b* is the weaker, or 'lunar' rime in a distich (since its second part is 'thrown away in the darkness'), while the a rime is 'solar.'

Can somebody out there try writing a poem in accord with these precepts?

I've mentioned two out of many — probably several dozen — events or explications in *Cities* that are likely to strike you as strange, passing strange. Each and every one of which, of course, was thought up, invented, made real through language, by Robert Kelly. And maybe that's really what makes this collection of sentences a prose poem.

Which is to say, for all the ways language is used poetically in *Cities*, it might be enough to say that the book's a poem simply because of the intensity of the imagination with which it burns, word to word, sentence to sentence, paragraph to paragraph. It never lets up. Okay, almost never. There are a few, a very few, somewhat ho-hum details. For example, most who've read any amount of comic books or sci-fi won't find much in the half-sentence about how residents of a certain city turn infra-red and become invisible.

But such pedestrian imaginings are rare. Essentially everything presented is something completely different. Reading it, I was giddy with amazement at the inventiveness, and just when that sensation was about to pass, Kelly would lay on something more. You turn a page and holy E-ticket, here's the narrator relating the circumstances of how he left a particular secret city:

> They made me mount a brightly painted wooden merry-go-round horse, whose pommel was of thick braided gold. The chamberlain whispered a word into the horse's ear, and I found myself high above the city, streaking through the sky. I was in Irkutsk within the hour; the horse left me at the airport, in time for the weekly jet. Spring opened its gooseflesh arms to me in Moscow.

In these few sentences Kelly gives us a string of events (the painted carousel horse, animated by a whisperer, that flies to the gooseflesh

Moscow spring) that any good surrealist (cf. Lautréamont's umbrella, sewing machine, and dissection table) would love. Or for that matter, any poetry lover (cf. Pierre Reverdy's assertion that images are strongest when the associations of ideas are distant and accurate).

May I provide another example of the poetry, the intensity of language used? Here's the narrator's comment about what he felt when a vast and dazzling city vanished entirely as he turned around to take a look at it from an exit gate:

> There is no need to give any account of the self-evident and predictable tenor of my thoughts — write them up for yourself, reader, or assume them as delivered and signed for; we have all looked on emptiness, we have all plummeted in heart's bathyscaphe to a deep current where demonic luminescent enigmas grin at us in the pressurized cabin of our isolate despair. I have no wish to detain you with the obvious.

I find absolutely extraordinary Kelly's extended metaphor with the heart's bathyscaphe, the deep current, grinning demonic luminescent enigmas, and the pressurized cabin. When I first came upon it in the book, I just stopped, and read it again, and again, and then one more time. And who wouldn't do the same, even though (and this is funny, and another sign of the genius of this work) Kelly's narrator, in the sentence following the extended metaphor (and included in the excerpt above), insists he has no desire to detain us with what we have just read!

Of course, after a suitable pause to admire the beauty of the metaphor involving the bathyscaphe and other watery matters, I continued to read *Cities*. I assure you, as unlikely as it may sound, that within a page Kelly had again blown my mind, so wondrous was what happened next and how Kelly's words made it happen.

Yes indeed, *Cities*, a work about travels that is written with language that transports the reader, is one truly trippy prose poem. And really, that should be all that needs to be said.

Go seek Kelly's book, kind readers.

STEVEN FAMA

A Note on the Cover Design of Cities

Per the credit on the copyright page, the design of *Cities*, including presumably the cover, is by Ron Caplan. The cover's striking combination of black letters on white background is similar to three other Frontier Press titles published at around the same time as *Cities* including their re-print of Williams' (as they called it) *Spring & All*.

The lettering on the cover of *Cities* is particularly brilliant. The book title is all capitals, C-I-T-I-E-S, but with an obvious and beautifully apt, twist: each of the I's is topped by a dot, the kind found atop lower case i's. They're no-doubt-about-it dots too, so perfectly proportioned, rich and black, that they dominate the top of the cover.

The blending here of upper-and-lower-case characteristics is unusual, of course, even odd. Yet that strangeness perfectly reflects the outré quality of what Kelly tells about in *Cities*. And the mix of letter characteristics also fits with the hybrid nature of the work as prose poetry. In addition, the dots on the cover, as round circles, suggest planets or other worlds. Places, in other words, that might be traveled to, which again fits with the substance of the book.

Finally, the cover just looks damn good. Bold and beautiful, the kind of thing you just gotta have. *Cities* is one book that you could appropriately judge by its cover![25]

25. This is a slightly revised version of an essay first published on Steven Fama's "the glade of theoric ornithic hermetica" blog, September 2009: http://stevenfama.blogspot.com/2009/09/truly-trippy-prose-poem.html

JOHN YAU

A MAP THAT NEVER STAYS THE SAME
ON *A LINE OF SIGHT*

Sun Tzu's Sixth Century treatise, *The Art of War*, is one of the precursors to Gertrude Stein's *How to Write* (1931). Written in different epochs, under different dark clouds, war either in progress or just around the fork in the road, these manuals are invaluable to an understanding of writing and the written, but in dissimilar ways. The primary difference is that Sun Tzu believed in narrative, with its carefully constructed beginning, middle, and end. It was an arc, though not a rainbow.

For Sun Tzu, the careful construction of a narrative arc — or arch through which the reader / writer passes — with its purposeful deceptions, was necessary to achieve a resolution to the text, wherever and whenever it was written. Obeying one or more of his rules, all numbered and set out in *The Art of War*, decisions were to logically follow one another as well as fit together, their seams not evident to the reader / writer sitting in the distance, whether on a horse or in front of his tent, watching his sentences move across — and mark — the earth. Otherwise, London Bridge would collapse, as the children's song insists.

Robert Kelly breaks rule 36 under the section titled "Maneuvering": "When you surround an army, leave an outlet free. Do not press a desperate foe too hard."

It is a rule that realist writers of every stripe have memorized, whether they know it or not. They do not want to write a sentence that stands by itself, with no outlet, isolated from home, and with no place to go to next. The realist gets on the uptown IRT at the bottom of Manhattan and minutes or years later he gets off. It can be 42nd Street or El Dorado, a place made only of words but that is as real as any world is.

"I live in an old house that has no address," Robert Kelly tells us at the outset of his prose meditation, *A Line of Sight*.[26] The reader wonders what can possibly come next. How will the writer get himself out of this cul-de-sac? This is the question I asked when I first read *A Line of Sight*. The copy of it in my possession is from the "Second Printing, May 1974."

---

26. Pierre Joris & Peter Cockelbergh, *A Voice Full of Cities* (2014) 410 ff.

I know that I read *A Line of Sight* when it first came out, some months earlier, and that I bought both thin, stapled editions at the Grolier Poetry Book Shop, 6 Plympton Street, Cambridge, Mass, which is the "oldest continuous poetry bookshop in the United States." I learned of the Grolier when I was in high school — I believe there was an article on it in the Boston Globe — and the one person near my age that I met there was the poet and translator Ammiel Alcalay.

Gordon Cairnie, who was born in Canada in 1893, opened the Grolier in 1927. Cairnie was around 70 when I met him, and had been running the store for 40 years. He was a friend of Conrad Aiken, who lived upstairs at 6 Plympton. Cairnie had gone to Harvard to study landscape architecture and ended up opening a bookstore that sold, as the hand-printed sign on the front door tersely announced, "only poetry, no text books."

Landscape architecture and poetry rhyme, as Alexander Pope knew when he entered a hidden passageway from the cellar of his villa at Twickenham, walked past the grotto he had designed — it lacked only nymphs, he wrote a friend — and entered a tunnel that went under a road and emerged in his secret garden.

We live in time. *A Line of Sight* is different from when I first read it more than 35 years ago and, needless to say, so am I. This is my first attempt to map a small territory of Kelly's that I have explored many times over the years, but until now I have written almost nothing down about my travels there.

* * *

At the end of the first sentence of Chapter I of *A Line of Sight*, the reader is directed to "Note 1," which begins: "A road, but no street. A street, but no number." According to the author, he has "computed that by the grid of the city down the river" (he is speaking of New York City, specifically Manhattan), he lives on 2097th Street, West 2097th St. "But," as he goes on to say, "that city is no longer anybody's system. The grid is more spacious now, builds up as well as out, comprises the nearer stars, has its roots in water." "The nearer stars," not the nearest stars. The former suggests a vastness that knows no end, while the latter points to an unstable limit.

"The house is dark most days," Kelly tells us in the second sentence of Chapter I. The fact that it has no address doesn't bother him because it doesn't actually reveal where he is in the vastness, of which we know only a tiny, perforated sliver. Even the city down the river — its storied gathering of money and power, and institutions, such as the Museum of Modern Art and the Guggenheim Museum — "is no longer anybody's system."

According to Kelly, who seems not to have left the house yet: "Years ago it had a name, 2, taken from the two lime trees that block the afternoon sun from the front windows, trees much sought by bees in May and June." I finish the third sentence of Chapter I before turning to "Note 2: a name, Erwin Smith the postmaster lived in the house around the turn of the century, and called the place Lindenwood, from the two in front, one at the side, saplings all around."

Kelly tells us

> The tree is Schubert's Lindenbaum, an aching song of nostalgia that summoned Hans Castorp back into the bourgeois world from the bourgeois dreamworld of Davos. I don't know much about Erwin Smith, but pieces of hardware from the original house turn up in other houses round about. A characteristic door-hinge. A hasp.

The "dreamworld of Davos" was where those with lung ailments went in the 19th Century. Robert Louis Stevenson and Arthur Conan Doyle spent time there. It is the setting for Thomas Mann's *Magic Mountain*. Ernst Ludwig Kirchner painted the mountains, before committing suicide there on June 15, 1938, five years after his works were condemned by the Nazis as "degenerate."

Is there an occult power emanating from this house, in which a postmaster and a poet — individuals who puzzle over words and are concerned with messages, origins, and destinations — have chosen to live? Kelly makes no mention of this because it is already there for us to read. Some rhymes do not need to end in a rhyme.

* * *

A Line of Sight is five short chapters, none more than a page. Chapter I is the longest at four paragraphs. The 12 "notes" are divided among the first four chapters, with no notes to the last chapter. The longest note is the 5th to Chapter I, consisting of four paragraphs. You read back and forth, stopping at the end of a sentence to turn to a note, before finding your way back. You both return and do not return to where you were. Heraclitus is precise about this. Along the way the mind drifts.

On June 5, 1967, Kelly wrote the poem "(Prefix":,[27] which ends:

> Finding the Measure is finding the
> specific music of the hour,
>   the synchronous
> consequence of the motion of the whole world.

I turned 17 on June 5, 1967 and would graduate from high school before the month was over. By then, I spent nearly every Saturday going by trolley and subway from my family's apartment in Brookline to Harvard Square, Cambridge, which was on the other side of the Charles River — always ending up in the Grolier. In my senior year, I met with my guidance counselor who advised me to join the army. He felt that I needed to learn discipline, that I wasn't ready for college and, though he hoped otherwise, may in fact never be ready for it. I chose poetry instead.

* * *

"History," Michel de Certeau writes in his essay "Walking in the City,"

> begins at ground level, with footsteps. They are the number, but a number that does not form a series. They cannot be counted because each unit is qualitative in nature: a style of tactile apprehension and kinesic appropriation. They are replete with innumerable anomalies.

De Certeau goes on to say:

> The act of walking is to the urban system what the act of speaking, the Speech Act, is to language or to spoken utterance. On the most elementary level it has in effect a threefold "uttering"

---

27. Joris & Cockelbergh, *A Voice Full of Cities* (2014) 687.

function: it is the process of appropriation of the topographic system by the pedestrian (just as the speaker appropriates and assumes language); it is a spatial realization of the site (just as the act of speaking is a sonic realization of language); lastly it implies relationships among distinct positions, i.e. pragmatic "contracts" in the form of movements (just as the verbal utterance is "allocution," 'places the others' before the speaker, and sets up contracts between fellow speakers). A first definition of walking thus seems to be a space of uttering.

Or, to see it from another angle, a first definition of uttering thus seems to be a space of walking, of moving from one place to another without necessarily moving, as Kelly writes,

> in an old house with no address, [where e]specially at the foot of the stairs it is dark, bottom of a dry well. On the wall above the last few treads is a large map of the Kingdom of Bhutan (Druk Yul), showing in monochrome relief the ranges and valleys and way stations. In the uncertain light that at times fall on this map from the opposite room, the tan spread of Druk Yul (isolated from the uncolored surround, India, China, Tibet) sometimes resembles a large cookie, 4 at other times a fallen leaf, which before withering rumpled into the crests and gorges.

Appropriations, realizations, contracts.

Everything Kelly observes is qualified, revealing that whatever place we consciously or unconsciously inhabit — call it a house or reality — is in a state of flux. The light that falls on the map is "uncertain." Druk Yul "sometimes resembles a large cookie."

Against this uncertainty Kelly juxtaposes another uncertainty:

> In one corner of the map there is a smaller replica, in outline, of the map itself. This diagram is called a Reliance Index, and shows sector by sector the confidence, expressed in percentages, 5 that the viewer can feel in the information

sketched or verbalized in the large map. It is to be wished that every map conceded in such a way the inevitable inadvertency of its parts.

A Line of Sight is a provisional map of a hallway and staircase in Robert Kelly's house with no address. If there are other hallways and other staircases in the house, they are, for the moment, the "uncolored surround." We are at the "bottom of a dry well." In Note I to Chapter IV, we learn that "[o]ften it is stifling at the head of the stairs, the long hall to the bedroom lined with books and maps. By the doorless doorway, the heat is gentler. The bed is cool."

* * *

Ralph Waldo Emerson observed: "I am not solitary whilst I read and write, though nobody is with me." We learn from the five Notes to Chapter I that Erwin Smith, Franz Schubert, Hans Castorp, John Navins, Helen's Great Aunt Malcha, Diane Wakoski, Beethoven, La Monte Young, Diter Rot, Richard Strauss, Rossini, and Pradyumna P. Karan, the "cartographer of the Druk Yul map," are in the house with Kelly.

Within the framework of uttering, the walker, in relation to his position, creates a near and a far, a here and a there. (de Certeau)

There is no there there. (Stein)

Within the framework of walking, the speaker, in relation to his position, creates a here and a there. (Yau, after de Certeau)

> In the hall there the map of Bhutan is large, and under it the map of Yucatan *1* is small but colorful, with tiny pictures of temples and deities marking the sites. In that specific sense, the god was flayed in the hallway, in the half light, or in the evening ugly yellow glare of the three overhead bulbs, Uxmal was built. (Kelly)

Uxmal means "built three times" in the Mayan language, although some scholars dispute this derivation.

At the end of Chapter II: "Note 1: Yucatan. The neighborhood has a number of spiritual links with Yucatan, and at least one unpublicized telluric *nadi* or geo-astral vein unites the two terrains." If, for the moment, you have lost where you are and are not sure where you are going, you might remember that you are looking into the dark hallway of a house on West 2097th Street, which is, as Kelly tells us at the end of Note 1: Yucatan, a "northernmost outpost of the Mayan Empire, a ruin like the rest, surrounded by dense thickets and a quiet swamp with very black water."

The Mayan Empire and Manhattan share this house with no address. Arthur Machen is the one taxi driver who can get me there without the help of a GPS. His cab is green and white with a red dragon painted on its sides. He directs my attention to the sign receding in his rearview mirror that says we have passed Mill Haven and Castle Rock. He tells me not to worry, because many different people — the Manhicans, Wappingers, Irish, Hittites, Cimmerians, Varangians, Crusaders, Venetians, Genoese, Welsh, and Chinese — have all driven down these roads at one time or another, leaving a network of astral tracery. Kelly is waiting to see what other guests will arrive as the nearer stars begin taking their place in the sky.

* * *

Chapter III's first sentence:

The point is, that these objects are not alone in the hall, by any means, but are the ones that can be seen, wholly or in part, from the yellow armchair *1* that stands at the end of the music room *2*, close to the one window the sun reaches, but divided from window and sun by a square small table covered with cactuses, some living, some questionable, some dead.

In Note I for "yellow armchair," I read: "The armchair is by the window. For my present purposes (if these discursions may so be dignified), this chair is important. For one thing, it is the one armchair in the house in which I'm comfortable."

From where I am sitting in time and space — in a brushed aluminum chair in an apartment on 29th Street, Manhattan, across the street from a hotel — I see a man in his late 30s sitting in a yellow armchair. He is looking at what is in front of him. "To the left of the map, and somewhat above it, there is a fierce grinning bright polychrome demon mask of unspecified origin, clearly enough the product of some tantric intelligence of the mountains."

(Across the street from my apartment, there is a blow-up of Allen Ginsberg's black-and-white photograph of Harry Smith high on the wall just past the entrance to the lobby. Smith is the hotel's official greeter. He is seated at a table, pouring a glass of milk, which in all likelihood he did not drink. He died in the Chelsea Hotel, which is six blocks south of here, on November 27, 1991. According to the autopsy, his death was due to "bodily neglect.")

* * *

After talking with his dispatcher, Prince Zaleski, Machen assures me that we will be in Annandale-on-Hudson shortly. Am I the only guest? Have the others already arrived? Or are they, like me, speeding through the thickening dark?

* * *

In his book, *The Practice of Everyday Life*, de Certeau appropriates two military terms, "strategies" and "tactics," to distinguish between those who are in power, high above the city, and those who walk its streets. He defines "strategies" as repeatable methods (actions or Speech Acts) based on an overall narrative or totalizing viewpoint, such as "the author is dead."

"Tactics," on the other hand, are the anarchic individual's use of any mode of action that is likely to gain an advantage or success. The walker in the city goes his or her own way, ignoring the directions offered by the city's grid. One stops to look in the windows of the stores closed up for the night. Another places chrysanthemums by the handprints of Anna May Wong pressed into the wet cement outside Grauman's Chinese Theater.

(Dietrich felt that Wong repeatedly upstaged her in *Shanghai Express*, the train that traveled across a back lot in Hollywood. Josef von Sternberg, who directed *Shanghai Express*, gave Dietrich a Chinese doll, which she kept in her bedroom the rest of her life. There is a photograph of Wong standing between Leni Riefenstahl and Dietrich, taken by Alfred Eisenstaedt in Berlin in 1929. Walter Benjamin wrote about meeting Wong and Carl Van Vechten photographed her. As far as I know, the Benjamin piece has not been translated into English).

* * *

A few blocks from where I live is a hair salon that is open, the sign states, 24/7. At night, walking the dog, I almost always see a woman sitting in a large upholstered leather chair getting her hair done, her back to me or to the window, preferring for the moment to face the mirror — it was both reasonable and practical for her to make an appointment at this hour. Across the street a large silver truck covered with pictures of steaming plates of rice and meat sells Styrofoam containers of halal food to the taxi drivers that have emigrated from Pakistan, India, and Bangladesh. My dog lifts his head, his wet nose quivering. Sun Tzu would have taken a different road to Bhutan.

When the dog and I pass between the hair salon and food truck, we are a few blocks away from the Empire State Building, which was built on the land where a three-story manse owned by the Havemeyers once stood. Henry Osborne Havemeyer founded the American Sugar Refining Company in 1891. Louisine Elder, his second wife and niece of his first, was a friend of Mary Cassatt.

Henry and Louisine gave the Metropolitan Museum of Art many of its Impressionist paintings, including works by Manet, Degas, & Monet. According to the museum's inventory records, nearly 2,000 works in the museum's collection were once in the house on Fifth Avenue.

"Believers identify the mask as the face of an adept holding back his semen, swallowing the world. The face is the brightest object in the hall at the foot of the stairs." (This is the last sentence of Chapter I).

Whatever the address, every house — old or new, small or big — becomes a museum or what Robert Smithson called a sarcophagus, which comes from the Greek and means "flesh eater" because the limestone was thought to decompose the flesh.

> Because of man's sins he perceives the sphere as a circle. Reflected from its convexity, the items of the wall and hall arrange themselves, maps and beasts and masks, thermostat and architecture. The lintel says this is where the wall ends or the door begins. Or the door ends, and no man can pass by. Because of his sins. In the sphere of sight, every object becomes a surface, a surface becomes a word. The word, because of his sins, wanders down the centuries between what we laughably call its root and what we, half-ashamed, half-hopeful, call its

obsolescence. The word wanders, meaning only one thing to him at a time. Because of his sins. Sin, says Clement, is inadvertency. (This is the first paragraph of Chapter IV, the second paragraph is less than half this length).

Let me pause for a moment before continuing.
Reading *A Line of Sight* is to accompany the author on a walk whose only destination is under the sign: Keep your eyes open and pay attention. He seems to stay on the same street, but it keeps changing and diverging. Maybe the path is an illusion.
Tu Fu: "I set out to find you" and "I set out."
One day the author walks to "the old Barrytown post office by the unused depot on the river" and finds in the "postcard rack a view of this very house, E. Smith's Lindenwood." He buys it for "a penny."
Between its root and its obsolescence, the word (the author) wanders, meaning only one thing to him at a time.
Stein sums up the difference between Kelly and herself in the following sentence: "I like a view but I like to sit with my back turned to it." Not all views (as Stein uses the word) are picturesque. In this instance she is conventional in the way she thumbs her nose at being conventional. She has left the path where the word means only thing at a time. *A Line of Sight* keeps opening new doors, keeps drifting and sprouting in unanticipated directions.
On the way to Annandale, Machen introduces the idea of the Holy Grail's continued existence in popular literature. (In another story, Machen recounts how he, Javier Marias, and Stephen King enjoyed a Mexican version of a *Hasenpfeffer* with bottles of wine from Chile's Aconcagua Valley.) Robert Kelly is sitting in his yellow armchair, wondering for a brief moment why his guests are taking so long. He is reading the entry on Edmund Burke in the Eleventh Edition of *Encyclopedia Brittanica*, printed in 1910—1911:

Burke could do nothing,
his hand so far from his head.

The penultimate chapter of *A Line of Sight* is titled "Quintessence." It begins: "It is the last hour of your life. Turn down the thermostat."

4 · A BOOK ON NARRATIVE

Thank you for giving me a moment to catch my breath:

Beyond Bhutan, exactly where you can't see it, is the cabinet of alchemic texts, the red telephone you can't use, the painful manuscript, the air conditioner plugged into the circuit too low in amperage to power it. The chemical lamp, all unseen things. The Brave Soldier has come at last to the bottom of the well. And finds himself in another house, just like all houses, every house. The wall. The wall might be the surface of what the Greeks, in nervous fear, ingratiatingly called the Hospitable, the Euxine Sea, a smiling most dangerous flatterer. We call it Black, and have forgotten to be afraid. The wall wants me to forget everything beyond its so casual opacity.

THREADS 17: ROBERT SAYS

"There's a wonderful story by Borges ("El Aleph") about people going down into a basement as in the "Cask of Amontillado," but the point of it is that the aleph is the single unspoken. In this way he's close to Cabala, the unspoken sound of which all sounds are manifestations. Aleph is the first letter in the Hebrew alphabet. It has no pronunciation in modern times, and if it indicates anything, it is the absence of glottalization. I guess Greek would call it a smooth breathing. Just an open. And as such, the most important of all letters has no sound for them, and they derive tremendous cabalistic satisfaction from this, a negative definition of God that can only define God by what he is not or it is not. That privative definition is God is silence. Every time the line stops I think I'm somehow honoring God or God would manifest himself as the Cabala in the world of melody making music out of language. Since that which distinguishes poetry from prose in all of the linguistic discourse that I know about is the deliberate intervention of silence, the deliberate shaping, the organizational principle that silence is, and I find that enough, I've never found it really necessary to use rhyme or metrics. Although I've played with them, I've never found it necessary to use them. I think people with good ears, what you call good ears, are really those who have a taste for silence and can recognize and place it [...]

A line is what occurs in the midst of silence. You know that image of Nut, the goddess of the starry night that the Egyptians used to paint inside their coffins, so that when they lay in the coffin her feet would be on one side of the horizon, and her head on the other, stretched over the sky? Beautiful, beautiful image. Well, I think of silence as being *like that — holding the line, embracing it, sexually embracing it. So I can get off on single lines. I think that since the time of Pindar and his friend Æschylus that most poetry has depended fully on the crutch of meter to order its sense of substantiality. I think that's the great thing we've been doing since Whitman. We've rediscovered what substance there could be apart from that, and it's a substance that the body of Nut does beautifully comprehend [...]*

As I talk I'm trying to figure out from your point of view where to locate the silence. The first successful line that in the poem, that which will then be the measure for the rest, does set up a system of expectations in my ear and all subsequent lines play off that, somewhat, even though I notice as I look through the book, that typically the first line is quite a bit shorter than the last line. With poems, the lines have a tendency to grow larger, and I don't fight that. I don't mean that in a Pindaric sense, that that first line sets a measure which has to be recurrently revisited, but it does set up a system of expectation that I try to dance with through the rest of the poem. Let me put it another way: Sometimes I think of the line as the smallest number of words that can meaningfully interrupt the silence. I always want the line, of whatever kind, in whatever poem, to be able to be extracted. I define it to myself in a way like this: if, God forbid, the angel of death should visit me as I'm writing the poem, and I have written one line before another, I want that line to be capable of being put on my tombstone as evidence of what his last utterance was. I want every line then to have that degree of completeness."

in conversation with James Stalker
[ca. 1980]

5.
A BOOK ON THE OCCULT / KNOWLEDGE

CHARLES STEIN

RE: THE OCCULT
ROBERT KELLY AND THE ESOTERIC TRADITIONS

1.

> the origin, far side of a lake
> is always shadow

begins Robert Kelly's first major poem, "The Alchemist."[28] It continues:

> the voice goes around
> it easily in one hour

That Being itself is occulted and yet yields its apparencies to poetry will be an inalienable attitude throughout his work. That there should be a tradition of spiritual practice that has come to know itself as "The Occult," "The Hidden," of course, will remain forever in the corner of the poet's eye. The many senses in which Being is hidden. The many ways in which poetry allows its revelations.

2.

I once said to a friend who was critical of the magnitude of Kelly's work and his apparent unwillingness to edit it down to a circumscribable *œuvre*, that you do not edit the ocean. Themes, attitudes, modes of invention, formal explorations, recur with minute and grand variations like waves in the sea.

The poems not infrequently allow the sea as a figure for poetry itself, for language, or for Being. There are other figures of similar power and generality. Language itself, for instance; or mind; or matter; or the body — each another life-long thought-experiment, another figure covering what is. Kelly's is perhaps the first major life-work to exhibit what radical Catholic theologian David Leahy calls "polyontology": a proliferation of ontological visions and a refusal to establish an over-arching ontological assertion.

---

28. Robert Kelly, *The Alchemist To Mercury: An Alternate Opus: Uncollected Poems 1960—1980*, ed. Jed Rasula (1981) 1.

Correlative to this visionary profusion is the fact that what I will be calling the Kelly Poet is concerned with ultimate questions on the most intimate terrain: each poem finds itself as if between Being in the raw and the immediate impulse to utterance. The avidity for what presents itself, what comes to hand or comes to mind, for meanings, for speculative possibilities — again and again return the poet from the success of his own articulations to the immediate ocean or ground or *ungrund* of inquiry and concern. Currents and waves languaging Being abound. One current would be "The Occult."

3.

In a short piece titled "RE: THE OCCULT" written for the one-issue magazine *AION: A Journal of Traditionary Science* that I edited in 1964 largely under Kelly's supervision, the poet said that such sciences "represent at best that empirical speculativeness which constitutes our best mind — study thereof can make us perceptive of conditions, states, rhythms we are no longer *in our bodies* conscious of."[29]

4.

I met Kelly in June of 1960 when I was not yet 16 years old and he was in his mid-20s. Our friendship took off two years later when I became, for a spell, an initiate in an esoteric order directly descending from "The Golden Dawn" of W.B. Yeats, Aleister Crowley, Charles Williams' fame. For the next four or five years I was a regular guest at his home at Bard College. Our conversations ever-returned to "occult" matters: alchemy, kabbalah (Jewish, Christian, occultist); *haute magie*; Free Masonry; the tarot cards as a symbolic system; Rosicrucianism; astrology; ceremonial magic; Paracelsian and homeopathic medicine; theosophy; "Theosophy"; the esoteric strata of Buddhism, Hinduism, Taoism; Platonism(s); Christianity in its more Romantic guises (Charles Williams, Rudolph Steiner, Jacob Boehme, William Blake) as well as Anglo-Catholic and even aspects of Roman Catholic orthodoxy.

---

29. Joris & Cockelbergh, *A Voice Full of Cities*, 85 ff.

My initiation consisted of a correspondence course and participation in a weekly ceremony in New York City. I received lessons in a variant of the syncretic system organized largely by MacGregor Mathers and Wynn Wescott and reworked by Paul Foster Case. For me the possibility of participation in these lessons was their truly participatory character. One was presented with the details of a grand cosmography in an organized fashion, but study involved integration of it into one's own sense of things in a way that was more participatory and intuitive than dogmatic. Since the system was a synthesis of symbolic materials from the above-mentioned subjects, initiation was essentially a formal practice of imaginal elaboration.

The lessons proposed connections between different topics on various planes of correspondence in the manner of the great Renaissance compendia of "Natural Magic." How those connections could be established involved the active imagination of the initiate. *Why* was metallic mercury coordinated with the planet and the god of that name? Examine a dollop of it; observe how it breaks into droplets and recongeals; learn something about the erratic orbit of the planet; meditate upon the stories about Hermes-Mercury; speculate regarding the metaphorics of the correspondences and record your thoughts in a diary dedicated to such matters.

Every symbol in the syncretism was subject to this sort of participation. One even attained the ineffable acme of the system by imaginal means. What passed beyond imagination was summoned into one's ken through the work with images. One's own mind would be the site where the hidden, even as hidden, would be revealed. At the highest grade of the cult one reconstructed the system itself on one's own terms. The latter-day variations on this material — those of W.B. Yeats, Aleister Crowley, A.E. Waite, Paul Foster Case, Frater Achad, Gareth Knight, Dion Fortune, not to mention Austin Spare, Harry Smith, Kenneth Anger, Gerrit Lansing, Harvey Bialy, and most recently Robert Podgurski (there are no doubt others) — are testimony to this procedure. The tradition itself was a "rumor" — a "fama" as indicated in the famous "*Fama Fraternitatis*" of the Rosicrucians — a rumor propagated by those capable of carrying it further through creative participation.

Robert, I think, was fascinated by *my* participation. I would present him not only with something of the substance of what I was being taught but the results of my own deliberations: poems, remarks, experiences, speculations. I in turn was fascinated by the challenging fact that Robert seemed to be able to generate something very much like this hermeneutic process in relation to whatever came to hand or came to mind from his reading or in his daily life. Robert challenged the conventional character of the systematic initiation while at the same time furthering its essential work. Poetry was already initiation, both in the sense that its composition drew the poet into practices analogous to "occult work" and because poetry itself — his own and a certain strand within the received poetic tradition — initiates the reader into the speculative connections forged by its inner orders. The intuitions, insights, assertions, animadversions, abrogations, appropriations of the poetry as it was written, seemed, I think to him — but particularly to me — a continuously evolving initiation of an order I only hoped my practice with the formal cult would lead me on to.

At that time Kelly was fond of repeating a dictum of Robert Duncan's, itself quoted somewhere in *The H. D. Book* from lessons of another, probably quite parallel, initiatory cult: "A man is no wiser than the book he has written." The book in the quotation was in fact the "book" of one's own being, but both Roberts took it literally as speaking of their poetry: the aspiration to insight, *sophia, gnosis*, had its native home and test in the quality of one's writing. As I was a poet, Robert did lean on that injunction. But there was a complementary point here: that the manifest insight of the work did or might bespeak insight attained in one's being.

Creative activity was therefore of an alchemical nature. One was oneself transformed by the transformations one wrought in the materials of one's art: there could be no insight of a subjective character unless it stem from and be manifest as objective work. The work was a mirror of inner unfolding; inner life the condition for and product of its articulation. The relation between one's being and one's poetry was intransitive, mutually mirroring, mutually transformative.

5.

The Kelly Poet

The alchemists say "solve et coagula": dissolve and cause to congeal. The "Kelly Poet" — let me call him that — in his magical performativity continually performs both. He causes the conventional to vanish or transmogrify; he makes the unheard of connection arise and appear.

5 · A BOOK ON THE OCCULT / KNOWLEDGE

I have been insisting of late that the practice of contemporary magic (I abuse "alchemy" and write it in this context interchangeably with "magic") is not at all the miraculous manipulation of material phenomena without technological con-trivance, but the power to originate an ontological perspective and make it stick. In this there is a natural affinity with poetry's ontological concern — with or without the will to impose. Poetry is *onto-poietic*: it *forges* being. Blake's poet-figure, Los, is a smithy. Hermes, a god of heady poetry, is also the father of lies. That is, poetry is *phano-poietic:* it causes Being to come to apparency and, conversely, to fall under occultation. But in regard to this heady philosophical agenda, if it is an agenda, one can find in Kelly a library of passages that deny that the poet is a philosopher. The Kelly Poet does not assert something. The Kelly Poet lets words speak — lets them come to form. That is its ethic, its poetics, in a rubric. Responsibility is exhausted by responsiveness to that which arises and the attention that bestows form. In this spirit, the highest matters can be treated in a deceptively playful guise. Much of later Kelly-poetry is playful in a grand and lofty spirit. One likes the work if one is in the mood or can summon the capacity for such play.

But such play is not without its provocations, its consequences. What is ever-at-play in this liberal giving voice to language itself is the entire play of mind and sensibility. Whatever comes to perception and to the full range of fantasy, association, affect, intuition, concept, conceit, will be allowed articulation in an ever-expanding gamut of rhetorical modes (traditional or invented first time out) with every imaginable species and degree of enframement, complex textualization, "forest-path" (Heideggerian), and other metaphorical meanderings. If this is not philosophy, it nevertheless poses for the philosopher the question of her own mode of Being, the ultimate ontological import of any utterance, the nature of our engagement with the matter of how Being takes on appearance through the formation and formative processes of language.

The Kelly Poet is no philosopher, but the philosopher who is sensible to the famous "linguistic turn" in the thought that continues to torque from the 20th century would do well to reflect on the Kelly Poet. And if I am not too far off in my conflation of contemporary magic with the *onto-poietic*, the contemporary philosophic agenda is implicated in this poetry and its esoteric abrogations and affinities.

6.

"One Poem a Day or Else Two."

I don't think anyone who knew Robert Kelly's first wife Joby during the early 1960s would have thought that she was Robert's Muse, however much what Robert wrote in those years was profoundly supported and first heard by her. The mutually imagined mythologems that seemingly ordered the Kelly household had her as a Himalayan yak (the portly character of both members of the couple was reflected in that figure). But the thing about the yak was that it had to be fed daily; hence the yak's motto: "One Poem a Day or Else Two." Robert wrote every day. Every day there was a time when the yak was to feed — when Robert would read what that day had been written — to Joby and whoever else was present in his living room.

What survived his marriage to Joby was the dailiness of writing. Behind every poem of Robert Kelly one can feel the presence of that activity. Not so much an image of a man at table writing in measured hand and elegant notebook, though not infrequently that is there too, but the intimate presence of a mind at the site where language becomes text.

The Saussurean terminology of "Langue et Parole" itself might serve as metonym for this phenomena, though no theory of language or single languaging of its nature will subsume the ontological matter intimately at work, in evidence, in every moment of Kelly's *œuvre*. Every utterance and every form can be felt as metonym for this emergence of manifest speech from the sacred if enigmatical, or the enigmatical if sacred, *ungrund* that will not refuse being called language.

Yet the emergence of form need not, indeed cannot, be local, immediate, instantaneous *only*. It arrives as already breaching the radical transiency of concrete event. Yet it is always local, immediate, wedded to its moment, *too*. Extended form may preside over its coming to appearance in the manner of inner instruction or demand; that is, as that which elicits an obedience to its own insistency so that its arrival through, in, and as immediate utterance will appear without remainder in the form unfolding as the poem.

Hence the complexity of the connection between divination and poetry — the solicitation and the reading of signs. Indeed, the occult in traditions throughout the world, almost unexceptionally provide divinatory practices. But divination quickly transforms, for the Kelly Poet, to instances of the solicitation of meanings from that which comes to hand. I remember a story Robert wrote but never published in which a kind of sibyl had a big pot filled with an "infinite tarot deck" where the individual cards were marked with ordinary or extraordinary practical objects: a "five of desk chairs," a "nine of fountain pens," an "ace of bombs"! Each thing solicited its meanings from the sibyl's attentions. Divination was no more nor less than the sufferance of meaningful language to arise and take form.

7.

However. The manipulation of Being through the allowance of form in speech evinces an ethical crisis that is surely perennial in Kelly's poetry. For the power to effect the appearances of Being is itself fraught with the ethics of that power — personal, political, cultural, religious, magical. And the wielding of such power is intricately woven with the act of giving form. How does ontological efficacy — the power to effect the way Being shall effectively come to appearance awaken responsibility? For it is the *effective* coming to appearance of Being that is the problematic of giving form. It cannot be wielded heedlessly or abrogated simply. Thus the religious currents that move throughout Kelly's work — Christian, Jewish, Pagan, Sufi, Hermetic, and after the early 1980s, Buddhist — are present at the very site of their practice. How one lives out one's power to give form is an essential site of a more general ethics of form and power. Magic here is not a term of valor. It is the condition of a responsibility. One might research Kelly's work for traces of this responsibility. One would find an encyclopedia of magical ethics: the ethics of the imposition of image on person; the abrogation of the will to such imposition or the refusal to perform the same; the compulsion to do it; the rectitude of doing it. The rectitude of refusal. The turpitude of refusal. But also the darker exigencies of the entire problematic. The consequences for one's own being; for one's relations; for the world itself.

An example, with characteristic *apparent* levity:

RURITANIAN ELEGY

If I were a semi-suicidal poet in a small country
using a frail endangered language only natives love,
my fragmentary observations would become
a guide to life and death for all occasions
and lead countless intense young readers into hell.
How fortunate for my karma and the world
that all my propositions and discoveries
are embedded inside a formidable castle of text,
almost unreadable experiments, unbearable
revelations of the most trivial desires, heart
attacks of sheer prose. My readers uniformly
fall asleep before they ever reach my bad advice
then wake up with a start, vaguely comforted to know
that somewhere someone loves someone, maybe
even them, silhouettes hard to make out
coming over the crest of the hill in morning fog,
sea-bell bonging, nothing clear,
and nobody's really ever figured out
how much good love does anyhow.[30]

A fable of abrogation. A claim of ignorance. But the performative manifestation of mysterious silhouettes over the hill in the fog.

8.

The Voice of Hermetic Gnosis

The fables and "*récits*" that constitute a considerable part of Kelly's work allow a number of voices to speak which are variously aligned on the personality of the Kelly Poet himself. The Kelly Poet is something distinct from his local voicing, as in the above piece. He is the intelligence of

---

30. Robert Kelly, *Lapis* (2005) 45.

the poem's and indeed the life-work's construction, though intelligence that is certainly very different from that invoked by demiurgic design. But one poetic voice that speaks at times through the Kelly Poet is of particular interest. It does not belong uniquely to Robert Kelly. It is neither the "voice of true feeling" nor the voice of the identity of the poet, not even really one of the Kelly Poet's personae. It does not speak for the poem's well-crafted articulations — though its words are consummately well-crafted indeed, to the point of having the character of an oracular utterance. Nor is it — and this is of particular interest in Robert Kelly's work (since the overriding poetics would lead one to think otherwise) — "language" speaking, though it does bespeak language and disorders any assurance one might possess regarding just what language *is*. I identify it as the voice of Hermetic Gnosis. It can be heard in alchemical literature. It speaks in Blake, Yeats, Duncan, H.D., Jack Spicer, Gerrit Lansing, Stephen Jonas. It speaks with an unabashed authority but never in the name of an authoritative institution. It is enigmatic, challenging, rarely expansive, and can seem to be direct and indirect in the same utterance. It speaks to the receptive substance in the reader's being that is capable of entering upon the mysteries it articulates. That is, simply to *hear* it is to risk becoming an enigma oneself: the possibility of an untenable identity, at once too comfortable and impossible to carry. The Kelly Poet assumes this voice with a suave assurance; dons it as if it were a garment; removes it as the ontological weather changes. Hears it. Then hears something else. Finds contexts for it. Transforms it. Never abuses it. Abandons it. Lets it speak. Leaves it be. Lets it stand.

One might say that the occult tradition transmits itself most authentically and indeed most problematically in this voice. We are invited to the inescapable provenance of a certain intelligence, a certain possibility. When insight at that pitch and register threatens to rise in the mind, it is this voice that will bring it to articulation (whether in a poem one is reading or a dream or meditation one is undergoing). One might not hear it as one's "own" voice, but, with whatever resistance, reluctance, enthusiasm or indifference one attends it, if allowed to speak, it comes replete with a kind of knowing that, in its moment, seems to cast all other knowing aside. Then it has vanished. But the site in the mind from which it spoke or at which it was heard will be returned to, and its utterances remain lodged there, if also hidden, lying in wait for further occasions of relevance and use. Its patience, if inaccessible, is also inexhaustible. When it speaks as the Kelly Poet, it does not refuse the impression that it speaks for the inner meaning of the Hermetic tradition, since it recites what even the Hermetic Tradition leaves unsaid, or points to a further unsaying, a region beyond all doctrine where what all doctrine really might intend impels toward speech. For instance:

17.

In that country there is a hoof
that comes down from the sky once in a while
and just stands there
a hoof and a slender furry shank
going up as far as they can see

they come and stand around the hoof and argue
this is Pan's foot
or this is the foot of her cow or this
is herself's own footstep

and when the hoof is gone
disappearing sometimes in the middle of their talk
it leaves a crater filled with milk

each drinks from it or abstains
in accordance with his nature and beliefs
about the nature of the hoof

the milk tastes like any milk
somewhat sweet and flat and when
night comes it shows the moon clearly
bobbing on the pearly surface like a nervous mouth

from "Postcards from the Underworld"[31]

---

31. Robert Kelly, *Under Words* (1983) 51.

9.

Regarding the specific doctrines of the multitude of disciplines listed above having bearing on "the occult," no doubt scholars will discover in Kelly's work a corresponding multitude of specific references and allusions to the literature of Western Esotericism. In general, I think, these matters will appear under three typical modes of treatment: antithesis; amplification; deepening.

When a given doctrine seems unexceptional or an established part of ontological consensus, counter-examples or untoward consequences will be elicited. Here the Hermetic voice plays the Trickster or imp, teasing — even menacing. Or the Kelly Poet would dislodge or make difficult the site in the consensus occupied by the doctrine. Here, an attitude antithetical to "The Light" itself is struck.

WASPS

> I stood at the window cursing wasps
> because they fell for the same tricks;
> the light *(Mehr Licht)* was thick,
> they thought it glory but it was prison
> because they believed in it. He
> worshipped its color. But the light
> persisted in its mystery, was question
> not answer, effect not cause.
> *More light!* Goethe called, but *No light,* the Rabbis knew, *No light at all.*[32]

When the doctrine is already apparently untoward, it is amplified or taken in further untoward directions. What seemed unlikely opens onto a set of ramifications that renders it pertinent to a world that comes to seem unaccountably unexceptionable. Hear how the poet positions himself oblique to the actual matter of traditional concern that he is at the same time amplifying. The poem almost alludes to an early passage in *The Zohar.*

---

32. Robert Kelly, *The Convections* (1978) 41.

STILL LIFE: ORIGIN OF THE ALPHABET

Between the fading fuchsia-spotted lily and
the budding iris, I am like some florist's fern
(from northern California rainwoods rustled wet)
shoved in a glass jar by brutal ikebana
to show off someone else's colors. I am no rose.

Back in the bathroom the alphabet's still ripening,
waiting for Ancient Semites to wake up and notice
hello, these birds *leave* their shadows on the ground
behind them when they fly away. Kabbalah
is the art of wondering where the birds are now.[33]

Sometimes the doctrine is taken at face value and deepened. Or what the doctrine is is obscurely alluded to but taken implicitly as harboring some verity. Its center is at first displaced but then shown to appear at another more powerful, profound, or simply interesting site. It is Being, or the nature of mind, or thought, or language itself that is under review, solicited for revelation, initiation — Being's own centerless center rendered available enough to contradict, amplify, or deepen; unavailable enough to establish ontological movement, poetic kinesis, volatility.

JOHN YAU BY CANDLELIGHT

I caught your face once
between two flames,
hell's choir boy
you looked to me,
a meditator,
a young prince of between.

---

33. Robert Kelly, *Lapis* (2005) 66.

As between Aix and Avignon
a ruined castle stands
much visited by swallows
who hover high
unbeatingly on a thought of air

for thought is warmth.
A thought is a face
between two candles
stuck in the dark,

a face that looks back at you
as if it knew something
nobody can possibly know.[34]

10.

Ontological Originarity

    Textuality itself in our time withdraws from the global scene just as the noosphere becomes global through electronic media. But what the ultimate denouement — if anything like an ultimate denouement is imaginable — will be — for the position of language and its involvement with sentience itself, on earth, in the cosmos, in Being — does not seem to be determinate.

    The noosphere — the global collective as the play of thoughts and modes of consciousness — can easily be read as fixated on forms of positive knowledge whose guarantee is technical efficacy; but the ontological underpinnings of this are not known, nor is the future of its unfolding. However, the emergence of forms of Being, of forms of intelligence — and hence of ontologically originary poetry — cannot cease to animate possibility, no matter what the denouement.

    The vast proliferation of poetry today with no ontological concern in this sense matters little. There are many conditions under which the difficulty of the possible must reside. It is not a bad thing that what is most of use in these times be difficult of access.

34. Ibid., p. 72.

> No one listens to poetry. The ocean
> Does not mean to be listened to.

Jack Spicer says in *Thing Language*.³⁵ The point of such lines of course is a call to listening. "What is most thought provoking in this most thought provoking of times is that we are not yet thinking," writes Heidegger, in a book I know Robert Kelly enjoyed when it appeared in English in 1976 under the title, *What Is Called Thinking*. A call to thought.

Everywhere in Robert Kelly's writing is the call to thought; the resistance to the finished item of belief, of intellect; the closure of "single vision" (Blake); everywhere the provocation to intuition and further intuition; the engagement *with* and responsibility *for*. For the attentive reader is brought into the arena of the problematic that is the writing itself: the matter of ontological originarity, of the potencies of speech; of the volatile, the primordial, the incomprehensible, the unevadably ubiquitous; the transiency of the impregnable.

11.

Transmission

The Occult Tradition in the West or its rumor shows no particular consistency over the question of its transmission from master to disciple. There are hints of it in alchemical texts. Once historically visible initiatory orders appear, there is some sense of mastership and tutelage. The idea of "the Craft" echoes through the occultist modalities. As it does through the lineages and practices of the arts. In poetry the sense of lineage and master-disciple transmission is as shadowy as it is in the occult traditions. And yet there persists a sense that what has been achieved, either in art or in Being, by effort, intuition, by grace, can by effort, intuition, and grace be passed and carried on. Kelly has been as prolific a teacher and indeed a source of initiation as he has been as a poet. I often feel that

---

35. Poem beginning "This ocean, humiliating in its disguises," originally in *Language* (1964). Later in *The Collected Books of Jack Spicer* (1975) 217.

the contemporary university (whether or not technically "for profit") is a purveyor of professional licenses masquerading as initiations. Perhaps the masquerade is vanishing. Degrees bestow debts and careers. Period. But to be or have been a poet and student of Kelly is to have been the recipient of an initiation indeed.

I will end this piece with a poem of Robert's from the early 1970s that perhaps touches upon what is at stake in his pedagogy.

THE CUSTOMS INSPECTOR

Everything starts in the same way.
The eye grows weary
of checking where they hide their diamonds.
These amateur smugglers
put them everywhere
but mostly in the same predictable places —
in vulva or anus
armpit, shoe (how can they walk?)
perineum behind scrotum
(how can they sit down?)
in their mouths so that they mumble
in their ears so I have to shout.

They're smuggling diamonds from the East
but most of them, maybe all,
have forgotten they're doing that
& mostly think of themselves as innocent —
it's been a long trip.
Where's the diamond? What's a diamond?
that's what they tell me
yet when I look at them quietly
my eyes not accusing, just being clear
on them & at them,
they get nervous, anxious, soon reveal
where they hid the stone

or where — without even their full
conscious awareness — the stone
was hidden in them by professionals
or for all they knew
maybe it hid itself in them.

I can tell by the way they squirm
what part of their bodies it's hidden in.
And then I have to call it out,
treat them carefully
& make them discover the stone themselves.
They feel better when they find it.

I'm not supposed to touch them
but sometimes their grace or awkwardness
touches me, & I move to help,
be of help, remind them of all the places,
dark hollows of themselves.
Sometimes I reach in and touch the stone.[36]

Barrytown, June 2014

---

36. Robert Kelly, *The Mill of Particulars* (1973) 40.

TAMAS PANITZ

A NOTE ON ROBERT KELLY'S CALLS, AND THE ISLAND CYCLE

Calls is the fifth and final long poem of what Kelly has called The Island Cycle (this includes: *Fire Exit, Uncertainties, The Hexagon,* and *Heart Thread*). As with each of these books there is a formal constraint, here found in the form of three-line stanzas. Throughout the cycle Kelly has explored a vision of number as an emergent quality, one that has its own agenda, and is encoded into our reality, everyday or otherwise. There is a twoness, threeness, fourness, etc. to which historically, and also spontaneously, the innumerable things respond.

Where Kelly attends *eights*, in the preceding book, *Heart Thread*, he is forced to deal with issues we might find, for example, while contemplating Gurdjieff's eight-fold ray of creation. Both of these eight-forms concern themselves with all of experience, and it is the diversity of eightness in anything and everything that Kelly's study of the number reveals, rather than the mere numerical fact of there being eight things, or eight themes identifiable in creation; in fact, Kelly's use of number is paradoxically non-configurative, and it is only by what presents itself that we find any order suggested. His are numbers without self-consciousness. Angels.

Here are three sections from *Calls*:

>2.
>
>The calls are causes
>listen to me
>three times round the island
>
>and stay your hand
>no one is guilty
>only the gull can look down on us
>
>*angustia* that narrow thing
>angina, a squeeze, *anguis*, a snake,
>anxiety the coil of worry
>
>round the moment when
>every stroke of time wants to be free.
>Be me (I wanted to tell her)

be me looking at you,
watching the slither of your absence
the panoply of human evidence

but these are fancies
bred of remembering too well
what I should never have seen in the first place

now I am a slave to what I observed.
Serve it, serve
the imaginary perceiving we call real.

3.
Every wall has a door in it
waiting for the door
not easy to find

every wind has a door in it
every air
or open the light and go through

it is all about doors today
the number three
the in the out and the between

daleth a door they say is four
I counted three
for *aleph* is zero, what has never been said.

4.
Ice was. And then.
Refrigeration. Engineering
grandfather. Great circle.

We are here on the boat,
boat on the water, water on the planet
the boat goes round.

There are religious reasons for everything
the serious ton of local conversations.
"Thoughtful" was a word I overheard.

> Lighthouse lovers estuaries
> youthful voices of old men.
> Community a kind of song,
>
> living out loud all
> the special anxieties of music
> among the animates.

Threeness. Kelly has pointed out to me the inherited three-fold division of Roman society, the invention of the concepts past, present, and future, among many others. The Scottish *glamour* (magic, enchantment), as in *to cast the glamour*, is a variant of *gramarye*, from English *grammar*. Grammar is itself an enchantment upon words, and our world and number is another kind of grammar.

There is a threeness in *Calls*, which may be found tercet by tercet, but this number comes with another sense, that of a trinity, which is a sublimation of each precedent part whose enchantments linger on in the whole.

I wonder if the threes of *Calls* perform in the diverse registers of the whole Cycle. *Calls* does not particularly read that way, despite the idea's obviousness; rather closer to the truth is that since this is the fifth book of *The Island Cycle*, it is ruled by the number five, which proves itself to be deeply concerned with threes. Nonetheless, we might contrast it with Zukofsky's *A24*.

A24, "*L. Z. Masque*" is a musical arrangement of previous sections of that same long poem, along with selections from his other works, and the music of Handel. These are organized into five voices by Celia Zukofsky. Five threads move simultaneously through the *L. Z. Masque*, resounding with each new context in flashes of multidimensional significance. I find it is worth mentioning, as the only corollary I know of to this last book of the *Island Cycle*, though I don't mean to mislead: *Calls* does not read as if it were from five distinct places, and these projects are not obviously similar on the page. *Calls* remains ever at the level of the immediate, to such a degree that the moment itself becomes something sensuous. The *L. Z. Masque* is a conscious fabrication, something put together, arranged, and presented as such. *Calls* on the other hand, if it can be said to contain The Island Cycle's previous measures *as such*, does so organically, prehensively: so that we cannot be sure the poet, intrepid voyager, was aware of the sublimations these threes wrought.

The Island Cycle has a noticeable organic evolution, and shows clearly Kelly's visionary attitude towards these forms: one book comes from the next, harmoniously, though without intellectual overdetermination. I am not the only person to have visualized several books of *The Island Cycle* at once in an archetypal, crystalline form.

A curiously prescient and very similar description to a vision I have enjoyed of these texts is found, perhaps unsurprisingly, in Kelly's early novel, *The Scorpions*:

> My mind saw a five-pointed star tracing itself luminously, silver on dark blue, and a deep voice in me said this is the Jesus pentagram, draw it, make it, worship it. Desperately I tried to trace it, from bottom left to apex, down to bottom right, up to upper left, across to upper right, back down to lower left again. But this was not a simple star, it was a great expanding pattern, proliferating parallels out in all directions, parallels that yet had to join at the apices, figures impossible on a plane surface, yet I saw them there in all radiance; they were to the outline of a five-pointed star as a tesseract is to an outline square, yet I seemed to see every line, joining, extension of the figure. Each time I tried to trace it, after endless miles of joining parallels, always I would falter as the last line leapt down leftward to the starting point. Tormented and obsessed, my mind grasped the word *pattern*, saved itself, *refused* to follow the lines, *refused* to draw the pentagram. Instantly the lines vanished, the weight of the cross eased. [...]

Kelly's poetry, though erudite, suggests itself to intuitive understanding not only at the level of the line, or stanza, or book, but *from book to book*. This achievement cannot be overstated as an evidence of the living work, and the lived work, and few are the parallels in American poetry, that great academy of eternal masters not on earth.

SYLVIA MAE GORELICK

KELLY AFTER NIETZSCHE:
ON "HER VOICE IN ALL THESE YEARS"

Her Voice in All These Years

Robert Kelly

In blue depeynted
throned erect
in her own nakedness —
the inner robe or chlamys
perfectly translucent blue,
the blue of summer morning
just before the pink of
sunrise alters it,
        no
passion yet,
        the outer
robe or circumstance
October blue
of cloudless apple weather
and she rides the sky
unmoving.
        And up to her
you find climbing all her dears,
servitors, abstainers,
absconders of her wisdom,
Heraclitus gazing at her lips,
the moist refulgence of that health
from which she speaks,
but she is silent in your moment,
Empedocles is climbing
old-muscled slow up
along her left thigh to
hurl himself one last

time into her lap,
perish in the heat of her
union of wisdom and compassion,
all-knowingness and rise as
somebody else some other time

but now applaud,
    he's on his way,
way down below
very near us,
        Friedrich Nietzsche
has risen already
from his strange Lutheran grave
and sits, silent as she,
on the instep of her great
naked foot, his back
turned to her, turned away
from all her other lovers
disposed about her body
and the shining landscape she
begets around her
wherever she travels,
    and yet his eyes are open,
back turned in denial,
fearful of that
    passion to be shared,
that *Mitleid* that made him mad
at Wagner,
        mad because he took,
mistook, compassion for pity.
It is not pity.
It is feeling what you feel
whoever I am.
    Leid is suffering,
sorrow, passion, *mit* is with,
in compassion I feel what you feel
and you feel me,

5 · A BOOK ON THE OCCULT / KNOWLEDGE

it is a path, the only path
to knowing everything
by way of knowing everyone.
Color means the shape
or body we inhabit,
it is translucent
to our hopes and fears
but perfectly transparent
to compassion.

But he is a child down there,
he turns away
closes his eyes so he won't be seen.
The mirror phase is broken,
her body, even the least of it,
sustains him,
   if he opened up
he would see the host of her deniers,
Saul of Tarsus on her other foot
and his eyes are closed too,

for all of them belong to her too,
   how could they not,
the muses mean her
   and money is her shadow,
the queen of coins *is* the queen of swords,

I have found you poking around
in my orchard,
   rifling my desk,
opening up my cupboards
and pulling out my deck of cards.
my silver dollars,
   my map
of purgatory, *Fegefeuer*,
my father's green tweed suit,
Now everything you find is yours
because you looked for it

I hear her say
far up above us both
I want that kiss too
her playful lips
her words inside us
strangely spoken
as if we were her too,
all of us,
open all our eyes,
the truth is only in the other ever.

*

  I received this poem from Robert Kelly during my senior year at Bard College, while I was finishing writing a vast project on the young Nietzsche eventually to be called *Songs of the Last Philosopher*,[37] which concentrated particularly on Nietzsche's profoundly personal relationship to the Presocratic, or as he calls them, Pre-Platonic philosophers. The beauty and singularity of this relationship can be more or less grasped by thinking together two phrases of Nietzsche's, both posthumous, the first written in a series of notes for a course on philology in 1871 and the second in an 1872 notebook. The first announces the condition and the act of all philology: "*Comprehension of Antiquity*, full penetration of love."[38] The second outlines a vision of history as composed of the intimate and secret communication between geniuses across it: "There is an invisible bridge from genius to genius — that is the truly real 'history' of a people."[39] It was this same love and this same communication that I had the ambition of resuscitating in my project toward Nietzsche. My year was punctuated with equally occasional and thrilling meetings with Robert during which I would sporadically share thoughts and he would bathe and turn them over in his wisdom — they were conversations

---

37. A title by no means uninfluenced by the poetic community at Bard, not only Robert but also Ann Lauterbach, Michael Ives, and Tamas Panitz.
38. Friedrich Nietzsche, *Introduction aux leçons sur l'Œdipe-Roi de Sophocle et introduction aux études de philologie classique*, tr. Françoise Dastur and Michel Haar (1994) 93.
39. Friedrich Nietzsche, *Unpublished Writings from the Period of Untimely Observations*, tr. Richard T. Gray (1995) 3.

kept alive by a great mutual admiration, and by a common will to understand and to experiment, to rethink history and its truths. These meetings provided me with great spiritual encouragement and always made me return to my writing with new eyes. "Her Voice In All These Years" was the last of three poems that Robert sent me over the course of the year directly concerning Nietzsche,[40] as gifts of profound inspiration.

The body and soul of the poem are constituted by a transmuted figure of the eternal feminine, the trans-temporal and trans-historical double source of love and truth into which all true philosophers have plunged — the main gesture of the poem consists in making love mean truth and truth mean love in order to explain Nietzsche's mistake to him and, beyond that, to rectify it for us. In *The Birth of Tragedy*, Nietzsche had marked the difference between the artist and the theoretical man, a new type that arrived in ancient Greece through the figure of Socrates, by their attitudes with respect to truth: "Whenever the truth is uncovered, the artist will always cling with rapt gaze to what still remains covering even after such an uncovering; but the theoretical man enjoys and finds satisfaction in the discarded covering and finds the highest object of his pleasure in the process of an ever happy uncovering that succeeds through his own efforts."[41] It is the will to strip truth naked that distinguishes the theoretical man, this manifestation of a new drive (*Trieb*), the drive to knowledge, from the artist, who strives toward beauty, toward appearance, and who thus weaves ever new veils to cover the enigma of the truth. Kelly achieves at the opening of the poem a synthesis — a poetical *Aufhebung* — of these two perspectives, simultaneously unveiling truth, that "nude goddess"[42] and restoring her many veils to her, on the inside:

> In blue depeynted
> throned erect
> in her own nakedness —

---

40. Robert sent me the final version of the poem on April 5, 2013.
41. Friedrich Nietzsche, *The Birth of Tragedy*, §15 in *The Birth of Tragedy* and *The Case of Wagner*, tr. Walter Kaufmann (1967) 94.
42. *Ibid.*, 95.

>   the inner robe or chlamys
> perfectly translucent blue,
> the blue of summer morning
> just before the pink of
> sunrise alters it,
>   no
> passion yet,
>   the outer
> robe or circumstance
> October blue
> of cloudless apple weather
> and she rides the sky
> unmoving.

She first appears to us throned in her nakedness, yet this nakedness reveals another layer of covering — it reveals an "inner robe" — an inner chlamys prior to the "outer / robe or circumstance" that comes with day; hers is an inner blue, translucent and matinal, before the exterior blue of October. The nudity attributed to this *her*, whose name we do not know, is also pre-passionate; it is a nakedness before love, a pure interiority whose music is monodic and solitary, whose heart is immobile. Then her adorers arrive, scaling her naked body, searching it over; Heraclitus "gazing at her lips," thus seeking himself, and Empedocles, the two purest of the Presocratics and also the two that Nietzsche took most strongly as his predecessors. Empedocles climbs up her thigh to plunge once more into the volcano of her lap — "perish in the heat of her / union of wisdom and compassion" — the return of Empedocles into Etna is here made eternal under the sign of her. And here she appears in her true form, in her welcoming of others, in the eternal opening of her inner chlamys: the first crystallization of truth and love comes about in the coincidence of σοφία (sophia) and *Mitleid* (which Nietzsche understood as pity and which Kelly will translate as compassion) at her center. Kelly answers in this way Nietzsche's famous question in the preface to *Beyond Good and Evil*: "Supposing truth is a woman — what then?"[43] The poem proposes a new figure for truth, and she is a woman, but in order to be truth she requires love, not just love to be given but love to be shared. And for this

---

43. Friedrich Nietzsche, *Beyond Good and Evil*, tr. Walter Kaufmann (1989) 1.

it is necessary that at her source she incarnate not only this self-veiling truth, the matrix of wisdom, but the very heart of equal loving. And such a face for truth — a face human, all too human and at once more than human, being the other of every lover of wisdom — destroys any notion of a single, stable truth. For the reaching of this truth, not only a synthesis of the artistic and theoretical perspectives is necessary, but a surpassing of the point of fixity to truth that opposes them; the truth is constantly fleeing, hiding herself as an enigma because she is beyond us — she cannot be caught but in her multiplicity, that is, in the fact that she is only alive through love. Empedocles shows us this by sacrificing himself in the volcano of her, and thus experiencing the correspondence between wisdom, the possession of the truth precisely that truth is only multiple, only in the fire between *two*, and compassion, which hence becomes the very movement of truth.

Then arrives Nietzsche on the scene, an event arousing applause — he has risen from the grave to join his true companions, whom he called the *pure types* of philosophers before Plato came along to mix doctrines, to find his place on the body of this woman. Yet he sits silently "on the instep of her great / naked foot, his back / turned to her, turned away / from all her other lovers" and turned also from the "shining landscape" that she births "wherever she travels" — he is unable to become part of this great eternal community thriving in the union of truth and love, and this because of his "denial." In essence, Nietzsche cannot join in the eternal community of these philosophers because he denies its principle — that is, he denies compassion, the root of truth.

>and yet his eyes are open,
>back turned in denial,
>fearful of that
>>*passion to be shared,*
>that *Mitleid* that made him mad
>at Wagner,
>>mad because he took,
>mistook, compassion for pity.
>It is not pity.
>It is feeling what you feel
>whoever I am.

What Nietzsche had attacked in Wagner's *Parsifal* as the highest, most dangerous value of Christianity and as the mark of decadence, this *Mitleid* in which he saw the motor of *ressentiment* working triumphantly as the force that negates life, the force of nihilism that treats weakness and pain as virtues, Kelly rethinks and retranslates this pity as "*passion to be shared.*" In *The Antichrist*, Nietzsche writes: "We are deprived of strength when we feel pity. That loss of strength which suffering as such inflicts on life is still further increased & multiplied by pity. Pity makes suffering contagious."[44] Pity as this perpetuation of suffering resulting in the progressive weakening of human life is reversed by Kelly into the experience in common, the experience *with*, *Mit*, another of *Leid*, "suffering, / sorrow, passion" — hence, compassion, that reciprocal love that gives rise to its own truth. And by blinding himself to that truth, Nietzsche denies himself the wisdom that would allow him to adore her along with Heraclitus and Empedocles. This compassion is the way that leads to a transfigured notion of absolute knowledge: "it is a path, the only path / to knowing everything / by way of knowing everyone." This position, that to know everything can only mean to know everyone, coincides with the perspectivism of Nietzsche's thought and his insistence on the multiplicity of knowledge by virtue of the multiplicity of perspectives and, hence, too, of truth. In the *Genealogy of Morals*, he writes: "There is *only* a perspective seeing, *only* a perspective 'knowing'; and the *more* affects we allow to speak about one thing, the *more* eyes, different eyes, we can use to observe one thing, the more complete will our 'concept' of this thing, our 'objectivity,' be."[45] This perspectivism is introduced as a weapon against metaphysics and the "contradictory concepts" that it preaches, such as "pure reason," "absolute spirituality," and "knowledge in itself" — contradictory because they "always demand that we think of an eye that is completely unthinkable, an eye turned in no particular direction, in which the active and interpreting forces,

---

44. Friedrich Nietzsche, *The Antichrist*, §7, in *The Portable Nietzsche*, ed. and tr. Walter Kaufmann (1954) 572—573.

45. Friedrich Nietzsche, *On the Genealogy of Morals*, Essay 3, §12, in *On the Genealogy of Morals* and *Ecce Homo*, ed. and tr. Walter Kaufmann (1989) 119.

through which alone seeing becomes seeing *something*, are supposed to be lacking"[46] — an impossible eye, the fictitious eye behind which the mechanics of knowledge *an sich* would operate. Nietzsche thus protests that it is only in the wide variousness of different perspectives, *different* eyes alive with the forces of action and interpretation, that knowledge can be sought.

Kelly proposes *Mitleid* as the only means to reaching other perspectives; only through shared passion can we see the seeing of another eye and know the knowing of another mind. Only in this way can the gradual constitution of a totality of knowledge — an "objectivity" — be reached, an objectivity, however, whose secret is its own impossibility. This impossibility is twofold: first, it is the impossibility of concordant views and concordant truths held by each eye — perspectives are by nature irreconcilable with one another; secondly, it is the impossibility of a finitude of perspectives — it is because theses eyes proliferate infinitely that knowledge can only be an infinite task. And yet, from Kelly's standpoint, Nietzsche is incapable of exercising his own perspectivism — blind to compassion, hiding in fear of any shared passion, his heart is closed to others, and thus also to the truth. This point touches on the limit that the transvaluation of all values unveils — the limit between, firstly, the values of Christianity which must be surpassed, values based upon *ressentiment* and the negation of life through the valuation of weakness over strength, and secondly, the values of the future, to be established. And the reversal of *Mitleid* as pity into *Mitleid* as compassion is perhaps one way to move from Christianity's system of values to a new constellation of new values — *perhaps*. Such a reversal would depend upon a full exit from the physiological forms into which these Christian values have molded men — that is, from forms of progressive weakness. In order for pity to become compassion, to transform from a mutually weakening value to a mutually strengthening value, from a value that says *no* to life to one that says *yes* to life, the body must already have attained great power. In the light Kelly throws on it, the body is fully penetrated by compassion:

---

46. *Ibid.*

> Color means the shape
> or body we inhabit,
> it is translucent
> to our hopes and fears
> but perfectly transparent
> to compassion.

In the shared experience of *Mitleid*, the heart is sounded, past the form or façade of body, color, shape — compassion is the force, then, that itself overcomes weakness by mutually strengthening the hearts that share in it, the transformational force of the value it names. In an aphorism from *Daybreak*, Nietzsche explains that what we refer to as pity, *Mitleid*, is not in fact true *Mitleid* — acts that claim to be performed out of pity are in fact a reaction of self-preservation in face of the sight of weakness and suffering in another. "Pity" is a reaction provoked by the *fear* that one's own "impotence" or "cowardice" will be revealed if one does not help the sufferer. Simultaneously, acts of "pity" are performed out of a desire to be glorified for one's heroism and charity. What passes, then, in daily life, for *Mitleid* is falsely named — it is not suffering *with* another but simply suffering oneself, solitarily, as a reaction to the sight of another suffering and the acts that result from it are not acts of pity but acts of pure selfishness.[47] Such an assertion opens another possibility, that of a true *Mitleid*, a compassion that would do justice to its name — a true *passion-with* in which the solitary self could dispel its fears of weakness and overcome its vanity to feel with another. Not to feel pain, suffering, and impotence, but to feel the strengthening force of *shared passion*. This would require that the relation of mutual necessity and constant, reciprocal creative action that Nietzsche had envisioned between man and woman and, by extension, between the gods Apollo & Dionysos in *The Birth of Tragedy* be fully realized between humans, and that it be given the name of *Mitleid*. Unthinkable reversal in the context of Nietzsche's own œuvre and yet —

Nietzsche often spoke of the drive to knowledge and the will to truth as destructive forces capable of leading mankind to suicide — in

---

47. Friedrich Nietzsche, *Daybreak*, ed. Maudemarie Clark, tr. R.J. Hollingdale (1997) §133, 83—85.

an early fragment, he writes: "In knowledge, humanity has a beautiful means to perish."[48] Is this not because truth is supposed by humanity to be a woman in the sense of the dogmatists? A glittering object that must be stripped bare to be discovered? Following in Nietzsche's own inversion of Platonism,[49] could we not say that this new *Mitleid* proposed by Kelly, this new identity of love and truth, is the inversion of Platonic love? For it no longer ascends the Platonic hierarchy of loves from the basest love to the most pure, which coincides with truth but on the contrary, this *Mitleid* plunges into the person of the other, into the mind and heart of the other to find a *perspective* truth, a truth embedded in the being of the other only born out of the contact in passion that the *mit* represents. It is just possible that this new conception of truth, truth as born of the contact in common love between two beings could arise as the beginning of a Nietzschean future for humanity, in spite of Nietzsche himself. It would require that the *mit* shatter the individualities of each of the two in order that new forms of life, new forms of passion, be born of their union.

The poem ends with the sound of her voice and its result resounding in the heart of an I:

> *Now everything you find is yours*
> *because you looked for it*
> I hear her say
> far up above us both
> I want that kiss too
> her playful lips
> her words inside us
> strangely spoken
> as if we were her too,
> all of us,
> open all our eyes,
> the truth is only in the other ever.

---

48. Friedrich Nietzsche, *Le Livre du philosophe*, tr. Angèle Kremer-Marietti (1969) §125, 86.
49. In a fragment of 1870, Nietzsche writes: "My philosophy is an *inverted* [*umgedrehter*] *Platonism*" (Nietzsche, *Unpublished Writings*, 13).

These words that she speaks, her only words, could be a translation of Nietzsche's rhyme of *The Gay Science* called "*Mein Glück*": "When I grew tired of searching / I learned how to find"[50] — she tells us that what we find is ours because we looked for it without knowing it was *that* which we were looking for. This completes the circle with Heraclitus' "ἐδιζησάμην ἐμεωυτόν" — "I have searched myself out"[51] — the circle of seeking, which is, perhaps, the practice of philosophy — a seeking that is always its own riddle and which retains the unexpected truth of finding. Her voice in its own enigmatic interiority moving across history enters into us to speak the words of this riddle. And then the truth that she incarnates is transfigured once again and she is "all of us" — from here the perspectivism that the poem creates, born from the figure of truth as a woman in eternity, the welcoming center of love and of truth, opens wide and makes itself clear. The exercise of this perspectivism, one that is both Nietzschean and far beyond Nietzsche, in a future he prepared without knowing it, and at his own cost, requires that we "open all our eyes" to receive the secret and key of the poem, the secret that her voice announces in us: "the truth is only in the other ever." This truth is folded into her heart and ours — it is the birth of a survival of the human past its time — the new double life of knowledge and passion in the opening of an eye.

50. Friedrich Nietzsche, *The Gay Science*, "Joke, Cunning, and Revenge," 2, in *The Gay Science*, tr. Walter Kaufmann (1974) 40—41. (Translation modified.)
51. Giorgio Colli, *La sagesse grecque*, tr. Patricia Farazzi (1992) 50. (My trans.)

ALANA SIEGEL

THOUGHTS ON THREAD

I read Robert Kelly's *Heart Thread* on the precipice of leaving for a three-year retreat. I am leaving in 3 days, but I feel like I've been saying goodbye for months. "Heart Thread" feels to me to be a book all about goodbyes, but also about beginnings, and the space each of those moments share, occupy. I've been thinking about goodbyes, not understanding the nature of them. I've been thinking about last words, and how a poem feels. When I said goodbye to one of my best friends a couple weeks ago, we were at an event turned into a party in a crowded new museum and after we hugged goodbye I said, "see you in letter form" (I mean in the exchange of written letters) and then as I walked away, I added, "or in astral form." We were now a good distance away from each other, and over the clamorous crowd, my friend, having not heard me, shouted, "What did you say?" "In astral form," I repeated. Because I knew these were the last in-person words spoken we would share with each other, each pronouncement — my declaration of seeing him in "letter form," and then my echo of "astral form" embossed a meaning into our friendship circulating these resonances.

I was speaking with Robert once, sharing a story of the first time I had met someone, and he leaned over and emphasized that the first moment of meeting someone is when the karmic eye opens, when, what we know most commonly as "the first impression" is made, and your vision of your whole relationship with that person is revealed before you there. Because I've been saying goodbye to people in the last months, I've been adapting this same logic to endings, but endings seem more difficult to fix in place than beginnings. You say goodbye to someone, casually, knowing you will see them next week, or tomorrow, or assuming you will. You say goodbye to someone when you're going on a flight, or getting off the phone. You don't know if you will see anyone ever again, but you can think you know, or feel you do.

The poems in *Heart Thread* can be held in the hand, as they are held on the page, separate yet alive to one another. I imagined each poem as a person, reciting the first words that came to mind upon being born, or the last words said, in this or that moment. The poems are numbered, and you can have the book with you when you're walking or riding on a train from one place to another. And when the world frees you from it for a moment of waiting, or traveling, you can read a poem and linger there, in these studies of beginnings and endings.

What is the difference in a beginning and an ending, saying hello and saying goodbye? I keep thinking about this, and it confuses me, relieves me, suspends me in a whirling curiosity about the nature of time and meaning. Chuck Stein, a friend of both mine and Robert's said to me one day that he felt like all his life he had been walking down this path and then when he reached, I think 50 he said, or an age around that age, he felt like he turned around and started walking back down the path from which he came.

The title of this book struck me because a couple of years ago when I was beginning to learn Tibetan, my Tibetan teacher in one class said, "there is no word for 'love' in Tibetan." I was enthused, drawn in, seeking out this exit, this answer above all the desire and pleasure but pain that came in that magnet of the world of that word. My teacher followed with a semantic break down of one of the Tibetan words for mind, which he translated as "heart rope." So this must be where the title of this book is drawn from. I was thinking about it today in the car, and the willful statements in this book, clear and concise in their purpose of writing down what is heard in the mind. There seems to be a vast neural network that is being laid out — a company of minds to think in rather than a single mind in time being thought — not a nervous will unhearing its own monologue — but an availability — a freshness — as this book in so many moments makes clear, that it is for "you," — it is not for itself — or itself is the linkage of this habitation in which a clearly distinct movement is being propagated, grown. It is like each poem is a seed, the restfulness of a beginning and an end not needing discrimination, and the harmlessness of language being shared, as a place to live in, rather than the fiery furnaces of opinion that arrow into the air and provide no shelter from any storm.

My friend whom I mentioned earlier said to me recently that he writes poems now only in an offering of consolation. I feel this way through how some of the images in *Heart Thread* seem to make my body disappear. What comes to mind most readily is the microwave that becomes a moon. This simple image, not simple at all. This glorious feeling, experience, of the mind's capacity to make a thing in the world other than it is, to make it like something else, is small and dazzling, is large and tingling. There is a consolation, a company, when a moment in a poem can let you be lost in it, where "sharing" is not needed anymore, the injunction toward it, or the shadow of its absence. You are initiated, naturally, in how the words proved your ability to be moved into them, by them, taken out from the vectors, the hurtling trajectories of will and intention, and hovering.

I am imagining my heart in my body, and my opening questions about ends and beginnings like hearts in the bodies, of myself, or anyone else. Floating, attached, full of function, hot, and yet invisible to me. You don't know, and because you don't, you go, out from yourself, into the thoughts of another, or yours, in the form of a book.

There is an intelligence in this book, in the intense engagement with every thought and feeling, understanding each as not isolated, but of a fragile framework being experienced by others, and how many others? This book is deeply concerned with how it affects people, but not in any overly careful or cowardly way. This book is an accumulated study of what seems to be trying to find the words in a single line's attempt, that can elevate as many souls as possible, somehow twisting, or trying to slake off a culture's associations into a purity of verse that can liberate a mind in any human being from their ideas of themselves. A poem serving as a discerning force, like a thread that can weave what you need to keep you warm, a rope thrown to get you up the massive mountain you are in the middle of climbing.

And this is thought, in the process of finding it's true intention, it's deepest purpose and need, through the fields and travails of so many vocabularies and other places and times, searching out that garment or geography that doesn't need any other name than the one you are told in the moment of hearing it. It's like the first time someone tells you their name, and in the great rush in skull of meeting them and taking in all the energies of this new soul before you, you forget their name, and have to ask them as you are leaving, "What's your name again?" And they tell you.

Galatea Resurrects #26 (2016)

THREADS 18: ROBERT SAYS

"So each age deserves the art it gets, obviously. Our own age, so overwhelmed in its attention, so fearful of loss of memory, with Alzheimer's Syndrome as the typically most feared fate, will naturally enough go for, be forced to go for, short-attention-span effects. To combat that a little, to give ourselves a chance for something more continuous. That would be my hope. The Continuity. Paul Blackburn's wonderful poem of that name a million years ago. The continuity — that's all we can hold onto. That's one reason I urge my students to the longest sustaining attentions they can manage — not for esthetic principles, but for simple physical hygiene, like brushing their teeth. Listen to operas, listen to Bruckner, read War & Peace, *study Pound's* Cantos, *go for the biggest systems, learn chemistry. Modernism began with the sense of 'shoring' fragments against our ruin. And now everything is fragment. So the angel we need is the energy of sustained alert continuity. But don't memorize anything. Memorizing destroys the moment.*

So the poem now is of now — all the poem happens just in the happening — Clark Coolidge showed the way — line erases the line before. And one day I found I had written at the end of a poem: there is nothing to remember.

So there is nothing to predict — just bare luminosity — which is the charged notice of what's passing. Maybe that's the greatness we can aspire too — and it's not so very different from Dante's resolving, forever unresolved image: the yellow in the heart of the sempiternal rose. A thing is passing, and we are possessed by it utterly and are utterly clear in our apprehension of that moment. And then another thing is passing — and that's it — nothing but what happens now.

in conversation with Simone dos Anjos
and Pietro Aman
The Modern Review (2006)

In a different sense, that's what poetry has been doing all through the centuries — slowing down the reading. Prose needs that too, and one way to accomplish it is by presenting fragments; it forces readers to string the beads themselves. I don't mean cruelly to manipulate the reader — I love the reader! But I don't want the reader to read too quickly and smoothly.

in conversation with
Larry McCaffery (1988)

6.
A BOOK OF READINGS

EDWARD SCHELB

HOME MOVIES OF THE ANGELS: *SONGS I–XXX* AND STAN BRAKHAGE'S CINEMATIC DANCE

Guy Davenport once wrote of Robert Kelly that "He has the Chinese sense of bringing diverse things together into a stark symbol, and is happiest when he himself can't quite see the meaning of the sign he's made. Thus his poems are mysteries to be pondered, something to dream on rather than to puzzle out."[52] The filmmaker Stan Brakhage also felt drawn to the mystery of certain of his films that escape analysis, obscure even to himself. He called them "ghost films," and he praised them for their ability to defy language and exist profoundly beneath words: "Only a ghost film could possibly break through thought-bonds of language & exist as, say, movement haunt, tone-texture haunt, ineffable haunt."[53] Kelly and Brakhage were both engaged in æsthetic experimentation in ways that profoundly dovetailed. Both sought a kind of organic knowing and poetic immediacy that Charles Olson called for in his manifesto "Human Universe": "The process of image ... cannot be understood by separation from the stuff it works on. ... There is only one thing you can do about kinetic, reenact it. Which is why the man said, he who possesses rhythm possesses the universe."[54] In the work of both Kelly and Brakhage, beneath the junkyard heap of mythic images, the swirls of color, the glyphs scratched in celluloid, body parts, cosmic spasms, there is the music that eludes categorization, evades naming. It is the rhythm that persists in a ghostly way, burying deep, but it is also the fundamental motion of what Brahkage called the "meat mind," the embodied perception that produces a "chamber-music-muscularity of throat apparatus, tongue, teeth ... exquisite grunts of meat-thought staccato" (*Telling Time*, 47).

At the time he met Kelly in 1963, Brakhage lived in Robert Duncan's basement. He was absorbing the vibrant poetics not only of Duncan and Olson, but the experiments in time and repetition of Gertrude Stein.

---

52. *Vort* 2.2 (1974) 164. Cited parenthetically hereafter.
53. Stan Brakhage, *Telling Time: Essays of a Visionary Filmmaker* (2003) 86.
54. Charles Olson, *Selected Writings*, ed. Robert Creeley (1966) 61.

Kelly described Brakhage as an initiate into mysteries of his own making — a characterization that also applies to Kelly himself, as he was already steeped in alchemy and myth and engaged in poetic initiations largely homemade. At the same time, Brakhage was completing the Prelude to *Dog Star Man*, a stunning orchestration of images in transformation that *enacted* Olson's poetic knowing. Not only was Brakhage able to assemble images into quicksilver sequences, he was also an animated polemicist and homespun theorist in ways reminiscent of Kelly's own forays into poetics. Kelly had not only begun to assemble vast occult and philosophical learning, he was investigating ways in which to embody those emblems and ciphers. He sought what the Greeks called *chros*, the "face of the body's / joining with the world, membrane of the self / at the brink of the gap." He wanted a kinetic immediacy, imagery in movement that reenacted the mind's flow. Quickly Kelly and Brakhage began a process of poetic cross-fertilization, resulting finally in Kelly's *Songs I–XXX*, his cinematic exploration of the "extended lyric."

Brakhage and Kelly saw themselves in occult terms, with the extravagant theosophy of Duncan intoxicating both. In many ways, it was the alchemy of the record player. The hermetic tradition with a soundtrack by Bach, with even Bach (in Brakhage's characterization) becoming an early instance of Projective Verse, "helping to defeat dominance of brain wave's math in music, giving excuse perhaps for ear-regularities and/or impulses of a non-brain origin" (*Telling Time*, 32). Naturally, the shamanic and visionary masks they assumed were also part of counterculture tribalism — Brahkage's letters from the period are full of free love and hallucinogens, Vietnam and racial antagonisms (as, beneath the surface, the racial tensions in Boston in the mid-1960s exist as raw material for Kelly's alchemical excursions). But what attracted Kelly was the technique of *Dog Star Man*, which Brakhage's formal adventurousness, with its intricate composition and rapid cuts, superimpositions, use of color filters, scratching and painting on the film itself. In *Dog Star Man*, a great number of the techniques Brakhage would exploit in his later, more abstract films, combine with a simple narrative of struggle, as the Dog Star Man journeys through a bleak landscape that finally overcomes him.

Importantly for Kelly, *Dog Star Man* did not move through the machinery of plot; as Kelly argues in his "Notes on Brakhage," these early films "broke the illusion of personal narrative. It is not that he destroyed the line, but (like our master Kandinsky) moved off from the line into continents of color, geologies of mass and bodily shove." Elemental images abound in *Dog Star Man* — solar flares, sex, the pulse of blood vessels, mountains, the orbiting moon, — as well as gestures that elude strict definition. All are orchestrated into a "cosmological epic" where images are shaped into an organic sequence. In his poetic assembling of images, Brakhage followed Olson's lead: "The mind's flow of (thus) moving images, transformative images which are metamorphosing and (thereby) reflective of the sensual world, is (as Olson's dream has it) designate of knowing..." (*Telling Time*, 10). Kelly ended up dedicating the *Songs* to Brakhage. He called the poems "parts of a continuous process of finding each day's song," and within the volume he consciously explored a poetics of the fragment. (Slightly earlier, Brakhage had characterized his own work as *Songs*: "I carry a Camera (usually 8 mm) with me on almost every trip away from the house ... and I call these home and travel movies "SONGS," as they are to me the recorded visual music of my inner and exterior life — the 'fixed melodies' of, the filmic memory of, my living").[55]

Kelly's entire song cycle was structured as a series of quick glimpses and rapid transitions, where images constantly transform and mutate. Like Pound's ideograms, Kelly shows the truth of the momentary in a dance of the intellect among words. Interestingly, Brakhage himself saw the Chinese ideogram as a type of film: "The pictures themselves were enjambed, that the eyes might flick one t'other, in a two or three frame 'movie' construct, yes! so that this surfacing of the brain (which eyes are) must shift viscerally back/forth in reverbatory dance of conception" (*Telling Time*, 11—12). Within the *Songs*, Kelly offers meditations on Brakhage, draws parallels to their respective methods, evokes certain image-strands in *Dog Star Man*, particularly in his moon rhapsody, and allows the poetics of film to resonate within the *Songs*' cosmology.

From the opening lines of Kelly's *Songs*, the universe is seen cinematically. Each song moves with a kind of associational logic, as image begets image, and each possesses a surface of rapid and enigmatic transitions. Like the root system of plants, the images entwine; nodal points break

---

55. Stan Brakhage, *Brakhage Scrapbook: Collected Writings* (1982) 168.

off into branches that in turn couple with other points, establishing a vast dendritic network of correspondences similar to *Axon Dendron Tree*. Or, to shift metaphors, they can be seen as a series of isolated notes and disjunct melodic passages that obscure the underlying structure, much like tone-row compositions in music (in fact, Kelly cites Schoenberg's unfinished opera *Moses and Aaron*, perhaps identifying his debt to the composer's dissonant surfaces). Historical figures come and go sporadically, cinematically, as the poems reduce history into an elaboration of the present moment.

Within the songs, systems of knowledge and historical epochs intertwine; as in Pound's *Cantos*, all ages become contemporaneous. Moreover, they become incarnate, inextricable from the rhythms of the body. In Brakhage's description, poetic time is recognized as "relative to the organic perceiver, to the very beat of the heart (which is not a drum or a drummer, but rather a collection of squeezer/releasers, down to each cell-of-it, which surge to various agreements of variously complex pulses always subtly at odds with clock or metronome" (*Telling Time*, 15). That rhythm is bound to mortality — one is reminded of John Cage's listening to the beat of his own heart in the absence of all other sound — and not to an abstract, universal ordering of pulse. Instead, both Brakhage and Kelly seek something like the rhythm of decay and transmutation, envisioned at a level far beneath the surface of things.

Central to the *Songs* is Giordano Bruno, the Italian Dominican scholar burnt at the stake in 1600 for heresy. Kelly was drawn to his intoxicating mixture of troubadour longing, word-magic, allegorical extravagance, and embrace of infinite worlds. Kelly had ventured into Pound's territory, and the *Songs* attempted to make peace with Pound's *Cantos* and their deep conservatism (Confucius appears a few times in a delightful sidestep of Pound's obsession with money). While certainly one can sense Pound's technique in these poems — with his tessellated *Cantos* — one can also sense the mechanics of film, raised to a metaphysical level. The body of Bruno becomes an alchemical emblem as it burns — like the burning salamander or corpse of kings in *Atalanta Fugiens* — as it emits light, "a controlled radiance." The body is dissolved in light, and that light is also the light of film; in Brakhage's words, "All interference with The Light (all shaped tones and formal silhouettes) ought to be an illumination of source-as-light" (*Telling Time*, 51). Thus the burning martyr's body, in the logic of the poem, is a promise of purification, an alchemical sublimation. In their quicksilver progression of images, the poems mimic the flickering tongues of alchemical flame — images are burnt at the altar and become nearly a wall of fire in their incandescence. In this vision, he comes close to the filmmaker Hollis Frampton's definition of the image as being "like a radioactive substance that gives out energy and is diminished and needs to be augmented."[56]

Kelly merges this martyrdom with the dance, as if the twitch of flesh on its pyre hovers beyond each ecstatic whirl and turn. Dance and martyrdom are each metaphors for the incarnation of meaning; and Kelly's Christian alchemy hearkens back to the "Rosy + Cross" (as Jed Rasula has argued of Kelly's work, "... Mystery is at the heart of it, the mysterium tremendum of sanctity and grace, the burden on man of making love salvation").[57] Again, Brakhage's thoughts on the kinetics of "cinematic dance" dovetail with Kelly's:

> But cinematic dancing might be said to occur as any film-maker is moved to include his whole physiological awareness in any film movement... I practice every conceivable body movement with camera-in-hand almost every day. I do *not* do this in order to formalize the motions of moving picture taking *but rather* to explore the possibilities of exercise, to awaken my senses, and to prepare my muscles and joints with the weight of the camera and the necessary postures of holding of these postures through my physiological *reaction* during picture taking and to some meaningful act of edit.   (*Brakhage Scrapbook*, 123)

Interestingly, in relation to Kelly's work, Brakhage speaks of both the immediacy of picture taking *and* editing. Kelly's *Songs* are not merely notations of what occurs immediately on the street or on the bus, but also the immediate decisions made when putting together the welter of images.

---

56. Quoted in Stan Brakhage, *Brakhage Scrapbook: Collected Writings* (1982) 176.
57. Jed Rasula, "Ten Different Fruits on One Different Tree: Reading Robert Kelly," *Credences* 3.1 (1984): 127–175. See 141.

In the context of Kelly's opening poem, what is central is Bruno's belief in an atomistic universe, where each part contains an animus, a spirit (akin to Brakhage's rhythmic cells). Each particle pulses with its own energy, and from that energy arises an obligation to experience everything, to destroy the images that inhibit a full embrace of the cosmos. (As Walter Pater wrote of Bruno, "To shut the eyes, whether of the body or the mind, would be a kind of dark ingratitude; the one sin, to believe directly or indirectly in any absolutely dead matter anywhere, because involving denial of the indwelling spirit.")[58] In this exuberant embrace, Bruno was an iconoclast — twice questioned by ecclesiastical authorities for casting away images of the saints — and thus a threat to dogma, not only in his pantheism, but in his allegorical savagery worthy of a Gnostic. (Interestingly, Brakhage at one point coined the term "imagnostic" to describe his own work). Kelly reaches for the fragment, and the triumph of the fragment is at the expense of grammar and illusions of language. The rigidity of grammar — with its laws governing identity and the ordering of perceptions — is a false unity, an imposed coherence that limits the ability to know.

In this opening song, Kelly rejects Nietzsche's god of grammar in favor of the paradoxical clarity of broken syntax. He assaults the sentence, which he sees as mirroring a certain ontology in its form: "Nothing / clearer than fragment. / No syntax / less than all" (9). For Kelly the stability of representation — the illusion of permanence fostered by language — is the central object of alchemical dissolution. In "Song XVIII," for example, Kelly explicitly links Bruno with alchemy; his martyrdom is a fiery cleansing of words, stripping them of their literality:

> ... root with no stem or stalk or flower .
> dissolve & find the words,
>   the word's fix . "Thrown on the wall of the mind"
> Bruno's shadows of ideas, one picture
> to seize the world . in flames
> the years ago . solve the world . he said . to the crucifix
> *I will not look upon that image . the fire shapes my eyes*
>
>   (*Songs*, 57/58)[59]

---

58. Walter Pater, *Giordano Bruno* (The Project Gutenberg Ebook: July 9, 2009).
59. Robert Kelly, *Songs I–XXX* (1968).

Bruno joins Moses, whose "pure / Lack of word" opposes the "tablet / of specific laws" as a destroyer of images, and the "rune-makers," who assert the play of images outside truth and know "words / could come before things & give comfort" (*Songs*, 18), as a liberator of images from the natural order. For Kelly the soul seeks its essence in the sword or the *labrys*, the two-headed axe of the labyrinth, severing image from context.

In other words, Kelly identifies with Moses as visionary, but struggles against the translation of vision into Law. His allegiance to Moses the Law-Giver falters. He partakes in the orgiastic dance before the Golden Calf. After all, a revisionary reading of the Exodus story reveals a mythopoetic energy in rejecting the Law, the tainted commandments of Moses, the vestiges of the corrupt priestly castes of Egypt. To deny the pure ecstasy of the idolatrous dance is to engage in monotheism's oppression:

>   ... the priests will refuse to take delight
> in the variety of god,
>   will not let him show
> her faces, her hippo head & small
> taut wet girl's belly   (14)

Better to be a "wild voluptuary of the polar vault," a mad allegorist making unmaking meaning in speech that borders on inarticulate grunts and cries. Better to embrace what Brakhage called a "Kali-like æsthetic" that permits "some reference to what's being transformed as well as the process of disintegration/transformation — in avoidance of re-formation" (*Telling Time*, 69). In fact, Kelly argued of the use of double-exposure that "Brakhage's genius lay in showing us this minus that minus those, and making those subtractions, which became additions, into a complex manifold in which we found ourselves seeing nothing of what had been shot, but only what had been resurrected, multiplied, into seeing. Literally (to use the word that links alchemy, Olson's poetics, and any film) projected."[60]

---

60. Robert Kelly, "Notes on Brakhage," *Chicago Review* 47/48 (2001–2002) 164–170. See 140.

For Kelly, such alchemical projection recalls the dance of Shiva and its dual nature: *tandava*, the powerful rush of violent energy, and *lasya*, the soft and lyrical expression of tenderness.[61] *Tandava* accords with the dance of fire that burns itself up in its execution, leaving nothing but a residue of silence; it is a dance that points to the void in its consummation: "*I burn the shadows / of the dancers, from Sinai I deny / the pattern of the dance, / art of the dancer*. What's left when the dance / is danced away" (*Songs*, 20). *Tandava* is the dance of Williams' path of the death of images, while *lasya* arises from delight and forms the weave of the imagination:

>   Make
> bodies of flesh, rub the fur of the velvet
> back & forth in the light,
>   feel the light
> as power of the cloth to yield or capture (*Songs*, 13)

Like the bellows of the alchemical forge, Kelly's songs alternate between these two rhythms of the dance: the contractive and the expansive. In terms of Kelly's mythology, his songs move to the rhythms of the "anguished journeymen / who have no masters" (*Songs*, 42), who conform to the arc of the sun and unite with the earth showered by the sun's divinity. An alchemical dance beyond nature and the certitudes of meaning:

>   Behind any light there is light behind any color there is
> light .
>   a dance ...
>   of being mountains &
> valleys . being earth & being each
>   thing that is on the earth & being
> vulnerable as earth .
>   Ode
>   in the measure of the Eye of Horus
> which is the resting place of those who do not rest
>   & the sun
> struck on the flint of the horizon)   (*Songs*, 43–44)

---

61. For an extended analysis of this distinction, see Heinrich Zimmer, *Indische Mythen und Symbole: Vishnu, Shiva und das Rad der Wiedergeburten* (1991) 168–194.

Earlier in this Song, Kelly writes: "For man dances maid & the dance / has nothing to do with it, nothing to do / is the consequence of their delight and not its cause" (13). The violence of the gaze, of desire, must be purified in ways antithetical to what Brakhage called "the spiritual tearing asunder [of] every vestige of lie to its cellular heat light" (68):

> Nymphs take us
>   on, flee back from our identities
> to water, the vast, the unspecific. It shines   water
> & while I think of the word
> the garbage truck surfaces outside, growls,
>   takes
> something away. Nymph because
> nymphai, dymphai, lymph of the earth. Not blood   Names
> of a subtle devious & colorless
>   moisture
> rides all night through the body, knows
>   no morning, no dark,
> look
> on water, turn into water. (17)

The traditional image of the nymph, an image of violent fixation, is transformed to lymph, the colorless liquid that transports waste away from living tissue.

Thus the poison becomes the cure in a carnal homeopathy. By becoming water, Kelly would evade the Law of the father and the rigidity of the Law that permeates the very structure of language. As Brown and others have argued, language hierarchically orders the body through the linguistic economy of the Œdipal complex. To transcend Œdipal desire, the unity of self and its corresponding body-image must undergo a form of alchemical dissolution; the body itself becomes the *lapis*. The unity which precedes the formation of the rigid, genitalized self — the amorphous and multiphasic world of fluid exchange before the erection of psychic boundaries — can be restored through the progressive shattering of borders and divisions in a world of fragments and body parts and co-mingling organs.

For Kelly, alchemy is a physical process, as fully embodied as cutting and splicing mothwings and plant specimens onto film. As Jung wrote of the physicality of the alchemical imagination, "The *imaginatio*, or the act of imagining, is thus a physical activity that can be fitted into the cycle of material changes, that brings these about and is brought about by them in its turn. In this way the alchemist related himself not only to the unconscious but directly to the very substance which he hoped to transform through the power of imagination."[62] And for Kelly that substance is language. In "An Alchemical Journal," he links alchemy and experiments with syntax: "It may be that every man is set upon the earth to find one new method of divination. That is, to write one sentence whose syntax is total. Because (this idea is familiar) syntax is at the heart of divination, to locate the function of a thing in the structure of process" (68).

As evident in his earlier *Axon Dendron Tree*, Kelly's awareness of syntax was integrally related to alchemy. Its polysyntactic grids and word-chains are indeed an approximation of "total syntax," and esoteric texts rewarded him with a Nibelungen hoard of images, granting him *permission*, in a sense, to deepen his understanding of the body and its relation to words. Like Siegfried, Kelly bathed in the dragon's blood and was reborn into the spheres of alchemical violence. In Brakhage's terms, the "meat mind" abolishes the hard lines and divisions of geometry: "Very little of geometry survives 'translation' into organic thought ... the meat of the mind ... puts curve to linearity, blurs hard-edge perception" (*Telling Time*, 79). Kelly's alchemical dissolution is in many ways equivalent to Brakhage's desire to recapture the full continuum of sensory experience, as when he envisioned "an un-nouned, non-dichotomous series of light-glyphs available for arrangement of cathectic exchanges which directly reflect each person's synapsing inner nervous system" (*Telling Time*, 86). Here we find the polymorphous perversity of film.

Similarly, Kelly envisions a carnal New Jerusalem erected through the Word. His prophecy resides in the configurations of the body — "every orifice is a sybil's cave / in which informations from an alien order whisper" (*Songs*, 74). If the artificial boundaries of the self — with its body marked by prohibitions and tattooed by guilt — can be overcome

---

62. *Psychology and Alchemy* (1944) 246.

in the breaking of phallic language, erotic play would be restored. "Every hole / is Delphi, each mouth takes in the sun, every / cunt gives birth to sunlight in the dark, messiah / snowheaded, blue eyes of ice" (*Songs*, 74). Identity would be dispersed in a refusal of sublimation, and once more the paths to the universe of prophecy would be cleared.

Yet *Songs I–XXX*, despite its erotic, liberatory intentions, appears to be a troubled recapitulation of Œdipal anxieties. Kelly's attempt to transcend the limitations of genital sexuality serves only to restore its efficacy (indeed, the figure of Bruno may be seen as almost a transcendent phallus governing these songs). His songs show the limits of his alchemical method; they trumpet the internal dilemmas and resistances that resound throughout his entire alchemical corpus. That is part of the drama. As Kelly noted poignantly of *Dog Star Man*,

> Brakhage not only gives us permission to stare, he demands that we do. But our stare must become dance, an active gesture, no more a passive gaze. Our stare must dance, a stare-dance, star-dance, the Dog Star Man struggling up the mountainside, tortured and restrained by colors, images, deliquescences.
>
> ("Notes on Brakhage," 167–168)

Central to Kelly's poem is also the figure of Faust, broken and left on the dungheap. While blasphemy is for Kelly here "to learn / the name of the god before we make the god" (18), the alchemical process often ends in a fetid mess. Throughout the *Songs*, creation can also appear to the impotent self as a cosmic crypt in all its suffocating vastness. At times the distortions sever the "full circuit of object, image," in Olson's phrase. As Brahkage argued, "I think there is some 'short-circuit' of light pouring into the eye, as it meets that person's output / memory's discharge, and that we SEE in midst of a smoldering fire of cross-currents."[63]

While Kelly's primary impulse is toward crafting the image — "Enact what is. / This is alchemy, / here is where you'd look for measure, / in which a spirit is / called down into the stone" (31) — what is enacted can

---

63. William Wees, *Light Moving in Time: Studies in the Visual Æsthetics of Avant-Garde Film* (1992) p. 92.

be the process of transmutative thought, with poems becoming almost like field notes of discovery, registering sightings of deities like new species of seagulls. Almost all the poems are a search for occult knowledge. Some elaborate upon an image to see what it will yield, to subject it to poetic scrutiny until it becomes emblematic. From the rain, rune stones and birds with diamonds in their beaks. From the "milk-soft light" of November, fertility goddesses. From a Schubert song, Persephone. From a subway, devouring goddesses and constellations. Likewise, what is enacted is *the making itself*; the cutting, splicing, and ordering required to stitch together these songs. Here the immediacy is of a different order — the intuitive ordering of materials, its compression into what Brakhage called "an absolute glyph-of-the-whole available in reflective variations forever compounding (through near repetition) into the greatest simplicity imaginable" (*Telling Time*, 118). When alchemy fails, what remains is the immediate charting of failure. One can feel the urgency to be immersed in paradisiacal forms and to create lovely patterns, particularly when the material resists. The *Songs* begin to assume the emotional logic of a Puritan divine, ceaselessly scouring the world (or at least's one's work table spilling over with coiling film reels) for signs of grace. The world — and self — must be constantly sanctified anew, as the unregenerate world of things threatens to obliterate all.

Thus in "Song X," the subway remains a subway. In "Song XI," there can be no "marriage" to things (only a voice enjoining one to wear the "cloth in glory"). In "Song XIII," Faust dies on the dungheap, bereft of song. In "Song XVII," the poet hangs in his bones like a tree, waiting passively for what will come. In "Song XIX," continuity does not arise (this is Kelly's song of the montagist at work), and the poet can only mimic the sun. In "Song XX," voices are not heard, and the poet enjoins himself to "catch / starlight where it impregnates the pool. / let / the gate tower crumble as the word / articulates among the trumpets" (65), where there is neither starlight nor trumpets. In "Song XXI," the dream turns to hissing serpents, and chivalry is dead. In "Song XXVI," the poet doubts that his words, bereft of fire, can illuminate Time. In "Song XXVIII," the water birds chant, "This is not your country." Many of the poems document the resistance of the material to ordering and the poet's struggle to establish connections in what Brakhage called "an ever expanding dream-web of God's dreamt tree" (*Telling Time*, 138).

Perhaps the most remarkable instance of struggle is the 21st song, which is a meditation on the Fort Hill watchtower in Roxbury, Massachusetts. The song reenacts primal scenes that arise in the syntactical breaks and slippages of dream-associations. Its surface is fractured — the central images of the fortress and tower are like palimpsests or mythic ciphers and Tarot trumps and undergo a series of metamorphoses that indicate they serve only as a screen upon which to project fantasy images. Kelly's fantasy has many levels; the poem's opening lines recall the timidity of the prophet before God's injunction, as if the poet stood like a reluctant Jonah before the gates of Nineveh, and also the poet's burden of creation in the primal scene of instruction. In the coalescing dream-associations, the carnal act merges with the spiritual psalm:

> Not ready lord not ready . I cant get started . blow sweet . out.
> futter has a sound like an animal doing it . a church
> of the brothers & the sisters,
>   also amen . at Roxbury
>
>   (*Songs*, 67)

For Kelly, anterior images haunt the visual scene; the blow of inspiration recalls the coitus of beasts. As Kelly enters the imaginary realm of Eros, he finds — at the very origin of creation — the shadow of a more primary act.

In Kelly's song, the imaginative space of the poem is eroticized. In an early song, he had already revealed his belief in the essentially sexual nature of space. Behind one's orientation to earth and sky lies a woman's body. All motion is sexual motion; all sojourns are pricking on the plain:

>   ... in crystal
>   the recensions of space
>   I see the queen . in the tower
> that is her body .
>   map the intricate subways of her city
> chambers hidden below the rails ...
>   (*Songs*, 23)

Words charting the space of dreams are to Kelly a substitute for the primacy of the mother's body. They attempt to symbolically restore a unity with the mother by exploring the labyrinth of her womb. As in Freud, dreams for Kelly symbolically reenact primal incest, returning to unity and quiescence in the manifestation of the desire for death.

Dreaming is also the hallucinating of organs — actors upon the dream stage become *phalloi* in the mother's womb, and the dream process is governed by the laws of castration. "Every coitus repeats the fall," argued N.O. Brown in his analysis of genital sexuality's ambivalence, "brings death, birth, into the world. It is Sky descending into Mother Earth, ejaculating his powers, suffering castration. The staff that cleaves the water is the dead man's body, the corpse; the stiff that ejaculates the soul or semen is the penis. Penis or corpse, stiff as stone; a perfect erection or monument."[64] While a Jungian view of Kelly's 21st song might see the Roxbury tower as a mandala image — the city, body, and cosmos turning and turning about its axis — the tower is unmistakably an image of coitus: "it was the 18th trump / that conduit to such down starfire & bed in / earth, menstrum / fire and aer, i.e., / a green-eyed tower, mother moon" (*Songs*, 67). Again the merger of *anima* and *animus* — the tower made feminine — too literally follows Œdipal logic to warrant any idealizations; in Freudian theory, the child, desiring the mother, yet forbidden her, enacts an imaginary coitus. The phallic image, transfixing the mind, is a sign of the primal scene — the self splits, becoming observer, father and mother, receptacle and substance, vagina and penis in the primary dream of "self as embryo in womb = penis in womb = parents in coitus, the primal scene" (*Love's Body*, 57). Desire de-realizes the present and affirms the stranglehold of the past. Events are shadowed — *scotomized* — upon the stage of dreams.[65]

In his attempt to transcend Œdipal logic, Kelly conflates the mother and the phallus, seeking to transcend the crippling duality of gender:

>   phallos is woman & seeks her own . (shining!) . witness [...]

---

64. Norman O. Brown, *Love's Body* (1966) 48.

65. In *Love's Body*, Brown writes: "Psychoanalysis ends in the recognition of the reality principle as Lucifer, the prince of darkness, the prince of this world. The reality-principle is the prince of darkness, its function is to *scotomize*, to spread darkness, walls of separation and concealment" (150).

>   witness cycladic Afrodita, under form of an
> unhewn stone, up-pronging, jagged,
>   or Hermes' oldest hallows:
> column or quern, herm, that is
>   Hermaphrodite means
> Hermes is Venus .
>   (*Songs*, 68)

In alchemical texts, the Hermaphrodite is often central, representing a reconciliation of opposites in the restoration of unity. The hermaphroditic body symbolizes balance, exchange, a harmony of opposites. For N.O. Brown, however, it is merely the hallucinatory false unity in the violent oscillation of Œdipal logic; it attempts to "square the circle; the desire and pursuit of the whole in the form of dual unity or the combined object; the Satanic hermaphroditism of Antichrist ..." (*Love's Body*, 71). The alchemical squaring of the circle so integral to Jung's alchemy becomes merely a process by which the dreamer assumes both sexual positions: the father as phallus, achieving symbolic gratification of incestual desire, and the mother as *vagina dentata*, severing the phallus in bloody copulation. The primal scene for Brown is the battle for the symbolic possession of the phallus, a bloody battleground upon which the spoils of authority are won.

In the logic of Kelly's poem, the phallus is precisely what is denied; the tower becomes a symbol of repression and prohibition. The gateway to the tower is seen as an "old iron door bolted shut, / spikes driven in the masonry to hold it closed" (*Songs*, 69) Can one read this not only as a denial of access to the mother, but as denial of access to poetic authority, to the mastery of the father's voice? Firmly in place is the logic of castration and rebellion. Kelly establishes a mythopoetic correspondence between himself and the Egyptian god Set, dismemberer of Osiris, as well as adopting the persona of the knight wandering the plain in search of the Grail. The land is laid waste, and a ritual sacrifice is necessary to restore the land's fertility. Kelly's divided symbolic response first envisions a return to the plenitude of light and Adamic power:

> this is the point of likening, this is the world
> inside the mirror that is the mirror, the world that is the world
> but the say . of moving there . where . the light
> chooses to begin
>   (*Songs*, 69)

But along with this return to originary light, Kelly also flees from judgment, celebrating Cain's expulsion. And flight corresponds to Kelly's kabbalistic belief in the primacy of words over substance, *muthos* over *logos*, the desert over the garden:

>   but the say . of moving
> is . gold wire . the code spun spirals of . gold wire
> with Saturn's song . mark of Cain ...
>   ... fix . settle here to flee . everywhere, wander,
> shunted along the genetic warp . fix . cut loose, an identity
> thought the sun a lance . it is the gold heart of the target
>
>   (*Songs*, 69)

But even here rules Saturn, castrator of Chronos, while the origin of light remains a phallic lance. The alchemist's gold is not only the product of mercurial dissolution, but is also an image of castration — the gold plaits, the genetic warp and woof, the snaky hair of Medusa.[66] The tower becomes as well the stone phallus, frozen from the phallic mother's gaze. And in the logic of Kelly's song, Medusa devours. The Egypt of Thoth and Hermes Trismegistus becomes the Egypt of Set governed by laws of castration:

>   & all of us killers, "The
> city defended from this prospect .
>   black Egypt . black Egypt .
> sisters who have one   between you
>   mouth . mouth .
> (this is classicism, rift in the aithêr,
>   ether riff
> blow old white song)
>   in your mouth, one part between you all
>   ...
>   (*Songs* 73)

---

66. Brown summarized castration imagery: "To be the penis of the mother with a penis; both erection and castration. The primal scene seen is Medusa's head seen: a trophy, decapitated, and still potent, the female genitals with no penis, but snakes for hair" (*Love's Body*, 65–66). Brown goes on to describe further symbolic resonances: "*Hyphen, hymen, hymn, hypnos*. The net or nexus. Networks of affiliation: the filial relation is not natural but artificial, threaded (*filum*)" (74).

As befitting dream-work, the passage is highly overdetermined — black refers to the populace wandering the grounds, but also to Jung, who (unfortunately) saw the presence of blacks in dreams as indicating historical repression, as well as the alchemical idea of the *putrefactio*, while white is both spiritual purity and the spurting semen of ejaculation. Though the fortress soon becomes a sacred *temenos*, mirroring the "great Ocean" wound in a circle like the snake swallowing its own tail, the nodal point of the passage is the yawning mouth. Devour or be devoured, Kelly seems to imply. No trumpets of prophecy, but the old white song fellatio and the primal scene. "In corporation (introjection), seen with the inward eye, is always eating or swallowing," Brown argues. "In the primal scene a regression takes place ... and copulation is seen as oral copulation" (*Love's Body*, 70).

In "Song XXIV," Kelly makes the equation of vagina, dream, and devouring mouth even more baldly in a tapestry woven of genital nightmares: "hunters spot the electric stag but shoot into their own mouths. / we live / any dream to the end . it is a tongue we march on . lose footing up the slimy groove . double arched mouth / the Swallower / is patient" (81). Women become destructive, demonic figures in "Hieronymus' Dream" where the "veins of marble turn to living serpents in the urn, hissed / the secret name of his fascinations" (82). The fascination and repulsion of the primal scene doom Kelly to the "Rocky Law of Condemnation and double Generation & Death; which makes the Loins the place of the Last Judgment" (*Love's Body*, 49).

The rest of Kelly's 21st song revolves around the battlements — as Shakti dances, forming the healing "circulus mundi" with the genetic code "unraveling in her hands," and Seth's hot breath blows in from offshore (72). The poem finally ends as divided as it began. The world diminishes in strife, becoming convoluted and suffocating. In a moment of clarity born of desperation, Kelly recognizes his failure & the illusory nature of his union:

> Lord Aithêr do you hear me,
>   we are not animals doing it, [...]
> it was to come to a point .
>   genital organization, or by gender,
> or by . the generations .
>   it was to come to a tower . above the whole world . where the enemy troops my brothers were on the move against my brethren   (72)

His prayer points forward to the Civil War of *The Common Shore*, his fevered attempt to bring about symbolically the mystical body of Christ and heal the rifts caused by genital organization. But in the context of his alchemy, his songs demonstrate the flaw of his poetics — the violence of alchemy promises transcendence, but that promise falters in the numbing repetition of violence. Isolated acts of the Magi only restore the roots of sickness. Fragmentary disassociations of dream-work only reveal the tenacity of phallic power. Eros weaves illusions as surely as Vishnu. The flames of the alchemical fire can be a martyr's flames; the Mage's robes a coat of Nessus.

But, as profound as these poems of anxiety and failure can be, what endures in *Songs I—XXX* is really captured in "Song XVII" in the parable of the tree, where martyrdom dissolves into something quiet and lyrical:

> We had to go on simply
> over the crisis, break in the skin .
>
>   this going is our bridge,
> leaves are quieter now . I was not a tree,
> I hung in my bones like a man in a tree,
> the tree talked . I said nothing . the sun
> hurts money, rain washes value away . they
> call it a sand . dollar . it is beautiful
> in the ways of strange writings not on it but
> which are it, the words . we do not read ...
>   (53)

Brakhage once equated his experimental film practice as creating the home movies of angelic beings: "... all that we call psychological projections are the movies of the angels — the home movies of the angels are qualities of light held as if in midair — any gathering of dust motes in the light records the passage of angels" (*Scrapbook*, 142). Perhaps it is that stitching together of the intensely personal and the cosmic that marks the triumph of these songs.

The Adamic qualities of Kelly's project are clear — he wants always to start from scratch; to create meaning from a moribund tradition only through the fire of his imagination. But the grand myth-making always seems eminently personal, always bearing the marks of their creation.

In this sense, the *Songs* share those qualities that he admired in Brakhage's films, "the hand-made, hand-scratched, twisted, glued, hand-painted films — always the gesture of the hand, hand of the eye, a sign the seeing body recognizes...."[67] (In his more grandiose moments, Kelly does equate the alchemical transmutation of events to Christ's clearing the temple of money-changers, a cleansing that restores the primacy of love untainted by worldly commerce. As N.O. Brown cried out, the poet's task is "To redeem words out of the marketplace, out of the barking, into the silence; instead of commodities, symbols" (*Love's Body*, 258). But what remains are those more intimate signs, such as Kelly's evocation of Confucius:

> ... my fingers pleased
> with mulberry texture, silk-shot twenties & tens.
> But money is now.
> What draws us is the contour of our finish,
> last words, sarcophagus. (84)

Sarcophagus is literally "flesh-eating," from the belief in limestone's ability to quicken the decomposition of dead bodies (as in his evocation of Bruno early on). But these songs are more like portable altars. As Brakhage said of his own "Songs," "many 8mm cameras fit easily into a coat pocket or purse and are no more of a burden than a transistorized radio" (*Scrapbook*, 168). Except, like Orpheus' car radio in Cocteau's film, they transmit signals from another world.

---

67. Robert Kelly, "Brakhage, Spoken in Memory, 17 March 2003," *Millenium Film Journal* 41 (2003).

BILLIE CHERNICOFF

READING *THE LOOM*

The poem declares its quest in the first line,

> To find a place
> to talk to you

and deft as Penelope sends the shuttle back through the warp.

> or find
> a talk
> to place you in,

Much has been said of Robert Kelly's ongoing exploration of place (*A Line of Sight, Map of Annandale, The Common Shore, Hypnogeography*). Here, in his book length poem *The Loom*, a place to talk, a place *of* talk, to welcome you. The poet, ever a rover, is at home the moment the poem begins. Who is the you of the poem? The one taken in.

*

> starting with
> I love you

Where so often a tale ends. But how simple, even foolish, to begin with that tattered garment, that worn proposition, *I love you.*

> I love you
> where it all began

Where to go from where it all begins? The fool where he wanders, the magus where he wills.

*

I love you. Maybe all of religion is an attempt to solve for those three terms. I heard Kelly read the line aloud, not long after *The Loom* was published, pronouncing each word at the same pitch and volume, giving the same weight to each, eliminating any sentimentality and making it clear that the three variables are equals as well as constants.

    & that formulation
    still waits their
    reverentest minds

    And ours.

*

Chantefable, a medieval tale of adventure told in alternating sections of sung verse and recited prose. The word was used by the anonymous author of the 13th century French work *Aucassin et Nicolette* in its concluding lines: *No cantefable prent fin* (*Our cantefable is drawing to a close*). The word is from the Old French Picard dialect, *cantefable*, literally, *[it] sings [and it] narrates.* (*Encyclopedia Britannica*)

Or *No cantefable prent fin* as RK translated it back to me in earish: *no cantefable ever ends.*

*

    natural contexts
    growth & form

How readable *The Loom* is. All poetry is language poetry, turning scratches into music, and vice versa, understanding into disturbance and revelation. But Kelly's poems are never merely glamorous — even his most abstract work means *to talk to you*, talks to mean to you. To risk meaning is to risk relationship.

You, most and least personal of pronouns. Who is the "you" of the poem, or more accurately, who is the you of the poem *now*, specific yet changeable, the most elusive of creatures.

*

The poetry of *The Loom* excites and troubles, woos and lullabyes.

> ... calm hands
> of a man
> hearing music,
> hears it
> as it is,
> fold & unfold,
> two rhythms two
> motions, place
> & talk.

It is among the most musical of Kelly's works, with its rhythmic, almost syncopated phrasing, the witty pizzicato and graceful swoons of its *parlando*. It confounds me that the lengthy conversations of the poem fall so lithe into those narrow columns.

> to find a place
> to talk to you

Poem as place. There are few images at the beginning of *The Loom*, other than the print itself on the page: a Parthenon, chorus of oboes, auger (augur) making its way down.

At the beginning it's mostly music, syntax, mind.

*

On the women of *The Loom*:

Helen becomes *the Helen*, *this Helen*, and thereby more richly and radiantly herself. Isn't it the responsibility of poets and lovers to imagine each other?

> The only thing worse
> than an Imagined Woman
> is an Unimagined one.

6 · A BOOK OF READINGS

Kelly's work stays close to the body. But without fables, dreams, myths, we are *only carbon*. "The universe is made up of stories, not atoms," Muriel Rukeyser said.

The women who walk, ride, or sail into Kelly's *Loom*, who invent and announce themselves (Lady Isabella de Cabeza, Ariadne, Korinna, Lolli, and the Great Blond Lady, sassiest of equestrians, to name a few) are self-defined and explicit. Separately and in concert they speak for themselves. The muses muse.

*

In *The Loom*'s redemption of Ariadne we see how one myth undoes another. The poet rescues her from mythology, from her vague victimhood *among the fogs, awaiting an identity,* rescues her from the Hero, from himself, and finally from all rescuing. At last she is her own.

> I reach into my mind for you,
> reach inside you
> & display her,
> here, needing no Hero.
> A woman who is herself
> steps up
> from the murky shallows of the poem
> & on proud hips walks away
> from this & every
> mythology
> out into morning.

*

More on gender, and trans-gender. The poet of *The Loom* is a shape-shifter. Leave home. *Be the other thing.* A blond lady on horseback, with a Catholic boyhood.

> until the end
> *when the male*

> *becomes female & the female*
> *male, & we move*
> *naked at last*
> *beyond the garments*
> *male & female one*
> *& none.*

Consider that Kelly's meticulous investigations of our various masks demythologize both she and he, revealing the means by which we so poignantly pretend to be a man or woman, afraid to be that even more difficult and vulnerable entity, a human being.

> man & woman will be
> one, & none,
> when compassion
> does not mean sharing
> but a loving silence
> hears everything,
> no mind
> dumb to that dialogue
> & no heart deaf.

On the other hand, more than one thing is true:

> Men & women
> are different species
> from different
> places, join
> a little
> for their work on
> earth.

Then again, *Inside-out man*:

> (a woman's voice then,
> that I attend her necessities,
> that female presence

> in me or of me
> that also I have found outside,
> anima mea),
> inside outside,

Perhaps those propositions are truest which at once call their opposites to mind.

Write everything, the poet is instructed & instructs. There will be uncertainties, ambiguities, contradictions.

> All the pronouns
> live in me.

*

Cantefable.

Spoken prose narratives interspersed with short songs conveying crucial information, e.g. magical utterances, riddles, threats, etc...

The Magus or Magician of the Tarot is also called Artixano, Knower, Juggler, Deceiver, and Gambler,

> ...Robert
> le Diable, the gambler,

Magus: master of secrets and of technology *(o technology / you are so asthmatic)*, a manipulator of tools and of matter, usually shown with a table, or altar.

> ...for heart
> to speak to heart you need
> a table. A body. A body
> of work. A trade. A box
> of swiftian tools.

> We need
> the artifice of order, something
> to talk around,

The Magician escapes the constraints of time and of his own body, travels between worlds and returns able to teach and bless. He is the archetype of the will, of male energy, though not necessarily a man. His work is transformation, in particular of the self. He changes his mind, and therefore everything.

These fragments from Section 16:

> Is that an island where
> the mind is changed?
> By light & dark
> we seek an Other
> but the Other (feminine)
> waits for us
> across the bitter sea.
>
> Change your mind!
> I leapt over the side,
> paddled along beside the boat,
> one hand on the gunwales.
> I will take my brain
> & its old palimpsest of locations
> & find a world, ...

And from Section 17, speaking to Mary/Isis:

> Come to me
> as you came to Lucius
> over the sea
> & let your name
> be only the beginning.
> Let me pass through you
> & change my mind.

*

Readers and writers have spoken about having to come to terms with the vast quantity of Kelly's work. Not only is the volume daunting, but the work is so various it's impossible to find a poem that represents a school or movement of poetry, or that exemplifies the poet's own body of work or its poetics whole. Kelly doesn't write from principles or ideas. There is only the formality that the specific poem imposes on its field.

But large and complex as the œuvre may be, the work is immensely legible, both in the long and small poems. *The Loom* isn't difficult in the same way as Pound's *Cantos* or Olson's *Maximus Poems*, where the texts can be hard to follow through their giant leaps, obscure references, mind bending non sequiturs, and slips of the tongue into Latin, German, Chinese, Greek. Kelly does those things too, but even his most arcane poetry is so… readable. The poet sometimes annotates the work himself without losing the beat:

> Helen, whose name
> Homer puns on, to mean
> the woman who destroys,
> sets fire, ruins
> the fabric
> of that paranoid
> hero society: Helen
> destroy Kundry.
> Destroy Wagner.
> And if I am not more
> than the impress,
> sore spot left
> in flesh by those
> gleaming pebbles,
> no more than my
> images, Helen,
> destroy me.

I couldn't resist quoting the whole of that extraordinary ending of the first section of *The Loom*, in which the poet asks his Other to destroy him. But you can see how Kelly lends the reader a hand, via history or etymology, context.

Yet, Kelly's work is difficult. *Dense, intricate,* with its Byzantium of concerns, a maze, but if you go on you will come to a Virgil or sigil, guide or talisman, one of the truths or lies that show the way out, or deeper in.

> I propose a texture
> so dense, intricate,
> snaky with thread of gold
> & honest old scythian wool,
> that it will take your eye
> & hold it better
> the closer you look.
> While I, in my Arcane Apart,
> keep the structure up my sleeve.

The work can't be summed up. But even if you read it through quickly, without references or footnotes, without a detour to the library, you can still get it, the gist.

> Erlösung, to be
> loosed from every
> locked condition,
> locked part of me
> that does not mean.
> That does not love.

You don't have to know what *Erlösung* means. He tells you. Words in Kelly's poems, like all things of this world, are open secrets.

*

But I don't mean "get" it. And "gist" is a rough word for the secular mystery of Robert Kelly's poetry. Perhaps the particular challenge in reading Kelly is the soul work his poems ask of a reader, the willingness to enter into the text and feel one's way around, the familiar made strange, the strange familiar. The reader, like the poet, enters the poem at the risk of being lost and finding herself elsewhere, emerging someone else. One reads *The Loom* with the sense that anything might happen, not only to the poet, Hero or Lady, but to you, the reader.

*

Erlösung: salvation, redemption, deliverance, ransom, release.

*

Kelly never offers up the formulaic or repetitive, the familiar trope. He is almost superstitiously afraid of cliché, but never scared out of his humanity into mere linguistic event, non-saying. He says something else, something that he and we don't already know, that the poem discovers for itself. If the moon rises in his backyard, though it has risen in the backyards of thousand of poems, he doesn't say no to it, and it's not a moon that anyone, even Kelly, has said before. He breathes love into "love," reimagining and redeeming the "poetic" as well as the ordinary.

> But the shape of love
> like the loom of morning
> could cast before it
> a light on the shapes of things
> made *realer* by the goal
> towards which it & I & all
> hopeful things were moving.
> To make love.

*

In the 1970's, Kelly read the Austrian philosopher Rudolf Steiner closely, and I wonder if he absorbed some of his contrariness from Steiner, or simply met a kindred spirit. As Steiner has it, one looks out into the world to see the scape of the self. The world is a mirror. Likewise, one must look deeply into her own experience to see the other, and can only truly know the world through a fearless (though fearful) look within.

> & slipped
> over the
> whole
> world my
> skin

The most apparently autobiographical passages of *The Loom* may show you yourself (both where you recoil and revel) because the book is a whole world and therefore a mirror.

*

Autobiographical passages are more concentrated in *The Loom* than in much of Kelly's opus. Anecdotes from "real life," though not more true than his invented stories, abound: the tale of Kelly and Olson making a table dance, for example, or a sort of Proustian telling of a party and its catalogue of partygoers.

The experience of sexuality in early childhood is seldom remembered, even more rarely written. A tender and sensual passage in Section 8 recalls the poet in the kitchen with his nursemaid and her two friends. He is very young: *I feel like three.* It is the beginning of selfhood…

> I come back
> to that moment
> & know it is me.

…and of sexuality:

> But now I am at the table
> looking up at the three of them
> in turn, all smoking,
> all with red mouths. I say
> nothing. My penis
> (my witness) is swollen
> & I am at peace. Never
> to end.

It is also the initiation of a writer, a tantric moment in which sensuous & spiritual worlds come together in the mystical experience of language.

> I stare with wonder
> up at the mouths of women,
> at peace to smell
> the breath from their lips,
> rich smell of the smoke
> after it has passed
> through their bodies
> & comes out again,
> breathed, a blue plume,
> I see their words
> breathed, the mist
> takes me into itself
> & I can talk with them.

The child somehow knows that talk is his vocation, the power that will let him in, and let him stay:

> I've got to say something
> that will make them
> let me go on
> sitting at the ivory table
> hearing them, feeling
> them, taking them in.
> Something
> so that when it counted
> halfway across my life
> they would turn
> in time
> to take me in.

*

The Magician manipulates time and this thread runs through *The Loom* and throughout Kelly's work, *the secret work* that liberates being from the mechanical illusion of clock time into the real moment, into presence. Here, the child's first intimation that it is possible to bend time to another purpose:

> to foster
> in delight & demonstration
> the use of time
> to the secret work
> I felt then growing
> in their neglect
> of the clock,
> to tear the living body free
> from the gears of labor
> & sit beside it,
> flesh with flesh
> & welcome each life
> to the breath
> inside it
> & little by little
> lead it
> (breath by breath)
> to speak
> itself
> into the eternal air.

*

Tantra may refer simply to a treatise or exposition. But "tantra" may be translated literally as loom, warp, or weave, from the verbal root *tan*, to stretch, extend, expand, and the suffix *tra*, instrument.

Central to Tantric Buddhism:

Visualization of and identification with a deity.
Ritual use of mantras and mandalas.

The importance of a teacher.
Transgressive or antinomian acts.
Revaluation of the body.
Revaluation of the status and role of women.
Analogical thinking (including microcosmic or macrocosmic correlation).
Revaluation of negative mental states.
Imitation, esotericism, and secrecy.
(paraphrased from a Wikipedia article quoting Anthony Tribe)
These could be accurate chapter headings for a treatise on both the hermeneutics and poetics of *The Loom*.

A tantric route

> to call my mind back
> into the senses
> & to the sense of things as they are
> in themselves.

via song, incantation, process, the creation of mandala, or cosmos,

> Only (& everywhere)
> the intention towards Form

as lens, the better to see things as they are,

> The orders
> are elaborate;
> The strings are tuned.
> Inside every image
> another is visible.
> In the nucleus
> the whole world
> reposes
> on a tantric
> vivid leaf.

the world as it is.

*

And it is erotic. Tantric in its weave, its coming together, but of what? Eros and logos, sacred and secular, the self and its anima/animus, self and its shadow. Or simply (not simply) two people.

In Section 8, the child awakens to the mystery of at-oneness, a state of being in which the I both surrenders itself and is exalted. In Section 9 (*Essay on Form*), the I fleshes out that same realization, now as a man. The journey toward orgasm is told meticulously, as a moment-by-moment story, in clear, simple words that say the unsayable. It would be a crime not to include it whole, so here's the passage, from pages 113–115 of *The Loom*.

> Sometimes
> we've been making love so long
> we almost forget
> we're doing anything,
> & then an acceleration
> begins in my throat
> to find some word
> shaped like what it is
> to be me in you,
> that might answer
> all the subtle
> information
> to which your body
> all this while subjects me, learning
> while my heart & breath
> hunt for the word
> (it must sound like you)
> & when I look at your eyes
> sometimes open
> the humid fire
> so far below
> increases
> & I am urgent to say
> so that from an immense distance

further than any grief
a word begins to travel
through me, I can hardly
understand it, I am not even
interested in it, it approaches,
I want to brush it away,
I will not submit
to its definition, but its will
seduces mine, it has your
name on it but
is not yet your name,
I hold you tighter now
from everywhere I am
& will not be refused,
even, there begins
to be no longer any
part of me that knows
how to refuse,
I look at your closed eyes
& know
there's no hope anywhere,
what you are doing
being
now
is irresistible,
you declare a fire & a hollow
& a world
the precise shape
of what must come
now
leaping to fill it
& louder than I could
ever have imagined
it suddenly speaks.

*

Regarding "revaluation of negative mental states," one of the defining features of Tantra, Kelly's poetry says yes to what happens and to what happens after that.

*

It's not that the personae of Kelly's poetry, and of *The Loom* in particular, are never heartbroken or heartbreaking, terrified or terrifying — they are. But they find their way. The poet has too much imagination or compassion to let anyone stay lost alone in the dark for long. Something or someone comes along.

*

I want to emphasize again the poet's contrariness, the way he stands givens on their heads, contradicting even himself — especially himself. Kelly's work is constantly prodding the reader to think differently, to experience the continual delight and terror of the world as it is — never static, never finished, inexhaustible, unpredictable.

*

It is Kelly's obstinate refusal of the outworn and banal and his allegiance to the work of seeing anew that make his work so anarchic. Kelly's poetry is radical because it consistently denies the values of the state and its loci of power and establishes its own hierarchies. You won't get much commentary on the violent trespasses of the day (how many bombs, how many bodies — the manifestations of our tragic lack of imagination). Kelly draws our awareness back to the body, its beauty and humanity. He draws the mind back to naked mind, back to being. This is revolution, the refusal of language to serve any regime other than the truths it discovers for itself.

And when a reader enters the text, is drawn into the poem's argument, reading becomes tantric initiation, a radical, political, transformative act.

*

Among lyric epics, *The Loom* might be closest to *The Divine Comedy* in its weaving of sacred and secular, or intimate and mythic, in its keen and compassionate scrutiny of human nature, in the overwhelming desire of the poem and all its souls to converse, the wisdom and charm of its improbable guides, the poet exiled from his city who carries his city within.

*

Chantefable. What if the sung and spoken do not alternate in time only, but in space also — is it possible for opposing rhythms to be heard at once, an aural palimpsest? Take Section 18 for example, (*His Wood — Jesus's Song to his Rood*), the exact middle of *The Loom*, the cross pointing in all directions. The lines are nearly breathless, ragged, but heard against that crisis is the rhythm of what could be blank verse, alliterative, rhyme-full, the sound of Prospero almost, if you slip through the line breaks a bit. Read it aloud for the music, the counterpoint, and so as not to rush by this most acutely beautiful of love songs and leave-takings.

How many? the poem asks Christ. How many what? *Elements scattered?* How many prophecies fulfilled? How many nails? How many ransomed by his sacrifice? How many songs?

> until the both
> of us
> were only carbon
> & even that
> much of form
> defined a song,
> one
> that others
> have leave to
> sing
> since you & I
> are done.

Christ takes leave of his rood. *You and I / are done.* Is he speaking to the cross, the wood itself? To his body? To you (we) human beings, to the readers of the poem, to the poem itself? Do *you & I* dissolve because no longer separate, because one? Is that love?

*

Notes on The Hero of *The Loom*:

> He moves too fast
> to notice what he's doing.

In Section 7, the poet catalogues the Hero's virtues and describes his path:

> The Hero
> begins his research
> into the matter of dark woods.
> It will lead him
> to an act
> he will confuse with himself.

Or are we hearing a heroic understanding of a poet's virtues?

> a syntax
> elaborated
> a year & a day

Must not the poet also *suffer his appetite, to know… the people of earth, to be guileless, gracious to receive, who digs in his senses, responses,*

> & let him be moved
> by what he finds
> in him to move.

and from birds learn to

> yield, yield our yield
> all at once, keep

(keép, keep, keép, keep)
nothing,
hold nothing back.

*

The Hero reappears in Section 11 (*A Labor of Herakles, as it turns out*),

How precious
& how rare
human life is,
to be reborn a man
holding a conscious
chance,

an eastern that turns into a western, complete with bunkhouse, gravy, and a tuna can ashtray.

The poem, as a being, has both anima and animus (more than one). Here the animus labors under the burden of being both man and god, how to be manly and how to be godly. To act with certainty, though uncertain, unknown to himself, the dark wood of his research is his own mind, the *dark between his ears*.

He led them on
trying to think
what he was doing,
what
was being fulfilled
or what good it did
to whom. For whom.
Who was he doing
this for?

To expiate one's own brutality by slaying or subduing the beast within. Facing one's unconscious, one's shadow. Not without pity, especially for those whose somnolence he must disturb, the poem's Hero has some of the weary compassion of Lawrence's resurrected Christ in "The Escaped Cock." Chthonic. The heroism of bearing oneself, one's own violence, insanity, grief, bearing one's god and the labors s/he imposes.

> *The grace that comes*
> *to tolerate*
> *each effort, the grace*
> *to go on.*

To come to terms with one's mindless deeds, but not via intellect or understanding. Selfhood and redemption require the mindful *deed*, the ritual act, shamanic journey. Bearing one's own death, and the bardo within:

> *The sense of death*
> *is what I hold to*
> *to begin to move.*
> *To go on.*
> *And the Maiden,*
> *who has always*
> *belonged to death,*
> *the Kore, the*
> *Girl*
> *on her travels*
> *below,*
> *who goes with him,*
> *she is the same*
> *who beckons to me.*

*

In Section 12 (*Theory of Narrative*), a Greek chorus-like exposition on the nature of narrative, the poet gives us the image of The Hero imprisoned in the constellation of his story

> the way the Greeks
> saw their stories

> locked in the sky,
> unalterable narrative
> of the fixed stars

not only because he has been canonized/mythologized, but also because his tasks only multiply. The surrender of self must be reenacted because the ego is so easily resurrected. The Hero's battle is never over. Nor is the poet's.

> ... It has
> no end. Herakles
> goes home & finds
> his ten labors
> have changed to twelve,
> he's off again
> dragging a world
> out of his memory
> to meet it,
> outside,
> in the flat sunlight
> of wherever it is.

We meet the Hero again in Section 29 (*The Garden Itself*).

> That noise
> is a tomb breaking open,

He (Christ, Herakles, animus, poet) comes back, freed from the tomb and from the past — but not knowing it, imprisoned by his own beliefs and fears, his ignorance, and especially by his refusal to be known and thus made vulnerable.

> Predicament: to be free
> & not to believe it
> is worse than chains.
> Look who's talking,
> you who have become
> the armor you are.

The Hero returns to perform yet another labor, to die again in pursuit of the liberation of the ego. And as long as the Hero is trapped in the endless labor of becoming, the storyteller is trapped in endless telling. From the beginning of *The Loom* (*Helen, destroy me*), the I seeks its own destruction, relentlessly.

> The Hero
> cuts his breastplate loose
> & stands before her naked;

> …

> He lets out his breath
> & is a woman,
> the red serpents
> writhe up his spine
> & bomb his head
> with their darting
> faces, their tongues
> burn out his mind.

> …

> His knees tremble
> & he drops to his knees.
> They coil around
> the snakes
> for a little
> are confused,
> replace his lungs,
> no breath,
> then dart
> down again
> & thrust out of him,
> he becomes a man again
> & no one
> comes to the door.

Jung called the encounter with the shadow the "apprentice-piece" in the individual's development, and the encounter with the anima the "masterpiece." Through his encounters with the anima, the Hero is at last delivered from himself into pure form, into change itself. He is at one with his labors. Time and space, music and matter, are one. Just so for the poet.

> There was nothing to him
> but the changing.
> The sun.
> The oxen, delivered
> to his teeth.
>
> He felt his body
> was made of music
> & that made him easy
> in the dark of
> what he wasn't doing.
> The duty was flesh
> & just to be there.
>
> He felt the music
> & was content with it.

*

"In my opinion Orpheus was a man who surpassed his predecessors in the beauty of his poetry, and attained great power because he was believed to have discovered mystic rites, purifications for wicked deeds, remedies for diseases, and modes of averting the wrath of the gods…" (Pausanias)

*

> Now then at last
> the voice
> I kept talking
> to provoke
> spoke:

— What *do* you want?
— I want to learn the prayer
I must say in this place.

Whose voice? God's, now.

Section 35 (*The Voice*) is a close reading of The Lord's Prayer, translating from the Greek. What must be learned is the most familiar of prayers, to be made new in the poet's own vernacular, that is, in the context of this poem, new to *this place*.

*

Coleridge's conversation poems come to mind, each addressed to a specific "you," each beginning with a sense of place or some natural fact, winding through a meditation on nature, sometimes on the nature of poetry, leading to a change of mind. Poem as spiritual exercise. *And when I rose, I found myself in prayer.* (Coleridge, "To William Wordsworth")

*

The last section of *The Loom* begins with *the voice* that has been prayed to and provoked into speech, demanding of the poet,

> The leaf
>   I lent you,
> where is that now,

Time for the poet to account for himself, for his life and his gift, that is *only a loan at best,* fragile & temporary, *a tantric vivid leaf* (a page!) on which *the whole world reposes.*

The poet/Hero prepares to journey and to die again.

>   ... A death
> for Robert, to elicit life.

He begins in the present, the Magus at his table, *skull on desk* for a cup, *dried stalk of cholla* for *caduceus*, for wand. A few pages into his deliberations, *Which/direction has the music*, he begins to move, the table becomes a plain, a guide appears. *I followed/wherever it flew*. He moves through past and present tenses, through the chakras of his own body, over great distances, compelled to walk, to run, to walk again, to keep going until the voice speaks:

BUILD MY TEMPLE

Like Orpheus, the poet is able to discern the place for the building of the temple,

> Now there was
> clear space to work in.
> I was there, & knew it
> because I'd stopped moving.
> It was the place
> because it was the place.

and, like Orpheus, knows intuitively the rites necessary to complete the task,

> Or all I knew
> was to do. This.

and here in a dream-like sequence he does. But in truth, the building of the temple is the making of *This*, the poem, the place in which the Voice speaks, *a place to talk*.

*

Death, the poet's last and most vital guide, also speaks:

> *It is time & past time*
> *& the beginning of time —*
> *you have no one but me*

> *to show you the way*
> *but I can bring you close,*
> *or close enough. I am more*
> *than enough.*

The Loom ends with the Hero walking away from the reader, in a past tense yet into the future, toward a well (source, the unconscious, conduit to the unknown or underworld, instrument whereby Demeter calls to Persephone), *a place to talk*.

> Outside I found all round me
> that the desert had
> predictably but to my surprise
> after the heavy rain &
> warmed now by the sun
> crashed into flower.
> I even had to walk on some
> to get to the well,
> small ones, very bright red.

We see the flowers themselves, more real for not being named, one last sacrifice, the small, mysterious violence that is the ending of the poem (*red*/read), rooting both past and future in the present, the only path to the source, *where it all began*, is about to begin, is beginning.

*

> The voice instructs me:
> my inwards
> is outside,
> my table
> stretches before me blank,
> my need to fill it,
> the poem, always the poem.

The Loom is threaded with such scrupulous renderings of how the poem comes to be. Kelly tells you, and he shows you, nothing up his sleeve.

6 · A BOOK OF READINGS

Endnotes

Unless otherwise noted, all passages indented or language in italic incorporated into the text, are from *The Loom,* by Robert Kelly (Los Angeles: Black Sparrow Press, 1975).

Kelly himself has been vexed by the volume of his work. What to do with all those unpublished notebooks, some two or three thousand pages a year beyond the prodigious amount of published work. Now much of the unpublished work, including "outtakes" from published pieces, and some of the out of print books are available to read and download at the Bard Digital Commons site, under the auspices of Bard's Stevenson Library:

    http://digitalcommons.bard.edu/rk_manuscripts/

There, for example, you will find RK's long poem *Ariadne,* from 1991, and can see how she has occurred to him since her appearance in *The Loom.*

If you don't have a dog-eared, coffee-stained copy of *The Loom,* or even if you do, it has been reissued as a handy Kindle Edition by McPherson & Company, Kingston, New York, 2015, in which form the multiple columns vanish and the poem unfurls from the loom as one long scroll, whole cloth.

THOMAS MEYER

HIEROGLYPH OF THIS UNFALLEN WORLD

The Convections (1978)
The Book of Persephone (1978)

> The pattern on the carpet, yes, but the carpet is on
> the floor, a room, sunlight comes in and treats not
> all parts of the pattern the same.
>
> ("Waking to Haydn")

I love the syntactic pucker, the unexpected negative displacing the metrical pattern of the statement, so that the ear only notices what's happening when those last two words end the sentence, now rhythmically askew, on the half-beat. Before being interrupted by that prose, the poem opened

> Sun bright on powder snow,
> unnumbered. The classic style
> never further than the mind away.

Never further away than the mind? No further than the mind away? No further away than the mind? Turning to someone at dinner, how would you expect to say that about "the classic style"? Or in anger, or making love? The line as it stands, as Robert Kelly wrote it, is poised, as I hear it, on the very edge of what a native American ear accepts as English. The first line though is okay; we recognize it immediately as a poetically collapsed version of something like, "The sun shine brightly on the powdery snow." Powder doesn't seem right to me, but then I'm no skier, so it gets by on the strength of overheard ski reports. What's going on here depends upon the expectations set up by our intuitive feel for American English, and the fulfillment or thwarting, even disruption, of certain formal anticipations. Music, in other words.

About a hundred and twenty-five pages, Robert Kelly calls this selection of poems *The Convections*. Generously laid out, it is of a deceptively loose weave. Yet here, as in *The Book of Persephone*, a rich, intricate meditation unrolls like a Turkish carpet. Where the sunlight of my attention plays — and not by hazard, human perception knows no hazard — dappling a passage of this *mian farsh*, I'd like to hesitate a minute and try to pull apart the weft-threads that keep its pattern of knots firm, these "convections."

> At death to take away & Out that rhythm
> the living know as breath

Possible *mihrab*, 17 syllables (isn't that the haiku's count?) listed in the table of contents as "At death," page 116. All 17 syllables center themselves on the second natural phrase, "to take away," which as an infinitive implies in so brief a context an understood subject. Almost any pronoun qualifies; all immediate distractions have been lost to the awesome condition under immediate consideration, death. Nor is it far-fetched to overhear, half-anticipating it, this phantom subject become reflexive, while "that rhythm" teeters upon a suppressed relative. As though ambiguous, the verbal fragment attracts the closest unclaimed subject and object into its field, which in this instance are identical.

    This last hundred years our outside limits have opened up expanding into a considerable frontier for the poet to inhabit. Between microchip and trans-Uranian depth, questions about the propriety of scale visit and revisit American poetics like The Wandering Jew. Comprehend it or not, furthermore, Modern Physics insists the chair we sit on isn't a solid, foursquare density upholding us, but a compacted swarm of energy, a myriad of tiny hurricanes. So too Kelly's work, that it is composed of poems remains as coincidental to its dynamic as arms, legs, and struts are to a chair's. For him the poem is not an exercise in textual resolution, but the constant engagement of its reader's faculties on a level so fundamental we can almost call it subliminal. Or autonomic: our attentions hum, phonemes switch to morphemes generating an electro-magnetic field where syntax disturbs, and semantics interrupt our Edenic lull and primal coo with articulation. With what vista! Its reach stretches into and then beyond Whitman's. "Eternity here, beginnings and the fortunate / end compacted in a minute," Kelly calculates in "Newton," a vernal, yet smoldering poem.

Here we have a troubadour's passionate courtesy ending a poem like "A Road to Captree," and there, "To Persephone," the supplicant's yearning after his goddess' vernal returns, amid patches of the ordinary, tire tracks, and slush. Or like a pattern never completed nor repeated exactly, the poet sets "a realm of pure color" and pre-Socratic margin upon our perceptual world, referring to its possible access in "The Engine Driver Five Years Old" and its constant actuality "in all the continuous excitations of the senses" throughout. The stance, implied in poem after poem, is heroic: the opposition of man and his sensual world whose tensor is language, but whose declaration is its vector. Loss figures as well, loss as a primary, sensual lack — a Piaget image of loss which reflects, not nostalgia, but the developing process of cognition. Language makes all report unreliable, constantly interfering with the sensual, imposing its own inherent demands while at the same time refining desire by widening its capacities — the creation of imagination.

"It is too soon to talk about love," begins "The Beguiling of Merlin,"

> I think about children who show
> their hidden parts & call it sex
> that they are doing to each other.
> Later love. Or it makes them pregnant
> with a wilder child than they had ever been,
> delivered from the forests of their loins
> later, twelve to twenty, into the light.

That exchange of intimacies that complicates two lives, how to call it? Love? Sex? Desire? or name its withholding? "The Beguiling of Merlin" has six short sections and an unnumbered opening (or argument) from which the above passage comes. Merlin appears as someone whom desire awoke to love, whose passion was fed upon being answered, only to discover itself abandoned, then stultified by that attachment. He is no more magician; his power has been suspended, all his word-magic surrendered in inadequacy, but at last gratified.

> What did they show, those spellbound children?
> Their soft parts, folds & holds,
> meek epopteia of the schoolyard

flashed into (how can it be?)
forever the life of the mind.
Later they would tell.
And then a fate like Merlin's
silences their secrets.

(*Epopteia* is Greek for the full or greater Mystery shown forth at Eleusis, Samothrace, wherever, and apparently "unspeakable," literally.)

Merlin's fate is a condition of "spellbound" latency; the sexual overwhelms and immobilizes him, transforming excitation into glamour. He is sealed away in a chamber whose exit is lost, an untortured Saint Anthony, at the height of his temptation with the bewitching Nimue. Merlin and the children arrive at a shared condition from opposing temporal directions. Unlike theirs, his imagination isn't fed on mysteries of sex to come. No, he is left to review passions no longer applied, and from them invent a science. What more perverse repression could there be than a manual on passions, words in place of our most direct set of actions? Or is that assumption about nature and instinct another of Nimue's sorceries, that our carnality needs no education, nor our affections?

All this held in the pale stillness of Burne-Jones. No painter better captured Merlin, not only in this painting but throughout his career, vision after vision of frozen, held sensuality. The androgyny promises a riot of abandoned delight, something polymorphous, yet Burne-Jones' subjects have neither life nor its repose in their limbs.

Though this "Beguiling" whose nominal image is perhaps a simple, visual occasion (thumbing through a book, or a postcard in the mail) begins when the poet answers image with image: the children initiating each other on the playfield. Not an exclusive, personal, or biographical experience, it is very much a part of the modern American psyche, along with "playing doctor." The issue hangs upon social and personal manifestations of desire and how they mold the individual inside and out, obeying or disobeying their unique proprieties. This *epopteia*, the children's Epiphany, to paraphrase Jane Ellen Harrison, is the outward and inner goal of all purification, all consecration, not the enunciation and elucidation of desire, but the revelation, the fruition of passion itself. Is our relationship to one another social, and free of all but shared taboos? Can it be talked about, or them, thus ushering us into a private discourse?

The children and Merlin, the young and old, are two poles; between them the poem's charge will run. Or arc, the resulting spark won't necessarily complete a circuit.

Merlin's singular desire to be pure in his passions is his love's testament and Nimue's lure; consequently, it is the object of his desire that imprisons him under a stone. Her appearance (the third section) declares the complexity of the poem's issues as they emerge, predominantly emotional entrapment. In her hair she wears snakes lifted from Merlin; she has become distant, fallen out of love, what she wanted from it she has, and it was infinite: power over him. Desire loses its gradient and won't move, falling back upon itself, Merlin's lot under the stone. Hidden in the wide borders of this poem are shapes sketched elsewhere: loss, desire, the sensual, intellection, the child, and the haunting, intricate character of longing. Of them all, the last pair is most emphasized. The child motif is complete, filled in here having begun in earlier poems, while the consecration of longing has only begun.

Apparently Nimue took something like thought (or mind) from Merlin, why? Kelly wonders, with acuity, was it "to confuse herself / back into the humbleness of first love / when her life felt him on her skin?" The poet's testament avoids in such asides, second thoughts like these, the venom of bitterness. "She loved him once, I think / she was a better lover ever than he." Despite the mythologem, the image displays the possibility of elaborate, vital, and emotionally "real" considerations. How can the answering of separate needs be kept from deadening a relationship, dissolving it, or worse, rendering it an arrangement? Is fulfillment the deadliest of all fantasies?

Desire will neither be ignored nor resolved, it demands constant engagement, even if we dig a hole in our psyches and bury it, perception continually stores its charge there. So it is we discover, day in and day out, that desire (like the classic style) is never further than the mind away. The clarity of numbers is no less than those details that arouse us, a crooked elbow, the careless toss of hair.

> I saw the girl then, bent down to recover
> one of those dark blue flowers herself —
> half aloud she was asking Do they
> after all have white centers, white

> or pale yellow deep in the heart?
> The grace of her bending low
> to serve her intellectual desire
> gave me such pleasure that I took hold.

So sings Plutone (Pluto), his aria the third movement or chapter in the suite called *The Book of Persephone*. "Persephone is the woman buried / in ordinary life," its author tells us. Despite the glades and surprising meadows, this isn't a forest anyone can be led through easily.

Discussing *Her Body Against Time* (1963) in *Kulture* #14, Kenneth Irby cites Goethe on the Poet, in conversation with Eckermann (January 29, 1826), "as soon as he knows how to appropriate the world for himself, and to express it, he is a poet. Then he is inexhaustible, and can be ever new." An apt gloss for everything on the table here: A single human being's negotiation of his own experience, the struggle to appropriate his own perception. In such an exacting struggle Persephone embodies the refreshment restoring life to that desert our emotions become under the threat of constant self-examination, self-denial, or self-indulgence. Her curiosity, her wondering, the Lord of Wealth so prized he made her his wife, his world, relinquishing his plutocracy. "Persephone is candlelight on apples & pears." The hunting and haunting of shape.

> Sun bright on powder snow,
> unnumbered. The classic style
> never further than the mind away.
> When the mind had heart.
> And what have you? Tonality
> will always come back.

The tonic returns, the heart sounds its fifth, desire stirs, mingling it with intention, emotion, an energy.

G. E. SCHWARTZ

OF DROMENONS, SILENCES, SENTENCES, AND EMPTYINGS:
Robert Kelly's Spiritual Exercises

1. *dromenons*

I am reading "Cathedral of The Incarnation," which is housed in *SPIRITUAL EXERCISES*:

> Standing below the huge wooden crucifix,
> looking up, acute angle,
> close, looking up
> as I have always looked up
> in doubt or love distressed
> to see
> that man, a thin man,
> not like me,
> lifted up maybe but looks dragged down by gravity
> drawing me up also, how
>
> that this is what the incarnation means,
> or brings, this sleepy agony
> it looks
> above the world.
>
> (SE p. 27)

As I read it is as if I am reading the caption *YOU ARE HERE* fixed at the top of an arrow. HERE YOU ARE, beginning a *dromenon*, that dance movement of turning through a maze pattern on floorstones of cathedrals as Chartres; standing on a "therapy in stone" whose turning and stretching stimulate motor-perception, inspiring profound kinesthetic intuition — *that remembering of the original pulse.*

And this is a spiritual exercise, *telling* me where I am, evoking in its carved wood of words and painted objects of words, through all its abundant imagery, something of the incredible richness of the ancient *spiritual experience.* So many manifold deities seen as one; the gods & demons, male and female, principle and manifestation; and which answers in the most apparent and profound way to the variety of spirit in the outside world within. *YOU ARE THERE* it says, as in all of the old exercises, each of the elements, or what we now call by that name, are represented by actualizing words. This *here* made word can be seen, and communicated with, by us, as true as any explanation of phenomena, any way.

The poems of Kelly's *Spiritual Exercises* seek to accompany, making it easier for a pilgrim to pace out a path from village to village and through life itself, as once similar images performed a like purpose for the devout on their way to a shrine or holy place, as:

> from the mountains they come down chewing mint
> making their mouths pure for the celebration
> of this most common food that understands them
> into ecstasy to eat the body for which they are the soul.
>
> (SE p. 36)

The transmission: there is "this most common food that understands them into ecstasy" — as the lyrical creation is a means to carry the individual consciousness into the universal. Kelly, invoking the images, gives form to the formless. And, of central importance here: the image is not framed as poetic object, but as channel of contact with the ethereal, generating a power not often felt in images placed in a poem.

Here, as in all of the extraordinary texts of the past, life, words, images, and the spiritual are one. The creation of a poem is an act of worship in the true sense, in which the invisible becomes visible.

Spirit and image and word, forms and objects, representations that are the embodiment of emotions, of will and personality, unified. To turn to poetry, to make poetry of this, is an act of discovery that writes the human spirit with the numinous. *YOU ARE HERE*, shouts the poem "Sermon," then soothes us as:

> ... nothing comes easy but the wicked wonderful things
> when we roll over to each other in the dark and clutch
> to the warmth we find there and murmur dear God dear God.
>
> (SE p. 34)

Flesh, spirit, & word are one. Behind the artifice there are true signs and proof to be found in the texts of the past, in those richly articulated delineations of ritual, of intimacy displayed, which is so far removed from our own semi-detached curiosity and sentimental descriptiveness. These burnished poem/objects — but they are more than mere objects, more than mere poems — were once alive in ways that we have forgotten, and the voices within them heard now. Kelly synchs up, adjusts where necessary, and with the poems in *Spiritual Exercises*, points *YOU ARE HERE.*

Here, in these poems, as left often in recent times, we encounter the varied personality of the world which embodies, among other things, the principle conflict in drift, in the opposing forces of good and evil, light & dark, asking from "Elements of Moral Semiotics":

> Can design foregrounded in the sign
> liberate the carnal mind from such affections
> as liberate themselves the mindly hand?

Or:

> Can I speculate while making love
> the assembly of interactive powers
> who bask above us light in our dark mass?

Or:

> Can I know a circumstantial air
> such that the heart sign and number say
> isomorphic urgencies you understand?

(SE pp. 74–75)

This poem tells us by asking that much of our problem lies HERE: in the difference between the attitude of worship with its applied humility and reverence toward resident spirits; a reverence and humility that at once encouraged a confident familiarity with those spirits, together with a organic respect for their needed powers, and in which the poem participated; and our own modern attitude and practice of reducing everything to its particular function and direct usefulness to us. We are here in the difference where lies a whole shifting world of time & loss.

6 · A BOOK OF READINGS

To turn from that ancient sensibility to its characteristic modern counterpart, Kelly measures the abstraction and dissociation we have fallen into. This subtle change, and whose effects and full significance have in many respects gone unnoticed — is not lost on these poems:

> the way the moon answers the sun
> every week for two thousand years
> trailing behind the greek priest's wife
>
> or the way the grass looks between
> rain and rain starting again
> or sifting flour from the big drum
>
> or kneading it later in the big bowl
> until the work and the workman
> are the same color and texture
>
> than someone lured by the aroma
> knocks at the bakery door at midnight
> and is answered only by the bread
>
> (SE p. 39)

Here we are: involved with a crafty and Noachian paradox: while we talk at greater and greater length about all things spiritual, spirit itself, in its assumed sense, has retreated from us and before our very eyes.

Many of these compositions also speak to the loss of that ancient richness & companionable spirituality, each ruling some manifestation in the world and the world within, that all of this multiplicity, and the texts that came of it, should have degenerated into the *one*, the all-demanding, the righteous — with all its witherings:

> When in this temple
> they point to an iron flower
> growing out of an iron flowerpot
> they mean to remind you
> of the root oneness of appearances,
> contained and container are one,
> root and branch one, beauty

and utility, past and future.
Then they touch you on the hand
and say Come on, enough of that.
(SE p. 35)

Kelly points out again and again a vital and affectionate closeness to things, as from a deep historical past, and which has only recently lost its hold on the imagination. What I refer to can be felt, for example, in a few characteristic lines:

A ladder going up into the tree
it is France maybe
a person comes to pollard his pears
or train them espalier
to face the setting sun and now
sits in his house drinking cool water when
some boys come mischievous to delete
his step-up highway.
The tree is empty. The ladder
is shoved in a culvert.
God is alone with the pears.
(SE p. 26)

There is little that resembles this fluent familiarity now in English and American poetry.

But how potent was that influence, that familiarity and affection in the past, from Shelley on; and even in Ronald Johnson's work, whose subtle evocations of *you are here* have so infrequently been equaled in subsequent poetry.

If the lines I have quoted can be said to be representative of his certain acuteness of sensibility, Kelly has never stopped looking, never stopped listening. It is apparent to me at least that the cadence of such verses, and of the innumerable poems from the transmission to which they belong, must have derived from centuries of foot travel, from walking — at times as Romany wanderers — in the land, not driving through it or flying over it. Once more it seems to me, that with *Spiritual Exercises,* we are faced with that indivisible connection between the way we are here and the spirituality we must take onto ourselves to be here. From "A Carved Georgia Peach Pit":

> The hard facts of imagination
> sleep in that soft spring earth
> dreaming evidence.
> The God-cloning light is everywhere
> but everywhere mute we speak for it.
>
> (SE p. 52)

Reality had assumed forms we hadn't anticipated. But it is always so; the spiritual, such a baffled & refuted circumstance, has taken up residence in us, in our very house, as we become, not its master — at least not for this dance.

2. *silences*

It is because the spiritual is written in us that we respond to such spiritual exercises, which serve (in Platonic terms) to *remind* us; as we do to the word writ sacred, or indeed, to the deep insights of Dante and Rumi or to the Mahabharata. And it is surely only in the modern West that poetry and the sacred have become detached, and the very idea of temporal art has its appearance — art without inspiration. Kelly, so far as I know, is very alone in declaring that the inspiration of the poet and the celebrant are one and the same, and the root of that inspiration in the *Divine Human*, innate in all. In fact the separation of the divine and the human is an article of faith from which only a few mystics have deviated, like Eckhart, whose works were banned by the Papacy for declaring the divine principle to be within. Sufi mystics have been executed for saying as much, although in India the words *tat tvam asi* (that art thou) is a fundamental principle of Hindu sacred writings. But Kelly professes to the modern world which has nothing to fear but neglect and confusion. From the prose poem "The Tower of Babel":

> Heaven fell. Great flecks and patches of heaven dropped, landing on the tower or its builders. "We have reached heaven!" some cried. "Heaven is all over my hands!" one of them noticed.
>
> There seemed to be no further point in completing the tower. Or, more precisely, it was not generally realized that the tower

had never been finished; even the canniest builders tended to confuse the structure itself with the conscious goals they happened to have in mind. So as far as we can tell, the tower still stands unfinished, and no one can say where it actually could go. (SE p. 54)

"(The) tower still stands unfinished, and no one can say where it / actually could go," and the mystery of silences continues. To be sure, Kelly has devoted a great portion of his literary output to addressing the question of that mystery. He speaks of it through an *absolute metaphor* — *absolute* in the sense that the philosopher Hans Blumenberg has spoken of universal experiences when they are referred to in archetypal ways; for instance, Blumenberg has written about the image of a shipwreck as one that rouses an experience familiar to all, and as one that lies deep within the recesses of our consciousness, manifesting as a shared sense of history and narrative, as a kind of collective memory.[68] Kelly's absolute metaphor is wordlessness, an idea that the poetry in *Spiritual Exercises* explicates. Yet, like the palpability of an image such as a shipwreck, wordlessness reveals its universality gradually, the more one proceeds on the footpath into the book. Silence is one figure used to say the wordlessness Kelly intuits as the world. Another is emptiness. His embrace of emptiness, but even more so silence, not at all proposes a rejection of poetry, however. Words, spiritual expression, arise from silence, and at times also signify it. Like a deep meditation, silence can be particularly fecund, never inert.

3. *sentencing*

Indeed, as the starting point and provocation for his writing, which in turn leads back to it, silence is anything but inevitable — for the language that has emerged out of the silence is striking, as when Kelly, in what stands out as one of two monumental poems of the collection, "Sentence," a four-part, polysyntactic piece, printed in bold, interrupted occasionally by italicized non-bold:

---

68. David Adams, "Metaphors for Mankind: The Development of Hans Blumenberg's Anthropological Metaphoring," *Journal of The History of Ideas* (1991): 52.

> the pure consuming ardor
> that keeps a word crossed out
> lives longer than a lover than a son
> word I wont even say but harbor.
>
> (SE p. 84)

Silence is Kelly's vital cause, as much evident in his long poems as in his short.

Yet, what underlies this sentencing of silence, for Kelly, is the wordless word everywhere he turns, the words he apprehends are shadowed by wordlessness. That sentencing of wordlessness is universal is truly ironic- universal what, if there is no word? But for Kelly there can be no world without wordlessness. He defines a relationship between the actual word and a wordless word imposed upon him but which is not really present in his mind or in any actual word he experiences through his senses. Where could this word *be?* These questions Kelly finds irrelevant; all that is ultimately important to him is that in some way he discerns the unreality of the actual word and the truth of some other word he does not know.

> this kindlier magic that is our merchandise
> these tuned apocalypses are our ornament
> bring down ecliptic into beastly order
> and sell to you. They say so you will soon sing to us.
>
> (SE p. 89)

If this were the case, one could rightly ask, what good can such a point of view be in trying to live for that kind of word. Yet, in Kelly's poems, the word is precious, to be conserved. Indeed, the word is beyond all comparative value. This is so exactly because he senses a word other than the one before him. The realized word, the word spiritually exercised, then, may exist within the greater process of birth and death, appearance and mystery. The real, wordless word, lies beyond the knowing of it, as Kelly explains:

> finally utterly all the old gardens
> spectacular harmonies of what is seen
> till the spirit work thee in thine own deed
> exalted testimony of particular sense
>
> whoever is not mine is mine whoever

was going out is coming in geography enough
unanswerable door or sudden heart rain
wet hands simple to reclaim the fact.
(SE p. 98)

All words other than the real word eventually fall away, revealed as empty of answers, unanswerable. However, Kelly feels they are important; although he can only spiritually exercise the less than satisfactorily option of trying to speak of it as doubt; at the same time, he always wonders if it isn't that either.

4. *emptying*

The second poem that balances the book and concludes the volume, is "The Emptying." Its tautologies of spirit and flesh elicit the poet's intense concentration because they both express and are to be contrasted with emptying, a down-loading of polysyntax:

> ... here in criss-cross winter land
>
> from which he bends to drink
> chaliced in eternal emptying
> self into no-self till the sound
> we are empties out into his hands ...
> (SE p. 145)

For Kelly, this emptying can be a catchall or rather a conceptual wellspring that yields a number of protean ideas such as abstraction and randomness, finding both great strength and difficulty in ideas of space and time, spaces & times that are utterly different from our everyday experience. And, once again, there is a disclosure that the primarily tautological nature of spiritual and sensual experience:

> I understand this lute creation
> whose bowed belly circumstance I touch
> toccata watch every snow while hearing this
> metropolitan winter goes the tongue remembers ...
> (SE p. 146)

Here is an archeological dig, revealing a past, revealing a sense of a continuing present which made "this lute" always contemporary. To see this timeless presence in the ancient, the medieval, or the yesterday is also to realize that common sense has huge limitations; and though it may be in some respects what experience has taught us and conforms to experience, it is often our non-sensical experiences which are made, forged, to conform, in turn, to a common sense. In "The Emptying" sediments are brushed away, ensuring that artifacts of "Chinese icons," "boats," "tents of mercy" — surface unscathed, finding new alignment.

Interestingly, what leads Kelly to interrogate the conventional view of time is first of all a response to what he is witnessing that lies outside the grasp of intellect. His response is æsthetic, not cerebral, but then the implications of what he is seeing rushes in:

> **We are here to lead each other out**
> **the dark of Ulster ford full of bleeding** (SE p. 149)

These lines transcend the then contemporary strife in Northern Ireland, taking on the message and power of something approaching a psalm. There is a valley, the shadows, and the hope of deliverance all in play here.

The emptying — that is, the difference from our own lives — is rich and exciting and has much to teach us — writer and teacher alike. Each is a bottle the other is emptying to. In *Spiritual Exercises*, we pass — *by verbal entrainment of physical event* — through *the first gate of the spirit*, to an almost Pascalian mysticism when Kelly asserts — perhaps echoing Pascal's well known belief that God was a circle whose center is everywhere, and whose circumference is nowhere —

> **life itself is revolution and dark**
> **comes only as mazurkas do a change of order**
> **in the midst of order a new clean map**
> **bereft of boundaries only lissome rivers touch**
> **unseen edges of another world.** (SE p. 157)

Writer and reader are not at opposite ends of the poles. We are *here*, as good ignatians (small *"i"*), where we know we're thinking right, since we feel our bodies trembling, as our skin sweats because we are here.

13 February 2002
West Irondequoit

KIMBERLY LYONS

FALLING FLOWERS:
READING ROBERT KELLY READING LI SHANG-YIN

You here among the eternity of conversations, the line from Robert Kelly's poem "Reading Li Shang-yin: Falling Flowers"[69] (hereafter referred to as RLS) essentializes a condition of Kelly's poetics, literary communion enacted within the writing. In Kelly's constellation of concerns, the 8th century, Tang dynasty, Chinese poet, Li Shang-yin came before & yet is present in the now of the poem. As Kelly's "A statement for the Modern Poetry Conference CUNY"[70] (hereafter referred to as RKW) proposes: the poems and poets that precede him (and us readers) turn and force us to write. He states further:

> Some grand provokers — Pindar himself, Li Shang-yin, Lycophron, Hölderlin, Stein — still wait their turn, still turn us toward the poem we must write, the poem they force us to write, to make sense of what they do to our heads. (RKW)

Kelly has commented that RLS "is a meditation reading through the first six lines on of an eight-line poem translation of the T'ang poet Li Shang-yin" (Red Actions). In another context, he elaborated: "this text, written in the early 1990s, is one of the earliest instances of my writing-into an existent text" (RKW). *Writing to track what the reading has in mind.*

RLS wraps and stitches the Kelly poem around and within the prior text's (Li Shang-yin's Falling Petals) translated lines. I would argue that RLS not only initiates for Kelly a new practice of "impletion" of text, but that it is also a threshold poem of reception into the talk of another, as heard, remembered, and responded to within the poem itself. Throughout this poem, Kelly talks back to, brings in, other poetries — and not just of Li Shang-yin. The empathy for loss, the spatial placing of lyric clusters and free-play of conversation in RLS, conterminously bring

---

69. Robert Kelly, *Red Actions: Selected Poems*, 1960–1993 (Black Sparrow Press, 1995, pp. 330–336).

70. *A Voice Full of Cities — The Collected Essays of Robert Kelly* (CMP 2014, p. 726).

Kelly's poetic to a newly opened frequency in which the poet works, responds to the words of others as an enlivened stream. *An eternity of conversations* of course echoes William Blake, yet as RLS proceeds, the conversations in the eternity of a readerly space are not only between poets, but among lovers and companions.

This essay cannot take on the fascinating and necessary study of how Kelly's poems have conversed with, ingested, integrated, represented, modulated, heard, or purposely misheard the discourse of the other over the course of his work thus far, but it is this essayist's intuition (without having factually verified this) that in the early 90s there was a deepening reception to and change in Kelly's concerns around representing the language of the other.

The shape of RLS unfolds in variably positioned lines, renewing the visual measure of earlier poems, and departing from the condensed, compacted lyric of his work of the 80s. (Having made this generalization, let it be said that as every reader of his work knows, Kelly's poems constantly change-up to accommodate the poetic requirements of any particular instance; therefore, there are exceptions to what was just stated). RLS functions as a rupture in some sense and not as a new constant:

> *Even you* shaking myself out of the dust
> of all I need you
>   the differences, the terrible birds
> *you have quit my high pavilion*
>   the shadow of you

Placed as they are, the floating weight of these lines gathers restraint and suggests a delay. As falling petals twirl in air come to lie on the ground, signal a writing through time. *The shadow of you* emerges as counterweight to the *you* who has *quit my high pavilion*. This instability of identity releases the poet, allows differentiated sources to converse:

> *She tells me: I will never*
> *Take her back,*
>   *For all her cheating*
>   *Was a wound*
>   *In the flesh of my time, and time*
> *That heals all else, has not a way to heal itself.*

The poem's undulations condense the *you* of Li Shang-yin's "guest" gone from the chamber of red, the *her* whose presence winds through, *a wanton star*. The absent, remembered one emits a force that spreads energy through the poem. See how the urgently distraught telling of the *she* slips in, winding its way in Kelly's cadence and yet not. Kelly's poetic powers and the restraint of the authorial I, perhaps, allows that other *I*, that *she* space and duration in the poem:

> *So that the doorway*
> *In it*
> *Is only about her coming through?*

The doorway indeed of *her* coming through… Not to mention the revered Li Shang-yin! Such is the flexible generosity of RLS that Li Shang-yin's 8-line "Falling Petals" which RSL extends, flowers, and (re) lives in Lisa Raphael's translation within Kelly's poem. Conjoining across centuries and *on the phone Joan tells me: from the tall pavilion the guests have all departed / In the little garden, flowers fly, pell mell. / They fall at random on the winding path, / And travel far, sending off the setting sun. / Heartbroken, I cannot bear to sweep them away; / Gazing hard, I watch them till few are left. / Their fragrant heart, follow spring, dies; / What they have earned are tears that wet ones clothes /* . Raphael's translation freshening Witter Bynner's iconic readings of that line: "And nothing left but a tear-stained robe."

And what about the events of this lingering, elegiac poem with all of its twists and rebounding shifts? Plucking at it fails to retrieve the pleasure & wholeness in reading it through. Instead, I'd like to offer up a survey of impressions.

Flowers. From a geranium in winter, *a red flower on my window sill* to *the blue flower in one's hand. And twisted in cold evening, all lilac*. The Blue Flower of Novalis in one's hand is signal of Kelly's enduring link to Novalis's vision of a deep and far ultimate perfection of eternity:

> *Whose many petals, still red, dry*
> *And fall*
> *Onto the blue tile of the kitchen floor.*

Crushed thoughtfully *gently enough one leaf of it*. The poem declares its flower language deep inside its length: *finity where the flowers grow* alludes in sound to Dickinson. But, it also is an evocation of Persephone's domain, death in a winterish *disaster in Tivoli*. The poem ends *with shiny petals of our polaroids torn up and scattered on the floor*. Archaic or techno, the poet finds his flowers where they are. What else. Woodpecker's, *Terrible birds*. A witty turn on birds in which *princes of the air, clowns on the ground* alludes to Baudelaire's "L'Albatros."

Isolate woodpecker also... they apprehend (we don't)
And Crows.

the silver snow
to them
in a full moon time
is given.

Such casual and beautiful (and "Chinese" sounding) observations are in the mix. Curlot's *Dictionary of Symbols*[71] offers that crows represent ideas of beginning, demiurgic powers, messengers, creator of the visible world, foretelling the future, divination, nigredo, putrification, yang, "the isolation of one living on a superior plane." More in Hollo's *Corvus* and *Caws and Causeries*.[72] Finally in this stream: "This carrion mind" offers a nearly shocking figuration of the poet split-into the carnivorous bird devouring and the meaty mind. Ours for the taking if we wish, but not offered with any more intensity or foreground than any other element.

Also evoked are alchemical elements, metals, gems, cinnabar, copper, garnet, gold, brass, brass farthings, slab, slate, "old bluestone slabs." Things of the East, this poet's particular Dutchess County late-winter East. All the signifiers are interwoven. No big deal pointing to esoteric themes, the poem works as a factual involvement with a universe in which the elementals activate *like a procession of Grail knights/disappearing*. The core of the poem is *strung with that yearning*.

71. J. E. Cirlot, *A Dictionary of Symbols* (2002)
72. Anselm Hollo, *Caws and Causeries* (1999)

> For in my thoughts I have caressed
> the sacred geomantic precincts of your body.

An urgent admission. The poet of the 21st century writes what Li Shang-yin could not. What may disturb some readers, is Kelly's preoccupation, perhaps obsession, throughout the corpus of his work, with conjuring sexual encounter & fantasy. Writing that replicates situation in which an active male lover strokes the pliant, receiving female ground. This is an inarguable tendency (more evident in Kelly's work up until the mid-1970s) and having been worked through in the poems of the past two decades. (The present essay, sadly, cannot take on the fascinating study of how Kelly's poems have modulated in relation to female as object or subject). Look at it this way: what master poet starting with Sappho is not obsessed, really? Kelly has held fast throughout the development of his work to the sexual as just one of the multiple energy streams and sources of information working the poem *as from the bones of the body sounded*. That path alone has placed Kelly's work way outside the precincts of mainstream poetry but deep inside the universe of the conversation of the poets that has come down through the centuries. His poetry as a whole engages — and is transformed within and by — eros in all its dimensions. In "Reading Li Shang-yin," whose thoughts and of what gender are imprinted here? For it is via the braided, entwined lyric of at least three articulating sources stitched withal by brief glances from other poets, other poems, that density is made. I read the line *Reach for her return* as counsel to a female friend in regards to a female lover, urging submission to love's requirements; to sweep (or not) the petals of the broken syntax between. A gesture more necessary than patriarchal configurations. This is a quiet milestone in Kelly's work, the kind of realization to be found throughout his continuous opus and due further research.

Whereas in some instances, particularly the pre mid-1970, his poems may have evoked the erotic as a balm against isolation or emotional withdrawal, Kelly's work as whole has a richer, complex environment of relation that the poems work within and out of. So by the instance of the composition of RLS, a sweeter, sadder liquor is distilled from fallen petals:

This is our winter's tale
"We have *passed into distances*
    of each other"

One other speculative note: Kelly has noted in his notes to *Red Actions* that in 1990, the year proceeding the composition of this poem, he experienced three tremendous personal losses.

I can only guess that such a penetrating emotional experience tempers this poem:

and when we love
    what thing is left
That shapes the shadows

Falling petals may encode the slip of a robe left behind, the transitory nature of experience, the poignancy of time passing in the hours of change, but is there not the shadowing also of a Buddhist poetic that reads flowers falling off as the flesh passing over? Online I found this translation in Arthur Lloyd's *Poems by Buddhist Priests of Japan*, attributed to Bukkoku Zenji:

When 'tis seized,
Beware lest, in the hour of joy, you shake
The quickly falling petals from the branch.

And it is just such temporal and transcendental concerns that figure, however subtly, in Kelly's more recent *Fire Exit* and *Uncertainties*.

His is the mind which makes these poems *astir in fire*.

Brooklyn, NY, 3.27.13

THREADS 19: ROBERT SAYS

With poetry, the difference between ending and closure is the difference between Olson and Yeats. Olson seemed to have a miraculous ear/mind for knowing the exact momentum of the poem, when it ends, the exact moment when the poem reaches its end, its information transmitted, its neural arc closed. And there stop. As miraculous as Yeats's sonorous and incredible act of closure, the whole mind of the poem twanged to a stop with a rich change of key — the chestnut tree, the burning tower, the throats of birds. Olson, as so often, is the classical mind at work. When I first read The Librarian, *its ending made me remember 'our' earliest poem, the* Iliad, *with its heart-breaking, absurd, final line, cut off in the middle 'And that was the funeral of Hector, tamer of horses.' Homer taught us from the start that the poem — for all its narrativity or imagery or preachment — arises as much from silence, and to silence recurs. After the* Iliad's *last line, when you're a child, you turn the page wondering what would happen to Troy and the horse and the Greeks, but there is nothing! That is ending without closure. But what we would do to the* Iliad *if we wrote the ending now — how many epilogues and postlogues and afterwords and trumpets and flags we would have to include to end that work?*

in conversation with
Larry McCaffery, 1988

The poem is a wonderful place where things have and lose contexts. Poetry exists in a kind of emptying way. Emptying is a lot on my mind these days, not in the Harold Bloom sense of kineses, the emptying influence. In Galatians, Paul talks about how Jesus, to become man, had to empty himself.

That kineses, or emptying, is happening in the arts. Things have to empty themselves to become themselves, to transcend themselves, so the poet, amongst other things, has to empty himself of his own opinion to write. The Keatsian, negative capability argument applies here. But even in the course of the poem, the syntax, the sentence, the sentential, has to empty itself by way of the line, producing an endless series of these lapses which deny the meaning of the sentence even while taking part in it, so that simultaneously you have a complex sentential built up by lines which are sneering at, running away from, rejecting the very sentence that they are the building blocks of. I love that quality. That quality is part of what I would understand as the rules for lines. A line should not only be interesting, but it should be interesting in dialectic with the whole sentence of which it forms a part [...]

And that simple power that the line has of interrupting, almost like a child waving his hand, at the end of itself saying, "No, I'm, I'm what's being met, not this long sentence, this sentential, this opinion that the poet has to unload, but I'm what really counts — this line along the way." The line, then, is almost an endless series of Freudian slips. Freud uses a Latin word, lapsus, for what we call the Freudian slip. A line is a lapsus, an endless series of lapsii. I never made that connection before. It seems right to make it — an endless series of Freudian slips each of which reveals something that the sum of the sentential can't reveal.

in conversation with
James Stalker [ca. 1980]

7.
A BOOK OF LINE AND MEASURE

RON SILLIMAN

WHAT *MEASURE* MEASURES:
ROBERT KELLY IN THE SIXTIES

Parceled, not parceled, ever the light.
                          Trismegistus to Tat: our bones
  will want velvet,
               line decays, root your gods
in flesh & stock your flesh in
                    flame
(Giordano given over
              —ubi peccavit— he sinned in fire
tongue   word-thorn
             into fire,
                  17 February 1600
& the beam of light
             that is defining measure
—metre, the palladium
             yardstick only a curio
or orifice of
         measure a controlled radiance,
angstrom
       an infinity 'longer than point—
Punctum in Nihilo
            from which
It pours.
      Sentences by nature false,
'opinions' momentaneous murmurings
corpse-fat soft,
             saponification of the great poets
when it is
      Delight forgot—
                      Addio alla madre
I take
    this serious knife
               where Death is
& makes
     all sharp again
wretch of dull edge
            his knife I fight
bites mine. Crystals
            of damascene sever in air
: this silken
      kerchief divides the steel.

This passage, the first two out of eight pages, opens Robert Kelly's *Songs I–XXX* (1968). Typing these lines, I feel as riveted by them as when I first confronted this work nearly 40 years ago. There is in this verse something I feel is almost entirely missing from most of today's poetry — the measure of the line heard & understood as a mode of music. Melopoiea as Pound once called it. This use of sound is something that poets once took for granted as an option — there are moments in *The Cantos* when it is all that exists beyond the crackpot economics & dubious readings of American presidential history. Yet, somehow, after Robert Duncan, a master at this mode, you find Robert Kelly, with his exquisite conception of this music, and Kenneth Irby, with an ultimate ear for vowels, then silence. Or not silence, exactly, but rather a shift in the manner of music.

I want to look at the role that sound, melopoiea, plays in Kelly's work in three books that I read as a decisive moment in his career as poet, and at the role of mysticism within that commitment to sound (or perhaps it is the other way round). I want to suggest that they are related & that a decline in a concern for that which goes beyond knowledge — Gnosticism, mysticism, what have you — led directly to a shift away from sound as the driving force for much American poetry.

It was Olson of course, along with Creeley, who heard that other possibility in Pound's line & even more clearly in that of Williams, the intricate prosody of the spoken, the huffing of the line as breath — very nearly a poetics of asthma in Olson's case, the way so many of his poems start out with a long line only to find themselves narrowing as the words rush, repeatedly interrupted by the need to mark line's limit, to a literally breathless conclusion.

Thus, in the 1950s and '60s, American poetry found itself with not one, but three different tendencies with regards to the proactive use of sound in poetry:

1. the complicated rhythms of the spoken (Olson, Creeley, Blackburn),[73] which also included a number of relatively casual practitioners, such as Ginsberg, Whalen, Snyder & O'Hara;

---

73. Whose sense of the uses of transcription to spatially approximate aspects of speech is perhaps the most detailed of all the poets of that period.

2. a poetics predicated on measure (Duncan, Kelly, some of Irby);
3. a regularized metrics derived from the old formalism (Berryman, Lowell).

Of course, the great majority of poets fell into a category that could be triangulated between "a little of this & a little of that," those who didn't really care & those who were genuinely tone-deaf to their own writing.

Songs I–XXX was the third book published by Kelly in a two-year period of 1967–68 that to this day remains not just a great burst of poetic productivity — Kelly has been the Energizer Bunny of poetic production his entire life — but also a defining moment for a particular mode of poetics, one that was grounded in sound & turned toward alternative sacred texts as a primary concern.

It's worth noting Kelly's trajectory in that decade — it gives some sense of how rapidly the poetry scene was changing, as well as how completely it has transformed in the years since. Beginning to publish around 1960, Kelly within five years had brought out five books with small press publishers, been the focus of an issue of Cid Corman's *Origin*, and co-edited with Paris Leary, *A Controversy of Poets*, published as a Doubleday Anchor paperback original, a trade press with major distribution. While Leary's contributions have largely been forgotten outside of a few obvious big names such as Robert Lowell,[74] Kelly's contributors expanded the roster of the Allen anthology, bringing Louis Zukofsky, Jackson Mac Low, Jerry Rothenberg, Gerrit Lansing & Ted Enslin to a considerably broader audience than they'd previously experienced.[75] & by virtue of coming five years later than the Allen, several of Kelly's selections, such as of Jack Spicer's "Billy the Kid" or the complete "Biotherm" by Frank O'Hara — in 5½-point type — were notably stronger than their respective contributions to the Allen.

---

74. This isn't necessarily a criticism of Leary's editing. The Quietist tradition in American poetry has done a very poor job in preserving, exploring, or celebrating its heritage.

75. I've noted elsewhere that when Richard Moore's *USA Poetry* PBS television series first introduced me to the work of Zukofsky in 1966, the only volume that held any of his poetry at Cody's in Berkeley, then the largest bookstore in that town, was *A Controversy of Poets*.

So the three books that appeared more or less on the heels of *Controversy*, *Axon Dendron Tree* (1967), *Finding the Measure* (1968) & *Songs I–XXX* served to solidify Kelly's position as a major American poet, one of the first (along with Ted Berrigan) to attain this level of recognition within the post-avant tradition who had not been a part of the Allen anthology.

Kelly self-published *Axon Dendron Tree* in 1967 as *Salitter/2*, distributed through his other small press journal, *Matter*, as well as via the legendary Asphodel Bookshop of Cleveland. The stapled 8½-by-14 publication appears to have been mimeographed, a process that would have limited distribution to no more than 300 copies that were run from each paper master. The process also partly explains why the 80-page publication was printed only on one side of each page, which fattened the result to the equivalent of a 160-page book. Another limitation to its distribution lies in the binding, or non-binding — the book is so thick that extra-length staples have been driven in both front & back, but in no instance make it all the way through the entire volume — I have to squeeze them by hand back into place whenever I read from this volume. This is one fragile book. The title — centered on a strip of white paper, 11 inches high but only 2 inches wide — is glued along the left side of the cover's brown construction paper. The brush strokes of the glue have long since stained through on my copy.[76] Because of its size, this volume has spent 46 years sitting atop my book cases, never filed within one.

This is an awfully fugitive publication to argue as one of the defining poetic texts of the 1960s, but it certainly is/was such an event for my 1960s. In fact, it may have proven more so for me than for Kelly, who accords *Tree* just one six-page excerpt in his selected poems, *Red Actions* (1995). The differences between the 1967 edition and his 1995 description of it are worth considering. A note to the reader at the top of the dedication page reads as follows:

76. Abebooks.com listed seven copies available through used & rare book dealers, ranging in price from $40 to $275 (for a copy signed for Joel Oppenheimer) on January 23, 2013. The Oppenheimer copy was also available for that same price when I first drafted this note for my blog in November 2002. On the same day in 2013, there were 18 copies of *A Controversy of Poets* available, ranging in price from $1 to $30.

7 · A BOOK ON LINE AND MEASURE

Axon Dendron Tree grew out of my reading of that issue of *Poetry* [October, 1965] wholly & with immense rightness given over to one section of Louis Zukofsky's *A (sic)*. This poem began swiftly in response & dictated in the first few dozen lines its own formal procedure. To the extent that I had any intention, it was to honor Zukofsky by letting his measure foster a like but different measure in my utterance. The concerns of this poem are its own, and have no bearing on Zukofsky's there or elsewhere, apart from a few teasing relations.

Kelly discusses *Axon Dendron Tree*'s formal procedures in the notes at the back of *Red Actions*:

Axon Dendron Tree. A long poem organized on a numeric structure. Each section consists of 111 unnumbered stanzas; the first section's stanzas are nine lines each, the second section's of eight, and so on, diminishing to the last section, 111 one-line stanzas. In my own sense of my work, this is my first real achievement using any sort of compositional grid or organizational principal other than the Local Music, which has always been the self-arising guide of the poem.

The 999-line structure described here is certainly elegant. However, the opening section of *Axon Dendron Tree* is composed of stanzas of eight lines each, not nine. At least as published in 1967, the poem has 888 lines. *Tree* begins with, of all things, an image of golf:

> Tee
> off
> & be
> on grass
> this is
> start
> of eighty
> leven

pages
in the book
each
makes
a form
I counted
7 then
8 came

or hard
to render
stanzas
like boxes
each one
a line
of Wace
his Engles

while Laȝamon
his Brut
took
the augury
of heard
— sruti —
beginnings
frutti

Layamon — there are multiple ways to spell that name & Kelly picks one of the more difficult to reproduce — translated Wace's own French translation of Geoffrey of Monmouth's Latin history of Britain, *Brut*, into alliterative verse around 1190. Henry Wace, however, was a mostly 19th-century religious scholar who focused on early Christianity, a topic that also concerned Karl Marx's collaborator. So Kelly is almost instantly playing with several layers of connotation at once, the discussion of form cast into many directions from which the poet might then proceed. & does.

It's interesting to contrast Kelly's programmatic conception of form with that of his model. Zukofsky's *"A" — 14, 'Beginning An*, starts with four stanzas, even more extreme in their verticalism than Kelly's. Zukofsky proceeds with 169 tercets, all but one line containing two words, then with 247 tercets with three words — save for two "ringers," one a four-line stanza with one word per line, the other just two stanzas further on, a couplet, one of whose lines has just two words — before dropping back first to a tercet of two-word lines, and then two concluding stanzas of one-word lines.

Zukofsky's formal focus is very much on the line, Kelly's on the stanza — it's almost as if two men looked at one phenomenon with just slightly different lenses. Zukofsky's conception of form generates the line, perhaps, but Kelly's sense generates the poem. It's a critical, even decisive, difference. In *Red Actions*, Kelly again acknowledges Zukofsky's relation to the *Axon Dendron Tree*:

> The whole poem is dedicated to Louis Zukofsky, in thanks for his creative kindness, as a poet to us all, and as a man to me when I was beginning. He is one of the Four Masters (with Olson, Duncan, Blackburn) who boxed my ears.

One name Kelly doesn't mention here is that of Jackson Mac Low, whose work he certainly knew, having published several pieces in *A Controversy of Poets*, but whom I suspect Kelly must have seen more as a peer, given how late Mac Low got started publishing.[77] Mac Low's sense of program as the motive principle behind a text was already quite developed by the mid-1960s. *Axon Dendron Tree*, however, may be the first such attempt to "just write poetry" by such method without constraint as to how the vocabulary might look or sound. Where Mac Low was consciously striking the ego's presence in his work, Kelly gives it pretty much free rein. In this sense, *Axon Dendron Tree* is closer to two other programmatic texts that were composed in the late 1960s, Ted Berrigan's *Sonnets* and Kenneth Koch's *When the Sun Tries to Go On*.

---

77. At 48, Mac Low had published just four books. It's difficult to keep in mind just how marginal someone like Mac Low (or Spicer for that matter) was in the 1960s and well into the following decade.

Axon Dendron Tree thus represents a signal moment in the history of the American poem, the point when true formal procedure "comes inside." The poem itself is raucous & witty, a high point of the Projectivist tradition, which is so often accused of being ponderous — *Tree* is just fun. Kelly of course is moving quite far from some of his masters Olson & Blackburn in utilizing measure rather than speech as his modeling principle for language, but that is precisely what he takes from Zukofsky & Duncan. That push-pull aspect of the Projectivist tendency, which has never been fully explored critically, is nowhere more clear than in Kelly's work from the 1960s, and almost never to greater purpose than in this poem.

Although I knew his work from *A Controversy of Poets*, I didn't focus on Kelly's poetry until I got to know some of his then-recent Bard students: David Perry,[78] John Gorham, and Harvey Bialy, and through them Tom Meyer. All spoke glowingly of Kelly as a teacher. But it wasn't until I got hold of a copy of *Finding the Measure* (1968) that Kelly's poetry forced me to pay attention. The volume's preface — or as Kelly titles it, complete with open-ended parenthesis, "(prefix": — is one of the knockdown finest statements of a poetics I've ever read. Even today, 35 years after it was written, it stands up:

> Finding the Measure is finding the mantram,
> is finding the moon, as index of measure,
> is finding the moon's source;
>
>   if that source
> is Sun, Finding the Measure is finding
> the natural articulation of ideas.
>
>   The organism
> of the macrocosm, the organism of language,
> the organism of *I* combine in ceaseless naturing
> to propagate a fourth,
>   the poem,
>   from their trinity.

---

78. These days a therapist in upstate New York and not to be confused with the David Perry who has been associated with *Adventures in Poetry* over the past decade.

> Style is death. Finding the Measure is finding
> a freedom from that death, a way out, a movement
> forward.
>
>   Finding the Measure is finding the
> specific music of the hour,
>   the synchronous
> consequences of the motion of the whole world.

Style is death. Derrida would have a field day with that, coming as it does in the work of someone for whom measure — the line & phrase heard as units at once both of music & of meaning — is the compelling issue. What does Kelly mean to make so bold a claim?

The answer of course is to be found first in Kelly's assertion that there is such a thing as a "natural articulation of ideas," followed by his trinity of organisms. The idea of "natural articulation" may follow out of the old Imagist maxim that "a new cadence means a new idea," but Kelly weds it very much to an organic vision not only of the poem but of all existence.

It's interesting to map Kelly's trinity over, say, Roman Jakobson's six functions of language.[79] I always think of Jakobson's model as three axes, or as pairs of opposites: *addresser, address*; *contact, code*; *signifier, signified*. Kelly's trinity does fall neatly into those three pairs, especially if one goes back to Jakobson's own discussions of the signified as ultimately contextual, much broader than the notion of an object for every noun — Kelly calls it the "organism / of the macrocosm."

What Kelly describes as three axes "ceaselessly naturing" to pop out a poem rather the way a hen does eggs is the grounds for any articulation, not just verse. Is Kelly arguing after a fashion that it is this particular configuration of these possibilities that lead to the poem? Perhaps, but more important is the way in which this text privileges the "I" with italics only to deny its force one stanza later with "Style is death." But of course that kind of equation can work both ways: *Death is style* might be even more accurate. Phrased thus, we can see that Kelly is trying very hard to separate out the "I" of consciousness from a second "I," the superego

---

79. Jakobson, "Linguistics and Poetics," in Jakobson, *Language and Literature,* ed. by Kristina Pomorska & Stephen Rudy (1988) esp. pp. 66–71.

really, that would impose its understanding of tradition & history encoded through a process that keeps the word from somehow coming through directly.

That distinction takes me back to the seemingly self-canceling phrase "natural articulation." Such a concept implies a universe in which articulation would be unmediated & inevitable. Not simply that the flower of my sermon should be its own message, but that nature itself is just such an ultimate discourse. But Kelly's phrase continues: "natural articulation *of ideas*." Thus ideas themselves must exist both prior to & outside of any embodiment in words.

If the lion could speak we would have to write it down.[80] Kelly is aligning the poem here with a discourse that is literally inhuman — though not necessarily anti-human. Rather it exists prior to & outside of our merely secular discursive behaviors. The *mantram* of the first line is, if we follow this logic, a subliminal hum within the universe. The role for a poet is not to alter or direct that energy so much as to enable it to come through revealed.

All of which, I would argue, takes us back to the question in this poem of the moon. It is not only that "Finding the Measure is finding the mantram," but that it is also "finding the moon, as index of measure, / is finding the moon's source." The question of the moon, its relation to Sun (the absence of article here marking it as more than a little like an Egyptian god) & that mysterious idea of "source" traces the other thematic thread that weaves through this text. Read strictly, the entire line of reasoning about the trinity of organisms should apply only if Sun is understood as "source" for the moon. Moon of course being a loaded term for a poet who has already published a volume of short poems called *Lunes*.

On the one hand, the attributes of the tides & their impact on any number of worldly phenomena is certainly present, but at a level of obviousness that makes it a So What. Ditto the question of gravity from earth to moon or vice versa & of sun to either. At a more significant level, though, I don't think this image is decidable except insofar as it pins the question of articulation up into a cosmology of effects. The poem resonates precisely as that which cannot be reduced to an argument, a good test of any poem.

80. As indeed Michael McClure already has.

7 · A BOOK ON LINE AND MEASURE

The third book in this sweep of writing, *Finding the Measure*, is full of poems of great interest beyond the "prefix," only five of which (out of 43) make their way into Kelly's selected *Red Actions*. While the "prefix" is included, among my favorite of the excluded works is "On a Picture of a Black Bird Given to Me by Arthur Tress," as close to an objective poem as *Measure* contains. It opens:

> Raven   in Chiapas
> beak up open to
> flat white Mexican light
> against which an arch
> is breaking its back to join the broken sky
>
> barbs of its feathers hang down, it cries out
> for a world full of carrion
> but its claws
> hold firm & flat
> the top of the ruined sill

The poem demonstrates Kelly's ability to be far more than a poet of pure statement. The prosody of that first stanza is simply stunning — not a single syllable that does not contribute above & beyond the denotative level of the words or their connotative resonances.

Another wonderful poem can be found on the facing page, "To the Memory of Giordano Bruno," a poem in two columns, the right one of which has its lines, words, & letters printed in reverse, so that one need read it in a mirror. A third excluded poem that certainly had its impact on the young Ron Silliman as reader is "First in an Alphabet of Sacred Animals," a meditation on murder that begins:

> The ANT for all his history is a stranger
> & his message is the gospel of an alien order
> & his & his & his
>
> works are furious in the crust of the earth
> his house & his bread

(We must start with him because he is other,
he comes from a nowhere underneath us
& returns again & does not know us)

this is the easiest animal to kill.

Today I did not kill an ant
                        a great big black one
& it became necessary to think
of the price of an ant's death:
                        nothing we do
is without consequence)
                        & in the taking of an ant's life
is the taking of life

But the ant is not an albatross & dies easy
& soon his carcass is gone, who knows where they go
the bodies of insects we kill,
                        when we take life
                        what do we give?
— What is the price
of killing an ant
— What intricate microscopic karma do we fulfill
in crushing him
— What cosmic debt does he repay under my foot
— Will we notice the pain
with which we must one day surely atone for his death
— Or are there beings (& are there beings)
who step on us lightly as we tread ants?
that is the hideous question someone is always asking
Egypt after Egypt

& onward for another page before concluding with a section in prose. Kelly's thesis here, as elsewhere, is compelled not to argue for the ant simply for its sake, but to connect it up, here to Egypt & thus to that larger system within the word "Sacred" in the title.

7 · A BOOK ON LINE AND MEASURE

Also excluded from *Red Actions* is the 12-part "Zodiac Cycle," a series that is accorded pride of place in *Measure*, with each section — individual poems really — illustrated with its astrological symbol printed large in deep blue ink.

A closer reading of *Red Actions* would show that the elimination of a sequence such as "Zodiac Cycle" cannot be accidental. Kelly's writing offers so very many choices — *Finding the Measure*, after all, was the 14th book of poems of Kelly's published in just nine years; in his spare time, he also edited *Controversy*, wrote a novel, *The Scorpions*, and published a liturgy — that one could easily publish a half-dozen selected editions from this period, each of which presented a very different Kelly. Thus while the Kelly of *Red Actions* remains a man interested in the alternate wisdom traditions, the mysticism that was front & center in his early books is presented here as incidental.

My own interest in Kelly, as with Duncan, had more to do with measure than mysticism. To this day I have never quite understood why these two phenomena appear to be linked, inextricable. Sound, it has always struck me, is an ideal antidote as an organizing & motive principle for the poem to the shallow surfaces of an unreflective dramatic monologue. Among the many poets that Kelly is & has been, is a superb practitioner of melopoiea.

The poem that follows "First in an Alphabet of Sacred Animals," "Smith Cove Meditation," has a title reminiscent of Olson, but the text is closer kin to Gertrude Stein. It begins:

> Across the tone there is the one.
> Everything is easier if there are women in it
> but past the tone   there is the bone,
> inside the bone there is the one.
>
> One & bone; one times bone is bone, one bone.
> One & bone are tone. Going across
> is taking them away
> from each other. Orphan bone,
> widowed one. Up on the hill
> a widow lives, nurturing the tone.
> Her son the bone. From their garden

> on an August afternoon
> you can see the one out on the water
> all the waves & all the town's streets
> all the bright places & far
> people, o some of them are gone,
> gone to bone & gone to one, fallen
> the castle of the bone, fallen the castle
> of the enduring tone, the one
> is over the harbor.

Every plausible combination of "o" & "n" is brought to bear — one can almost feel the deeper resonance of "afternoon" the way one might individual notes of a carillon. One might here argue that the "tone" of this poem is the selfsame "mantram" Kelly writes of in the "Prefix" to *Measure*, and while it is a radically different music than the rich alternation of consonant & vowel in the description of the blackbird, what it demonstrates most clearly is Kelly's commitment to the poem of sound.

The timing of all this is significant. Right around 1970, a number of different events occurred that would transform the role sound played in poetry socially. Olson's death in January of that year, followed a year later by Blackburn, shut the door on any hard-edged conception of speech as the prosodic determinant of poetic form. Already Creeley had moved toward a more relaxed notion of the same in his 1968 volume *Pieces*, the potentially contradictory influences of Ted Berrigan & Louis Zukofsky combining to soften the tone of its linked sequences. When, in early 1971, Robert Grenier declared "I HATE SPEECH," in the first issue of *This*, he was already jousting with an opponent that had largely abandoned the field.

Similarly, Duncan's decision to not publish another book for 15 years after his 1968 *Bending the Bow* muted his enormous influence on younger poets. Combined with Olson's & Blackburn's absence & Creeley's shift, Duncan's step away from the scene transformed the role of sound in the poem — so prominent a feature in poetry for 20 years — into something of a non-issue in the 1970s.

But if *This* magazine's first issue proved functionally to be announcement of this shift in poetics, it was Kelly who had the literal first word:

> If this were the place to begin
> is not,
>
> starts with the disk-sun-boat — a journey we can share,
>   a precise
> boat — Gokstad, not metaphor —
> to our own country
>   following the line
> of tensions between the heard & the hard
>
> facts of the world,
>   perception. Stanza
> of particulars.
>   Lamplight half led
> onto my book & half held back —
> afraid of the white page
>
> My confession. The pale blue asters
> with dark hearts
> are everywhere these days.
> It begins to rain.

It is likely that Kelly and the editors of *This* meant different things by putting this poem first. As is so often the case with Kelly, tho, the evocation of "particulars" — in this instance the Viking vessel Gokstad — is something unlikely to be shared by many readers, serving less as a point of reference than as a demarcation between those in the know & those outside. It's in keeping with Kelly's own long interest in alternative systems of knowledge, and in the poet as shaman or priest. But, with some notable exceptions that would include Norman Fischer, Fanny Howe, John Taggart, & Nate Mackey, poetry's spiritual impulse was not much foregrounded for the next few decades. Thus, when the *Apex of the M* gang proposed, circa

1990, that langpo had short-shrifted the Gnostic, they came within a hair's breadth of identifying what I actually suspect could have started the very revolution in poetics they longed for, the flip side of the measure/mysticism coin. The poem as sound, as measure & song as much as speech, let alone the narrow gargling of the sound poets.[81]

& if such a poetics is again desirable, or even plausible, reading Kelly & these great books is one useful way back in.

---

81. Lisa Jarnot's biography of Robert Duncan confirms this, at least to my reading. With the bulk of Duncan's writing finally coming back into print, it will be interesting to see if a renaissance of this impulse is forthcoming.

JED RASULA

FLESH DREAM BOOKS

I first read work by Robert Kelly forty years ago, in 1972. It was my third year in college, and I'd found a hearty friend in Mike Erwin, with whom I shared a deep absorption in Pound but who knew more about contemporary American poets.[82] So visiting my parents during Christmas, I took a stack of books to read: *The Maximus Poems* by Charles Olson (the first volume only, in the Corinth reprint of 1960), *Bending the Bow* by Robert Duncan, *Gunslinger* by Edward Dorn (again, just the first installment as issued by Fulcrum in England), and *Flesh Dream Book* (1971) by Robert Kelly. These were all Mike's recommendations. On my own steam I'd also brought along titles by Pablo Neruda, Fernando Pessoa, George Seferis, and probably Eugenio Montale. Olson and Duncan I'd already dabbled in (*The Distances* and *Opening the Field*), so I had some sense of what I was getting into, and Dorn had made a legendary appearance at Indiana University where I was studying (I missed it, but my ears were full of the reports). Kelly, though, was a shot in the dark, fueled only by Mike's obvious & almost liturgical reverence for this intriguingly named book — a book, moreover, that was almost two hundred pages, and made a show of containing only two or three years' writing.

82. Mike Erwin and I subsequently embarked on a series of interviews with contemporary poets. The interviews that were published were with Kelly, Nathaniel Tarn, A.R. Ammons, Roy Fisher, Charles Tomlinson, and Peter Redgrove. Unpublished are interviews with George Barker, Edwin Morgan, Peter Porter, Jon Silkin, Adrian Mitchell, David Wevill, George MacBeth, and Theodore Enslin. We began with Americans on the East Coast, spent November 1973 in England, and were unable to continue as planned with more Americans because of Mike's untimely death in March 1974. As this list of interviewees suggests, we were aiming to talk to poets one or more generations beyond ours (we'd scheduled an interview with Auden, who died before we made it to England; and Bunting, misconstruing us as academics, denounced us roundly in a letter of refusal). It says much about the orientation of aspiring young male poets at that moment that we never considered interviewing women, nor apart from Levertov and Rich were we aware of any living women poets.

Needless to say, *Flesh Dream Book* was the fuse that lit the dynamite cluster of the other books. I didn't expect that an apparently tossed off gathering of poems by a guy in his early thirties would claim the exalted heights charted by Olson and Duncan and the others; but there was something deeply insinuating in that title, something leonine in the yellow-tawny cover, to say nothing of the bardic-bearded countenance of the poet himself in the photo that Black Sparrow routinely provided with its author profiles. It's hard now to imagine the impression of a book like that, because its impact came with the full force of its moment in tow. For a (or *this*) twenty year old male that moment reverberated with the seemingly endless ignominy of the Vietnam war (my draft number was just two digits above the threshold drafted in 1970), the squalid Nixon presidency, and the quaintly named generation "gap" that felt more like an abyss—to say nothing of that estimable triple crown (sex, drugs, rock 'n' roll) with which the Sixties has been branded and which by the Seventies provided an inescapable hedonistic countenance to countercultural life. Against that backdrop, contemporary poetry, *real writing by real living people*, was tantamount to the discovery of long lost Atlantis. *Flesh Dream Book* waved its obscurely ceremonial wand over this hidden domain.

Reading this description now, I can imagine a younger person assenting to the official version of the Sixties bending our heads out of shape. So I need to be precise about the magical procedures involved. I don't quite mean Magick in Aleister Crowley's sense, though that was much in the air and certainly courted by the references and vocabulary in Kelly, Gerrit Lansing, and others. The most succinct way to specify the aura is to challenge the term "recreational drugs": my point being that, for us anyway, there was no such thing. Drug use was part of a hieratic engagement, a spirit quest. An acid trip was a carefully choreographed itinerary of unabashed soul searching. And while smoking dope was more casual, it too contributed its share to one's discovery of the *calling*. (There was little alcohol, by the way, except when we danced with our girlfriends to Rolling Stones albums like *Sticky Fingers* and *Exile on Main Street*, chugging bourbon.) Call it quaintly period specific, but there it is; and arched over it all, like an inscription above a portal, those words, that mantra: *flesh, dream, book*.

So what was it in that book, in Kelly's writing in general, that led us on—led us *in*? Right there on the surface was the look of the poems, rang-

7 · A BOOK ON LINE AND MEASURE

ing expansively across the page. Where Olson had insistently expanded the visual coordinates of the poem by occupying the space of the page as force field, Kelly took an additional lead from Duncan's elegance (to use my coordinates at the time: I hadn't yet encountered Mallarmé's *Un coup de dés*). The result was that a poem by Kelly made a subcutaneous impact before it was read, like a hermetic barcode scanned with an adroit alchemical flourish over the alembic. Striking through the lines of "The Separations" from *Flesh Dream Book* gives you the poem's visual template, deftly released from margins, gently cantering left and right as if tracing the movements of a miner panning for gold in a Sierra Nevada creek:

THE SEPARATIONS

Such pages were paradigms of whatever "open poetry" connoted. (*Open Poetry* was an anthology edited by George Quasha, by then a Kelly acolyte.)[83] It meant, above all, openness to experience. What's more, in this book the poems were printed continuously; a poem as such had no privileged claim to start on a page of its own. This novelty had the effect of leaching a cornucopia surreptitiously into the textual sum.

83. Kelly addresses the heritage of this emancipation from the left margin in his conversation with Quasha and Charles Stein, "Ta'wil or How to Read." See *Vort* 2:2 (1974) 108–134; reprinted here 477–509.

Furthermore, Kelly's mind was so sharp, and his ear so refined, that this effortless resistance to the staple tug of the left-hand margin revealed a ballet of pure creative intuition. It constantly courted the moment-to-moment of a diary or journal with the tacit grail quest of process poetics. Robert Duncan's "Structures of Rime" and "Passages" sequences were evident models, but they were procedural gambits whereas each Kelly poem seemed the charter of some potentially new genre unto itself. In all of them, though, there was a characteristic melody of mind on the move — portending glimpses of what he called (echoing Wallace Stevens) "The Stream on the Other Side of the Mind."

The code words in Kelly's title speared three related fish. *Flesh* suggested the incessant immediacy of desire, but also the corporeal envelope of the world that Olson had anatomized in his "Human Universe" essay. *Book* was what you held in your hands as you read, and as you read it became the palpable emblem of desire, the residuum of foreknowledge in an almost alchemical sense: scriptural, without the scriptures. *Dream* was the crucial hinge. Where *flesh* and *book* seemed to rotate their respective beacons without overlapping, *dream* dissolved the Euclidean geometry and parsed everything in a fabulous nimbus of potential connectivity. *Tat tvam asi* (thou art that) has been a constant underpinning of Kelly's work — revenant of childhood Catholicism no doubt, but also trip-lever of perpetual discovery in the flow of analogies (re)inaugurated by Baudelaire. The book, scaled back, was a dream of flesh; skin, probed lightly, was a dreaming book. The dream folded flesh onto flesh and the book took flight.

I don't want to make too much of a single title among Kelly's sprawling opus. *Flesh Dream Book* was a portal for me, but it was shaggy and uncouth in a way befitting my own condition at that moment. Returning to Bloomington (Indiana) after the holidays, I quickly laid hands on anything else I could find by Kelly, and it was as if the very title (to say nothing of the contents) of *Finding the Measure* became my compass. Dig deep and open your mouth as wide as you can: that was the portent, or "permission" in Duncan's sense. Although I was far from realizing it then, Kelly's mouth-to-the-measure momentum constituted a poetics very close to Gertrude Stein's way of laying hands on the moment, as she describes it in "Composition as Explanation." Hard to see because of Kelly's thematic straining after orgasmic epiphany — whereas Stein, one might say, is all about multiple orgasms. But taken more broadly, Kelly's abundance is as *continuous* a composition as "Lifting Belly" or *The Making of Americans*. "There is no end to a Kelly poem," wrote Guy Davenport in 1974. "It is a cataract of energy."[84]

Just as important as the energy, though, was the flotsam of curious lore borne along as if with the casual gesture of some herculean fund of esoterica. Other poets in a more conservative lineage might make the appreciative nod to Mozart or Beethoven in a poem, but with Kelly you stood exposed to *Die Frau ohne Schatten* — one of the lesser known operas of Strauss — or more obscurely, "Mare Nostrum: A Sequence from the Piano Music of Frederic Mompou," a Catalonian composer better known now, but whose very existence I could not verify until long after this initial exposure in *Flesh Dream Book*. Kelly's work took the spark from Olson's patchwork bibliophilia in "A Bibliography on America for Ed Dorn" and "Proprioception"; and *In Time* seemed achingly poised on a threshold where any proper name or title could become a poem unto itself. This Olson Effect went well beyond Kelly, encompassing Howard McCord's *Gnomonology*, John Clarke's *From Feathers to Iron*, and much else. It infused a broader discourse evident in Richard Grossinger's journal of bioregionalism & poetics *Io*, in which the first translation from Foucault's epochal *Le Mots et les choses* appeared, as well as Rothenberg's *New Wilderness Letter* and his numerous anthologies. In many ways the slaphappy culmination was *America a Prophecy*, edited by Rothenberg with George Quasha, a singular apparition all too quickly forgotten.[85] Looking back now, it's apparent that this venturesome initiative of poets following the lead of Pound as grand wizard and grammar school headmaster was spurned in academia, which insisted on a strict division of labor whereby poets would supply product and critics seal the packages. It was this factor, more than anything, that made Kelly such an attractive portal to a poetry counter-culture with its own presses (e.g., Black Sparrow,

---

84. Guy Davenport, "Kelly in Time," *Vort* 2:2 (1974) 163–165.

85. *America a Prophecy* had a blurb by Hugh Kenner, but the anthology was dealt a lethal blow by Helen Vendler's front-page review in the *New York Times Book Review*. See Rasula, *The American Poetry Wax Museum* (1996) 334–338.

City Lights, Auerhahn, Oyez, Four Seasons, Jargon, Coach House in Canada, Fulcrum and Cape Goliard in England), its singular bibliomania, its cultural eclecticism, its grand sense of adventure.

An important factor in the glow Kelly emitted was the "company" in Robert Creeley's sense. Olson and Duncan, like Zukofsky and Pound, were conspicuous coordinates, but Kelly's own contemporaries were crucial portents of very different destinations. As companions in esoterica, Gerrit Lansing and Stephen Jonas and Kenneth Irby were promissory notes of their own. Clayton Eshleman's journal *Caterpillar* netted these and others with clear deference to the force of gravity Kelly exerted — a milieu in which Paul Blackburn also held court. On a somewhat different track were Jerome Rothenberg and David Antin, comrades from the beginning of Kelly's career who, by the late Sixties and the journal *some/thing*, were heading off in procedural directions owing more to John Cage and Jackson Mac Low than to Black Mountain poetics. That Kelly could serve as a roundhouse from which conceptual trains embarked on such variable destinations says something about his charisma at that time. Through Kelly you could get to — get *into* — all these poets, along with a younger generation (often but not always his students: Harvey Bialy, Thomas Meyer, Charles Stein, Bruce McClelland, Pierre Joris, and others), and even, through that curious Anchor anthology he edited with Paris Leary, *A Controversy of Poets* (1965), back into the conservative Hall-Pack-Simpson crowd. As dense and impenetrable as Kelly's own work could seem at times, Kelly the phenomenon was an agreeably accessible conduit to adjacent worlds. Certain of his works pointedly cohabited their sources as well: *Axon Dendron Tree* is the best poem Zukofsky never wrote.

And this is where the touted delirium of the long poem comes in. I can't overemphasize the aura of the long poem at the time of Pound's death in 1972. I'd only been reading *The Cantos* for a few years at that point, but in the lifetime of a 20 year old, that felt like a big chunk of my life. Olson had died in 1970, at which point *The Maximus Poems* seemed like late-term pregnancy, awaiting the final volume that wouldn't appear until 1975. Zukofsky's *"A"* was a momentous perplexity: we knew of it, its decades in the making, but it was unavailable until I nabbed the two volume Jonathan Cape edition in London in November 1973 — and it was only after the revelatory publication of *"A" 22–23* in '75 that the spigot turned full throttle. But these were ancestral examples. The long poem was a fixture of Eshleman's heralded *Caterpillar*, in which Theodore Enslin's *Synthesis* was being serialized, amidst a steady series of long poems by others.[86] As *Caterpillar* shepherded the 60s into the 70s, it seemed as if the whole mission of poetry was intent on abolishing the discrete private lyric moment, not denying it but enfolding it into a phenomenological continuum. For the prescience of that trajectory, consider that Michael Palmer and Ron Silliman first appeared in the pages of *Caterpillar*.

And then came *The Loom* (1975). Like nothing before, and nothing since (although it did seem somehow beholden to the installments of Dorn's *Gunslinger* that had appeared). If there is a lost grail of American poetry in the 20th century, *The Loom* is self-nominating. To be a partisan participant in a certain poetry world of the early 70s meant being exposed to installments of *The Loom* in *Caterpillar* and elsewhere. There was no mistaking the spellbinding insistence with which they came across as portents of another mission in poetry altogether. In time, I would recognize *The Loom* as an assiduous assimilation of alchemy, and a poetic companion to Jung's *The Psychology of the Transference* and his other studies in the hermetic tradition. Yet even as I came to appreciate the intertextual resonance, *The Loom* carried impetuously along like a tidal wave, its own unique *duende* was unmistakable.

Lore had it that the vastly overweight Kelly (obese when that was a distant gleam in the lecherous eye of fast food franchises) had been told he wouldn't live past 40, which would be 1975, the year *The Loom* was published. Written during Kelly's sojourn in southern California 1971—72, it was an acutely ontological reckoning with looming mortality. As it happened, Kelly survived — "you will not die," the Nurse confides in the poem (*Loom* 98) — and he eventually shed so much weight as to appear a different person altogether. In the process, his poetry changed as well. It's hard to tell at this distance whether the physiological transformation or the deflation of the 60s played the greater role.

---

86. I was sufficiently enthralled by the tide of long poems that I tried to fasten a theoretical cape around the phenomenon in "The State Meant" in my magazine *Wch Way* 2 (Fall 1975).

By the time Reagan took office, Kelly's poems had largely returned to flush left margins, as if chastened by former indulgences into a penitential compliance with Official Verse Culture. It was during those years that the clamorous challenge of Language poetry began to infiltrate the discourse, and while Kelly steadily plied his vigilant intelligence in poems and tales, he drifted away from the discursive edge he'd pioneered in the charters of *In Time* and "On Discourse" (in the Biopoiesis issue of *Io* edited by Harvey Bialy). He became, in other words, a straightforward practitioner, no longer an obstreperous agent of the broad poetic Awakening of the New American/Black Mountain lineage — a lineage subsiding into dubious relevance in the long interregnum after Olson's death in 1970, Duncan's principled refusal to publish another book after *Bending the Bow* in 1968, and the ongoing obscurity of figures like Robin Blaser, Kenneth Irby, Ronald Johnson, and others.[87] Kelly became just another poet, then, among all too many others, eventually disappearing altogether from the radar of younger poets.

An unkind attitude might peg Kelly's case up to the late 70s as that of a preposterously fluent instinct finding a voice, as the expression has it. In turn, this suggests that a recognizable Kelly voice is evident in everything since. The seeds for such a response were planted by Barry Alpert in his issue of *Vort* on Kelly in 1974, suggesting that "many resent the quantity of work he's published."[88] Many since then have thrown up their hands in defeat, acknowledging his impeccable ear while insisting that his publication record was unmanageably vast. There's some merit in this view, I suppose, but what I want to draw attention to here is the cornucopia, the vagabond potentiality, in that delirious mass of publications from the 60s into the 70s, when Kelly could toss off a book length sequence like *Songs* as if it were an aside. The phrase that comes to mind is *possibilities of poetry*, for that's what it all amounted to. But these were not possibilities as in false starts, shots in the dark; rather, they were thoroughly habitable instances in the life of poetry as *the truth and life of myth* in Robert Duncan's sense, or *going down in the world's books* as Melville so sportingly puts it.

---

87. See "Note on Ongoing Obscurity" at the end of this essay.
88. Barry Alpert, "Robert Kelly's Reputation," *Vort* 2:2 (1974) 166.

In the long poem "The World," Kelly unabashedly stakes the largest possible claim for the ethos of that time:

> there is no
> form not
> organic no
> mind not mine [89]

Organic form was the rallying cry behind the New American poetry, and Kelly here affirms it while abolishing it in the mode of Hegel's *Aufhebung* — cancelled in preservation/preserved in cancellation. Even more boldly, his declaration of omniscience insinuates a cohabitation many readers might not want to share, and leads directly to Kelly's characteristic sex obsessions, flamboyantly expressed in "Ode 6":

> Every branch I pick up's a cock
> & wants to come I rub the wet bark
> rainblack opulent with crumble. Come!
> Aither light & shade & spurts
> the glad rollicking masturbant of earth
> disguised as human love & harvest. [90]

This emphatically male orientation smacks in hindsight of the sexism insidiously rampant in the heyday of free love and patchouli oil — despite which the poet's fecundating vocabulary proves irresistible. Deep in the inner sanctum of these reveries played out under the tutelage of the Great God Pan, there was the androgynous model of the alchemists, one of the grand themes of *The Loom*, and also strikingly evident in Olson's final days when he surmised that a sex change operation might save him, transforming the liver cancer that was killing him into Lady Live Her. As if under the spell of Olson's last hope, and with explicit guidance from alchemical tracts and the renegade Thomas Gospel, Kelly envisions a gender switch as the grand finale of terrestrial matter in *The Loom*:

---

89. *The Mill of Particulars* (1973) 129.
90. Robert Kelly, *The Alchemist to Mercury*, ed. Jed Rasula (1981) 211.

> *when the male*
> *becomes female & the female*
> *male, & we move*
> *naked at last*
> *beyond the garments*
> *male & female one*
> *& none.*
>   (*Loom*, 19)

The path forged by this revelation is what Kelly calls "polysyntax," "the permission to take any or every word or phrase as linkable to what comes before, or to what comes after, or as capable of bearing meaning while standing alone."[91] In light of the above, I note the pressure of the otherwise innocuous verb *comes* (Kelly wrote a book-length poem called *Comes* which I aspired to publish at one point). But there's more: "So any continuous text," he suggests, "is in fact rife with moves, forward, backward, stopping and recovering — syntax reaches as far as our lust for meaning lets it. And that's the joy of it." Joy: *jouissance*, that opulent word Roland Barthes never stopped fondling. And *lust*, that *must* to which Kelly's polysyntactic aspirations aspire — on which they expire? The passage I cite concerns *Sentence*, a 1980 portent of a more recent book-length poem revealingly titled *Uncertainties*, disclosing polysyntax as procedural equivocation. Does polysyntax answer to all that was promised so long ago? I can't say, but in its depths I hear the old Wagnerian hammer hearkening in *armed descent*:

the sun is your mother's hand

held high to shield you from the dark
like a hammer grieving for its nail.[92]

I've opted in the foregoing pages to address the crystallization of a moment in a mind — a mind seemingly capable of moving through language with sinuous serpentine ease, in a moment at once vexed and

---

91. *Red Actions: Selected Poems 1960–1993* (1995) 395.
92. *Uncertainties* (2011) 122.

privileged, a moment when the vectors of historical possibility had not yet become unilaterally *global* as they are now, a moment in which the palpable residue of the past hung enticingly over those alert to its endless potential. That moment ended, and its termination ushered in the age of self-perpetuating contemporaneity. The internet and cell phones and unalleviated connectivity were all far in the future, but around the time *The Loom* appeared, an entire initiative in poetry culminated and vanished all at once. Kelly's epic was squeezed through the doorframe along with the final volume of the *Maximus Poems*, *"A" 22–23*, Spicer's *Collected Works*, Dorn's *Slinger* and his *Collected Poems*, and most consequentially for what has followed, *Self-Portrait in a Convex Mirror* by John Ashbery, which won all the big prizes (deservedly, if oddly, considering the competition), crooning a deep and unsettling new tune into the inner ear of poetry's body politic. What I'll always recall as the signature event marking that cusp, however, is a reading I arranged in conjunction with an exhibit I organized in spring 1975 at the Lilly Library, the rare books collection at Indiana University. *The Loom* wouldn't appear until that fall, but it formed the core of Kelly's reading to an audience of about 30, only a few of whom had ever read his work. It was the only reading I've ever attended that could be called spellbinding in the strictest sense: when Kelly stopped, after 40 minutes, people applauded, but not a soul left the room. Spellbound.

Note: "Ongoing obscurity" extends beyond that moment. Blaser, Johnson, and Irby are nowhere to be found in the 700 pages of *The Oxford Handbook of Modern and Contemporary American Poetry* edited by Cary Nelson (2012). Kelly is only mentioned in a footnote, as is Rosmarie Waldrop; and Alice Notley will stand here for all too many buried in the *et cetera* of a list. It's ironic, given Nelson's exemplary advocacy for the erased legacy of activist poetry, that this insightful array of articles would themselves collectively legislate a comparable act of erasure on a (I would say *the*) vital strand of late twentieth century American poetry. Among all too many others overlooked here are David Antin, Jackson Mac Low, Jack Spicer, Nathaniel Tarn, Clayton Eshleman, Gustaf Sobin, Clark Coolidge, Edward Sanders, Anne Waldman, and Nathaniel Mackey. Even Laura Riding has vanished from this account. In fairness, this sort of topic-driven omnibus is not intended as a comprehensive guide, but such conspicuous indifference to or unawareness of the field opened by Olson and Duncan is symptomatic of an unpleasantly evasive collective mindset.

Like similar compilations and histories, the *Oxford Handbook* jettisons even farther behind a rich tapestry of small press poetry that's highly instructive about the historical milieu; what's more, much could be gleaned about the practical coordination of poetry with an expansive outlook from a perusal of such titles as *Dawn Visions* by Daniel Moore (1964), *Ghost Tantras* by Michael McClure (1964), *The Tapestry and the Web* by Joanne Kyger (1965), *Provisional Measures* by Charles Stein (1966), *Not a Word* by d. alexander (1966), *Transmutations* by Stephen Jonas (1966), *The Heavenly Tree Grows Downward* by Gerrit Lansing (1966), *The Ladder* by David Schiff (1967), *Word Alchemy* by Lenore Kandel (1967), *Tombstone as a Lonely Charm* by d.a. levy (1967), *The Dainty Monsters* by Michael Ondaatje (1967), *Peace Eye* by Edward Sanders (1967), *Roads to Dawn Lake* by John Oliver Simon (1968), *The Ends of the Earth* by David Bromige (1968), *Fertilized Brains* by Brown Miller (1968), *A History of America* by Bill Hutton (1968), *Ing* by Clark Coolidge (1968), *Homestead* by Keith Wilson (1969), *Leaf Leaf/s* by Daphne Marlatt (1969), *Shining Leaves* by Bill Berkson (1969), *Yesod* by David Meltzer (1969), *Skull Juices* by Douglas Blazek (1970), *Babalon 156* by Harvey Bialy (1970), *Geode/Rock Body* by Gretel Ehrlich (1970), *California Poems* by James Koller (1971), *Desde Alla* by John Brandi (1971), *Maps* by Howard McCord (1971), *Nobody Owns th Earth* by Bill Bissett (1971), *Early Selected y Mas* by Paul Blackburn (1972), *America* by Victor Coleman (1972), *The Cargo Cult* by John Thorpe (1972), *The Spirit by the Deep Well Tank* by Drummond Hadley (1972), *Somapoetics* by George Quasha (1973), and *A Palaeozoic Geology of London, Ontario* by Christopher Dewdney (1973) — to give a symptomatic profile of books easily spotted on shelves next to now more familiar titles like *The Sorrow Dance* by Denise Levertov, *The North Atlantic Turbine* by Ed Dorn, *The Back Country* by Gary Snyder, *Rivers and Mountains* by John Ashbery, *Power Politics* by Margaret Atwood, *The Will to Change* by Adrienne Rich (this was a time, I might add, when Gilbert Sorrentino and Jim Harrison were primarily known as poets). I can't resist quoting Dennis Lee's recollection of a milieu in which "Everyone was scruffy and apocalyptic, making up our lives as we went along": exactly (Coach House Books website).

ALLEN FISHER

ROBERT KELLY: FACTURE AND RECEPTION IN THE FIELD

1. The Idea of 'Field.'
2. Encounters in London.
3. Explicit Attentions.
4. The Practice of Field.
5. Some Extrapolations.

*

1. The Idea of 'Field.'

English language poetry, with evident exceptions in oral and architectural traditions, typically uses the field of a page for its facture and reception.[93] The decision to facture on the page has often been accompanied by the use of a left-hand margin and horizontal lines, inherited from medieval manuscript scripts and the first printings of books. This facture was clarified by the inventions and first uses of the typewriter in the middle of the 19th century.[94] The typewriter also made the use of the tab key to facture one or a range of margins for the beginning of a line or the spacing within lines. The tab key becomes a tool and consequent feature in the facture of poetry and is a noticeable visual feature in the poetry written with typewriters after the development of the machines during

---

93. Consideration of this view might be tempered by attention to Jed Rasula & Steve McCaffery (eds), *Imagining Language. An Anthology* (1998).

94. The first typewritten letter of 1846 includes tabulated indentations after the initial address and at the signature. In 1883, Mark Twain's secretary, Isabel V. Lyon, typed up his manuscript *Life on the Mississippi*, which he then sent to his publisher. This may have been the first manuscript to have been delivered in this form. A facsimile of the letter appears in Julius E. Haycraft, "A Typewritten Letter of 1846," *Minnesota History*, Vol. 16, Nº 4 (Dec. 1935) 445–447.

and after WWII.⁹⁵ This helps to encourage the development of the idea of the page as a field for facture and reception. But the page-as-field is very particular and not readily transformed from the concept of the field in agriculture or the theories and practices in mathematics and physics, philosophy & psychology. In poetry the idea of field is both metonymic of the idea of field in other disciplines and metaphoric in the practice it orders. The typed or typeset page as visual display is also, of course, a parallel with collage and with painting practice.⁹⁶

Use of the idea of 'field' is considerably extensive, from initial applications in agriculture by farmers and poets (a piece of ground, open land toward an open-field system of agriculture, probably in the 10th century)⁹⁷ to the concepts of 'field' that describe new discoveries in the 19th and 20th centuries. In 1832, Michael Faraday articulated the idea of an electromagnetic force field and used the term in his 1845 Diary. This was both a visual presentation and a mathematical approximation. Both articulations explicitly described action-at-a-distance for charged electrons and protons. The electromagnetic field has force and a direction of acceleration. Simultaneously both articulations, visual and mathematical, describe interactions inside of descriptions of order and pattern. Many physicists, including Faraday and James Clerk Maxwell (in 1865), and then J.J. Thompson, Hendrik Lorentz, and Max Born, and many others, imagined the field to be real, which probably led to the concept of the ether, the medium for the field. The concepts for both field and ether are rhetorical constructions; as such they are both tools and traps that contribute to both human pleasure and human anguish. This is a rhetorical

---

95. I refer more specifically here to the use of the TAB key which becomes a tool and consequent feature in the facture of poetry and is a noticeable visual feature in the poetry written with typewriters after the development of the machines during and after WWII. James Koca's patent for the mechanism was 1940. It allowed the tab stops for each column to be set and cleared from the keyboard, eliminating the need for the writer to access the back of the machine to manipulate the tab.

96. A good description of this is demonstrated in Johanna Drucker, *The Visible Word: Experimental Typography and Modern Art, 1909–1923* (1993).

97. The Oxford English Dictionary.

device available for visual artists and poets, musicians and mathematicians, and indeed for theosophists (who begin to use the term in 1889) and, in the 20th century, psychologists.

The concept of field in mathematics was used implicitly by Niels Henrik Abel and Évariste Galois in their work on the solvability of equations. The use of the concept recurs in work on sets by Richard Dedekind, in the 1870s, in the work on domains by Leopold Kronecker, in the 1880s, and in the work on 'abstract fields' by Heinrich M. Weber, in the 1890s. In 1910 Ernst Steinitz published his *Algebraic Theory of Fields*. Subsequent works using the vocabulary of field increase exponentially through the early part of twentieth century mathematics and physics. In physics of this period, the field concept started to distinguish between 'Classical' and 'Quantum' and included a range of attentions from electric and magnetic to radiation, scalar, tensor and vector. It is little surprise to find not only parallels in the work of poetry and other arts, but also use of the terms as part of a rhetorical engine. It is also worth noting that, as Charles Bernstein put it, introducing Joanna Drucker's essays on books, writing, and visual poetics, "All language is visual when read."[98]

In *Un Coup de Dés (A Throw of the Dice)* (1897) Stéphane Mallarmé draws his words from a central margin, the poem moves left twice and then to the right followed by a margin cascade from 'l'Abîme' ("The Abyss") through six margins, then back then forward through a further two, then into a tighter set with seven margins and so forth. This visual paradigm is not really picked up again until the 1940s. William Carlos Williams makes his earliest use of field display in *Paterson*, but that is in the post-war period (1946). Mallarmé's procedure and display is not really picked up by Ezra Pound either, except perhaps regarding some of the displays in the post-war period with the *Pisan Cantos* and after.

Charles Olson's earliest use of field composition occurs in *Atalanta* (1941), with its offset stanza, "A Lion upon the Floor" and "Sing, Mister, Sing" (1945), with their two column arrangements interlacing the left margin text, and *Conquerer* (1948) with lines, George Butterick notes,

---

98. Introduction to Joanna Drucker, *Figuring the Word: Essays on Books, Writing, and Visual Poetics* (1998) XI.

"so long they can only be doubled-up at the margin" (1987: xxi)[99] until, finally, *The Kingfishers* (1949) and *The Maximus Poems* (from 1950 and until 1969).

Robert Duncan had already started to introduce ideas of 'field' with "An Essay at War" in 1950 (*Derivations: Selected Poems 1950–1956*). The term is, of course, made emphatic in his book *The Opening of the Field* (1960) and recurs in *The H. D. Book,* composed in the period 1959–1964, and which started to be published in magazines in 1966.

Significantly, Robert Kelly's first use of field composition appears in a poem dedicated to Robert Duncan in 1960, "The Alchemist," in which there are four indentations and in one place a displaced punctuation.[100]

2. Encounters in London.

The use of field composition in poetry and visual art had been apparent to a few writers and readers in Britain throughout the 1960s, but sightings of the work of Robert Kelly in the period was at a premium. Discovery of his work in those early editions became a shared experience, a sharing of rare sightings. In London, Better Books had started to provide the initial tasters. When in 1969 Nick Kimberley, then at Miles' Indica Bookshop in Southampton Row, published *A California Journal*, there were already 18 publications listed as works of poetry by Kelly, but most of these were not available. John Martin's Black Sparrow Press had become the main source, particularly with *Finding the Measure* (1968) and *The Common Shore* (1969). The Pym-Randall *Songs I–XXX* was also on the shelves. In 1970, Cape Golliard in London published *Kali Yuga*. Pierre Joris, an ex-student from Bard College where Robert Kelly was teaching, came to live in Britain in 1971. He carried with him some of the more difficult to find books. In particular at that moment, *Axon Dendron Tree* (1967). In 1971, Frontier published the extraordinary *In Time* and Black Sparrow Press published *Flesh Dream Book.*

---

99. George F. Butterick (ed.), *The Collected Poems of Charles Olson* (1987) XXI.
100. Robert Kelly, *The Alchemist to Mercury,* ed. by Jed Rasula (1981) 1.

This was followed by two substantial books that arrived at Compendium Books in almost quick succession: *The Mill of Particulars* (1973), and *The Loom* (1975). The task ahead for poets and readers then was overwhelming and necessarily formidable.

3. Explicit Attentions.

In 1960, in his "Notes on the Poetry of Deep Image,"[101] Robert Kelly provides insight into the necessary contradiction of his poetic thought. In one of the paragraphs sub-headed "The Line" he elaborates Charles Olson's "Projective Verse," "The line as set down on paper is an indication of the breath period, with visual & rhythmic considerations determining the visual notation." In the following paragraph he notes, after Arthur Rimbaud, that "Systematic derangement" "of standard speech rhythms, of the inflexibilities of our analytic grammar, is a sharp exploratory tool, and a means of locking images." The statement is an explicit juxtaposition for a definition of collage by Max Ernst in which the function of the work is "systematic displacement," but Ernst's proposition uses two images.[102]

Later in the same essay by Kelly, under the subheading "Deep Image," "The whole poem is more than the sum of its parts. Very important for this super-equivalence is the ORDER of images within a poem. The final quantum will vary with the rearrangement of the images and the images' fields of force. Every image has its field of force, it[s] shadow moving darkly through the poem, with which the poet must contend. ... The image is the measure of the line. The line is cut with image in mind."

And, under the subheading "Language," "The verbalization of the image comes out of the linguistic patterns of the poet's native language."

---

101. Robert Kelly, *Trobar #2* (1961).

102. Max Ernst sums up collage as "the exploitation of the chance meeting of two distinct realities on an unfamiliar plane, or to use a shorter term, the culture of systematic displacement and its effects." Max Ernst, *Beyond Painting and Other Writings*, tr. by Dorothy Tanning (1948).

and "Only in the native linguistic PATTERNS can the deep image communicate at full strength."

Later, in "Duende, Lorca's Dark Sounds," he writes, "Image, the unit of deepest awareness, the persistent and variable signal of the unconscious emitted into the field of the poem." [103]

In "Poem = Communique," "It is easy enough for the image to explode in its novelty, in the seductiveness of epiphany, but it must do more: with the same speed, it must open more than it closes, must open to what follows, respond to what follows, elapse instantly in the field of sight, linger as a controlled resonance." [104]

The rhetorical context enlarges in "Sermo,"

>   'We are each a field
> & also the limits of that field.
>   Above the
> field the sun rises & stays in the sky and falls
> to the inward west.

and:

>   We are
> haunters & haunted. We talk in our own fields.
> What is called Imagination is the harvesting of
> the field.

and:

>   'Memory closes the door
> of the body. Memory closes the gate of the field.'[105]

---

103. Robert Kelly, *A Voice Full of Cities* (2014) 54.

104. Kelly, ibid., 73.

105. Kelly, ibid., 105.

7 · A BOOK ON LINE AND MEASURE

In notes for a class at Cal Tech he finds himself "confronting

> ... polarity, the Descriptive vs the Prophetic,
> wch turned the question away from 'sources' ... and did accept the neurological-spiritual identity of any poet, i.e., he (sic) is what he does and what happens to him, since he is the field-of-event (whether the 'source' is book or dream or 'flesh', history or any other hallucination) ...[106]

In his "prefix": to *The Mill of Particulars,* he writes,

> Language is the only genetics.
>
> >Field
> "in which a man is understood & understands"
> > &becomes
> > >what he thinks,
> > becomes what he says
> > >following the argument.[107]

In a subsequent review of two books of translation, Stuart Kendall's *The Epic of Gilgamesh,* and Thomas Meyer's *Beowulf,* in 2012, Kelly writes,

> The solemn priestly tablets of the "original"... are transformed into communiques from the field of action: the page. / The page is the field. The page is spacetime itself, your moment. The page (since Gutenberg) has been the only time there is.[108]

And in his "Notes on Brakhage"[109] he writes:

---

106. *FLESH: DREAM: BOOK* is the title of a substantial collection of poems by Robert Kelly (1971).
107. Robert Kelly, *The Mill of Particulars* (1973) 11.
108. Kelly, op. cit. (2014) 549.
109. Robert Kelly, "Notes on Brakhage," *A Voice Full of Cities,* p. 565.

Mallarmé was fascinated, especially in his last years, with the visual field in which the poem is inscribed. It is a simple fact that in this apparently linear, successive art, one word after another, one line after another, we do in fact see more than we are reading. Poets are fascinated with these penumbral words that shimmer round the text in ocular focus. IT has been said, I don't know on what authority, that Mallarmé actually speculated about inscribing his great final experiment, *Un coup de dés n'abolira jamais le hasard,* as a film in that nascent medium, so the words and phrases could scroll by at a controlled rate.'

4. The Practice of Field.
A brief survey of the first 27 works by Robert Kelly.

The use of the term 'field composition' needs to be tempered in application to the work of most poetry. To state the obvious, in almost all of the examples of poetry by Kelly the text is at an orientation to make reading possible, horizontally displayed and usually read from left to right; what do shift, and articulate differently from much poetry, are the margins and the line breaks. As early as 1961, after the initial 1960 poem "The Alchemist" for Robert Duncan, Kelly published *Armed Descent*. The book makes extensive use of field composition, in the sense just indicated.

"How It Fell" has 3 margins, with 3 en spaces after colons.
"Early One Evening" has 2 margins and no punctuation.
"Parallel Texts" has two columns each with the same subtitle ("Figure"), each with 2 or 3 indentations.
The longer sequence "Measure Those Distances" varies its use of margins from three to none, beginning with 3 then 2 then one.
"This Visible World Seems Formed In Love" has four margins.
Sometimes, like the "Poem for the Jews" there is no indentation or margin for poetic effect, but rather an expedience for the typesetter to get a long line on the page.
"Spiritum: Two Excerpts" has a cascade which moves from right to left through four margins & which are partly out of line with a preceding use of margins left to right. The poem includes the use of a three-dot triangle.

7 · A BOOK ON LINE AND MEASURE

The following poem "The Exchanges" (1961), which Jed Rasula names as "Kelly's first major long poem," immediately followed *Armed Descent*.[110] In the poem there are multiple margins (5+) and indents, which are partly arbitrary regarding a position that varies from one publication of the same poem to another; also evident are displaced punctuation and specialized notation like three dots in a triangle.

In the 1962 poem "Thor's Thrush" there are 19 sets, 18 of which are subtitled 'Spel' and numbered in Roman numerals. The work uses a left-hand margin almost entirely throughout and uses punctuation occasionally: 'Spel II,' which begins in lower case, has a comma in line 4; 'Spel III' begins on line 4 with an indented colon and starts using commas at lines 12, 13, and 14 and then an indentation to end. The text also uses capitalized letters, which it hardly uses at all in a conventional manner, but rather in a specialized manner. 'Spel III' has:

'ble-a-ow
'taRa beast
'bite not gore not'

In 1964, *Round Dances* continues this æsthetic attention to field composition, continues, that is, to define what it might mean. In "Round Dance: The Ample," a poem addressed to an other and to a sexual act with the other, displays a range of phrases laid horizontal across a 72 letter space page, each phrase separated by a double letter space then a full stop followed by a second double letter space. The array here becomes a landscape or rather horizontal body-scape of phrases, sometimes four sometimes three to a line or carried over into the next line where the phrase has not concluded. The phrases are sometimes syntactical sometimes fragmented.

In "Round Dance: New Moon Harvest," the portrait page carries long breath lines partly using staggered margins and occasional clusters separated by larger spaces. The speculative is approached in this design as a series of fragmented or uncompleted small nocturnal speculations

---

110. The poem appeared in *SET* #1 and then fully in *Origin*, then in *The Alchemist to Mercury* (1981) 5–21. The sentence from Jed Rasula appears in the introduction, page v.

("moving of the night," "branched candlestick," "owls are quieting down now," "which / star is the pole star") contrasted within the same page to an ongoing single speculation, the projective attention to "The heavenly city," and "Jerusalem."

In "Round Dance: The Gamble," the margin shifts provide an open breathing, a cascade of again nocturnal spacetime actions as playing "cards fall" and as prediction or chance tunes the attentions until, in the last sentence, "The moon fights her own way up, the sky." A sentence which characterizes the attention in these poems when the comma-ed gap between "way up" and "the sky" provides a breath, but also a hesitant addition to the meaning from the assurance that "The moon fights her own way up' to the internal check, fights its way up what, yes: 'up,' 'the sky.'"

In "Round Dance: Haruspex," the stanzas are tighter and the margin shifts are used to focus on different spacetime attentions to the "unmerited." The reader is again taken by attentions to birds from the page "this as log-book" to "the skypath," from "I had written" to "a river" to attention to the poetic task "prepositional" and "metaphor" back to and from the title's attention to the speculative, the omenic.

In the two-page "Round Dance: Oracle" the speculative is addressed full faced beginning with "Delphos" and attention to the body & vulva and, on page two, "is the oracle virginal, self sybil priestess a, virgin?"

In the same year Robert Kelly innovates his field composition into a multiple form with *Enstasy* (1964) in which the column-like shape of the first twenty-two lines of text break out into prose for twenty lines, then a tightened central margined column for four lines and back into prose for a further twenty lines and then again column form against the lefthand margin for twenty lines of poetry until prose again for twenty-seven lines and a conclusion of twelve columned lines against the left hand margin.

In the same year (1964), *Lunes* (printed with *Sightings* by Jerome Rothenberg) was published. The verse uses a conventional design of three-line stanzas, using a lefthand margin, each stanza separated by a pronounced forward stroke mark.

Two years later in *Weeks* (1966) he again composes with a range of margins, cascading down from the end of one line in a typewriter form, and then returning to the margin, or carrying the next line on for a further cascade down and to the right. Occasionally, as at poem 3, there is an interruptive central column with eight short lines in two stanzas, or at poem 20, a column in the left margin of one and two word lines for ten lines. By poem 148 this field complex has become a considerable play with the poetic energy. Starting with the left margin, "The architecture of series," breaks down into a parenthetical two line hang from the line edge and then back to the margin to let the poem cascade to and then away from the left margin as it descends and concludes with a central column.

1967 saw the publication of *Devotions* (1967). The book is a selection of ten poems from a series numbered to (in this publication) XIX. They are printed from a typed copy (with additions of calligraphic lettering on pages 5 (two words in old Neuhochdeutsch), on 9 in enlarged italicized Greek, on 19 and 20 in near-type size Greek. The decision about margins varies. In the "Preface" a range of margin tabs are used and these are used with a consistency within each of the two stanza groups. In the last line of the first there is a gap between "devoted" and "from earth" which permits the preceding line "air fire water" to act as a kind of plug to the gap below.

In the first poem there is one indent of a brief stanza, but the poems (I, II, III & V [IV is not present]) are mainly drawn from the left margin. Then at VII (which follows V) the text opens again, beginning with a subheading. The mode is that of left margin with eleven indents at a range of different margins over 54 lines. At XII (which follows X [XI is absent]) a quotation of underlined text is wholly indented and later a parenthetic section is wholly indented. XII is followed by XIV which begins with a two or three word column, then longer lines partly from the left margin and picking up the column again for single Proper names in the next section. The following XVIII mainly uses the left margin with occasional indents. XIX uses the shifting method of leads from the left margin interrupted with indents that often line up vertically, but sometimes do not.

In this last poem the spacing couples to its devotion to listening and touching, to his lover and clothing and to the music he is hearing, the word "made" dropped down from the end of line 45 is then repeated back at the left margin on the next line, encouraging a change of emphasis in the word "made" which in the following line is then rhymed with "Getting laid."

In the same year *Axon Dendron Tree* (1967) appeared. The poem had been written the previous September. It is designed into long 295mm columns, usually no more than two, three, or four words per line. The field here is a vertical insistence, a Yggdrasil. The following substantive work was *Finding the Measure* from Black Sparrow Press and was the first general selection of poetry after *Her Body Against Time*. The work was written 1965–66, with an added 1967 prefix. The poem "Rivermarks" makes the device of shifting margins and approximation or notion of the physical world, where the phrase "waves against the shore" is shifted to the right and the phrase "vectors of a common motion" is centred. In the following "Of Earth" the phrase shift has more to do with a graphic indication and thus shift in language source and proposal. The phrase "Muskingum level, but the rains—" from the lefthand margin in line 3 is set before an indentation at line 4: "there are Jews trapped by levees." The phrase shifts also accentuate thought shifts and conjectures. In part (5) this shifting is made manifest and a detailed account might help. Line 1 indented to a centre margin begins, "But men do anything," then continued from the lefthand margin, "in the heat of it, heat of their flesh in the place" and then back to the centred margin for the next line, "earth takes them in." Line 4 in italics introduces a kind a grisaille or reverant, from the lefthand margin "*& paint their women, who have a bitter laugh,*" which is continued at line 5 from a centred margin, "*no one but women*" continued in line 6 from the lefthand with "*can laugh that way* at what has become of them," followed in line 7 with a thought shift, indented to the centred margin, "at what we have done to the earth." and then a further indentation with line 8 the emphatic, "On earth."

Line 9 begins from the centred margin, "This was the day" and in line 10 from the lefthand, "I learned to scoff at women's wisdom. Was it" and then line 11, from the extended indent, "a good day?" leading abruptly to line 12 from the lefthand, "since they hold the earth in mistaken hands," and concluding in line 13 from the centre, "intuit what is to come." (1968: 22)

"To the Memory of Giordano Bruno" (1968: 27) is set in two columns, the first using a lefthand margin, headed 'They say:' and the second, using a righthand margin, headed 'Angels answer' is in reversed type.

In 1968 *Sonnets* appeared; they display an array of lines. In "Sonnet 1," the first line begins fourteen en-spaces in from the lefthand margin, the second line begins flush with the lefthand margin and then drops at the end of the first phrase, to form line 3 and then line 4 returns to the lefthand margin. The form is redolent of *The Opening of the Field* by Robert Duncan,[111] but in fact has a differently ordered appearance. Lines 18, 19, and 20 are all flush left and then aspects of the earlier facture recur. Similar display facture is used throughout the eighteen sonnets. Because these are named "Sonnets" the reader is also alerted to the regular line count. All eighteen of the sonnets have fourteen lines flushed to the lefthand margin with other lines shifted into the page away from the margin. For example in "Sonnet 18, for Nerval, *le pendu*," three of the lines are in fact part of the lines they precede or follow. A quotation of the whole sonnet may make clear the proprioception of the activity.

> When they look they'll find it beautiful
> if they find it at all, a hand
> not getting any older, holding a weight
> as a woman would hold a sword
> tipping her hand to the power in it.
>   The cut.
> Weight that a man could balance on a leaf
> & still believe:
>   that much music was left in him.
> He started when he could. All the mythology
> weighed him also down.
>   Fell & the grass was cool,
> felt wet after the stone sky, intimate & free.
> Which is all he could ever have wanted to become,
> month after month all the way into evening,
> stayd there forever & lifted the weight of the hand
> he's found beneath him, a skin he always knew.

The shift from "a hand" in line two to "not getting older, holding a weight" in line 3 allows an unstated parenthesis "not getting older" and also rimes from "'older" into "holding" and then, at the edge of the line, "a weight," followed by another parenthetical "as a woman would hold a sword," with rimes of woman and would, would and hold, hold and sword. Then, at the end of line five, a drop to "The cut." & "Weight" begins the next line,

---

111. Robert Duncan, *The Opening of the Field* (1960).

which prepares the reader for "All the mythology / weighted him also down." This line end then drops to "Fell…" and then "felt" leading toward lines thirteen and fourteen, "lifted the weight of the hand, / he'd found beneath him, a skin he always knew." The proprioceptive shift is from expectation to surprise, from disconnection to riming connection, as if the facture had taken place in the process of a quiet dance.

Like *Sonnets*, *Songs I–XXX* uses long lines with drops from phrase edges onto a new margin. The work also makes use of the full stop bracketed in em-spaces that are not syntactic stops but are breaths, which recalls Duncan's use of this timed punctuation in his early *PASSAGES* from the 1960s.[112] For example in Robert Kelly's "Song XIV":

> …
> a process (for Kenneth Anger) of going
>   where you want to go
> & make the world . be there when you come
>   . a process
> (for Edward Kelly) of living your blood to the end & dying
>   with no
> comfort.
>   Behind any light there is light behind any color there is…
>   (1968: 43)

The following year, *The Common Shore* appeared, also from Black Sparrow. Books I–VI of *The common shore, a long poem about America in time,* celebrate field composition; the array evident in so much of Duncan's *Passages* and Olson's *Maximus*. The array is displayed throughout the books of *The Common Shore*, with poignant interludes or sections of single margined texts at page 32 (in book I), pages 71 & 72, and then on 74 and 75 (in book III) and almost entirely from 111 to 115 (in book IV) and again almost entirely from 154 until 157 and at 163 and 174 (in book V). The single margined text is also an integrated element such as the column of short phrases and words on 21 and 22, 27 and 28.

---

112. Collected in Robert Duncan, *Bending the Bow* (1971). For example in *Passages 1–5* on pages 9, 10, 12, 14, 15, 16, 17, 18, and so forth.

On page 64 in book III, the graphic emphasis is further signaled with the poem *"These images once incised"* which begins at an indent 'Every order of being' and then a double line space to line 2 from the lefthand, "an ancient name-of-itself," followed by two columns of identical text,

> a picture
> of a king
> on a horse
> holding a
> woman"

and so forth.

On page 97 in book IV, an aspect of the collage method combines with field composition. The top third of the page is set in three columns; the first or lefthand column uses a single line space & makes a number list from 1 to 4 under the heading "the few data:."

The second and third columns are headed by the word "PLEIS-TOCENE" and both columns use a centred justification, also both use a variety of lists. This first third of the page is followed by a centred paragraph of prose and this is followed in the last third by a poem using field composition over onto the following page. The whole effect anticipates the extraordinary book of collage and field composition *In Time*, that was to follow in 1971 and which develops some of the material in *The Common Shore*.

In the same year Nick Kimberley published *A California Journal*. The April 1969 poems set out from the left margin until on page sixteen with the poem "17 April 69 — Cuidad Juarez ..." (date of the poet's wedding), the lines begin to shift away from the left margin. On page seventeen the words in a displaced prose block form a bronze plaque in a waiting room. On page nineteen the whole page of prose is framed in a thin black line. "This is a darkness round a wedding, that wagering of ourselves before the civil powers..." Page twenty returns to California and, in the main, left-hand margins, with a few exceptions.

Kali Yuga, also written in 1969, followed in 1970. It is a considerable collection with a number of different field activities. Two examples take on a new departure with columned repetition. In "Running Eyes" a separated block of words is set between horizontal lines.

    Signing my name with a chisel
    I hear the blackbird
    trapped in the stone

          let
          let me
          let me
          out
of your stupid doctrine

---

and in the seventh section of "Pronunciation of an Unvowelled Text," "(to the memory of Jack Spicer),"

    ghost holes
    overtone
    from anguish of
    (in death the)
    phoneme,
    echoic
        (ghost)

    trace of a
    ——————— truth ———————

       true   false
       true   false
       true   false
       true

          he pulled the zipper
          the bird
          flew

In Time is the book which follows in 1971. It is usually listed as a book of prose, but the work is full of poetry and field composition. Most in particular, a central section, a double page numbered 34, is a field-map, a map in the mode of Charles Olson's *A Curriculum of the Soul* and texts like

A Bibliography on America for Ed Dorn of 1964 and *Proprioception* of 1965. In Robert Kelly the field purpose carries a similar testing energy, an enquiry and a set of propositions. The array has five columns, linked by signage, brackets, directional arrowed lines, underlinings, large-scale letter headings. Like Olson, the scopes are large, from mythologic Greek to the European Renaissance. From *Gilgamesh* and the Bible to Pindar, Sappho, Chaucer, Blake, to G. Stein and Ezra Pound.

Page 35 begins to set out the a basis for facture:

1) An age of analysis has ended.
2) the concept of form is a barrier to experience. This buffer must be destroyed.
3) Beyond form is the experience of complexity.
4) In Euroamerican society, the poet is financially & socially impoverished because of the prevalence of the idea that poetry is numinous...

Toward the end of the book a set of poems titled "Labrys: Twelve Matters." On the last page (all by itself), we read: "Language is space" dated 10.XII.70.

The last section could turn through two substantial volumes that precede *The Loom*, these are *Flesh Dream Book* and *The Mill of Particulars*.

5. Some Extrapolations.

What the idea of field proposes or provides for is a new practice in poetic facture. In its origins in the coherence of energy, in terms of pattern, order, and disruption, the concept encourages metonymic as much as metaphoric rhetoricity, that is rhetoricity that both stands for the energy and is metaphoric of the energy that it promotes. Robert Kelly's stance, which on one level may be characterized as "flesh, dream, book," is enhanced by his shifts between conventional layouts and field compositions. This is in part a new emphasis on eye sight within the poetic presentation, in English from left to right, which quickens as the line progresses and is given a quick return at the line end to the left-hand margin, is now given a new speed in the line break that drops to an indented line that changes the breath and potentially changes the nuances of the meaning. The syntactic break and shift from linear reading has an effect on the proprioceptive engagement, an effect that makes possible a new range of artifice. In a poetic facture that makes a demand on a large range of attentions, combining as it often proposes to, an array of engagements that, in Robert Kelly's vocabulary, include the physicality of the facture, the attention to language and philology and sometimes extensive artistic and esoteric knowledge, all connected to the publication of the poetry and its page design.

Each page in the work of Robert Kelly is potentially a field for a new attention to facture, both proprioceptively informed, in its articulation of breath and dance, and in the complex dialectic of experience and invention, of learning and play with language. The book provides a series or set of fields; it provides the opportunity to facture a focused array of patterns as well as the opportunity to connect a variety of fields. The articulation of the poetry engineered on the page, in the field, is identical to the field that energizes the facture. Reading the poetry across an array of fields is to experience an energetic transfer, of learning, invention, and engagement. The gift of that transfer to the reader is made possible through the articulation of the field, the field that makes the necessary æsthetic reception possible. It is the gathering of facture and reception that defines each book, each field encounter, and provides on each occasion, a different work of art.

March 2014

THREADS 20: ROBERT SAYS

TMR: So, to end on a more serious matter: if we find ourselves at a dinner party with Robert Kelly, what can we expect?

RK: He'd sit, eating placidly, somewhat indifferent to his food, till the cheese plate arrived. Unless of course lamb was on the menu, or Korean beef, or cod or hake or haddock... Then local enthusiasm. He would hope for good coffee, and usually be disappointed. But he bears such trials since at home he's been drinking it all day. So he can endure the meek industrial brown fluid that they'll serve him even in otherwise conscientious places. He will complain about the coffee, if the meal is in a restaurant, and it will be the only complaint he permits himself. Food is food, but coffee is a friend.

And so is tea. In fact, you'd be much more likely to find yourself with him and his wife at teatime, which strikes them as the best meal for meeting — strong tea (Darjeeling, Assam, or Upton's Scottish) and two kinds of cake. He likes seeing people in daylight, at the end of the day, nibbling and talking, so the food doesn't get in the way of the talk.

All through any meal, though, he'd talk a lot, incessantly, unless he can coax you into talking. He loves people who run the mouth, as we say, because then he can listen — listen to their words and think about their meanings (physical, mental, spiritual) and what they truly want, their Lacanian désir usually so ill-expressed by their conscious statements, and listen also to his own words rabbiting around inside him, answering them in himself and also answering themselves. A concert of voices it is to hear a person speak. He loves that. Yet he has this habit of deliberately taking people at their word. It's the safest thing to do, if not very adventurous. It is impolite to answer their désir when they're talking of something they think different, and seldom will he do so, unless moved by his own.

Dinner party, you say. Well, he'd try not to be there. Dinner is a sacrament, not a scrimmage. Best is a dinner of two, three, or four. Any more than that and angels would need to work hard to keep his interest. He'll either orate, arm raised and spectacles gleaming, or else sulk & think about far off things.

He has certain eccentricities. He doesn't drink alcohol, which makes him a deaths-head at the feast. He dislikes water unless it's carbonated — pétillante, say the naughty French. He doesn't like leaving wherever he is, so he will sit a long time at table, wearing out his interlocutors, and the poor waitress already late for her date.

What will he talk about? He'll talk about you. "Whoever you are," in Whitman's great tell-tale phrase. Despite the evidence of the endless pages of which these must be close to the last, he will not talk about himself. He will try to move the subject into your area of expertise, to learn. He will often lecture excitedly on theories that came just that second into his head in response to something you said. In response. Everything good that ever comes into his head comes in response. Thank you, he'll always be saying thank you. Thank you for asking. Thank you for making something happen in his head.

in conversation with
Simone dos Anjos and Pietro Aman
The Modern Review (2006)

8.
A BOOK ON HOW TO READ

PIERRE JORIS

A PRIMER FOR THE GRADUAL UNDERSTANDING
OF ROBERT KELLY

1. ENTRANCES [113]

(MARCH 1969, ANNANDALE-ON HUDSON VIA:
NEW YORK CITY / LUXEMBOURG / PARIS TO:
JANUARY 1974, LONDON, ENGLAND)

"It may be that every man is set upon the earth to find one new method of divination, that is, to write one sentence whose syntax is total. Because (this idea is familiar) syntax is the heart of divination, to locate the function of a thing in the structure of process. We must remember that. Who are we?"

In my notebook, on the page facing this quote from Kelly's "Alchemical Journal," (*IO* Alchemy issue #4, summer 1967) are the following lines by Robert Duncan, a juxtaposition that happened by 'chance' & makes sense:

"And this poetry, the ever forming of bodies in language in which breath moves, is a field of ensouling, Each line, intensely, a soul thing, a contribution; a locality of the living."

*

(Interpolation / the story so far:
                      I first met Robert Kelly & his work while studying at Bard College in the late 60s. I was then quite unable and unwilling to come to terms with Kelly's poetry. My own vision of the poet & the poet's concerns was still to a large extent caught up in that

---

113. All quotes, except where otherwise indicated, are from the work of R.K.

familiar European vision of the *poète maudit* à la Rimbaud, Nerval, Ducasse, etc. Thus anything related in any way to the 'academic' was suspicious. I was aware that the best energies in the field were in America, having been turned on to American writing by the work of Ginsberg, Kaufman, Snyder & Burroughs — the only modern Americans somewhat available in Europe at that time, & here was Kelly, a poet involved at least as much with the European as with the American Renaissance. I had gone to the US to get rid of a heritage I had felt hanging around my neck like a millstone all my life.

& I was suspicious of what I saw as Kelly's 'style.' "(*Style is death*)." Sensed a kind of 'high style,' something close to 'discourse,' a mode I saw as a root-symptom of European sterility in matters of literature as well as politics and life in general. Saint-John Perse came to mind, & Perse is the end of something, not a beginning, l'ambassadeur, the high-priest, the psychopomp...)

"European whiteness is sepulchre to us & European consciousness a museum." (Gerrit Lansing)

((The one Modern European I love, then as now, is Paul Celan. For my thesis I decided to translate his book *Atemwende*, and it was suggested to me that Kelly would be the person suited to supervise that project. Earlier on I had made the decision not to get too close to Kelly: I saw myself as a comet, a yet unsolidified gaseous mass, happily hurtling through the new spaces that had just opened up to me: the American Space. Kelly was too massive a star, surrounded by a powerful magnetic field — if I let myself approach too closely, get too involved, I feared I would get caught, pulled in, lose the precarious fire of my comet & become a dead moon on a fixed orbit circling a sun I wasn't even convinced was a sun))

A man almost himself is conspicuous, a man fully himself becomes invisible."

((I was wrong, working with Kelly on the Celan translations turned out to be one of the most exciting & fruitful periods of my education. What first made me like R.K. was his immense curiosity, a basic sense of wonder he had kept intact at a time when 'coolness,' a blasé stance of disconnection, an arrogantly assumed negativity, was the order of the day.

The breadth of his concerns. His vision of the modern poet as a man to whom all data whatsoever are of use, like Pound, Goethe, Coleridge, because "they do not have hobbies they eat everything."))

> "... the fact
> that there can be (& at historical times
>   has been, now is)
> a scientist of holistic understanding,
> a scholar,
>   a scientist of the whole
> the Poet —
>   be aware that from *inside* comes
>   the poet, scientist of totality,
>   specifically,
>   to whom all data whatsoever are of use,
> world-scholar"

((This realization, and the joy that comes with it, finally enabled me on my return to Europe to begin dealing with, looking at, those European roots of mine I had so frantically tried to shake off by going to America. And found myself able to read and love Kelly's work.))

*

aug 30th, 1969, Luxembourg

"It does not matter
if you do not understand, I am unfolding
a necessary story, putting the blocks out clear on the floor,
whether you want to or not, you'll pick them up
when need sings."

* * *

October 73, London

What is needed now, for anybody coming to Kelly's work for the first time, is a way in. The massiveness of the published work to date — 32 or 3 volumes — demands it. There are, to my mind, two distinct possibilities to achieve this:

— an essay (not necessarily of the 'critical' species) laying out the main concerns that Kelly brings to his work. To name but a few:

Alchemy (Kelly's notion of the "Alchemical Work," his vision of that Process trans- & in-forming his writing/life day by day)

Woman (Here RK irritates at times; too much mytho-logizing going on.)

The Hermetic Tradition (the main directions thereof, & K's use of these. Here Frances Yates' works, especially *Giordano Bruno & The Hermetic Tradition*, were of use to me, as were Gerrit Lansing's instructions in his SET essays)

Geography
Geomancy
Narrative
Ecstasy & Enstasy
     etc.

Until such an essay is available (& it ought to be available now, my hope being that the occasion of this issue of VORT, which is providing the locus and motive for such a work, has been taken up by someone), a new reader in need of a fix on Kelly's aims & methods ought to look at the various <u>Prefixes</u>, (specifically those opening Finding the Measure, IN TIME, and THE MILL OF PARTICULARS)

> "*The organism*
> *of the macrocosm, the organism of language,*
> *the organism of I combine in ceaseless naturing*
> *to propagate a fourth,*
>   *the poem,*
>   *from their trinity."*
>
> ...
>
> "*Finding the Measure is finding*
> *the natural articulation of ideas.*
> ....
>   *is finding the*
> *specific music of the hour,*
>   *the synchronous*
> *consequence of the motion of the whole world."*
>
>   *

"Language is the only genetics."

*

"... language itself is the psychopomp, who leads the Individuality out of Eternity into the conditioned
  world of Time, a world that language makes by discussing it."

*

"Eterntity, which is always there, looms beyond
the grid of speech."

*

— the second possibility for a way into Kelly's work would consist in setting out those works that stand out as his most successful attempts, the books / poems / essays in which he manages to state his vision most accurately and accessibly. My own choices for such a list would include:

Finding the Measure (Kelly's best collection of short poems to date, notwithstanding some excellent poems in his latest book, *The Mill of Particulars*, such as the "van Eyck Workings").

In Time (A book I turn back to at least as often as necessary. Some of it does infuriate me, i.e. his takes on Rome, Empire, the Emperor... "All feofs, forts & taxes to the emperor"...) I do not care for the politics that result from those takes, but most of the essays are illuminating, especially:

Re The Occult
Identity Preference
Temple-Complex
The Dream Work
Re Snow Job
Labrys: Twelve Matters

Songs I–XXX (the pleasure I get from these perfectly succesful 'experiments in the extended lyric' grows with each rereading.
The Pastorals (lovely, lovely, music? & it's all there, compact, clearly laid out, *no-blame*.

Axon Dendron Tree (Kelly's most successful long poem. A difficult work, & maybe 'a grreate book.' Also, a book that ought to be reprinted and made available on a larger scale.

Cities (An enchanting tale / a narrative of enchantment, I read it traveling on a train between two great European cities, and the tale transformed the cities. My heart beat faster than usual as I stepped through the gate, having finished the tale.

Alchemical Journal (a clear account of one of the major processes behind Kelly's work, or better, behind, in front, around, through, in & above his work.

*

May this list provide the 'Entrances' of the title, or at least get the 'second possibility' I spoke of, going. All these notes offered, therefore, as a possible chapter in an impossible book to be called
'A PRIMER FOR THE GRADUAL UNDERSTANDING OF ROBERT KELLY.'

*

July 18th, 1969 / Luxembourg

"*in front
of the agony of any being
we are stupid mute,*

*what is important to each man
he never says,
never learns it till the light
walks out of the sky
& he is left
alone with his failed utterance
impossibly clear in the dark*

*write everything
the oracle said…*"

*

8 · A BOOK ON HOW TO READ

July 18, 1970 / New York City

this poem ("Last Light") right now, for me, Kelly's finest single poem — the bones laid out clear — no unnecessary weighing down by knowledge esoteric or other — that wisdom I think of as the highest form of wisdom: namely, that wisdom without action is sterility.

"What is not here

is nowhere"

*

"*The anguish of the Work is the discovery of the correspondances. Once they proclaim themselves, they never let the Philosopher rest.*"

*

"*Bother with no writer who will not stand by his words, to death if necessary. Trust only the literalist, Take the words of Our Lord literally, Any Lord.*"

*

"*It is at some point, not first nor last, the healing of metals, curing the leprosy of matter, restoring the elements to splendor. Syntax lends its magic (= substance). The things that are said that cannot (Aristotle) be thought. It is commonly the 'words' that are blamed, or 'language'. Yet language is the only system in which truth is stated, Logos, or understanding what's happening, or making it up.*"

*

"*To stick to the work like a fish to water.*"

*

"*Alchemy is the science of associating yourself with the 'movements' of time.*"

*

"Alchemy is the science of having silent dreams, of having no dreams."

*

"Alchemy is the science of becoming aware of the body of information to which we contribute, becoming aware of the whole project in which we are engaged."

*

"Alchemy is the science of being used. Alchemy is the science of use. Its name probably means the art of the black, & alludes in all likelihood not to the black soil of Egypt but to the black blankness of the unknown brain, the 'silent areas' in which the Operator, bent night & day over his fire, eventually kindles a Voice, one that guides him in the science of penetration, science of final separations."

*

Westende / Belgium

10/IV/73 Dream-Log entry:

There is a party going on in the living-room. I move through it & out of the crowd, I am standing at the bay window looking down into the night. Across the street wedged between two buildings a green square with trees. A man steps in front of the little square. The moon is full & gives enough light for me to see that the man is Kelly. I wonder if I should call down to him, but decide not to. He moves into the square. Suddenly he begins jumping around, zigzagging over the grassy area, then throws himself flat down on the grass where he begins to roll around randomly, I realize that he is tripping, & I wonder at that, knowing that Kelly never thought much of drugs. But he seems to be having a great time & I can't help laughing out loud when I realize that he is wearing a black leather motorcycle outfit.

2/IV/73

Dreamed that I was walking around New York City, I know I was in Manhattan, because I had just come out of a bar I used to hang out on the West Side of town, but the place looked more like Brooklyn:

it felt seedier, older, and a great number of blocks had been torn down making the place feel like the east end of London after the Blitz. Then I noticed Kelly dancing in giant leaps across these ruins, jumping over huge boulders, cracking huge chunks of plaster with each step. It was late afternoon & the sun was closing in on the horizon. Suddenly Kelly stopped his dance & began running toward the setting sun along an avenue miraculously cleared of debris.

august 1973, London

from: <u>THE COMMENTARIES</u> (VIII)

Damn it,
RK,
I'm gonna
put an
axe
to your tree
— one of these
dreams —
last night
& the night before
you sat there
solid dream flesh
stolid image
extolling
till I fell asleep
in my own dream
& woke up
to the full moon
of an empty night
with nothing left
to do but read
you re dreams
the work of it
while waiting
for today's
penumbral
eclipse.

*

"...there is nothing of our own which may not become foreign to us; and nothing foreign to us which may not become our own..."
Giordano Bruno, *Cena de le Ceneri*

"the form of the poem must be our habit"
Gerrit Lansing

"The dreams that matter are the dreams remembered of themselves."

*

"We must now assert the autonomy of dream as ARTIFACT, legitimate product of psychic event, not record of it."

*

"Passer des mots aux idées il n'y a qu'un pas." (Comte de Lautréamont)

*

"There is no 'form' without the in-formation." (Ed Dorn)

*

"The poem takes form from its words, as love takes form from its acts, an imaginary conclusion. Of acts or of words A total vision. Exceeding the sensible." (Robert Duncan)

*

from : Journals / January 1973 / London

For a long time I waited for a poem of Kelly's to come along & hit me straight, full-blast, work me over. THE PASTORALS does just that; I hadn't expected it when I saw that the poem was "Book Seven of The Common Shore," as the first six books of *The Common Shore* had by & large seemed unsuccessful or at best uneven. But *The Pastorals* holds, &

clears up several points on which I had been doubtful, viz. my suspicions re politics, that 'empire' crap in *In Time* like, "The Emperor responds, We are here. The lot of us make the empire," wch is not accurate history, though it cld be mediocre semantics. "We" does not equal the lot of us, but is singular. The royal (or imperial) *we* is the arrogance of those who claim to be where they are by 'divine right' or similar abuses. "The lot of us make the empire" becomes / is the equivalent of "l'état c'est moi."

 OK, Kelly is right to put the finger on Gibbon, & show him up for the sterility and prudishness of his approach, & he's right to point out that 'decline' can also mean "to develop, to be possessed of qualities, possible gestures of freedom & responsibility, lacking in the original contract invented by historians for every state." That equation of decline — decadence — decomposition with a newly gained fertility does make sense — up to a point. & we do know that "imperial history is commonly written by such as hate the emperor," (&, it is my guess, they had damn good reasons to hate the emperor) but this does not permit the conclusion that the empire was vastly superior to the republic. ((Or is this just my own reaction, as a man raised in a country ruled over by a 'constitutional monarch,' & at present living in a country which still thinks of itself as an empire, feeling the presence of 'empire' like a man will 'feel' his legs or arms, days, weeks, or even years after they have been amputated. Though I was born in la France, on, haha, le quatorze juillet! ... or/and vice-versa, Kelly, son of the grreate republik is here 'romanticizing' about empire?...

 I dunno... But reading the PASTORALS today, has convinced me I misread him. Or that at least Kelly was imprecise & opaque on these matters in *In Time*.

> *"We want*
> *the whole body to erect, body politic,*
> *we want a revolution, a social erection*
>
> *to fuck the obscurity of life on earth,*
> *to burn up money..."*

 I never thought you would come out & say it so, Robert! So loud & clear, this time around, the literal man, the one you say is the only one we may trust! The poem has made my day.

*"Since work is passion, & passion being
serious about the world."*

*

*"Use is rarer than emerald, Use is never thought.
How to use our intelligent skin or make a song
or hear one, & how to use that? He has the tools
but lacks the skill, & skill is the habit of use
made perfect."*

*

*"The rest is politics, how to own & not to use.
The Greeks were bad at it but learned from Rome:
idleness is the end of work: that's their motto*

& no one lies down to love at all."

*

*"Sex (herself) would be our instruction , , ,
Sex is the only encyclopedia , . ."*

*

To you, then, Robert of Annandale, this curve thrown from London to America, the oldest country of all, with the hope that others too may make use of what you have laid out, so clearly, & make yr vision of the "scientist of the whole" the source of the Commonwealth.

*"But love does not want always to be spoken of. It
rests secure in the passing of time, speaks in nights
& days, is its own journal & night-book."*

London, 14 January 1974.

2. On Robert Kelly's *Red Actions* (BSP 1995)

There is a more or less fastidious ritual most poets submit to at one or the other time in their career. It's called doing the "Selected Poems," & can be initiated by either the poet or the editor/publisher & performed by either of these or a third participant/officiant. The reasons for this public ritual are manyfold: to make available poems from long out of print books & chapbooks; to present a "greatest hits" catalogue; to assess the trajectory & development of the work; to create an overview of a large opus; to bring out an economically viable or even successful book (thus banking on that American preference for the "digest" supposedly allowing in- & di-gestion of a given work in "handy" bite-sized form); to lay claim to status of poet or importance of the work, etc.

Robert Kelly waited a long time before submitting to this ritual, probably because he has always been more interested in the writing underhand, the poem to be written today, than in past achievement. A massive achievement it is, as chronicled in *Red Actions, Selected Poems 1960–1993*, a book spanning 33 years of work, a Christic or Dantean number to be sure. For anyone acquainted with Kelly's work, the concept of a *summa poetica* is a tantalizing idea but also a seeming impossibility; for anyone unacquainted with the breadth of the work, it is a seeming necessity. Thinking about such a book immediately suggests two major hurdles that need to be overcome for the project to succeed.

First, there is Kelly's early decision to "write everything," to write every day, which gives a certain processual shape of continuity to the work, suggesting or even demanding a reading of that order — i.e. an extensive reading in order to get to the true intensity of the life-work. The counter argument is clear: the individual books he has published over the years are in fact already selections from the much vaster store of daily work, & thus his own publishing practice gives him — & us — permission to take a *Selected* at (some kind of) face value. But the question remains: does this two-fold distillation give us the final, refined, pure extract, or does it just shake off the "dirt dangling from the roots" & thus falsify the essential process? The problem, starkly specific to this poet's output: how to select from 50 volumes behind which stand thousands of pages of (unpublished) work? I'm not exaggerating: in 1982, Jed Rasula estimated that the total published output up to that time came to some 3000 pages of poetry (not to mention some 750 pages of prose publications).

This work is culled from what Rasula estimates "conservatively" to be, for the same period, some 30,000 pages of typescript poetry! Nor is there a hint that in the ensuing 15 years this level of production faltered in any way thus suggesting that the 400 pages of this *Selected* were culled from some 40,000 pages of writing. Considering such an order of magnitude, does the aim of a *Selected*, which is always bound to play on some notion of "representativeness," stand any chance of being fulfilled?

Secondly: A *Selected* is most viable if the core of the poet's work consists of short, more or less independent lyrical poems, from which he or she is willing/can cull the best exempla (A method based essentially — as it is also with Norton type anthologies — on the "masterpiece.") But in Kelly's case, not only is there an implicit rejection — as in most other of the major "post"-modern poets — of the concept of the masterpiece, but also a sense that the long poem is essential to Kelly's endeavor. How can one deal with poems that are processes of several hundred pages in the context of a *Selected*?

Given these *caveats*, what then of *Red Actions: Selected Poems 1960–1993*? Giddy from juggling these figures while roaming through the book, culinary metaphors came to mind first: No, it's not a smorgasbord, in the use of that term to describe a confused & confusing medley of things; it would rather suggest an *antipasto*, hors d'œuvres (out-takes of the work; a manifold of appetizers, all selected from the full menu of possibilities). Better yet one could consider it as a "menu de dégustation," the chef's own choice, where the client submits & the chef shows his dexterity & art, presenting a vast meal including numerous small-portion versions of the full menu categories: hors d'œuvres, entrées, & *postres*. But these metaphors won't do either: poetry is not just food for the *intelletto*, though it be that too, but something else than a consumable quantity of which you partake till your appetite is sated. "A poem," Kelly says in a text not reproduced in this book, "any poem, is a deed for writer and reader alike. It is a shared dromenon, a workspace of more than mental and more than emotional activity: the movements of the eye, guided and inhibited by syntax, by space, by the look of silence, commit our bodies also to apprehension, the great alignment."

The poem, & by extension the whole field of the work, as a process of alignment, i.e. as orientation. And this book too, is best seen as such a possible sense of orientation — for the reader here, new to, or only partially acquainted with, that work. In 74, already suspecting that the massiveness of the work demanded some such orientating model, I had suggested the necessity for what I then called "A Primer for the Gradual Understanding of Robert Kelly." *Red Actions* can, I believe, best be seen as such an introduction or orientation.

The construction of the book is relatively straightforward. Kelly proceeds chronologically, selecting poems from his already published books from *Armed Descent* (1961) to *A Strange Market* (1992), while appending a 65-page selection of poems from 1991 to 1993. The only titles not represented here are *Enstasy, Weeks, A California Journal*, and the most recent *Mont Blanc*. He includes the seminal poems "The Alchemist," "Hui-neng Chops Bamboo," and "In June" collected in the Rasula-edited *The Alchemist to Mercury* (1981) & here restored to their original chronological order. The latter book remains an indispensable "alternate opus" to be read next to *Red Actions*, especially as it provides a range of middle-length poems or series of poems the inclusion of which would have made the present selection too unwieldy. Kelly further provides a useful ten-page section of "Devotions & Permissions," i.e. notes on some of the included poems.

The book is thus not the easy temptation it could have been, i.e. a *Selected Shorter Poems*, but rather an attempt to show the whole breadth of the œuvre by including selections from the long poems, most importantly from the long out of print *Axon Dendron Tree* (1967), and from what may be his finest achievement to date in that mode, *The Loom* (1975). Such inclusiveness arises from Kelly's willingness to present poems by partial selections only — & not just in the (obvious) case of the long poems but also in that of the shorter ones. The two sections of *The Loom* presented are in fact parts of parts: 3 pages from the 22-page 3rd section & 4 from the 7-page 12th section. And yet Kelly manages in those two short outtakes to present the two crucial aspects, what I consider the propelling tensions of the book: the transformative narrative of image, & the prospective-reflective meditation on formal concerns regarding both poem & life, thus clarifying the poem's intention & enabling a reading of the whole less likely to lose itself in the work's sheer overwhelming richness. Middle-length works are either shortened (thus "The Book of Hagar," here renamed "The Book of the Running Woman" from *Flesh Dream Book*, is reduced to its first two sections) or given whole, as is the case for "A Constant Telling of the Father and His Widdershins" from the same volume.

Kelly's concerns have not wavered over time, & his comment on the title of the just cited 1971 collection still holds, setting "the priorities straight," as he puts it: "The title *Flesh Dream Book* identifies the three great sources of human information: the flesh of sensory experience, dream & vision, & the holy book of tradition and learning, shared through time." This steadfastness of concerns has taken on a myriad shapes over & in time, and one of the successes of *Red Actions* is how the book makes the reader aware of these formal experiments, from the sharp image-based ("deep image," is how he & a few others talked about it back then) 13 syllable (a five-three-five pattern) *Lunes* to the highly complex informational mappings of later poems such as — to mention but one among many — "Man Sleeping." Or the different shape & feel of those poems arising from what elsewhere he has called a "ta'wil of the first line," for example the poem starting on page 344, arising from its title, the Tibetan character (the last of that alphabet) pronounced [AH], as against, say, "Sentence," his experiment with polysyntax, "the permission to take any or every word or phrase as linkable to what comes before, or to what comes after, or as capable of bearing meaning while standing alone."

Although the work's vastness & its constant return to those basic themes — love, vision, & language — is likely to hide this variety of means somewhat, Kelly, like others of his generation — Mac Low, Rothenberg or Antin, say, and more so than poets like Ashbery or Eshleman — has been an endlessly fertile formal innovator and experimenter. The book accurately maps these investigations & while there is no introduction to ease the inexperienced reader's difficulties, there are enough programmatic poems in the book for the reader to gain access to Kelly's poetics, with foremost among these "Prefix: Finding the Measure," "Against the Code," "Sonata in A-flat: The Essay on Form" from *The Loom*, and "Ode to Language."

Let me also say the pleasure I hope *Red Actions* will be for those who through this book will come to discover an *œuvre* without which the second half of this century would lack the American shape & depth it does have. May the book also have the effect all good *Selected Poems* should have, namely to send readers back to the books from which these selections are culled — or, pious hope, forward to some Pléiade-like *Collected Œuvres*, in as many volumes as it will take to get it all down.

8 · A BOOK ON HOW TO READ

3. On *the flowers of unceasing coincidence* (1988)

1. Here is a book of poems — or one long poem-sequence made up of 672 numbered chunks — you can enter anywhere. The coincidence turns out to be unceasing enjoyment, the movement — nomadic — that belies the linearity of number: this book is multidirectional at all points. Which makes for strange flowers: neither head nor tail, I mean this is not a stem-root-flower flower, the old botanical tree image as mimetic paradigm/alibi of human shape & act (hubris of Leonardo's renaissance male centrally inscribed in a circular cosmos).

2. & thus the book also proposes a disruption of our reading habits. No way to pull the petals one by one and murmur oh muse she understands me she understands me not or a little or very much. Can't eat this daisy by the roots. Meaning, that old conundrum, or at least any singular truth, always lies just beyond the horizon, a line of sight, a line of flight. But Kelly says as much clearly, leading us on & in: *don't make sense make difference* (7).

3. Beyond the horizon, or on it: tangential line of our laborious, straight minds touching the curved earth. Meaning as the spark of the meeting of what we imagine we think and what is. Meaning never more than this: sparks, shards of light, a breath held. You set out to find and what you find is:

> *world of soft grammaticals, fractals of typography*
> *cheating any horizon — geology of pure punctuation*
> *all you can hear is the gap singing* (327)

4. The book is full of flowers (*speed-well sweet-william saxifrage / little-sword chrysanthemum / I have said them before I will say them again / blue chicory New York aster lupine vetch* 197) which come to feel like the most solid entities when we encounter them at the turn of a verse (*me too little flower / as of roadside chicory* (228)). A solidity undermined by a Gertrude Steinian sense of play or play of sense playing between the thing & its name (*to know the name / of any flower is / to live in it* (265)).

312

5. The shape of the whole thing — if a botanical image has to be used — is that of the rhizome, i.e. a non-hierarchical space, a burrow where you, the reader, can go to earth, for as long or as little as you like. You can think of it as gnomic wisdom-shards (*language is the litmus of law / by it alone judge / the honor of thy State* (196)) or an epic bouquet of unheard-of flowers. But "flower" is a trope that names the trope of poetry, which brings to mind a book by Jean Paulhan, *The Flowers of Tarbes or, Terror in Literature* — but I will save that book for another time. Today, as the snow begins to fall, I'll keep the company of *the flowers of unceasing coincidence.*

4. FOR ROBERT, RE #95 OF HIS "CAPRICES"

> which has it:
> *"The priests say that's what*
> *purgatory's for,*
> *to end the game*
> *and settle up the score."*

I don't agree with the priests
purgatory's not
the end of the game,

in fact, purgatory's all
there is, heaven & hell
have fallen away or

never were, & we are
where we always were
& will be:

smack in the middle,
the in-between that is us
in the world

& the world in us,
misnamed by said priests, it is
what the poet Ibn Arabi called the

barzakh.

JENNIFER MOXLEY

CHARLOTTE'S CARDINAL:
SOME THOUGHTS ON ROBERT KELLY'S POETRY

My title refers to a bird that lives on Cuttyhunk Island, off the coast of Massachusetts, which happens also to be the location of a summer cottage that Robert Kelly and his wife Charlotte Mandell visit annually. Each year the cardinal returns to the cottage porch in search of seed. Over time the bird has come to trust Charlotte, to the point where he now eats from her open hand. Has Charlotte tamed the bird? Or has the bird tamed Charlotte? However we answer this question, it is an unforeseen relationship and a gentle coexistence — perhaps a bit like the one between Mandell and Kelly — if I may risk such an observation. I wanted to start my thoughts on Kelly's poetry with an account of this relationship, not only to conjure the Orphic tradition of Nature charmed, but also to evoke the image of a woman doing a simple, yet mysterious, thing: "everything that exists / is grounded in mystery and this mystery / holds your hand" (*May Day* (52)). The bird and Charlotte are each unique, apart, "other," if you prefer, though their communion does not *other* them. "From the first touch of you / I knew / I had the strength to be separate" (*The Loom* (34)). Bird and woman are separate. They share "neighboring solitudes," to use Rilke's term (*Letters* (150)). Their communion alters them. The bird must trust and the woman must sit perfectly still, like a statue or tree. In the stillness the cardinal's touch unfolds the woman's myriad selves.

> & each of us
> will only be alone,
> alone,
> in the incredible beauty
> of a multiplicity
> of different separate *ones* —
> to invent
> the plural of one, do you
> possibly understand me?   (*The Loom* (54))

"Possibly." It is such an interesting choice of words. Of course these lines are referring not to a woman and bird, but a woman and a man. A relationship which, in the linking of identity to sex and gender, many have come to believe impossible, or at very best compromised. *Vive la différence* is a bygone. If this is true, however, then why do lines like these feel counterintuitive, or at least dated, in their framing of this "difference": "Men & women / are different species / from different / places, join / a little / for their work on / earth" (*The Loom* (30)). Is it simply because we no longer feel comfortable when male writers articulate a difference between the sexes, having so long manipulated such rhetoric to their advantage? The current thinking proposes that it is only through narratives of *likeness* that we can come to know ourselves. What you know validated and reflected back. Experience confirmed. There is a lot of wisdom to this, especially for those who have been historically denied mimetic satisfaction. But the world is not only a mirror. Most are *unlike* ourselves — yet still we dream it *possible* that "you" can empathize with "me," and that a man and a woman can understand each other, can replace what Kelly calls "the complacent analyses / that pass for understanding / between the sexes" (*The Loom* (30)).

David Antin reminds us to steer clear of the term "understanding" (126–127). He suggests that we do not come to an understanding of one another, we *tune* to each other. This helpful corrective allows us to see that connecting to other people and to the larger environment does not come from an identity built on reflection (the perils of Narcissus). Rather, it is a matter of patterns and rhythm, of recognizing how discontent rises from *arrhythmia,* or to use a better word, free of the medical connotation, "*idiorrhythmie*" (Barthes 36 *et passim*). This is how we "join" together to do our "work." It is a question of resonance: "the image, after its first appearance as a dark sound, still lingers as a resonance."[114] Kelly's synesthetic logic baffles the word "image." Is it to dissuade us from thinking of the image as representation? "[N]ot only a vivid representation of sensory data but an evocation of depth" (Duncan, *The H.D. Book* (42)). The true poetic image does not reflect back but projects forward, it creates, to quote Duncan again, "the pulse of its own event" (42).

---

114. Kelly, "Notes on the Poetry of Deep Image," *Trobar* (1961).

Yet we still believe when we hear the word "image" that the poet will want us to *see something,* whether an "emotional complex" or imprint of the outer world upon our mind's eye. Modernist Imagist poems, influenced by the fashionable *Chinoiserie* and *Japonisme* of their time, succeed, like Japanese brush painting, as delicate scenes of visual intensity presented to us without commentary, their explanations await unlocking in the surrounding silence.

Kelly's poetry is not a poetry of image in this sense. We do find "the world" there, but rarely does it appear painterly or framed. What he allows us to "see," rather, falls loosely into the realm of abstraction: the movement and shaping of the mind as it abstracts (*abstrahere,* to draw away) from the particular, moves toward *cohesion* (*cohaerrere,* to cleave together), and *resonates* (resounds) past matter through present senses. What is documented in this motion is the poet's repeated intimation of a larger consciousness or cosmic whole, a kind of rhyme between the micro and macrocosm. This intercourse is perhaps best described by another writer with whom Kelly's work has a kinship, John Cowper Powys. The opening of Powys's novel *A Glastonbury Romance* is definitive: "one of those infinitesimal ripples in the creative silence of the First Cause which always occur when an exceptional stir of heightened consciousness agitates any living organism in this astronomical universe." Through the concert of this "living organism" with the centuries of "cultural matter" that have attempted to capture its "stir of heightened consciousness," in that moment when, Schleiermacher claims, "the object no longer dominates in any way, but rather is governed by thought and feeling," a poem resembling something akin to a small quadrant of an astronomical map comes into being (*Translation Studies Reader* (45)). Kelly describes this "rhyme," as I like to call it, in one of his many *artes poeticæ,* "Finding the Measure": "Finding the Measure is finding the / specific music of the hour, / the synchronous / consequence of the motion of the whole world" (*Red Actions* (80)).

Kelly's work is euhemeristic — for lack of a more precise term. It cannot be experienced, in the manner Michael Clune argues our time *insists* on reading literature, "as a reflection or extension of the actual" (146). Euhemerism is named for a Euhemerus, a writer from the 4th century BC who believed the Greek myths were based on actual historical events. We might cite the example of King Arthur in our mythic tradition.

H.D. is also euhemeristic. Eurydice is as real to her as is Helen, as is the evidence drawn from her own senses. The term is imprecise because I do not mean to say that these poets are engaged in a gloomy fact-finding mission to *prove* the historical existence of mythic or literary inventions — like those literalist digging up divers holy sites in search of the Grail — but that both embrace the pre-scientific mindset that sees in all of the written and oral record, imaginative and not, valid clues into a deeper knowledge of the mystery of life. H.D. and Kelly manage to make mythic figures *feel real,* as historically significant as any roman coin you could clamp between your teeth. When Kelly writes in "To Persephone," "tell her when you reach her house / how glibly she has been represented" the queen of the underworld ceases to be mere figure, or poetic window dressing (her function in so many poems) and becomes a real woman whose influence has been syphoned away by misrepresentation and disrespect (*The Convections* (119)). This is far closer to what we find in William Carlos Williams's *Kora in Hell* or *Spring and All* than in Duncan's use of myth, which, despite surface resemblances to Kelly's, tends to move in the other direction. Duncan's goddesses, his "Queen Under the Hill," are used as symbolic figures of his own psychic history, a private, occult mythos, rather than a public inheritance that any of us might draw from.

Kelly's poems connect the real to invention through *cohesion,* the second movement referred to above. He cleaves our sensual experience of the present to the rich mythic and literary archive bequeathed to us by the past so that the two resonate. The archive he prefers, though not exclusively, is that of Western antiquity and the Medieval period. Even names solidly associated with modernity fall into line: "Darwins, Freuds and quarks / just phases in Very Late Romanesque. / We breathe inside the imagery, we live / by images" (*Sainte-Terre* n.p.). The lovely way in which the word "to cleave" in English contains its own antonym will aid us in understanding this movement. When reading a Kelly poem often we find ourselves separated from the natural grain of the present (cleaved from our world) to be joined with the still living grain of the past (cleaved to it). This movement feels timeless, for, as Duncan, through Whitehead, never tires of reminding us, "the universe has only now in which to live" (*Selected* (12)).

It is the euhemeristic syncretism of Kelly's poetry that has earned it a reputation as erudite to the point of impenetrable difficulty, that same reputation for which Jed Rasula has no patience: "This is hogwash:

there are no difficulties Kelly inflicts which are not compounded in any of these other poets" — referring to Pound, Olson, Zukofsky, etc. (150). The risk of erudition in poems is that it can read as pretense or a needless display of "book learning," hampering the emotional immediacy of the poem. Kelly's poems do sometimes betray a tone of gentle schoolmaster, no doubt a residue of his Poundian inheritance, yet for the most part the learned references in Kelly's work are *not* gratuitous, but necessary elements used to breathe life into and illuminate the emotional depth of the poem. Given that today any reference can be cursorily traced in about one second through Internet search engines, no reader need feel locked out or put off because a poet mentions Kundry or Ariadne or Paracelsus. Kelly's religious, mythic, and literary vocabulary, while vast, is obsessive and repetitive. One read through *The Odyssey,* Ovid's *Metamorphoses,* Genesis, Exodus, the Gospels, Malory's *Morte D'Arthur,* Wolfram's *Parzival,* and Wagner's operatic response to it and you will be, for the most part, good to go.

But perhaps it is also a mistake, forgivable among scholars, to attempt to write or think holistically about Kelly's *œuvre*. It is my belief that this work can only be read *one poem at a time*: "The poem is only when it is. Only the going by right now" (*The Convections* (18)). In forcing it into one belief system, or in attempting to discover some grand notion of "structural apparatus" or underlying systemic knowledge we risk mistaking the impetus behind the work, and confusing its historical moment. Kelly's is not a modernist project in adherence to scientific formalisms or "experiment." This work was born in the post-war postmodern era during which such schemes had become rightly suspect. Rasula recognizes this, calling Kelly's work "ongoing but not summative, long eventually, but not striving after length" (133) and likening it to Duncan's *Passages* (though Duncan — perhaps made uncomfortable by identification or envy, or by the gimlet-eyed heterosexuality of the work, ungenerously said Kelly's poetry "bored" him ["Interview" 121]. I dare not speculate how many, striving to work their way through one of Duncan's books, haven't on occasion felt the allure of Morpheus). There are no systems in Kelly, at least not those we can ever hope to see in their totality. No matter now much we abstract ourselves, we cannot take in the whole lest we be taken in by it, deceived by the fiend of ideology. Instead, Kelly's poetry asks that we allow ourselves to be *taken in* from out of the cold desert of isolated self into something much more reassuring: the warmth of cosmic unknowing. I purposefully evoke the mystical tradition here in order to add a further distinction: even those who have experienced the "totality" through mystical vision cannot replicate that experience except through endless spirals of inadequate, if evocative, signs: small steps & intimations, something akin to poems.

As a poet of the quest Kelly is unsurpassed. His poems, from early to late, constantly evoke the long tradition of questing literature in the West. The English word *quest* comes from the Latin *quærere,* "to seek, to look for," but also "to ask, question, inquire." This is the double bind of Parsifal, the hero of the quest in the heterodox Christian Tradition. He must combine these two definitions in order to fulfill his quest. His name appears variously as Perceval (in Chrétien), Parzival (in Wolfram), and Parsifal (in Wagner) — Kelly prefers this latter spelling, which served as a title for a lengthy work of fiction he was writing in the 1990s. Parsifal is the young innocent who heads out into the world knowing and following nothing but his own desire — a disruptive desire that lives outside of the civil society's sense of right and wrong (if there's another kind of desire, "truly wot I never what it is" — as Malory would say). He initially fails in his quest because he does not question:

> The youth who had come there that night beheld this marvel and refrained from asking how this could be. He remembered the warning of the man who had made him a knight, he who had instructed and taught him to guard against speaking too much. The youth feared that if he asked a question, he would be taken for a peasant. He therefore asked nothing. (Chrétien (379))

The marvel he beholds is, of course, the ritual of the Grail and the Wounded Fisher King. Parsifal does not question because he is following the advice of the worthy or wise man Gornemant de Gohort (Chrétien), also called Gurnemanz (Wolfram; Wagner). He allows his education to override his compassion. Kelly's poetry often moves from the space of Parsifal's double bind to that of Gurnemanz's sage, if too restrictive, wisdom. His narrators and lyric subjects can take either role. They can wander in a space of wondrous confusion, and then suddenly display great wisdom. But in either case the quest and the question remain the drivers;

it is just a matter of *who* — lyric voice, narrative character — is placed in which role. This accounts for the disarming doubling effect of many Kelly poems: they can perform percipience dispensed with great confidence and then suddenly seem innocent and unknowing. They are peppered with questions. His 1975 epic *The Loom* is, arguably, *the* great quest book, but as late as 2006 Kelly, the 75-year-old innocent, can still ask, "When will my childhood end?" (*Sainte-Terre* n.p.).

From a formal perspective Kelly's actuation of "open field poetics" employs a narrative meandering indebted to questing literature and Medieval Romance, using episodic structure and encounter more often than apposition and juxtaposition. The figure of Ariadne, unraveling her thread through the labyrinth, is also an appropriate analog. Like Ariadne, Kelly knows intuitively (or is it through long reading?) how to guide us with his threads of syntax and grammar. One never finds formal devices or figures used as tricks in his poems, and even when he pressures his matter into predetermined forms, such as the five-line stanzas used in *Axon Dendron Tree,* the result *feels* organic and necessary. The work is earnest in its wonder, *foolish,* if you will, in the tradition of the Christian hero who baffles the militaristic Romans with his disinterest in politics & disregard for warcraft. His poems never cease to remind us that there are much more pressing things to attend to.

Kelly's publishing career spans 50 years, and the work of the sixties, while already well along its way to establishing his signature earnest tone, remains under the formal influence of his "company." I am thinking, for example, of the Creeleyesque lines in the 1965 book *Her Body Against Time* or Duncan-like gestures in the 1964 *Round Dances*. The work of the 1970s, notably *The Loom*, is brilliant, if occasionally marked by "period style." Unlike Ginsberg, or other poets who could never be of any time other than the one that produced them, Kelly is at his strongest when he eschews the jargon of his day. Colloquial outbreaks, such as the following from section eleven of *The Loom*, "because she was the first / pair of tits he saw," fall flat when placed beside his more typical use of literary, though not necessarily ornamental, diction. By the 1980s Kelly has freed himself of his elders, as well as most traces of period style, and begun to stretch out in the full comfort of his formidable skill at weaving narrative and metaphysical complexity. There is, at the heart of this lyric writer, a raconteur, a poet with a deep knowledge of the power of prose as well as its mechanics.

Women have a central role in questing literature. They play the role of prophetesses, guides, or disruptors (*femmes fatales*). There is a mythic trap to this, much documented and rightly objected to by feminist criticism, and which Kelly recognizes from early on:

> A woman who is herself
> steps up
>   from the murky shallow of the poem
> & on proud hips walks away
> from this & every
> mythology
> out into morning. (*The Loom* (66))

Yet in spite of these liberationist lines, if every woman mentioned in Kelly's poetic *œuvre* got up and walked out, little would be left for us to read. For this poet, who wrote with some degree of pride and scolding toward other men, "I'm never surprised at the wisdom of women" (*The Loom* (75)), women are central, real and mythic, desired and desirous, divine and mundane. As in the quest, they guide and baffle, but ultimately (and quite in contrast to the emotional frustration they cause, say, in a Creeley poem), they almost always serve as a catalyst for "meaning making," that is to say, they give the poet and the poem a "motive," to use Nicole Brossard's word for *what keeps a poet writing* (74–75).

It is beyond the purview of these notes to globally address the representation of women in Kelly's poems, so I'll limit myself to two striking instances. In the first woman, or the "feminine," exists and exerts itself *inside* the male body.[115] In the second, the poet identifies with or even inhabits the role of the mother.

---

115. Though I am choosing to go in another direction here, issues of masculine and feminine principles, as well as sexuality as a spiritual gate, can also be read through Carl Jung's thought, as well as various Eastern religions and practices. For those interested in these aspects of Kelly's poetry, Edward Schelb's article "The Charred Heart of Polyphemus: Tantric Ecstasy and Shamanic Violence in Robert Kelly's *The Loom*," may be a good place to start. Jed Rasula's article "Ten Different Fruits" is also very insightful on these issues.

These lines, from book two of *The Loom,* are typical. In this instance the internalized woman acts as muse:

> A voice from inside me
> I hear far away,
> up the canyon, over the mountain,
> over the ocean, Write Me,
> Write Me
> (a woman's voice then,
> that I attend her necessities,
> that female presence
> in me or of me
> that also I have found outside,
> anima mea) (*The Loom* (26))

In other parts of *The Loom,* the poet calls on Helen to destroy him, and Kore "beckons" to him as this far away voice (22; 124). In book 14, the male rejection of the internalized woman is shown to be at the root of men's violence against women, a sort of self-hatred driven outward: "A man who tortures women / is inaccurate; he is trying to beat the woman inside him ... I beat the woman to make me speak" (171). At times the "woman inside" is the man's conscience, soul, or heart, as Athena was for Zeus or Brunhilde for Wotan: "woman inside, my soul, / mi alma" (*The Loom* (190)). Kelly's complex thinking about the internalized female presence in man is most compellingly and revealingly represented through his use of the figure of Orpheus. In a poem from his 2005 collection *Lapis,* the Bacchantes stand in for "all the women of his life," and perform a brutal psychological tribunal with their "hands deep in him." The question is central to this disturbing poem — though he leaves out the actual punctuation mark: "how could women tear a man apart unless they had their hands deep in him" (108). This image of the woman inside the man is repeated in "The Ear of Orpheus," though in this instance it is Eurydice: "she died into him (I die into you) / her life is in him now (I live in you)" (*Lapis* (119)).

Kelly's interest in the role of the mother can be directly connected to, among other things, his preoccupation with questing literature. Mothers in questing literature, while key to the hero's formation, tend to be forgotten or neglected. They try and fail to protect their sons. Odysseus's absence is lethal to Anticlea, as is Parsifal's abandonment of Herzeloyde (heart's pain). These are mothers who die alone, and whose deaths are unwitnessed by absent sons. "Who can watch his mother die? I kept trying to understand, and there is so little to," Kelly writes in his notes to "Afterdeath" (*Red Actions* (396)).

Catholicism also provides a lens through which Kelly seeks and questions the deeper meaning and sensuality behind the mother. The focus in the Catholic narrative is, of course, on the relationship between mother and son. The divine father is absent, the human father irrelevant. He explores this theme in his "Marian Hymns": "alone / conceived / this fatherless Who / had to have, had / Reality for father / no realler really than She…" (*Red Actions* (120)). The Virgin as desired lover/mother is also the complex center of a species of erotic worship in book seventeen of *The Loom*: "let me come to your thighs, / dark nipples / that swell when any mouth / comes to your breast" (218). In "The Long March" the father is mentioned in the opening line as having "made me begin thinking in the body of my mother," but then is quickly forgotten as the poem follows the body of the mother which "carried me patiently," and "writhed" for "three days" to bring the narrator into the world.

In the opening book of *The Loom* the narrator, listening to Wagner's *Parsifal* on the radio, too loudly, and to the consternation of his lover, channels Kundry's complex maternal role: "linger / until I come / at the end of the world / to be healed in you, / in no one but you, / & I will be your mother" (18). We recall that in Wagner's opera, Kundry uses Parsifal's memory of his mother's love and body as a method of seduction: the quasi-maternal breast of the mature woman, offered to the pubescent boy, serves as the initiation into the pleasures of the flesh. Parsifal is saved from giving into his confused desire at the last minute by shouting out the name of the wounded king and father figure, "Amfortas!" Throughout his poetic output, Kelly repeatedly returns to the Grail quest in all its various forms, including Wagner's retelling of it. Yet paradoxically, he has no patience for these tried and true Grail themes of woman as sinful seductress, male chastity, or an exclusively male company represented by the "no girls allowed" policy of the Grail Knights: "I hate a place where I'm alone with men, / whether they're friends or not," he writes (*The Loom* (190)). Repeatedly Kelly fights against the hatred of Eros and severing of the sexes in the Christian tradition, most pointedly perhaps in

"Meditation on a Well-Known Phrase of St Augustine." The poem bemoans Augustine's turn against sexuality, which results in the desexualizing of Christianity as a whole. It asks, "O my Christ how did they blue you so / into an enemy of ecstasy," before drawing a moving scene of the would-be saint leaving the bed of his long-term lover and the mother of his child: "... The sadness of leaving her / he redistributed over the act of being inside her. / He built the Church of St Sorrow, the grief / was the last thing he remembered of the silk" (*Kill the Messenger* (129)).

The quest, the internal feminine in man, and the centrality of the mother, all contribute to the power of a poem from Kelly's 1992 volume, *A Strange Market,* titled "From the Resting Place of the Grail." Humankind's "stardust" origins, implied by the already quoted lines, "join / a little / for their work on / earth," return in full force as a man (first person speaker) and a woman (second person addressee) stand together at the legendary and mysterious Glastonbury Tor, supposed burial site of King Arthur and, as the title tells us, resting place of the Grail. The woman is sensually described: "bronzed shoulder bared intimating braless lushness." The man feels the ocean stirring his "back hairs." The speaker (assumed to be Kelly) asserts that the "Random jests of rock whereon we live" were likely created by an "afterthought" had by the "architects of space." The moment is perfect, described as "paenecrepuscular, postnatatory," as the two gaze out onto the archipelago of "frail delights" and hear the voices of "beach revelers." The poem's commitment to the knowledge of the body gained through Eros is decidedly contrary to the religious doctrine upheld at Monsalvat — the castle in Wagner's *Parsifal* where the Grail Knight community hides itself from women. "There is a final message... cloaked in the sweetest merest lodging of our flesh — / That Body is innocent, and on high." "That Body" could be the body of Christ, the divine cloaked in flesh, the "sweetest merest lodging." A transient gift of pleasure, of pain. The poem then changes tone as the speaker rebukes the woman standing beside him for questing after wrong knowledge. Her question clouds the experience of that magical place. He cuts off her foolish cry for the father:

> But you, you want to know the fuselage markings on some
>
> Turbo saucer that brought our race to this planet, you
> Want to know your father's name. Be ashamed. A body is enough to have.
> Stand with me on Glastonbury Tor inside St Michael's roofless tower

And look up: the patch of sky you see is your real home. I also
Fell. Suppose our heads tilted up without effort, gazing
Our way beyond the blue veil. The clue falls from your hands.

Kiss me. My mouth is the lips of your mother before you were born

(79–80)

The cunning line break around "I also / Fell" seems to contradict the optimist gnosis implied by the earlier description of flesh as the "sweetest merest lodging." But this is a pure Kelly move. The "fall" is not into corrupted matter, it is not a *down*fall, it does not sever us from "gazing / Our way beyond the blue veil." The flesh *is* our way back. The poem's outdoor setting encourages us to understand "blue veil" as a poetic description of sky, yet it cannot help but symbolically gesture toward the Virgin as well. Suddenly we are in the position of the Christ Child gazing up at the mother's angelic face, perhaps even reaching up with our small hand to give her an erotic "chin-chuck," as memorably described by Leo Steinberg in his book on the Renaissance Art, a gesture which designates "Mary's son as the Heavenly Bridegroom" and Mary as "his eternal consort in heaven" (5).

"The clue falls from your hands" functions as a syncretic segue when we remember that "clue" once commonly meant a ball of thread used to guide one out of the labyrinth. Ariadne, a central figure throughout Kelly's œuvre, is suddenly standing on Glastonbury Tor. But now the way "out" is "upward," promoting a spiritual escape. The thread is momentarily unnecessary. The poem's final line is a "Bridge Perilous" of sexuality, combining masculinity, maidenhood, and desire for the mother in the vocative to astonishing effect. It is a variation on the "shut up and kiss me" motif of pent-up desire, a harkening to the poem's earlier claim that "Speech when it listens / Says everything." To kiss the lips of one's own mother "before you were born" is a paradox (before we are born, our mothers are *not* our mothers), and a parable of the transfer of desire. Your lips may be those of a mother yet to be, the woman inside the man you love may in fact be your own mother. The collapse of time promised by the embrace pays homage to the cosmic powers of the place.

The conclusion of "From the Resting Place of the Grail" recalls yet complicates Kelly's phrase from *The Loom,* "the plural of one," quoted at the start of these notes. Myriad selves unfold. Time collapses. The poem follows the movement of image outlined above: it *abstracts* from the particular of a place, moving from the Tor, a fixed point on the map, all the way out to the larger universe. It creates a *cohesion* between the history of that place and the history of all mankind, and finally it makes the past *resonate* through the present via the erotics of a shared kiss. The micro and the macrocosm rhyme.

In "From the Resting Place of the Grail," as in so many of Kelly's poems, the mediator of "cultural matter" — of stories that we have told ourselves for centuries — becomes the portal through which a greater wisdom about our place in the cosmos is gained. This is quite distinct from Romantic communing with the sublime as filtered through nature, for there is no flight from history or culture here, no noble savages. Kelly's is a deeply literary poetry, one that admits little or no distinction between experience drawn from the senses and that drawn from deep reading. Kelly's literariness, his erudition, is a form of spiritual survival, not an elitist display. Therefore, his evocation of tradition has little in common with Eliot's use of the literary past to "escape from personality." Rather, Kelly's work shows us how tradition can help us learn how to ask the right questions so that we might deepen our emotional knowledge, and by extension our compassion for the other. Only through the understanding of what has preceded us can we gain the empathy needed to ask the Wounded King "what ails you?" and rejoin what has been torn asunder. Only then can we resonate with each other across the distance of our difference.

And where is Charlotte's cardinal? He is tuned to the nourishment-bearing woman on the deck of the beach house in Cuttyhunk. He is allowing himself to be fed by returning to the yearly offering placed in the outstretched hand. And so shall we allow ourselves to be fed, like creatures tuned to Orpheus's lyre, upon returning to the pages of Kelly's poetry. We can chose to follow his words like Ariadne's thread through the still growing labyrinth of his life's œuvre, hoping one day to get out, or we can take the poet's own advice and, letting the thread fall from our hand, read with resonant abandon. We can learn to stop demanding answers to our questions and enjoy the complexities of the never-ending quest, the wisdom it affords along the way, for as Kelly reminds us, "The grail found is no grail at all — the heart's ease is in the seeking" (*Sainte-Terre* n.p.).

Orono, Maine 2014

Works Cited

David Antin, *Tuning* (New York: New Directions, 1984).

Roland Barthes, *Comment Vivre Ensemble* (Paris: Éditions de Seuil, 2002).

Nicole Brossard, "Poetic Politics," *The Politics of Poetic Form,* ed. Charles Bernstein (New York City: Roof Books, 1993).

Michael Clune, *Writing Against Time* (CA: Stanford University Press, 2013).

Chrétien de Troyes, *The Complete Romances of Chrétien de Troyes,* tr. David Staines (Bloomington and Indianapolis: Indiana University Press, 1990).

Robert Duncan, *The H. D. Book* (LA & London: University of California Press, 2011).

——, "Interview with Robert Duncan," Michael Andre Bernstein & Burton Hatlen, *Sagetrieb* 4.2/3 (1985): 87–135.

——, *Selected Prose,* ed. Robert J. Bertholf (NY: New Directions, 1995).

Robert Kelly, *The Convections* (CA: Black Sparrow Press, 1978).

——, *Kill the Messenger* (CA: Black Sparrow Press, 1979).

——, *May Day* (Ontario: Parsifal Press, 2006).

——, *Lapis* (Boston: Godine, 2005).

——, "Notes on the Poetry of Deep Image," *Trobar* (1961).

——, *The Loom* (CA: Black Sparrow Press, 1975).

——, *Red Actions. Selected Poems 1960–1993* (CA: Black Sparrow Press, 1995).

——, *Sainte-Terre or The White Stone* (NY: Shivastan Publishing, 2006).

——, *A Strange Market* (CA: Black Sparrow Press, 1992).

John Cowper Powys, *A Glastonbury Romance* (NY: Overlook Press, 1996).

Jed Rasula, "Ten Different Fruits on One Different Tree: Reading Robert Kelly," in *Credences: A Journal of Twentieth Century Poetry and Poetics,* 3.1 (1984): 127–175.

Rainer Maria Rilke, *Letters of Rainer Maria Rilke 1892–1910,* trs. Jane Bannard Greene and M.D. Herter Norton (NY: Norton, 1969).

Edward Schelb, "The Charred Heart of Polyphemus: Tantric Ecstasy & Shamanistic Violence in Robert Kelly's 'The Loom,'" in *Contemporary Literature* 36.2 (1995): 317–349.

Leo Steinberg, *The Sexuality of Christ in Renaissance Art and in Modern Oblivion* (Chicago & London: University of Chicago Press, 1996).

PETER MONACO

"WE ARE ALL MADE OF STARS": THE DEMANDS OF "READING" ROBERT KELLY

"...I want the reader of my poems to dance, if not with me, then with the poem..."
    — Robert Kelly, *Brooklyn Rail* interview with John Yau, David Levi Strauss, & Phong Bui

"Working with deep image is the development of a 'basic imagination.'... The present and necessary function of poetry is the transformation of the perceived world... Poetry is concerned with things transforming and transforming things, with the whole picture in mind. We are given: 1 world to transform, 1 language to transform it with."
    — Robert Kelly, "Notes on the Poetry of Deep Image"

"Every night I tell myself 'I am the cosmos / I am the wind'"
    — Chris Bell (Big Star), "I am the Cosmos"

Robert Kelly's work makes a certain kind of demand upon readers; namely, readers are implicated in the act of making meaning within the compositional space of the poem. "Reading" Kelly's work demands a physical, psychical, and intellectual dance among faculties and senses. In the following meditation on Kelly's forays into deep image, as well as some of the work that comprises his first two decades including co-editing *Trobar* and his study of the Ta'wil in the work of Avicenna, I will argue that the language and compositional space of a Kelly poem is a living, breathing, organic part of the living WHOLE or "cosmos" which "composes" both poet and reader. In this sense, I define "cosmos" as the space of infinite chaos and creation, akin to the space of the poem, in which Kelly seeks "the transformation of the perceived world." This is the same "cosmos" or charged energy that surrounds us and creates us, and Kelly's work is an attempt to tap into or engage directly with this charged "cosmic" energy in the space of the poem's composition. A Kelly poem is an esoteric, para-archaeological site, where he believes truth emerges from the very act of composition, in which the reader is implicated. Thus there is "work" to be done when reading a Robert Kelly poem, and it is not an act of explication or literary analysis; it is the very real task of creating "meaning," relentlessly digging for "truth" as it emerges in the space of the poem, and the very real transformation of the perceived world.

In the *Contemporary Authors Autobiography Series,* Vol. 19, in section 10 of his autobiography, Kelly writes:

> At twenty-three I dedicated my life of work to God. To benefit the world was how I thought about it. At forty-six I dedicated it to the enlightenment of all beings. It seems ambitious and possibly pretentious to want these things, but I mean them with everything I have that can mean anything. My search in 'flesh, dream, book' has been for ways of saying, ways of saying that benefit beings. Searching now in language to unsay my 'self,' & thereby say the truth, or say toward it (183).

The literal religious conversion alluded to in this passage is seamlessly juxtaposed, between the literal lines, to Kelly's "coming-into" a poet who is concerned with dissolving his own "self" into language itself, the very structure that orders our personal and collective identities, our cosmology. The "poetry of desperation" and the demand for a poetry that "transforms" found within the few pages which constitute *Notes on the Poetry of Deep Image* will follow Kelly in one form or another through to the work he continues to produce without fail. In section 17, he writes:

> Here is the story I have tried to tell: Armed descent, into her body which is my talisman, my weapon against time. Against time these round dances, the movement around the core of myself that is my entasy — the opposite of the ecstasy people are always raving about or hoping for. I wanted entasy, to stand inside, to be incarnate as myself, in all the full intensity of feeling *in full consciousness* from this place outward. Above me the stages of the moon declare their lunes, which are their measures in us too, the tuneful amazements of the soul's calendar. Words are forever in service of this going that is my knowing… I can admit it now — my work *has* a meaning to declare (186).

Kelly's conceptualization of the deep image in his *Notes on the Poetry of Deep Image* as well as comments on the image in Postmodern American poetry that he makes in an interview conducted by David Ossman, published in his collection *The Sullen Art*, considers the poem as "a happening in itself," poetic language via "vision" and "perception." In *Notes on the Poetry of Deep Image*, Kelly asserts that "The present and necessary function of poetry is the transformation of the perceived world. This transformation orders the known world into an effective and coherent universe" (14). Thus Kelly is concerned with moving beyond the surface language to the *perceived world*, which requires a process of "illumination." Kelly considers the surface world, the supposed "truth" of reality, to be, in a sense, virtual, a construction predicated on the imposition of power and approved discourses of knowledge. He writes "Poetry is concerned with things transforming and transforming things, with the whole picture in mind" (14). "Reality" as such is a fiction; it exists only in so far as it can alienate and subsequently suppress or silence competing and multiple discourses which are always already part and parcel of the "whole picture." The key to dismantling this imposed, virtual "reality" is an understanding that the literal material of poetic language, the language of "transformation," is also the same language by which certain totalitarian and dogmatic discourses order "reality." Kelly seems to suggest in his *Notes* that there is a mode of reading or perception that is organic, he sees poetry *as an act of transformation* that is *process*, it "involves truth as emergent from process and not distinct from it"(14). One cannot dictate truth; it emerges.

From 1960—1964 Robert Kelly and George Economou, along with Kelly's then wife Joan, edited the little magazine, *Trobar*. The name of the magazine comes from the troubadour tradition in Old Provençal, a form of song associated with courtly love. "Trobar" is literally defined as a mode of poetic composition in which the content is "found" or "sought out." Thus it implies that there is a search or probing of "depths" inherent to "trobar" or "poetic composition" as a practice. However, both the magazine *Trobar* and the troubadour tradition move beyond the conception of "love songs" and "little magazines" to the extent that each occupies a more significant place in the history of contemporary poetics. Likewise, both the troubadour tradition of Old Provençal and the mimeograph "revolution" in New York's Lower East Side in the early sixties, out of which *Trobar* emerges, are an extension of a larger discourse surrounding poetry's relationship to the "other" discourses that are commonly associated with philosophy, science, religion, and politics. Western philosophy and the history of the development and use of written language has all but relegated the poem to the margins of so-called "public language," the modes of speech and writing that occupy more "serious" areas of knowledge and learning. What Kelly and Economou initiate is a poetics that not only re-charges poetry with depth & energy, but a poetics that explodes how language is deployed and experienced. In the editorial statement introducing the first issue of *Trobar* (1960), Kelly and Economou seek the "... primal gestures of language: ox foraging on the grassland, the archer pulling his bow with all his powers" (2). The magazine's content, and more importantly the approach to contemporary poetics that it champions, attempts to capture the "primal" energy in language. This "primal" energy, according to Kelly and Economou, is rooted in the unconscious, not unlike a rock that is partially buried beneath the ground — "not till the rock is pulled from the ground is its size or nature known" (2). Similarly, Kelly and Economou reconcile the material "ox" and "archer's bow" with language; they insist on the materiality of the words themselves being as "real" and "concrete" as the "ox," the "grassland," and the "archer." They reject language's objectivity, its supposed impartiality as merely a signifier of objects and the verbal or written expression of thought & ideas. For Kelly and Economou, the poet's role is to discover the "deep images," what they define as "... the substance and bearings of those roots which are inescapable content of dream and discipline" (2). There is a power and intensity in poetry that calls attention to the idea that language, as opposed to being fixed, is dynamic and moving, shifting and changing, a living breathing piece of a larger "whole," or cosmos.

Returning for a moment to the title *Trobar* and its connection to the troubadour tradition, one must already dig deeper than a cursory understanding of Postmodern American poetry or its seemingly divergent counterpart, the troubadour poem/song. The troubadour poetry of Old Provençal is almost exclusively associated with the existence of "courtly love." Courtly love is defined as the poet's idealization of a specific woman who occupies an exalted or privileged position; she embodies the perfect union of body and soul. The troubadour poet thus seeks union with this woman not for the sake of quelling passion and desire, but more significantly, as a way of reaching a state of supreme moral excellence.[116] This idea certainly complicates the nature of the concept of love in the history of Western culture, but more importantly, it charges the troubadour poet's language with the goal of achieving a higher state of mental & physical being. The poem is not a vehicle for mere self expression, but the means by which the poet attempts to connect to an "Other," a woman who simultaneously occupies the physical world and a more exclusive or "deeper" spiritual, "creative" or "imaginative" psychical realm.

Although the concept of courtly love survives in histories as the major impetus of troubadour poetry, this does not do enough to explain its privileged position over the course of the history of Western poetry. For example, according to Economou, in his introduction to Paul Blackburn's translations of troubadour poetry, the recognition of the troubadour's influence "begins during a serious reading of Dante, who acknowledges and manifests the importance of the troubadours for him and his work" (Blackburn XIII).[117] The historical and literary figure of Beatrice, as the exalted "Other," fuels both Dante's passions and his textual journey, particularly as pilgrim in the *Divine Comedy*. It is, among other things, the loss of the literal Beatrice to death which demands that Dante make a spiritual and poetic descent into the Underworld in the *Inferno*. Her death also brings about the journey that will lead to a deeper and more substantial questioning of the interconnectedness between, for Dante, the physical and spiritual realms, and perhaps for some contemporary investigative poetry, the connection between material language and the

---

116. See Ezra Pound's work on the troubadours as detailed in Hugh Kenner's *The Pound Era* (1971). Kenner notes that for Pound, "A binding, a having-to-do-with, that joins in likeness, in difference and in modulation all the poem's materials, through which interactive web the syntactic movement flows, abandoning nothing: [...] is the deepest, the most persistent Provençal intuition" (84). Pound's influence on Kelly and Economou is tremendous. However, Pound is most interested in the more formal elements of the troubadours, where as Kelly and Economou will develop a more "Gnostic" reading of the troubadours work, in which "desire" functions beyond the scope of courtly love to more strongly reveal its relationship to language and thought.

117. See Paul Blackburn, *Proensa: An Anthology of Troubadour Poetry*, ed. George Economou (1978) xiii–xxiv.

language of the unconscious. The seriousness of this task is left to the poem; it is poetic language that will lead Dante and his readers through the journey. In the *Divine Comedy*, poet and pilgrim are ONE. The text intercedes between the physical and spiritual, between what is intelligible and what can only be imagined without resorting to literal death.

It is difficult to imagine the significant influence of the troubadours to contemporary poetics without looking beyond the concept of courtly love. It is necessary to explore what is best described as the two sides of the same troubadour coin: one side being that which is dedicated to courtly love, the other to the more elusive side of troubadour poetry, namely the side concerned with hermeticism and magic. In the history of troubadour poetry, there exist two versions of the same genre, though they are never mutually exclusive. A great debate raged circa 1160—1210 CE between *trobar leu* ("light" and "easy" troubadour poetry concerned with courtly love), and another version called *trobar clus*, associated with magic, hypnosis, and hermeticism. If *trobar leu* is the love song, *trobar clus* is the spell cast in lyric that allows the poet to perform a kind of descent into the darker regions of the soul.[118] As mentioned in the above passage, these two kinds of troubadour poetry seldom appear mutually exclusive, although it would seem that the *leu* (light, "love song") version is the one that best details a contemporary understanding of troubadour poetics. However, keeping in mind the example of Dante's *Divine Comedy*, his lyric surely embodies a combination in influence of the two forms of troubadour poetry, and it is this combination that brings us back now to Kelly and Economou's own conception of poetry in *Trobar*.

Kelly and Economou declare in their editorial statement that "Poetry is itself a power of life" and that the poem's strength is drawn from "the deep image as a mode of working within the poem, as statement and vision" (2). Just as the troubadour poet charges his work with the task of uniting with the woman as "Other" in order to transcend the physical realm, thus achieving "moral excellence," Kelly and Economou believe that it is through the poem that contact between "the perennial strength of the deep image" and the contemporary world can be achieved, and to

---

118. See *The New Princeton Encyclopedia of Poetry and Poetics*, eds. Alex Preminger & T.V.F. Brogan (1993) 1308–1310.

a particular end. In their closing statement they insist: "The purpose of *Trobar* is to publish American poetry of intensity and immediacy, apparitions of the native duende, articulate in the power of word, dynamic in the space of music, made with all the powers of poetry, moving alive and passionate" (2).

Over the course of *Trobar*'s short run, a new poetics of vision, energy, and risk is established.

In David Ossman's interview with Kelly, Ossman follows a line of questioning that attempts to link Kelly's concept of the deep image with the publication of *Trobar*. More specifically, Ossman presses Kelly on how, in light of his and Jerome Rothenberg's then recent explorations into the deep image, image comes to bear on the process of poetic composition. For Kelly, the work published in *Trobar* was to be "poetry that qualified by being alive in one sense or another" (Ossman 33). The image, as it is deployed in a "deep image" poem, is considered the life-force or energy charged with the capability of literally, certainly in conjunction with and in response to Charles Olson's "projective verse," "breathe life" into the poem, to channel the simultaneous energy of the poem's composition and discursive space from both "inside" the depths of the poet's psyche and "outside" into the physical matter and conceptual space that calls the "world" into being.

In the Ossman interview, Kelly will bring together Olson's "push" with Pound's division of poetic powers into the three categories of *"logos,* or word — word-magic, ... *melos*, the musical gist ... really — sound; and third, *phanos* ... equaling for Pound, 'throwing the image onto the mind'" (Ossman 33). This, Kelly asserts, "is the intellectual and emotional tone of the poem" (33). Kelly does not order Pound's "trinity" hierarchically, but rather, develops deep image poetics around how these three powers, logos, melos, and phanos, interact and engage with one another. Since "poetry deals with word, word is its ground," Kelly calls language "the mystical hypostasis of all poetry" (33). Language is the mystical "essence" or real, material base of the poem; melos he regards as "the space-time of poetry — its line, extent, duration" (33). However, he insists that "phanos, the image, has gotten rather slighting attention" (34). In regards to deep image poetry, Kelly insists that he is not considering poetry that is dominated by image, but poetry in which "the rhythm of images ... form the dominant movement of the poem" (34). Image is a vehicle, a machine that functions as "a vehicle for Vision" into the primordial realm or "floating world" (35). "Vision," Kelly explains, "discovers ... explorations of the real world, discoveries through perception" (35).

The development of both deep image and Kelly's lifelong vow to a poetics of transformation can certainly be traced through the influence of Robert Duncan on Kelly's work. In his essay, *Poetry Before Language*, Duncan seeks to rediscover poetry's roots in the body before conscious thought, to a time which he describes as when "The brain in those days was of ordinary service, a mere clearing house for parts of the body" (60). He argues that before what he refers to as the development of "the minding brain... in the happy concourse and democracy of what we do not mind, hand, arm, leg, foot, finger, stomach, bowels, liver, heart, lungs, brain, skin and bone made their way together. There was no sense of anything, not even common sense; all sense was in the senses" (61). In short, Duncan is reaching back to a moment in human development when the body and the world around it were perceived, defined, understood, and most importantly *made* through the physical senses. More importantly, he reaches back before the Word, before a name, and subsequently a "definition" was given to all sensory perceptions and feelings. As Self develops, there is a demand for meaning to be made of simple physical desires as well as the desire for an understanding of the world, and meaning is produced in the act of naming. Duncan feels that much like the imposing Self's desire to name bodily functions and desires, so too does it give poetry a "name." Thus by *naming* the poem, which like Olson and Kelly too insist, comes from the body, the poem is no longer action; it is no longer physical; it becomes a thing. This concept will prove fundamental to an understanding of Kelly's coming to deep image and a charged poetics of transformation of the perceived world. In *Poetry Before Language*, Duncan writes:

> I want to describe Poetry as it was before words, or signs, before beauty, or eternity, or meaning, were. Poetry would not allow the brain to falsify what it was in giving it a word or a 'meaning'; and so the 'meaning' of the word 'poetry' or name 'Poetry' is a making. The organs of the body not only communicated but all the organs made things. The act was dancing, the product of the act was the dance, poetry. In one kind of dancing the hand

and the eye danced together. Thus the hand 'saw' the stones and sticks, and the eye 'felt' them ... The happy brain — this was the brain before it grew upon its self — and the heart danced in concourse, and as the brain danced, hand no longer determined, nor eye determined, nor ear determined, but all became attentive to the full complex of the sum of all their dance (60–62).

Movement, process, and Duncan's "dance" make their way into Kelly's development of deep image. More importantly, each of these actions involves a "whole"; in Duncan, the entire body, physical and psychical, is involved in the "dance" that is Poetry. In *The Sullen Art*, David Ossman presses Kelly on the origins of his *Notes*, when he asks about the relationship between image in poetry and film montage through the work of Eisenstein. Kelly's answer will not only illuminate his coming to deep image; it will also bring together the significance of Duncan's "dance" and Kelly's insistence that "image" is action, or in his words "process." Kelly insists that in film, it "starts out with a *known* reality: the reality the camera faces" (Ossman 37). The images that come together in a filmic montage, like those employed by Eisenstein, are at least situated against the backdrop of the "known reality" as seen through the lens of the camera. As the images are received, there is still a semblance of order and a known reality that will emerge in the art object. However, as Kelly states, "There is a Mystery in poetry, and I really mean this with a capital M, a darkness, an atmosphere in which the author composes the Images before he really knows what those Images amount to" (37). He then connects this "darkness" and "Mystery in poetry" to process: "The poetic Image is not a thing. It is process and a discovered identity. It discovers its being in its function ... Image is the rhythm of poetry" (37). So then, one can bring together Kelly's assertions and Duncan's observation that "the product of the act was the dance, poetry" by considering image as not simply something that comes across the literal field of vision related to the eyes. Image, for Kelly, is Duncan's "dance" of the total body; image is perceived by the entire body; the poem is composed by the very rhythm of the image. Kelly states "the Image itself, in its development, constitutes the fundamental, basic rhythm of the poem, which all other rhythms — sound rhythms, stress rhythms and so forth — must subserve" (38).

Duncan's essay, *Towards an Open Universe*, locates the physical body and the body that is the poem within the larger framework of SPACE or cosmos. In the opening passages of his essay, Duncan relates the very moment of his birth, citing both date and time of day, as well the domestic objects that line his sight and make up his SPACE, his surroundings; he goes so far as to launch from the hour of his birth and "the tree at the window, the patterned curtain, the table and chair" all the way out to "The shining planets and the great stars, the galaxies beyond us" (76). This identity with the "cosmos" alongside the specificity of images provides a powerful indoctrination of the "imagination" as conceived in Kelly's coming to deep image. Duncan continues:

> The imagination of this cosmos is as immediate to me as the imagination of my household or my self, for I have taken my being in what I know of the sun and the magnitude of the cosmos, as I have taken my being in what I know of domestic things (76).

Duncan raises the issue of consciousness, and he asserts that "the poem as a supreme effort of consciousness, comes in a dancing organization between personal and cosmic identity" (78). Toward the conclusion of his *Notes*, Kelly locates this "dancing organization" in "verbal expression," and reading Kelly through Duncan suggests that both "personal and cosmic identity," as well as consciousness itself can only be fully expressed or communicated through language. He writes that "Verbal expression of the image demands an urgency and directness that only the spoken language of poet and reader can supply, the language of here and now" (*Notes*). Ultimately, the "Open Universe," including "personal and cosmic identity" for Kelly is expressed through the deep image, which is itself expressed in language. The deep image is linguistic: "In the poem built from the deep image, the image itself bears an enormous weight, for through it and its connection with the rhythmic sequence of images, the flow of the image-conditioned word and music, the meaning of the poem exists, *all communication takes place* [my emphasis]" (*Notes*). Both personal and cosmic identity are joined in language, and consciousness is also structured in language; for Kelly and Duncan, the poem then is the ultimate expression of creation, of the interconnectedness of all things. Thus the radically charged space of the poem, what Kelly refers to as the "tension in the work itself" which "cannot be exaggerated," means that "The language of deep images restores the poetry of desperation" (*Notes*). This "desperation" can be understood when Duncan writes in *Towards an Open Universe*: "Each poet seeks to commune with creation, with the divine world, that is to say, he seeks the most *real* form in language," since communing with creation through the compositional space of the poem ultimately means having the potential to transform the "world" (78). As articulated by Kelly: "Poetry is concerned with things transforming and transforming things, with the whole picture in mind. We are given: 1 world to transform, 1 language to transform it with" (*Notes*). As Duncan declares in *Towards an Open Universe*: "To answer that call, to become the poet, means to be aware of creation, creature, and creator co-inherent in the one event" (81). In the same vein in which the space of composition is considered in Kelly's *Notes on the Poetry of Deep Image*, Duncan writes: "Perhaps we recognize as never before in man's history that not only our own personal consciousness but also the inner structure of the universe itself has only this immediate event in which to be realized" (88).

A closer look at some of the poetry that comes during the immediate moment of deep image poetry further reveals how time and again, Kelly will return to the poetic and intellectual spaces out of which the deep image first emerged, as if to say "often I am permitted to return to deep image." Echoes and reverberations of his later work, and the preceding discussion which sought to begin to trace the origins and future returns to deep image, can be felt in the poems which come in Kelly's first collection *Armed Descent* (1961). From "Measure Those Distances," in the section titled "Of this night":

> Here and now she becomes alive
> a roar of things out of the streets
> for the first time covered with skin
> moving for the first time with the train of waters
> here this body is me (15)

Kelly announces the arrival of the poem, its coming to life of its own accord. He gives no indication that the poem was necessarily something of his own creation, but rather, a complex gathering of individual charged particles, of "things out of the streets" coming together as a living, breathing animal "covered with skin" moving steadfast "with the train of waters." And the poem takes its own shape, one image following another; the image of "the train of waters" suggests that the poem arrives and takes the shape of its vessel, much like water taking the route of a predetermined path. The body of the poem, the poem itself, is also poet: "this body is me," here in the compositional space. Kelly is, from Duncan, "co-inherent in the one event." The poem continues in a series of lines each beginning with "being":

> being out in the open without terror
> being out in the parklands hunting for meat
> being atlantis unresurrected and carelessly swimming
> being navies and heavily-armed convoys
>   being decked out with banners being
>   sudden in an animal, being dark (15)

The repetition of the word "being" in these lines works on a number of levels. The first two uses of "being" denote a literal place; they locate poet and poem first "out in the open" and "out in the parklands." However, beyond this literal use of "being," there is a deeper resonance that locates "being" as also pertaining to a state of mind or consciousness. The poem/poet is exposed "out in the open," yet it also stands physically and emotionally fearless "without terror," and "out in the parklands hunting for meat." This is significant for a number of reasons, beginning with the personification of the poem; it is an animal following its unconscious "natural state." Kelly then has allowed the poem to take a physical form, and stemming from the preceding inquiry into personal and collective identity, as well as the cosmos, as coming from language and the literal space of composition, Kelly blurs the "distance" between human and animal as well as personal and collective identity. Also, the poem is "hunting for meat"; this ACT can be read through Kelly's *Notes* when he discusses "force" and the order of images as they appear in the poem. When Kelly writes in his *Notes* that "The final quantum will vary with the rearrangement of the images and of the images' fields of force," he is setting the speed and purpose of *Of this night*. This is the deep image poem in action; it is a physical (thus "armed") descent into the very space of creation, the "cosmic WHOLE." Kelly composes in a vernacular that is both human and animal, that blurs the distinction between the two as much as it blurs the distinction between poetic and "everyday" speech. As he writes in *Notes*, "Only in the native linguistic PATTERNS can the deep image communicate at full strength" (*Notes*).

Kelly is heavily "armed" in his "dissent"; he is "navies and heavily armed convoys," and he is a "thirsty and savage... animal" (15). However, he is also "atlantis unresurrected," an allusion to his willingness to engage the myth of Atlantis as readily as any other so-called rejected or occult knowledge. He does not distinguish between myth and reality since he has already determined that both are constructs of language; all being and understanding occurs in language. He will not subscribe to the notion that some discourses are "true" and others "false."

Another way of considering the lines in *Of this night* which begin with the repetition of the first word "being" is one that considers the lines as marking, in the space of the poem, the evolution of the "poem" as a discursive space that is as much alive and breathing as the poet who composes it. As noted at length in the preceding discussion, Kelly's concept of deep image is predicated on the charged, living percepts that "rise from the unconscious or from the retina of the awakened eye... the percepts, in order to be communicated, are fleshed in language" (*Notes*). The descending lines beginning with the word "being" are each examples of how Kelly attempts to achieve the "continuum" of "the ACT of relating word to percept, image to image" (*Notes*). Each line contains a montage of percepts that come to full energy and full dimension through their simultaneous presentation. Thus the line "being steps and an entrance to a living house" weds the more literal images, "steps" and "house," to the conceptual "living," achieving a continuum that attempts to operate at "maximal communicative force" (*Notes*).

Serving as both Kelly's first collection of published poems, as well as an inaugural work in the push toward a poetry of deep image, *Armed Descent* reads much like a series of canvases or filmic montages. The poems come at the reader, and they make demands upon the reader: that the reader be fully engaged as a co-contributor to the space of composition. Often, one must read and read again, only to come to the realization that each subsequent glance at the poem changes how it is perceived. One can argue that so-called "outside" mediating factors, such as a change in season, mood, or weather, coupled with the charged energy emanating from each line, will affect how the "fundamental rhythm of the images" is perceived during the act of reading. The concept of the deep image will morph and change, and grow in complexity and form over the course of Kelly's work, and *Armed Descent* captures an ephemeral snapshot in time, in the development of a transformative space of poetic composition.

As Kelly moves beyond the literal, historical moment surrounding deep image, and expands his concept of the space of poetic composition as being one of transformation that directly implicates the reader in the making of meaning, he engages with another significant mode of transformation, namely alchemy. He is looking well beyond "image" to song, spirit, and language at both the verbal level, as well as the physical materiality of words inscribed on pages, palm leaves, cylinders, and tablets. This phase of his work is developed over a series of poems and longer collections, but it is *Finding the Measure* (1968), and its "Prefix," that comes closest to a manifesto of sorts:

> Finding the Measure is finding the mantram
> is finding the moon, as index of measure,
> is finding the moon's source;
>
>   if that source
> is Sun, Finding the Measure is finding
> the natural articulation of ideas.
>
>   The organism
> of the macrocosm, the organism of language,
> the organism of *I* combine in ceaseless naturing
> to propagate a fourth,
>   the poem,
>   from their trinity.
>
> Style is death. Finding the Measure is finding
> a freedom from that death, a way out, a movement
> forward.
>
> Finding the Measure is finding the
> specific music of the hour,
>   the synchronous
> consequence of the motion of the whole world.

"Finding the Measure is finding the mantram" or sacred words used in meditation, on language, the body, the poem, and world and their synthesis as the true real. For Kelly, the poem becomes, over the course or process that is its composition, an investigation, examination, and provocation of the above mentioned "material" that constitutes reality. It is in *Finding the Measure* and elsewhere, where Kelly's writing and the reader's interpretation converge in an act of call and response that together constitute and actively engage the very discourses (including language, image, and sound broadly defined) that constitute a perceptible reality. To perform the "mantram" of writing and reading is to admit that there is no "outside" to the language of the poem; the text is as much a part of the literal, tangible material that constitutes reality as such. And the texts that inform Kelly's work, in this case the *Prefix*, are often at odds with so-called "sanctioned" discourses. For example, for Kelly, Finding the Measure "is finding the moon, as index of measure," and from a Jungian perspective, the moon acts as literal "prima materia" in the alchemical process. The moon, according to Jung, "represents the unknown substance that carries the projection of the autonomous psychic content" (*Psychology and Alchemy*, 317). And although it is named, or "marked" as "moon," it is, according to Jung, "impossible to specify such a substance (what constitutes 'moon' as prima materia in the individual psyche) because the projection emanates from the individual and is consequently different in each case," inferring that each individual reader will always create new knowledge in the collaboration with Kelly in the making of "meaning" (317). Thus, meaning is not fixed, it is dynamic and changing; it explodes beyond the confines of time, history, memory, space, geography, and the like. Considered against a socio-political-religious backdrop that demands allegiance to a single narrative or "truth," dynamic meaning is a threat and must be suppressed whether it be via enforcing a strict interpretation of what constitutes a "poem," relegating poetry to a space of leisure, or censoring and devaluing a series of writings or the work of unsanctioned writers and thinkers. This is evident when considering the line "index of measure." An "index" can refer to a reference or operative symbol, yet it can also be read as the list of books that were forbidden to be read by the Roman Catholic laity.

Kelly argues in the *Prefix* that the measure is not fixed: "if that source / is Sun, Finding the Measure is finding / the natural articulation of ideas," ideas which speak, are expressive, yet "articulation" can also refer to the connecting of different parts. The "articulation" is the joint; it is the moveable hinge which links together the ideas and gives them life and mobility, action. "The organism / of the macrocosm, the organism of language, / the organism of *I* combine in ceaseless naturing / to propagate a fourth, / the poem, / from their trinity," writes Kelly. It is here that Kelly locates the physical body and the mythological origins of the human body and universal soul in the act of composition, in the act of making. In Jung's most elaborate and at times overwhelming study on alchemy (much more esoteric and demanding than *Psychology and Alchemy*), and perhaps the culmination of his life's work, *Mysterium Coniunctionis*, where in chapter five, titled "Adam and Eve," he explores the figure of Adam as both first "man" and first, or potentially, universal soul. Adam has a "polarity," according to Jung, that "... is based on the contradiction between his physical and spiritual nature... in the Islamic view... Adam's soul was created thousands of years before his body and then refused to enter the figure made of clay, so that God had to put it in by force" (408). According to Jung, Adam is both "from whom the macrocosm arose, or who *is* the macrocosm. He is not only the prima material but a universal soul which is also the soul of men" (409). That is to say, Adam rejects his less than suitable clay body, perhaps incapable of fully expressing and experiencing the sensuous dimensions of a physical presence in the material world, and he is eventually forced into a physical form, and so it is potentially with great pleasure that he, with Eve, eats of the tree of knowledge. In fact, according to Jung, "According to the teachings of the Bogomils, Adam was created by Satanael, God's first son and the fallen angel, out of mud... Adam's inner connection with Satan is likewise suggested in Rabbinic tradition, where Adam will one day sit on Satan's throne" (409). So then, in Kelly's *Prefix*, "the organism of the macrocosm" or Adam as both physical body and spiritual/universal soul, and "the organism of language" and Kelly's individual psyche or soul, his "I," are the trinity by which the poem emerges. The reader is the macrocosm, is language, is body, as is poet — all are essentially one and the same in the making of knowledge. Also, in just this single stanza, by going much deeper than a cursory glance, Kelly's poetry takes a left hand, or rebel stance against any and all institutions and boundaries which prohibit the movement, energy, and dynamism of thought and language.

Thus he declares "Style is death," since style constricts and delegates that the image (not of the deep variety) must be consistent and maintained. Adam as "first man" is also "macrocosm"/universal soul, and simultaneously the figure of Satan's son, rebel angel who defies *God*, the transcendental deity or figurative force that, albeit veiled and unspoken, often underlies the demands of conservative æsthetic, religious, and political institutions.

In a conversation published in *Vort 5* (1974) entitled "Ta'wil or How to Read," Kelly insists:

> I've talked before about why poems are hard and have to be hard and have to get harder; that if they're not hard they're no good, and about how 'poem' replaces 'religion,' I mean as its enemy — that it represents the development of the growth of our consciousness that we can transcend the religion that purports sacramentally or magically to perform an act for us, and instead forces to the point of performing it for ourselves, transmutatively (115).

Reading Kelly's work is a process that allows the reader to enter other or disparate concepts, images, and melodies into the space of the poem. Each reading should produce something else; it should create an extension into other areas of inquiry. The poet does not *do the work* for the reader. In Kelly's poetry, reading and writing are intrinsically linked — two actions that pervade the event of the poem's reading and composition. As he insists in the preceding passage, the word "poem," as a designation, becomes the 'enemy" in the compositional process. What Kelly aims for are poems that are "events" that must be attended by reader as well as poet. "Poem," like "religion," determines that something has value; when an object is presented under the guises "poem" or "religion," it proclaims or purports its own value as inherent. However, the "poem" as an object holds little value as such; it is a poetics of process, a communion between reader and poet that "sanctifies" the space of poem and creates meaning in Kelly's work.

The real or perceived world exists in such a way so as to suggest that its origins, natural laws, social structures, and the like, have already been "figured out" or approved by post-Enlightenment reason or religious dogma. However, the very languages that constitute & compose reality produce an excess that cannot be contained or conceptualized according to the above schemata. This excess discourse locates itself within the gaps, aporias, and margins of contemporary reason and religious dogma — the very spaces out of which poetic discourse emerges to engage so-called "reality." In these cracks and crevices in the surface of the real, hidden and suppressed languages and marginalized discourses of thought and intuition, philosophy and speculative science, political and social theories, are brought to light via the poet's engagement with these "others" in the act of poetic composition. The poetic process provides the means for a direct conversation and mediation with these alternative discourses, these poly-vocal "others." The existence of this excess *other* demands interpretation; however, this demand does not and cannot conform to rational modes of thought already weighed down by the very language it employs in order to seek an understanding of the world. Instead, this demand calls for another mode of thought, one that simultaneously charges readers with the responsibility of both interpreting these discourses of "otherness" and developing the very mode of thought or process by which these discourses are to be engaged. In a sense, poetic discourse, in its direct conversation with the other, subverts on one level and calls into being on another, the reader and poet's "I" or subjectivity. This "I" is the critical consciousness that calls the subject into being and allows the subject access to and demands responsibility for the creation of what is referred to as "reality." Without this delicate balance, both subject and "world" are susceptible to totalitarian and dogmatic modes of thought based in prevailing ideology.

In "Ta'wil or How to Read," Kelly continues to contextualize his relationship to the poem and the reality in which it enters, reflects, and transforms. The poem, according to Kelly, "doesn't ask anything of me, except to write it or drive it or use it or whatever. Because I do sense reality as a task" (118). In this sense, Kelly as poet becomes the medium for a language that will transform what he refers to as the "perceptual world." Understanding or making the "perceptual world" intelligible is the task of the poet or according to Kelly "anybody else who wants to play that game" (118). Designating "reality as a task" raises the value of the poem from the placid drudgery of object to the intense field of things. Also, Kelly begins to distance or disrupt the relationship between the poet's ego and with it an individual desire to objectify reality and the poem, which takes on a collective desire to admit all things simultaneously into the space of its composition. The poet's responsibility is to "drive" the poem, meaning Kelly must maintain a consistent level of intensity during the act of composition. This intensity forces an incision into reality; it creates an additional or alternative space from which to view and engage the "perceptual world." In this respect, Kelly's poetics not only "MAKE IT NEW" but MAKE IT POSSIBLE for a myriad of alternative discourses to commune in the task of perceiving the "real" world. His poetics initiate both the reader and writer's critical consciousness, creating spaces for new thought and subsequently action & transformation of the perceived world.

Kelly's reflections on process in *The Loom* celebrate the spontaneity of narrative and his inability to stall or subvert the process, the composition. The "recital" of the poem, borrowing from the Ta'Wil in the work of Avicenna, selects one "seed" to grow, and Kelly insists it often appears during the composition of the poem that "the other seeds do not" (122). At the conclusion of the poetic composition, Kelly stands in awe. Although it appears the "Recital" has only allowed one seed to develop, nevertheless, "it's all there" (122). He reflects:

> And I stand in awe of that narrative process. Because that's [writing the sections of *The Loom*] really the first time that I came to know about the spontaneity of narrative. I mean of course certain kinds of narrative do tell themselves — fantasies or dreams or whatnot — but to have the power expressing itself right in the moment of one's conscious, most alert activity, where I'm thinking about vowels and its thinking what's going to happen, seems to me so extraordinary (122).

Kelly's poetics allow the narrative to "happen," and because of this, the poem not only allows marginal discourse or "other seeds" to enter the composition, it also develops its own method of attending to all of the possible "seeds" in a single poetic field without boundaries.

The poetic process is not to be confused with "procedure," or something that can necessarily be directly applied to other acts of writing and reading. Kelly insists that the terms used to describe his poetics, "the Recital," are "non-paraphraseable" (130). This attempt to paraphrase poetic process, Kelly warns, "gets painfully close to the problem where process becomes procedure. Or where, in talking about one's process, one could seem to be talking about a procedure that would be transferable as a method, to somebody else" (130). Turning "process" into "procedure" stifles the composition by setting up arbitrary boundaries or a prescribed method that must be followed in order to achieve a so-called "successful" poem. The poem would retreat back into object, into "enemy," if the process of its composition is no longer a task. If the action that the poetic process implies is limited by the restrictions of method, the arenas of potential risk, discovery, and inquiry are also then limited or disengaged. In short, the potential of the field or space of the poem is short-circuited; the energy of its language falls flat on the white, cold page.

Actively reading Kelly implies active participation with the poet and an approach to the poem and the world which it passes in, through, on, and about as "task." In his *Autobiography*, Kelly admits "and I am with you reader, really, for writing and reading are the same act, only different phases" (186). He implies that reading & writing require the same energy because both produce the potential for thought and action. Also, both reading and writing occupy the same psychical space. The reader bends & shapes the poem around their own subjective experience, interaction with the world, and the multifaceted development of their sense of perception. Similarly, the reader engages the poem in a specific instance in time, different from that of the poet, and may recognize varying linguistic, discursive, and melodic aspects of the language of the poem. Any time a reader returns or re-visits a Kelly poem, their relationship to the text, their reading "experience," and their active engagement with the poem as an event, will change.

Kelly's act of composition and the reader's initiation into the act of reading, another "phase" of the writing process, allows access to a direct communion with charged creative or "cosmic" energy that often proves to be new, strange, and revelatory. The effects of this process of reading, and thus composing, alongside the poet extend then beyond the æsthetic dimension and permeate other discursive fields. In short, something, a process, a "task" occurs as Kelly and reader share in the making of the poem's knowledge, and subsequently "the transformation of the perceived world."

Works Cited

Chris Bell, *I Am the Cosmos* (Rykodisc: 1992).

Paul Blackburn & George Economou, "Introduction," *Proensa: An Anthology of Troubadour Poetry* (Berkeley: University of California, 1978) XIII–XIV.

Phong Bui, John Yau, David Levi Strauss, "ROBERT KELLY with John Yau, David Levi Strauss, & Phong Bui," *The Brooklyn Rail* (January 31, 2013).

Robert Duncan, "Poetry Before Language," *Fictive Certainties: Essays* (NY: New Directions, 1985) 60–64.

——, "Toward an Open Universe," *Fictive Certainties: Essays* (NY: New Directions, 1985) 76–88.

C.G. Jung, *Mysterium Coniunctionis: An Inquiry into the Separation and Synthesis of Psychic Opposites in Alchemy*, tr. R.F.C. Hull (Princeton, NJ: Princeton University Press, 1970).

——, *Psychology and Alchemy*, tr. R.F.C. Hull & Gerhard Adler (Princeton, NJ: Princeton University, 1980).

Robert Kelly, *Finding the Measure* (LA: Black Sparrow, 1968).

——, "Notes on The Poetry of Deep Image," ed. George Economou, Joan Kelly, and Robert Kelly, *Trobar* 2 (1961): 14–16. Reprinted in *A Voice Full of Cities*, pp. 9–12.

——, *Red Actions: Selected Poems, 1960–1993* (LA: Black Sparrow, 1995)

——, "Robert Kelly," *Contemporary Authors Autobiography Series*, Vol. 19, ed. Joyce Nakamura (Farmington Hills: Gale, 1994) 179–206.

David Ossman, "Robert Kelly," *The Sullen Art* (NY: Corinth, 1963) 33–38.

George Quasha & Charles Stein, "Ta'Wil or How To Read: A Five-Way Interactive View of Robert Kelly," in *Vort*, Vol. 5, ed. Barry Alpert (1974) 108–45.

PETER COCKELBERGH

"DAY BY DAY. MAKE IT NEW."
ON SEARCHING FOR RK STARTING POINTS
AND TEACHING THREADS

Reading "Robert Kelly" might seem like a daunting enterprise... There's so much around, i.e. there's so many books — I for one have literally lost count —, so many Robert Kellys (or Kellies?), too. It is, at any rate, a reaction I often get when introducing Kelly in my classroom: over eighty books? Where to begin? And yet. Simply starting, as the cliché goes — starting anywhere — actually suffices. In what follows, I would like to trace one trajectory, one thread as it were, I happened to take with students — a haphazard thread, in the sense that it has a random starting point. (Even if it turned out to be not random at all in the long run.) Before starting off properly, it is, perhaps, important to mention that the aforementioned classroom should be taken as just that: a high school classroom, filled with 16 to 18-year-olds who happened to have chosen literature (instead of PE, Spanish, sciences, philosophy, economics, or music) as their optional. Anything "literary" can therefore be part of those classes: Harold Pinter's *Revue Sketches*, sessions of experimental translating, Baudelaire's "Les bijoux," MF Doom's hip hop lyrics, Donne and Marvell, *Un Chien Andalou*, or a month devoted to one author, of whom at least one book is read and thoroughly discussed... In this case: "Robert Kelly month."

As said, the starting point of my "Robert Kelly month" was to be a random one. (By the way, at two time slots per week, "Robert Kelly month" lasted eight times fifty minutes.) And so, as announced the previous week, upon entering the classroom four books were indeed waiting for my students in the four corners — *The Loom* (1975), *Sentence* (1980), *Threads* (2006), and *Uncertainties* (2011). The idea being that they could examine and browse through them, in order to select one together, as a group. Of these four RKs — why four? Simply because of the number of corners available in my classroom —, *Threads* made it almost immediately: something about the size of the book, but also the title, cover, and look of the poems running lightly down the page. And there you have it, the first Thread — "A ship on the estuary" — as a starting point to begin reading "Robert Kelly" for a month.

8 · A BOOK ON HOW TO READ

The first thing we noticed was the lack of punctuation marks — merely two commas and above all a colon at the end of line 16, which seems to cut the 37-line poem in two halves. Much like translating or performing, form and rhetoric hunting always is a good activity to explore a poem a bit more. What caught our eye next was, for once, not so much the sound patterning, as the subtle play of variations and repetitions on sentence level: for instance, anaphora with "because" initiating lines 11, 12, and 16 (the line that ends with the colon), or the repetition of "one" making a first appearance at the onset of lines 8 and 10, then midline 11 (after "because"), a repetition that is echoed in a reverse "one," i.e. "now" (lines 12 and 15), itself in turn echoed in "know" (line 11), "knowing" (line 9) and "known" (line 15). Here's the first half of the poem:

> 1 As a ship beating up the estuary
> crimson sails disposed to take
> advantage of so contrary a wind
> brings you an awareness
> 5 that comes across an almost endless plain
> every day a new geology
> brings so many things to tell you
> one has come here to you
> by the act of knowing
> 10 one comes to enquire
> because one wants to know all
> because everything is now
> about the little world that isn't you
> the angel said,
> 15 now you can be known
> because you live in ordinary miracle: [119]

What attracted our attention then, was a fourth punctuation mark (easily forgotten, there's a full stop at the very end of the poem only), another anaphora ("brings" at the beginning of lines 4 and 7), and the question of what it all actually *means*?

---

119. Robert Kelly, *Threads* (2005) 12.

One astute student was actually struck by the very first word of the poem, "As," which, combined with the ship and its sails, made him think of that other complex long poem we had read a canto of: "And then went down to the ship, / Set keel to breakers, forth on the godly sea, and / We set up mast and sail on that swart ship." But an "As" is not an "And," in the first place because the former usually signals a simile. The difficulty in this poem is working out that simile, as it seems to veer off in different directions at once. One possibility is to bring the anaphora of "brings" into play: "As a ship ... brings you an awareness ..., so every day brings so many things to tell you." The problem, however, lies in the other potential syntactical offshoots: "a wind brings you an awareness," too, much like "a new geology brings so many things" (in the latter reading, "every day" complements the "coming across the almost endless plain" of the water surface?) and so on.

This veering off of lines, or line halves, is of course related to Kelly's complex take on how words, phrases, lines, line breaks, sentences, stanzas, and poems all dynamically relate to one another. The "Foreword" to *Threads* already hints at this, too: "Sentences have always haunted me. [...] Words strung lightly on a sense of form. *Threads* is my fealty to the tyranny of sentence."[120] To get a good idea of the importance of these complex interrelations, it is good to add a couple of quotes into the mix, such as the following one, taken from a 1980s conversation between Robert Kelly and James Stalker:

> [E]ven in the course of the poem, the syntax, the sentence, the sentential, has to empty itself by way of the line, producing an endless series of these lapses which deny the meaning of the sentence even while taking part in it, so that simultaneously you have a complex sentential built up by lines which are sneering at, running away from, rejecting the very sentence that they are the building blocks of. I love that quality. That quality is part of what I would understand as the rules for lines. A line should not only be interesting, but it should be interesting in dialectic with the whole sentence of which it forms a part.

---

120. Robert Kelly, *Threads* (2005) 9.

This dialectic is also relevant in two other books that were to be found in two other corners of the classroom: *Sentence*, and above all *Uncertainties*, and the blurb actually entirely applies to *Threads*, too:

> Formally, the poem engages with one constraint: each line wants to be semantically intact — ideally, any line could stand alone, be my Last Words, my epitaph. Yet it also must link syntactically or narratively with the line that follows. And each stanza must stand in like relation with the stanzas before and after. This requirement extends to line structure something that I've worked with for years (usually furtively): hypersyntax, where phrases link with what comes before or after, or plausibly stand alone. *Uncertainties* tries to use these strategies in "mental strife," to solicit the dissolving of certainties—in between the in-breath and the outbreath, where nothing is fixed, and freedom begins.[121]

Take out the stanza, i.e. the couplet in the case of *Uncertainties* or the quatrain in *Sentence*, as an active building block, and hyper-syntax, or poly-syntax as Kelly also calls it, is the active constraint that causes to dissolve syntactical certainties in *Threads*, too — whose poem sections are, incidentally, more or less of similar lengths to those constituting *Uncertainties*. This is what opens up the poem's space, all the more so as hypersyntax is, of course, also underpinned by Kelly's already observed use of anaphora, repetition, variation and so on. And their combined effect is what turns his poems into such extremely fluid, or gorgeously supple constructs, which, reminiscent of Mallarmé, make the reader's head whirl as her eyes try to thread a way along.

Hypersyntax, then, also in part explains the title of this book: *Threads* consists of 33 untitled poems or "threads of meaning" running down the pages in a single, complex hyper-syntactic sentence per thread. In that sense, it's a title that also calls to mind other Kelly books — most notably *The Loom* (1975), or the more recent *Heart Thread* (2016) —, hinting at a crucial concept in RK's poetics: that of weaving, in the sense of using

---

121. Pierre Joris & Peter Cockelbergh, *RK1 — A Voice Full of Cities: The Collected Essays of Robert Kelly* (2014) 705.

language to weave "the fabric / of the story," as "the stand / of any story / is our shared / knowledge of the world."[122] Such weaving of words with syntactic threads into the fabric of stories obviously also recalls the etymology of "texts," from Latin *textus* or "tissue," and *texere*, "to weave."

It is in this sense that *The Loom*'s well-know axiom to "say it all" and to "write everything," also helped to shed more light on our first Thread. Before establishing a link, however, it was important to unpack this dense statement, and realize how ambitious its scope actually is. In a conversation with Bradford Morrow for *Conjunctions* (№ 13), Kelly states the following of his adage:

> [N]otice that Write Everything! is not the same as, is in fact the strict opposite of, Write Anything! Write Everything means: Devote yourself steadily to language to express the whole. [...] The whole capacity of human perception, the whole faculty of human expression, the whole infinity of human aspiration. As simply as I can say it: to deny no aspect of human enterprise.

A bold statement indeed, for it implies that the full multiplicity, the infinity of being, not only can be written, but actually is to be written: "To say it all. // Everything, / in twig or fruit or flower, / whatever stage / of its juvenescence, / perfect or not. / Or the only perfect / thing is something that / is."?[123] (Having read this, "being" turned out to be a major motif we started to trace in *Threads*, too.)

The next question then became how as a writer one goes about such an ambitious project? Kelly often refers to this as a vow he took early on, in October 1958 to be precise: "To write every day." This is what "autobiography" means to Kelly, too: it is "the life that writes itself," in truth, "autobiography is now-writing."[124] Which is the reason why Kelly speaks of a vow, and why his project as a poet is so ambitious: it is not writing some verses in one's spare time, or dabbling in form, it is a life-long, daily commitment to writing the infinity of human being, of life and our surrounding world:

---

122. Robert Kelly, *The Loom* (1975) 148.
123. Ibid., 232.
124. Joris & Cockelbergh, *RK1* (2014) 683.

To write every day was the method. To attend to what is said. To listen. To prepare myself for writing by learning everything I could, by hanging out in languages and enduring overdetermined desires, by tolerating my own inclinations as if they had the physical accuracy of gravity. To listen, and say what I heard.[125]

Or, again in *The Loom*'s words: "La Vérité / is day by day."[126] — a statement made with great panache (note the rhythm, and cross-language rhyming), and above all a commitment that truly impresses young adults. My same astute student again linked this to Pound's adage: "Day by day make it new," day by day look for new forms to write down everything, to write down the now.

Time to come back to our first Thread, because the second part of the simile suddenly became clearer: "every day a new geology / brings so many things to tell you." And the following lines also made sense now — the links between "one," "now," and "knowing" can be understood from Kelly's remark on writing everything, & expressing the whole. For that brings to mind that other infamous concept of his, explained in the "(prefix:" to the early essay book *In Time* (1971): "the poets (now) / last scientists of the Whole"[127] in an age of overspecialization.[128] It is that knowledge of the whole, at present, now, expressed day by day, one — i.e. the reader — comes to these pages of *Threads* for: "one wants to know all," and so "one comes to enquire" in these pages how everything is now, how the now can be known, the now as the ordinary day by day miracle of living and (human) being (perfect or not). It also makes clear the incessant recurrence of a "you" in the first half of the poem (five times in sixteen lines!). Even if an ambiguous "you," it certainly (also) addresses

---

125. Ibid., p. 684.
126. Robert Kelly, *The Loom* (Black Sparrow Press, 1975) 109.
127. Robert Kelly, *In Time* (1971) 1–2. And: Joris & Cockelbergh, *RK1* (2014) 82.
128. When teaching RK, I find it's always useful to have a set of "(prefixes": or poem statements and *Loom* sections at hand — whether to help shed light on an older or a more recent poem, they always do just that... shed light. Which in turn testifies to the tremendous consistency of Kelly's poetry & poetics, even if spanning some sixty years of writing everyday. A truly remarkable feat in itself.

the reader, who can be known to herself only upon knowing "about the little world that isn't you." That is what "writing everything" means as an axiom to an entire, and therefore incredibly consistent œuvre, made new day by day, from October 1958 onwards, till this very day, materialized in 80-odd books, among which the recent *Uncertainties* (2011) — lying in the left-hand corner of my classroom — that reminded us once more of this axiom, too, for the motto to that book (still) is "*Tout dire.*"

This brought us seamlessly to the second half of our diptych: lines 17 to 37 of the first Thread, "A ship on the estuary." For at this point, we had hinted only at how it might mean — uncertainly, i.e. openly —, but we hadn't yet said anything about what it all means. Here they go:

>   that things take up space
>   exist in places
>   and places extend through time
> 20 meaningful and with their various colors
>   new country for you
>   to be sure,
>   she went on, information must
>   be broken before it can be given away
> 25 or even checked out for an hour
>   like a chess set in Marine Park
>   for play on concrete tables permanently marked
>   with the alternating signals of the endless game
>   white square dark square
> 30 sparrow droppings random on terrazzo
>   your life also is a table or
>   something measured on a table
>   something shown
>   and now this also datum
> 35 this given thing
>   no longer sounds like only language
>   has time to give to you.[129]

---

129. Robert Kelly, *Threads* (2005) 12–13.

We could simply pick up now where we had left off — the poet as "a scientist of holistic understanding, / a scholar, / a scientist of the whole." For as Kelly explains in another programmatic poem of *In Time*, "re: Snow Jobs / we have got:," the poet as a "scientist of totality," as "world-scholar," is someone "to whom all data whatsoever are of use." Having understood where the idea of the scientist of the whole comes from, we now also understood why "all data whatsoever" are of use to that poet, and why the first Thread talks about information & data in the context of knowing, and coming to these pages to enquire.

There is, however, something strange about this: as the "information must / be broken before it can be given away." It is the image expounded in the following lines (25–32) that allowed us to fully make sense of this. The chess sets in Marine Park have their chess grids permanently marked into the tables, allowing players to come and go, playing sheer infinite sets and sequences of chess contained only by that grid — a founding measure or constraint that allows the game to be played *überhaupt*. For no grid means no infinite sets and sequences, no game, no players. Similarly, human life — all of it, its infinity of daily possibilities and beings, perfect or not — makes sense, becomes meaningful only when "measured," i.e. by *saying* what is heard (instead of just listening), i.e. by being written down, or told as story in poetry.[130]

And so we stumbled upon another key concept in Kelly's poetics, one that is yet again explained in a programmatic poem, attached yet again as a prefix to an early volume, the "(prefix:" to *Finding the Measure* (1968). Here's the crucial second half from this poem:

> The organism
> of the macrocosm, the organism of language,
> the organism of *I* combine in ceaseless naturing
> to propagate a fourth,
> the poem,
> from their trinity.

---

130. It would have led too far in the classroom, but as it happens, *The Loom* also expounds on the importance of tables, their relation to inside / outside, the heart and the voice, or even a Kelly poem called *Tabula*. The table as a place of weaving, and therefore as writing table, too. Cf. Robert Kelly, *The Loom* (1975) 26–33 ff.

> Style is death. Finding the Measure is finding
> a freedom from that death, a way out, a movement
> forward.
>
> Finding the Measure is finding the
> specific music of the hour,
>   the synchronous
> consequence of the motion of the whole world.[131]

The first stanza was, at this point, clear enough: the macrocosm of the world, the identity of the I, and language make for the whole that is triangulated in poetry. The way poetry does this, however, is precisely by "Finding the Measure," which brings us back full circle to the hyper-syntactic structures underlying *Threads* (but also *Sentence* and *Uncertainties* and so many other Kelly books). For doesn't the line "Finding the Measure is finding a freedom [...], a way out, a movement forward" recall the way in which hypersyntax dissolves easy certainties, so that "in between the in-breath and the outbreath [...] nothing is fixed, and freedom begins"?

To fully comprehend this, it proved interesting to read Kelly's seminal essay "Notes on *Line* for *Epoch*" (1980), in which he elaborates on the complex dialectic between line and syntax, which generates both music and meaning. RK's basic conception of the line is that of "a cut of sound," seeing that it is "bordered by silences," literally being "the shortest distance between two silences." In that sense, it "is the *cut* of a line that counts, that makes it count," and finding that *cut* is, of course, Finding the Measure with which to compose the poem. The measure, allowing for composition, is therefore what poetry and music have in common: indeed, a line is "a musical event," it is "how the music happens," because a "line is shaped time" as "music shapes its verbal onwardness." Yet "measure" as a temporal element, also engenders and shapes measure as a spatial element, especially so when writing in short lines raining down the page. Such short lines are "shaped time itself shaping space," to begin with the very space of the page, which "makes a world the line explores" — the image of the page as a world obviously being a crucial one.

---

131. Robert Kelly, *Finding the Measure* (1968) 1. And: Joris & Cockelbergh, *RK1* (2014) 687.

In short, the line as interruption, as a way of Finding the Measure, is how poetry becomes "the hypersyntactic organization of language. Where hypersyntactic means 'subject to a principle undetermined by linguistic rules.'"[132] The musical composition of a poem — its dialectic between line and silence, between line & syntax —, is the way in which the complex relations between the poem's constitutive elements, i.e. its morphemes, words and phrases, are woven to form the fabric of the story, and that story "is our shared knowledge of the world." Kelly's relational view of syntax therefore is a very dynamic one, in which sentences are "wired, wired to move as a body could."[133] What is more, such dialectics, and the complex relations they have to establish always all over again, are a different version of the method of "writing every day" in order to write everything — or, as the nineteenth section of *The Loom* sings it (a section appropriately titled "To say it all"):

> Method: By moving it
> in relation,
>
>   by comparing.
> By contrasting. By putting
> it in you or you in it. By
> writing it down. Erasing it.[134]

This measured combination of language, the macrocosm and the *I* is what informs our first Thread, too: breaking up everyday information is what the poem's measure, i.e. its hypersyntactically, or musically composed lines do, so that the poem finally becomes a given, a datum that "no longer sounds like only language," but "has time to give to you," and shows something, offers knowledge, or truth, and not just facts. In short, life as "something measured on a table," for the measure is what makes it so that *everything* is written — instead of just writing *anything*.

---

132. Joris and Cockelbergh, *RK1* (2014) 699–702.

133. Robert Kelly, *Threads* (2005) 9.

134. Robert Kelly, *The Loom* (1975) 235.

Suddenly, another part that had as yet remained unexplained in the first Thread made sense, too. Writing everything, day by day, means just that: measuring in poetry's language the world's time and place... For a line is that double thing for RK, as he explains at the very onset of "Notes on *Line*": "A host of content and a cut of sound." Poetry isn't just language about language, or music for the sake of music; its cut of sound is precisely what tries to measure up the "macrocosm" and the "*I*," that, broken up, make for the poem's content, as a gift or datum of meaning(fulness) to the reader. In other words, hypersyntax, by means of the line, time and again takes those measures, and breaks the information, day by day, into *datum* — that is the beauty of musical composition. Though the forms differ day by day, this commitment is — in part — what lends Kelly's œuvre such consistency. And sure enough, in an attempt to outsmart each other, a second perspicacious student noticed another parallel with Pound, and his "poem containing history."

It is interesting here, too, to recall the etymology of "datum," literally something given, with *data* also being a medieval Latin formula used in dating letters to record a particular time or place, as in *data epistola*, "letter given or delivered." And isn't this exactly what the first Thread says itself: "that things take up space / exist in places / and places extend through time / meaningful and with their various colors." The ambiguity of whether this concerns the miracle of the whole, of day by day life, or the knowledge thereof offered in the poem itself, or the spatial and temporal dimensions of the line, is all the more interesting.

It shows us at any rate a poetry fully anchored in time and place, in everyday life and its coordinates — as the first five lines of the first Thread actually directly indicate, as well. For those first five lines had remained enigmatic up until now: a last bit of fabric to unthread, as it were... Not that it is in any way truly relevant to those lines, "Thread 16" possibly gave us a very concrete idea of the exact setting in place: Cuttyhunk Island, where Kelly indeed regularly spends time. After a bit of Google mapping, nosy students concluded that the "Marine Park" from line 26 might therefore very well be the New Bedford (MA) Marine Park, where the ferryboat for Cuttyhunk moors. Whether or not originating in that specific place — say, New Bedford —, these first five lines gave us above all a very concrete and accurate image — deep and / or other —, that seizes a visual particular in language: one easily sees the billowing sails, making us aware of the opposite forces at play here, wind, water and land all beating up against each other. It is *that* awareness that is brought by the ship, a datum or given, which brings knowing, and which sets in motion the poem, and the whole volume, in as far as a first poem sets the hypersyntactic, or musical measure for the coming 32 Threads. The subtle, triple use of the verb "to come" not only opens up the syntactical relations, it actually also underpins the movement initiated by this image: "awareness that comes across an almost endless plain" of the ocean (lines 4–5), "one has come here to you" (line 8), and "one comes to enquire" (line 10). That is precisely what Kelly means in his Foreword with sentences being "[t]he bones of meaningfulness on which scraps of flesh or silks might drape for a moment."[135] It might be that an everyday observation in New Bedford gave him this image, setting off his day by day writing, but that is actually irrelevant: its information having been broken and cut up in lines, what counts is the ensuing datum offered to the reader, here in the form of a powerful image conveying contrasts, knowing and measure.

Having thus established a seemingly random starting point, and having found a measure for the remaining Threads, what remained was simply reading and enjoying "Robert Kelly," spending time with him and tracing our own trajectories, whether it was the Hammerkopje in the second Thread — only one of the many birds one finds in Kelly's work, undoubtedly instigated by bird observations on Cuttyhunk Island —, the reappearance of "an old ship still beating / up the estuary" in the seventh Thread, or the two Threads (9 & 10) dealing with Achilles and war — yet another form of contrary forces, conflict and Heraclitean strife —, two threads tying in nicely with the 2009 poem "The Will of Achilles" or the wonderful Cross Cultural Poetics conversation on this poem between Robert Kelly & Leonard Schwartz,[136] offering us a different perspective on the Homeric epic, and on not so long ago US wars. While in many ways, of course, still a very basic RK reading level, this is how far we got at the end of "Robert Kelly month."

---

135. Robert Kelly, *Threads* (2005) 9.
136. Episode #202: Path and Counterpath (December 3, 2009). "Robert Kelly reads from his new long poem 'The Will of Achilles,' available on Web Conjunctions." https://media.sas.upenn.edu/Pennsound/groups/XCP/XCP_202_Kelley_12-03-09.mp3

THREADS 21: ROBERT SAYS

When I was fourteen, I climbed the side steps of the great New York Public Library and demanded a library card [...]. When I was filling out the application, the blank space beside "Occupation" I paused over — certain of the answer, but timid of inscribing it — then wrote down Writer. I have tried to live up to that commitment. Through the years, I have felt more and more the centrality of writing to my task. I'm told I'm a good conversationalist, and I enjoy talking and discoursing — and listening — for hours. But nothing of that really counts until it's inscribed. Yes, I know that what one says, and perhaps even what one thinks, gets inscribed somehow in the spaces of the world — the Akashic record of the old Theosophists, perhaps. But what mattered to me is getting it written down. Writing is from writan, *to scratch something in. No wonder I like pens.*

Once it's written, I'm not so studious to preserve it. I can enjoy the thought of Li Po writing poems all the drunken night and setting them to sail away in the river. Once it's written, the text takes care of itself. Habent sua fata libelli.

But get it written down. Words start speaking in me, and I write them down, and wait for more. After a while, as words come and I begin to write more of them down, the sense of form begins to declare itself. Form is a physical presence, form is a big animal close to my chest and arms, pressing on me. In resisting it, the work under hand takes shape. For a while, I don't know (don't think about, don't care) whether it's what will get called a poem or fiction or prose or essay. That's up to it, as it discloses itself to and through me [...]

But to the terms of your question: no, I don't think my sensibility had matured. I hope it has not yet even now matured. I mean I hope there are some more turns in the fabric before the garment is finally cut into permanent form — and thrown away. But the poems in Armed Descent are part of my work, and seem accurately to lead into most of what I've been learning and doing since then. But as I say, there are poems in it that no longer please me (though they too were doing their best in heading toward something or staking a claim on territory I would come to inhabit or at least explore.) There's even a poem or two in it that I feel pointing toward a kind of poem I have not yet dealt with, let along mastered — a kind of dream narrative caught on the wind.

in conversation with
Simone dos Anjos and Pietro Aman
The Modern Review (2006)

9.
A BOOK OF BIRD'S EYE OVERVIEWS

JED RASULA

TEN DIFFERENT FRUITS ON ONE DIFFERENT TREE

WRITE EVERYTHING

The injunction appears in "Last Light" — "write everything / the oracle said" (FM 84) — and is repeated in *The Loom*, section 16 ("I change my mind"):

> ... Say it all
> over again,
> but say it all.
> Write everything.
> In ten thousand years
> we have only scratched
> the surface.
> In another ten,
> the surface itself
> will be worn away.
> Will we get to
> the fruit we posit
> beneath the rind? (L 209)

The rind is of particular concern in the years following the composition of *The Loom*, particularly in The Convections and "The Stream on the Other Side of the Mind" (AM), where in a slightly giddy fantasy Kelly poses as lecturer:

> ... The mind is
> its "local fact," I argued
> & I agreed we have moved from the nucleus or yolk
> out through the nourishing clarity of the classics & work now
>   year by year
> to break the shell of objective fact. (AM 187)

Omnivores that poets are ("they do not have hobbies they eat / everything" Kelly wrote in *In Time*, p. 25), the goal is not pursued to the neglect of the intervening obstacle, the shell:

> I worked with my delicate opposing thumb
> pausing from time to time
> to eat what I peel off the wall. (AM 188)

The biggest problem for potential readers of Kelly (not the real readers, for whom this can hardly be troubling) is that such uninterruptible digestion deposits a mountain behind. The common theme of the critical appraisals and personal tributes assembled in the Kelly issue of *Vort* in 1974 was "there's so much!" And remember, this was a year before *The Loom*'s 400 pages appeared. Jonathan Williams admitted "The size of the work scares me away..." (83). Guy Davenport claimed, "He has written an Ohio River's length of poetry" (165) and placed Kelly in the post-Olsonian camp of barbarian invaders. "He gets a lifetime of work into a year. He has Picasso's energy and fertility of invention" (164).

Let's address the situation now, June 1982, with the following facts. In the titles published under Kelly's name since the first book, *Armed Descent* in 1961, there are some 2,600 pages of poems. There are in addition about 400 pages of poems published in periodicals from 1958 to the present which do not duplicate material in the books. So Kelly's poetry published to date claims 3,000 pages.

The published prose is substantial, though not to this degree. There are the fiction titles (*The Scorpions*, *Cities*), with the few pamphlets and magazine publications amounting to about only 50 pages. There are the theoretical and speculative prose writings of *In Time* and *Erin Tantra America* with roughly an additional 75 pages of magazine contributions (on poetry, film, theater, translation), as well as the little fantasias *A Line of Sight* and *Wheres*. It's likely the least known aspect of Kelly's prose consists of the various tributes to other writers, reviews of their work, and critical appraisals. The 30-page essay on Zukofsky (1963) remains his only extended critical analysis, but the later tributes to Enslin and Irby are incisive, and the prefaces to books by others are notable (Bialy, Blackburn, Jaffe, McClelland, Meyer, Quasha, Yau). These and occasional reviews amount to about another 100 pages of prose. And finally, there are the interviews, six published between 1963 to 1981, constituting upwards of 75 pages. There's a miscellany of published letters and incidental pieces, mostly from the early to mid-Sixties, bringing the total of Kelly's prose publications altogether to approximately 750 pages.

For anyone who's been through a sizeable chunk of the published material, it should be apparent that Kelly's energies are not parceled out here and there, but have flowed in all directions unbounded for nearly 25 years. It should then be less surprise that the great mass of writing remains unpublished. The Poetry/Rare Books collection at SUNY, Buffalo acquired, in 1981, Kelly's notebooks which are literally the collected writings. Through the past two decades Kelly's practice has been to collect typescripts of all poems chronologically into spring-binders, with the exception of certain larger projects which have similar binders of their own (*Texts*, the unpublished *Comes*, and *The Loom*, for instance). I have no estimate of how much material there is in all, particularly in that different weight paper stocks have been used, and binders of comparable thickness may contain surprisingly different numbers of pages. But in 1980 I did have the opportunity to read through about seven years' worth of work in bound typescript, ranging from the late Sixties to the mid and late Seventies. So I can offer the following observations.

From my examination of the shelves of typescript binders, it was apparent that Kelly has filled at least three of them each year for as long as he's been published. Some years fill as many as five or six. A rough estimate is that each binder contains between two and three hundred pages. A conservative estimate would place the number of typescript pages from 1960 to the present at about 30,000. This estimate includes only poetry. There is a considerable amount of prose, including the "prose transformation of Parsifal" which exceeds a thousand pages, or so I've been told.

Kelly writes poems (stress the plural) every day. One finds in the typescripts many days with half a dozen entries, all reasonably filled out poems. It should be emphasized that these typescripts contain no notes, drafts, shavings as it were: every page is a poem, not necessarily 'fully achieved' but nonetheless complete as stands. The proportion of published poems to unpublished is, in fact, minuscule. One can read through hundreds of pages in the binders before coming across a published poem. The quality of the material is fairly uniform. Kelly's mode of writing as daily practice has meant a relatively even modulation of attentions.

Reading the typescripts can be unnerving, because the habits and obsessions of the man are so plainly evident, even oppressive. But that's to be expected in any body of work attended to day by day. Much as I've admired Kelly's collections through the years, I found my admiration for their assembly substantially increased as a result of reading the typescripts, because the mass of material he has to deal with is awesome indeed. The articulation of a collection like *The Convections*, for instance, out of a few thousand typescript pages, is exquisite. *The Convections* contains work of 1973–75 (some dozen binders), but the published book fills only 125 pages. There is a tone to the book (elegiac, as it happens, to the end of a marriage) which is carefully composed, and not at all 'representative' of the great mass of poems written during that period. This is unlike Spiritual Exercises, where Kelly carefully & accurately notes that "the tone of the book is the tone of its time." The two collections most representative of the range and variety, as well as the highs and lows, of the typescript binders for their periods are *Flesh Dream Book* and *Kill the Messenger*.

"Write everything" was a prescription Kelly had filled many times before he came to articulate it that way, and has continued to fill since. His revisions have been artful but selective; his approach has generally been to write and write and write and trust in having plenty to choose from when the time comes to gather poems for a book. The size of the resulting work is such that it can even defeat Kelly's perception of it as well as his memory of what he's done. This is what compelled me to assemble the outstanding poems published in periodicals over two decades that hadn't been reprinted in books, presenting that "alternate opus" as *The Alchemist to Mercury*. At this point the concerned reader, knowing the true size of both the publications and the writing itself, must take it on faith that Kelly's representation of himself in print has been accurate to his concerns and indicative of his talents.

POEISIS

Kelly has been a formalist poet all along, in the following sense: that the poem is approached as a work site, where the energies brought to verbal articulation bear the formal imprint of their materiality. Each poem a seal, stamped with whatever signet, poured from the same wax.

Kelly has thus written laterally, engaging in his poetry the poetry of others, contributing toward a massive superstructure which is Poetry, like the anonymous builders of the medieval cathedrals invoked in Songs.

Poeisis, or making, has been at the heart of his concerns from the beginning. His earliest presence was as a theorist of "deep image," with emphasis on the practicality of making the poem come alive by accurately opening oneself to the deeper images that the act of composition draws forth. Taking the cue from Nicolas Calas, the 1960 deep image position was that "The fundamental rhythm of the poem is the rhythm of the images...," augmented by rhythms of breath and phrase (or texture), resonance, acoustics. "Every image has its field of force, its shadow moving darkly through the poem, with which the poet must contend." Transformation and process are other terms invoked; the primacy of perception is the base. But "Poetry cannot exhibit naked perception. The clothed percept is the image." The second Trobar editorial (1961) stresses deep image in its connection with vision. The efficiency of these statements at the time was that they underlined the poetry of *Armed Descent* and the long poem "The Exchanges," making clear what the practice rested on and strived for.

Only a year later, in 1962, the theoretical position had been clarified considerably, in a statement for *Nomad* magazine. Kelly is no longer promoting the concept of deep image, as such, though he provides a succinct definition: "deep image is the functional perception of all dimensions beyond the surface." "It is for the poem to move among facts so that the entirety of the visible is visible." "We have not yet clarified our sight, & see still too much out of memory, & not enough by sunlight." "So facts are not just surfaces." Deep image in this context appears to be the visible in its extensiveness, internal and external, where the depth of the image's penetration restores to the poem the condition of light. Visible realities are spiritual clarities. "The gateway is the visible; but we must go in."

The 1962 "Statement" stands as a credo for what is to follow, although it doesn't stand in so prescriptive a relation to the poems as the deep image theories do to *Armed Descent* and "The Exchanges." This may be because Kelly has never had much interest in theory, as such; his poetics is milked out of the overarching cow of the body of his work, and as the years have gone by, his pronouncements on poetics have most often (and most lucidly) occurred within poems. He is not unlike a T'ai Chi master, speaking about the practice while demonstrating the form with his body.

Not surprisingly, then, the next significant enactment — to call it that — of a Kelly poeisis is in a poem called "Commentary on the Gospel According to Thomas" (AM 51) (remember also that *Armed Descent* prints two passages from the Thomas gospel on its title page). This has to do with his repeated epiphany of "the elephants' graveyard" as he has called it, "the silent places / behind the brain" where the images die, "where our lives are slain / minute by minute," in a "brightness of organic event / crossing into the dark." The poem then goes into the image of Christ as the bodily capacity to resurrect the images by tending the physical garden with love. This is a stance which has continually informed Kelly's poetry, and it is a stance, not an idea. It led almost immediately into the watershed composition of *Weeks*, a 180-page poem that decisively inaugurates a new phase in the work (leading directly to *Finding the Measure*, which many would still regard as Kelly's finest book).

The compositional process of *Weeks* is, in effect, an ongoing poetics unfolding from within the sequence of poems. It is all rigorously tied to a proprioceptive awareness of the poem as the issue of physical dynamics, in the sense that it issues from sexual and sensory stimuli, and in the sense that what is at stake is the issue of any stimuli transformed through the act of writing into a dance of words on the page. On one level, *Weeks* consolidates the elegant symmetries of shifting margins and dropped lines, internal spacing and nuances of the phrase that visually characterize many of the poems of this period, particularly *Songs I–XXX*, up through the poems of *Flesh Dream Book*. On another level, *Weeks* was clearly a process of saturating the poetry itself with its own principles, such that it is impossible to extract or condense a poetics from the work. Every day, every entry, every week, is affirmative of the condition of its own articulation. Kelly's poetics are pervasive in *Weeks*, as are many of the thematic episodes, images, and moments he will return to again and again. (The fact that the poem has not been available for reading has, in the end, not been detrimental, because nearly everything it contains has been resurrected elsewhere. What the reader of *Weeks* gains is the realization that what would appear to be an unfolding of themes over many years was all explicitly brought together in this one large scale effort of 1964–65).

"I am interlocutor of the Dream / Work" Kelly wrote early in *Weeks* (p. 19). "The Dream Work" is one of several speculations on a poeisis of dream written in the early Sixties, and the only one to be reprinted later

(*In Time*, 19–24). The premises are that the dream-world is a fully structured interior realm, and that we experience dreams as artifacts, products of psychic event, not simply records of it. Dream is related to Old English drēam, "joy, gladness." "The problem of the Dream Work is not æsthetic, then, but logistic" (22). The acting of the dream and the working of it are two gates pivotal to Kelly's later practice. In *The Loom* particularly, the talismanic provocation of the dream as act issues in a series of narratives which are the dream work, the dream continuing to work as text. It would appear that through careful consideration of the issue of dream and writing here and elsewhere in the mid Sixties, Kelly was able to stabilize his somewhat ambiguous urge for deep image by relating the work of the poem to the actual basis of autonomous psychic production happening all the time. The poetics as articulated in "The Dream Work" and in subsequent texts disavows affiliation with any practice (surrealist, for instance) which seeks to approximate the dream state. Kelly's drive has clearly been to make further contributions to the dreamworld even while awake.

Most of the speculative writings collected in In Time date from the mid Sixties, and the book remains the propositional storehouse of many of Kelly's motivating ideas of that time. There is in fact nothing in the book that is not instructive as well as helpful to readers of his work, difficult though much of it is. But more often than not, Kelly's concerns as articulated there have to do with lore and information rather than any poetics relevant to his stance as maker. The real contribution to poeisis is "Sermo" (27–28), on the cultivation of an inner harvest in the field we are and the field we make. "Those things we make on a frozen earth / free us inward." The image of the field ("What is called Imagination is the harvesting of / the field") turns out to be apt, since in a very real sense Kelly's practice has been to attend to restoring depleted minerals of the field after each harvest, to rotate crops, and to create the inner space for sowing and reaping. It's a paradigm that informs his practice, and while it's less evident recently, images derived from the field-work saturate the later Sixties.

Finding the Measure is as clean an enactment of the poetics of the field as Kelly has given us. It is, properly, his equivalent of Duncan's *The Opening of the Field*. The "prefix" to Finding the Measure is the single most central epiphany of Kelly's poeisis to date, and is reprinted and discussed in the 'fruit' here, called *Finding the Measure*: The reader may even turn to that now and continue this exposition of poetics after absorbing the material presented there.

In 1968, when *Finding the Measure* was published, Kelly complied with a request by John Martin to contribute some assessment of the early Sixties years, the deep image context and associations with New York poets Rothenberg, Wakoski, Schwerner, Antin, Economou, and Eshleman. This brief pamphlet[137] effectively concludes that period of Kelly's life & the poetic community that nurtured him. Written with the considerable achievements of *Finding the Measure, Axon Dendron Tree*, and *Songs I–XXX* behind him, his analysis of deep image conclusively ends his involvement in public theorizing. "Where we were wrong," he writes, "was to speak of deep image when the word we wanted was depth / thing, tehôm. We could have spoken better of the opening door, or the wellhead, or the well to which the hawk swoops to drink, joining air & earth & water with his own fiery nature. The word image botched it, when generations of critics have debased that word into an easy theory that denies intellect & denies music. It was the deep thing we meant, that the poem was itself the battle with Kur, or with the dragon of the deep waters who locks up the fertilities of earth." Even in this retrospective assessment, the context of its time is now evident. The alchemical images guide the analysis and color the perspective in a way that they would not, some seven or eight years later.

If *Statement* closes one phase of public theorizing, *Finding the Measure* opens the mode that has continued to be predominant — a book of poems with a kind of credo attached. *Flesh Dream Book* lacks such a statement, but I would suggest "The Wall" (93–94) as an enactment of poeisis by virtue of the intensity of its resolution of the abiding images of the wall of orgasm and the apples glimpsed on the other side. The next collection, *The Mill of Particulars,* opens with a "prefix" called "Against the Code," an enigmatic series of propositions (beginning with "Language is the only genetics") that squarely place the burden of eternity on language — both as tool for dealing with time, and principle for apprehending eternity. The book also contains "The Mill," a parable which is, like the "prefix" to Finding the Measure, as pervasive an articulation of

---

137. "Statement," Black Sparrow pamphlet, 1968. Reprinted in RK1, 144–151.

Kelly's poetics as we're likely to get. Again, I've provided a deeper entry into this here in the section "Whatever He Thought to Bring to Grind."

Contemporary with *The Mill of Particulars* is *The Loom* which, like *Weeks*, continuously rehearses the principles of its poetics as it goes along, though section 12, "Theory of Narrative," is the most detachable single statement. More fundamental even to both *The Mill* and *The Loom* is the angelic visitation in the prose narrative concluding the long 1971 poem "Injune" (AM 151–159). The angelic visitor reproaches Kelly with a dislike of narrative, which he says portends an unwillingness to be responsible for human actions. A spate of heated argument follows, which is concluded by the angel maintaining that the horrors of human behavior can only be changed by conscious awareness, presaging not only Kelly's assumption of the narrative burden in *The Loom* but that poem's central motifs (to have a way with things as they are; and to change the mind). Anticipating *The Mill*, the concluding image has to do with material thoughtfully stored in the vessel: "Or you are a jar into which all the honey of time has been poured. When time ends, the jar will break & there will be left only the honey you've gathered or restored" (KM 159).

The next collection, *The Convections*, affixes no "prefix" but rather slips it in quietly after the first four poems. It's titled "Purity" and marks a shift in Kelly's attentions from writer to reader, following the general drift of continental theory of the Seventies. "The integer of poetic composition is Interruption," he writes, adding: "A poem is a controlled interruption of the reader's associative mental life." Clear enough, but the piece ends on a true enigma — "So the blank page must have words on it" — linking it with a trio of profoundly elusive statements (or reveries) on poetics: "A Simple Horn,"[138] "A Plucked Flute," and "Piano Tuning" (unpublished, which Kelly was considering as a Sparrow pamphlet but was advised against, owing to the difficulty of its propositions).[139]

The complexities inherent in articulating a poeisis at this point (1973–74) issued in these enigmatic pieces which attempt to coax theory out of image, proclamation out of evasion. "The point, I think," wrote

---

138. "A Simple Horn," *Fiction International*, Vol. 3, № 4 (Fall 1974).

139. "A Plucked Flute" and "Piano Tuning" have since been gathered in RK1, 737–740 & 746–749.

Kelly in "A Simple Horn," "is to wake up in the middle of it (a text) without too vivid a persuasion of how I came to be there. Read my way in... What matters is confusion, a word we need to honor more. To stand in the middle. Muddle. ...To stand confused in the middle of a text, like a man suddenly in a Wyoming meadow..." Ironically, Kelly's poems of this period seem less confused and more lucid than ever. In "A Plucked Flute" he proclaims for the present that "This is a generation of timbres. The old melodies die back, climax vegetation of the great Eur-American plain, after the ice." Revisiting the dictum "write everything," Kelly insists that "To hear is to heal. Who listens, hears everything." The timbres, scales, and capacities of the instrument are the thrust of it: a simple horn "to wake the words," and a "plucked flute" which could only be something like plucking heartstrings. The poetic credo which attends these pronouncements is the concluding poem of *The Convections*, "Orpheus," where "Song is Risk" (C 133):

> aieee or aiooo
> we have achieved
> you & I
> an enviable condition
> called Recency
> known in acute stages as Now
> where his music
> summms around your partials
> & resolves
> what had never even once been risked
> he risks now! (C 132–133)

What sounds like throwing it all to the winds is perhaps a realignment on the question of measure, giving more room to the processual energy by allowing a primacy to words which the 1968 position on measure hadn't been quite committed to. "That we can think our way along a process, processing, and pluck the flute, and go on to witness the ordering of these sounds by the grace of our thinking and feeling in the behavior of the instrument. A proposal, to all kinds of our mind" ("A Plucked Flute").

Readers inclined to confusion by such elliptical propositions were to be left little doubt as to the earnestness of Kelly's position on matters of poetics, when in 1974 three interviews with him were published in the issue of *Vort* devoted to his work, and some 35 pages "On Discourse" composed in 1973 appeared in the Biopoeisis issue of *Io*, edited by Harvey Bialy.[140]

"On Discourse" seems so weighty and impenetrable in some of its propositions the reader is likely to miss the fact that much of it is simply off the cuff, spearing in the dark with a barb for any passing meat. Certain other points are so stimulating they cry out in their brevity for expansion (fortunately the interviews often do just that). It is here in "On Discourse" that we read Kelly's insistence that a poem is not long or short but only "as long as itself" (13). He advocates an art not of objectivity but of the "precise subjective" (18), by means of a "writerly language" (24).

A proposition elementary to the poems of this time — particularly "The Stream on the Other Side of the Mind," "The Convections," and "The World" is that "life can be penetrated from every side" (29). "What is the other side of this place?" he asks, immediately followed as if by an afterthought, "Or the pronouns, to know who they are" (remember that the exacting specifications of I and You date from the poems cited above). Penetrating the matter from every side — essentially finding the measures — is to recognize the Atlantis of personal consequences, "mirror convections of the seafloor below my floor" (31), which, again, provides one of the essential moments in "The World" (MP 152).

It is here in "On Discourse" that Kelly first broaches the notion of the poem proceeding from its first line as self-exegesis, in the manner of ta'wil as studied by Henry Corbin (and gone into at length by Kelly in the *Vort* interview with Stein and Quasha). The concept of ta'wil is vital to *The Loom*, the revision of which Kelly was completing at about this time.

Finally, the topic of the Middle Voice arises here (22–23, 33), which has continued to be evident in Kelly's interests since 1973. He sees the collapse of the middle voice into simple passive as that which is responsible for reducing men to objects, inert material within a field. This vanishing of the middle voice (as in, "I wash myself") he regards as the death of Pan, "one of the profoundest evidences of the departure of the daimones, the 'obsolescence of oracles,' the loss of direct awareness of the spiritual (dynamic) spaces & their occupants..." (22).

---

140. Cf. RK1, 266–289.

At the close of "On Discourse" the middle voice is hailed as reflexive, the "deed for the sake of the doer," "the within for its own sake being within" (36). The within which is the issue is most artfully presented and cannot be paraphrased here. But the interactive discipline which is writing — especially as unfolded by means of ta'wil from the first line of a writerly text — is an other, an outside, an elsewhere which is 'without,' not within; yet without this gift, this extension of the within, it is without even the recognition of what, or how, or what it is without. "Words are the gods of Without." We are reminded again that "the blank page must have words on it."

Since these propositions of the mid Seventies, there has been little manifestation of Kelly's ability to define his practice in poeisis. The *Texts* of 1975 of course are tightly coiled around propositions of textuality and texture, reading and writing, source and substance — too much so to recapitulate here. Some few of the later *Texts* appear in *Kill the Messenger* and are at least solid imaginings within the space of a poeisis, as well as the poem "I would like to find a thing I can talk about" (KM 30–31), which veers as close as anything else in the collection to the nature of a "prefix" like those in *Finding the Measure* or *The Mill of Particulars*. But for my part, I must admit to having once misread the title *Kill the Messenger* as *Kill the Measure*.

While *Spiritual Exercises* also lacks a "prefix," Kelly did take the precaution of appending a statement to his biographical note at the end of the book. He wants to stress that "a poem, any poem, is a deed for writer and reader alike. It is a shared dromenon, a workspace of more than mental and more than emotional activity; the movements of the eye, guided and inhibited by syntax, by space, by the look of silence, commit our bodies also to apprehension, the great alignment." With this we are, clearly, back to first principles and the 1962 "Statement": "The gateway is the visible; but we must go in." He continues in the note to Spiritual Exercises: "This verbal entrainment of physical event is the first gate of spirit — hence the title, which alludes with respectful tongue in cheek to the ignation meditations, where you know you're thinking right if you feel your body trembling and your skin sweating." The note begins by stating that this book, *Spiritual Exercises*, "is a moment in my work that wants to stress" all the things I just quoted. It strikes me that *Spiritual Exercises* stresses these less than any other book of Kelly's, so it's just as well that he closes the note by specifying exactly what does demand a deed or enactment of writer and reader: "The book balances on two experiments in polysyntaxis: 'Sentence' and 'The Emptying.'" Those two long poems are in the fullest sense the shared workspace Kelly invokes in his note. Their intractability makes them impossible to extract a clean poeisis from, other than to intone them exactly as they are in the silence they force on the reader. "The Emptying" is the clearer of the two, aided perhaps by its central movement being condensed to two pages in the poem "Text for Palm Sunday" (SE 24–25).

Wherever it is readers of Kelly feel themselves to have arrived by following his work out to this promontory, these latest "experiments in polysyntaxis" — with their vital interlooping of poeisis and praxis, text and demonstration — are certain to continue to feel the compelling undertow of the man's work, possibly in such a sense as indicated by the title of his next collection of poems, *Under Words*.

CATHECTED WITH COMPLEXITIES

The reader struggling with "Sentence," the most recent of Kelly's difficult poems, arrives surprised at the claim that it is really "a simple poem cathected with complexities" (SE 85). Cathected — from cathexis, Freud's term for intensive psychic energy — usefully returns the reader to the substance of the difficulties, which are maelstroms of psychic energy rather than hermetic lore. In the late Sixties, after publication of *Finding the Measure* and *Songs I–XXX*, when the "Alchemical Journal" and similar publications in magazines were at the forefront of Kelly's work, the convenient claim for inattention was hermeticism. And certainly there are poems that light up fully only to someone conversant with that lore, with the cathexis of textual energy hermetic texts arouse. But it was not much noticed that the real 'difficulties,' such as they were, extended back to the clearly image-based poems of the first book, *Armed Descent*, and to the long poem "The Exchanges," whose Christ theme should have alerted readers to a discernible thread through imaged-based or hermetic difficulties.

There are not, actually, difficulties in Kelly's work; there are mysteries, because Mystery is at the heart of it, the mysterium tremendum of sanctity and grace, the burden on man of "making love salvation" (SE 154).

There is a chalice, a grail cup which is a body or vessel that fills and overflows, spills and is drained away, emptied. This is a cycle of redemption plainly written into Kelly's poetry from "The Exchanges" (1961) to "The Emptying" (1980), through the large mediating axes "The World" and *The Loom* and rehearsed countless times in shorter poems over the years. The short poems are frequently modes of idling, like an engine; but when Kelly shifts into gear the poems enact the same cycle, the passion of the nuclear blaze of the upright impaled man gushing redemption through language.

Publication of *Spiritual Exercises* in 1981 made the underlying nature of this cycle easier to see in the previous work. It doesn't dispel the considerable difficulties, because those difficulties are the reader's share of the work, not to be lightly put aside. Kelly's difficulties, after all, are rarely lapses or confusions (when his attention lapses, the poem becomes prematurely easy): they are instead condensations, saturations, modes of congealing and forming a mass of palpable (sensual) resistance. There is as far as I know nothing in the way of hermetic lore Kelly's work would lead you to which isn't well worth the effort of knowing.

The nature of the difficulties clarifies aspects of Kelly's hermeticism. His work is alive with pagan energies, but the Christian Passion is always the (sometimes invisible) thread stringing the pagan epiphanies together. The simplest advice to a reader prone to be befuddled with the occult strata in a poem is to permit the Christian imagery we're all saturated with to pour into the text, released from the fixity of pure iconography, allowed to be limber enough to trickle or gush as the case may be into the textual receptacle. They will find a place and provide an alignment, an orientation — enough at least to move forward on. I don't advise this as a general approach, but in moments of bewilderment, it is a real handle.

I am not suggesting a Christian 'interpretation' of the work (after all, Kelly in Spiritual Exercises is providing just such an exegesis himself) — remember, I only offer a guide, an aid to reading here — but rather attempting to illuminate the gestural repertoire that underlies it. It must be remembered that Kelly's Christ is private sanctity, spiritual vividness imaged forth as a man. Jesus, that man, is *homo maximus*, archetypal human, Adam Kadmon even, who is always and only a personal configuration, never the administrative property of Church or State (see Kelly's exact position in an interview in the first issue of *Callaghan's Irish Quarterly*,

1981). The rituals that are appropriate to religious practice are agencies of an increase in the participant's awareness, but what is perceived once the ritual is interiorized differs from each to each. And Kelly's work does not duplicate the classic lyric invoice that reports what came in, in what quantity and for what cost; its lyricism is always responsive to the depth to which whatever comes in has to sink before it can be reanimated and returned to text. The reader is of course always subject to that darkness and depth, the alchemical *nigredo*. But the reader should never confuse that depth with strictly informational or textual difficulty. It is, as in "Sentence," a simple poem under hand, whose difficulties are cathected or riveted with psychic energy. These difficulties are not alleviated by the fact that Kelly is a poet of consciousness, offering little lapse into the libidinal pleasures of purely unconscious or free-association fantasies.

When the psychic energy enters a narrative mode, readers have no trouble at all absorbing even the most intractable series of images derived from Hermetic wisdom. Readers of *The Loom* can comprehend the poem and feel satisfied with that comprehension without ever knowing they're seeing an immense catalogue of occult data pass by. The details of *The Loom* are so obedient to the Great Work of the alchemical transfiguration that, in effect, the reader innocent of that is subjected to a kind of brainwashing, whereby the process is inserted directly into the depths without giving any room for quibbling about surface hermeticism. "Who can read this text?" Kelly writes near the opening of "The Book of Water," the most recent narrative, perhaps to remind readers that the ease of story facilitates difficulties that the reader's own prejudices would otherwise filter out. And for a reasonable cause; Kelly, after all, is not much concerned with indoctrinating people into occultism — "for me cosmology is still psychology, my cosmos still psyche" he writes introducing "The Book of Water" (Sparks of Fire, *Io* #29, p. 252).

The most disquieting thing about complaints of Kelly's 'difficulty' is that they often come from competent readers of Pound, Olson, Zukofsky, Duncan et al. This is hogwash: there are no difficulties Kelly inflicts which are not compounded in any of these other poets. In poems like *Song I–XXX* where the actual textual interplay with hermetic material is constant and functional, the reader is aided by a consistent clarity of sensuous imagery (the alchemists used the emblem-book format for a purpose); again, to remember the Christ figure in such circumstances is also to remember the body, arms spread open, completely visible and accessible. "It is the empire/ of the simplest signs" (FM 122). This is from "Opus Leonis," one of Kelly's most difficult hermetic poems, whose lore and physical imagery tells the same story: "& what was baptism / but cold water / thrown on a sleeping man" (FM 122). The water may be cold but remember: sleepers can't read.

NONSTOP IMAGERY OF MAKING LOVE SALVATION

If it were a tribunal, what could be brought out by way of accusation? Kelly cites "the usual nostalgic poem" — "Hearing this / I thought of you / & want you / right now" — and asks "Who of us has not written that poem a hundred times?" (*Credences* #7, p. 125; RK1, p. 241). He asks this rhetorically, and as if in exaggeration names a hundred transgressions. In his own case, it could be reported in the tribunal, the number might easily be a thousand.

I find it not especially rewarding, but an obvious enough task for detractors, to extricate certain principles from Kelly's writing, apply them to his work, and find him lacking. In *In Time*, for instance, Kelly included some observations on America dating from the early Sixties on "Identity Preference Temple-Complex." There he wrote that "The yoga of the west confers identity upon each man in consequences of each man's ability to make Acts of Preference (much of our lives is given over to development & training of that ability). We are trained to discover our identities as products of all we prefer: we are the sum of our preferences" (IT 9–10). "Americans are the least materialistic of all historic peoples." And they are most absorbed in the cult of preference, identity by choice of consumer items. Poets or makers in any sense are materialists; as he ended his 1968 *Statement*, "Last of the materialists, the poet salutes the morning alone."

Now — and here is the clue for the detractors — turn the principle back on its maker and find all the instances in Kelly's work where he ardently joins the cult of preferences (there are many, you can't hope to cite them all). Find all the occasions in which the materialism he reveres becomes a farcical substitute for preference, that is, a fetish.

Turn again to the same essay in *In Time*. He asks "Who is it in me that desires" (IT 7)? It's a question of much import for Kelly's work.

It is the obvious assumption behind the concomitant search aroused by the question "Who is it that I desire"? The dignity this polarity imparts to the work may become indignities in personal relationships and an affront to readers for whom Text is not, strictly, primacy. The hyperbolic ventilation Kelly's poetry establishes between 'I' and 'You' often works in the mode of the "desiring / that contaminates its object and then falls sated back." But it is also this which gives the drive and energy of the work the feel of austerity which most characterizes Kelly and Stevens, candidate for his closest twin. They are the grand poets of American solipsism, most disarming and solemn prophets of the strength of singularity.

The difference between them may finally be that Stevens was mastered by his tone, where Kelly's mastery has always played off the tone, submitted to it often enough, but remained free to assume other proportions. Without that freedom, that disengagement from habit, preference and the solipsistic engines of 'open poetry' (as it came to be called at about the point Kelly was, in the late Sixties, its foremost practitioner), *The Loom* could not have been composed. *The Loom* stands high among Kelly's books not only for its relentless epiphanic drive, but for its commitment to the cosmetic (from kosmos: making up) properties that compel the poet to balance every vision and every triumphant perception with some registration of failure, incompetence, deceit. The wall of women's breasts and hips and thighs moving down on the poet in reproach (L 388) is the only fitting authentic outcome of all the deliciously dizzying fantasy encounters with women which have generated throughout the poem. What can be brought out in reproach by readers who have not penetrated *The Loom* to that point is that these 'encounters' are demeaning to women, that Kelly is something like a colonialist of the imagination (comedian as the letters RK), practicing deceptions on the female natives and consoling them with the notion that sex is a Universal Principle.

This reproach can be addressed to the body of Kelly's poetry in general. There are equivocations of sexual issues throughout; the practice, one feels, is to sanction whatever is desired at that moment, then repudiate it later on. The cycle that this establishes is, not surprisingly, Christian in its exultations, Islamic in its reprisals. Again, to detractors: find the proof of this.

Whatever can be brought out by way of reproach, it is not that there has been any effort at concealment on Kelly's part. Whatever one would fault him with is written clearly again and again throughout the work. He is his own most accurate critic, as when he observes that "I've always been much too willing to jettison the specific place for some lyric observation comes to me out of it" (*Credences* #7, p. 122). It cannot be said, as he has written it of Goethe's creation of Helen, whom "Faust / watched the glory of & forgot to sing" (*Songs* 41), that Kelly has held back anything. The rebuttal is on the contrary that it has all been dispensed too generously, so that the principle of concealment, such as there is, lies in there being too much to have to sort through in order to arrive at any synthetic or analytic grasp.

The single dominating theme of Kelly's work also suffices as the most exacting pronouncement of his poetics: "nonstop imagery of making love salvation" (SE 154). A visionary appetite can engender material abuses, and while some may read love as the heart's gift of a salvation made or attained, others may cringe at 'making love' as anybody's mode of salvation, particularly as a practice of 'nonstop imagery.' But the accurate undecidability here is — let us be reminded — Kelly's. And if we struggle exasperated or flushed with excitement as the case may be, immersed in the materiality of his visions, we are in the end left with the image of Kelly buying a pair of needle-nosed pliers and spark plugs in a hardware store, "as if I were a man on earth" (C 44), likely to be moved or aggravated, according to our lights, by the stubborn grace of his *as if*.

FINDING THE MEASURE

Not the least of the potencies inhering in *Finding the Measure* is the fact that Kelly most clearly articulated his poetics in the book's "prefix." Since the book has been out of print for some time, it seems advisable to reprint it here:

> Finding the Measure is finding the mantram,
> is finding the moon, as index of measure,
> is finding the moon's source;

>   if that source
>   is Sun, Finding the Measure is finding
>   the natural articulation of ideas.
>
>
>   The organism
>   of the macrocosm, the organism of language,
>   the organism of *I* combine in ceaseless naturing
>   to propagate a fourth,
>   the poem,
>   from their trinity.
>
>
>   Style is death. Finding the Measure is
>   finding a freedom from that death, a way out, a
>   movement
>   forward.
>
>   Finding the Measure is finding
>   the specific music of the hour,
>   the synchronous
>   consequence of the motion of the whole world.

Now, this "prefix" ends on nothing less than a renaissance of attention to the music of the spheres. As the contents of the book *Finding the Measure* reveal, Kelly is most at home in the medieval world of the books of hours, the body as a zone of astrological inscriptions and humors, the mind the organism of ascent through the plectrum of the stars. With the processual flexibilities of 20th century poetics in hand,[141] the universe is open at every turn. This very clearly is the basis for Kelly's abundant hermetic compositions of the mid-sixties, centering on *Finding the Measure, Songs I–XXX* and "Alchemical Journal" (in AM).

---

141. Poundian poetics may be more precise. Through the 60s Kelly's practice is deeply indebted to the prosody of *The Cantos,* and his medieval affiliations and pagan energies place his work squarely in the Poundian realm of the book of rites, cycle of seasons, fertility, harmony and justice.

Finding the Measure is in the first, literal, sense a process of modulating the rhythms of both language and attention. So the phrase 'Finding the Measure' is applicable to those moments in Kelly's work where the measure, once found, permits notable acts of ongoing attention. The measure thus found is a mode of tuning or attunement, as well as a mode of address: *Weeks, Songs, Axon Dendron Tree, Sonnets, The Pastorals, Sixteen Odes, The Loom, Texts, Sentence* and *The Emptying* are all indisputable instances of finding and then following a measure. These are to be distinguished from the many other modes of working; the following poems or cycles are more properly work-spaces within which any number of measures might occur: *Round Dances, Lunes, Devotions, Lectiones, The Common Shore, A California Journal*. The centrality of the notion of Finding the Measure to Kelly's canon is evident in the success of the poems with measure found, and the relative confusions or diffusions of the work-space texts.

Measure is claimed in "Opus Leonis" as a universal force: "sun who knows / to measure the year" or "Maya she is, / mayati, he measures" (FM 119). Keeping in mind the cosmography of the spheres' music, the measure is musical base (or bass), and any trope is a turning in a universe continually returning to its utterance of measure, or scale and proportion. (Somewhere Kelly writes of scale and proportion as the only things that can, or should, be taught.) Kelly's measure is, like Pound's, attributable to Confucius' dictum that the model for carving an ax handle is never far from the site of the work proposed. So in "The Sign," two pages after the "prefix" to *Finding the Measure*, we find that in Ireland the mason

> carved the woman part
> in the cornice stone, fitted
> his own prick to the artifact
> glad
>   to have an easy measure
> a touchstone of good work, a
> rule of more than thumb. (FM 4)

The touchstone, the image, the poem, like

9 · A BOOK OF BIRD'S EYE OVERVIEWS

> Sex
> is a process of alignment,
> a magic
> of summoning the electron ghost
> behind the molecule machine (AM 126)

Alignment is orientation (for which the reader should be directed to the writings of Henry Corbin, on the personal orientation or awakening to the Orient of the soul's journey). Kelly fancies the relationship between dead and living to be a reciprocal orientation.

> It is this way with the dead
> that they turn
> back from the doorway & gate of Horn
> to look down our long streets
> like men sighting
> true north along a tricky needle.
>
> They do not leave us willing.
>
> So this earth, our life
> is their compass. (FDB 158)

The needle is the thorn piercing the tongue in "Sun of the Center" (AD) and "The Exchanges" (AM), as well as the compass needle of "The Alchemist" riding "northward through the hemispheres of his brain" (AM 2), guided by "the needle stuck in his brain / inventing true north."

Dream and sex are the firmest needles, Kelly's constant themes & sources from the earliest work on.

> The alignment a dream promises
> opens out from the magnetic altar,
> the old stories linger
> to instruct the dreamer
> how to build the dream
> that teaches him to build. (AM 126)

Readers of *The Loom* will recognize here the source of the temple-building skull-viewing dream that concludes the poem. In terms of the singular orientation proposed by the North of the spiritual Orient (see Corbin's *Man of Light*), sex as a process of alignment is the alignment a dream promises. Sleep is libidinal ravishment, as sex is abandonment to the fulcrum of unconsciousness opened in dream.

> men must have looked the first time fire,
> each time man covered girl in darkness
> his open eyes focused in the dark
>
> ... is it what
> we see when we look in the fire
> what we see in the dark
> moving to the immediate rhythm of the visible
>   moving to the hidden rhythm of the real   (AM 9)

In the coalescing of images here in "The Exchanges" of 1961, the principles elicited continually in *Finding the Measure* five & six years later are articulated.

The piercing thorn recurs to open "The Emptying" 20 years after "The Exchanges": "this will shed light the measures / from before a thorn set out of Jewry" (SE 145). The tongue pierced both by speech and taste is itself a pure measure,

> exactly as a cantaloupe at its
> ripest moment allows itself a gap
> through which its secret flesh transpires
> scent by motion into barren air
> and all some women passing by do note
> this motive and this measure it releases
> always covertly to the place where longing
> knows itself a taster and a taken in
> so opens wide to that which gently
> exudes the meaning of its measures kept
> so long lightfooted by the original stone
> stationed to let no sleeper pass
> this is the original country and you dream   (SE 146–147)

As with the Irish stonemason in "The Sign," in this journey "the rod in your hand is a real measure" (SE 147). As the luminism of sex and dream disclose, an undercurrent of alternating gleam & dark enlivens all. Or in "Song IX," "Certain / measures ride from a disordered past / beat below our ears" (S 30–31). Finding the Measure is there given a further prescription:

> Enact what is.
>   This is alchemy, — here is where you'd
> look for measure,
>   in which a spirit is
> called down into the stone.
>   The altar must be stone
> or enclose a stone. (S 31)

At the end of *The Loom*:

> These things I measured
> in the doubt of time
> using the yardsticks
> my body gave me
> & the shadows
> each stone or construct
> cast — from those
> I learned direction.
> I had no wish
> to impose.
> I found it
> as it was… (L 410)

Finding the Measure, remember, initially locates the moon "as index of measure," lit as it is by the sun, shadowed by earth.

Measure is recognition of the ascent and descent of what is made in what is being made up.

> What happens is that men
> make things up .
> Up is this down to which it comes
> when it comes down . (AM 206)

The function of the yearning poetry obeys carries an injunction that "this fact of love does not stay just a fact on paper... recording the ups and downs of never getting there at all" (KM 31). When it comes down it comes as lightning striking the horizon, a bird in the head loosening the hand, or in the hand — to return to that Confucian image — an ax:

> nothing in this world is
> mine but my action
> yet even then, when
> I have raised the hatchet
> & let it fall straight
> onto the seasoned wood
> whose is the hatchet sun-glinting as it falls,
> whose is the blow?   (FM 97)

In the old lore, *Finding the Measure* was taken as a matter of course: the bodily humors pulsed to the music of the planets in motion, a universal composition in which all things bore signatures of their ascent or descent through the spheres of manifestation. "Through the mists of interstellar energy drifts / the great ones come unfleshing their masks" (FM 63). As for instance, "Venus a young girl bent to peer into the locker room."

> ... "we
> are the flesh of the gods," I told you, did I know
> what I meant? Mars takes it off the wall
> pegs it in to nip Ott at second but his head is buzzing
> is it 1940 is it 1965 is it a day in Thessaly
> an unnamed god is dancing west by south strung out by women
> who will devour him.   (FM 63–64)

The central epiphany of *Flesh Dream Book* is in the poem "The Marks," where it becomes clear that the apparition any process of energy assumes is itself, also, a measure.

> Mask-confidence,
> mask-fear.
> I am the wolf I am the sudden wind

> scattering cloud I am the dreamer doubting his dream
> the dream-carver hollowing a mask
>   that will fit anybody's face
>   The power
> is in that hollow
>   The mask makes noise
>   when the wind blows through   (FDB 92)

The shell of life, any life, is hollowed out to become instrumental to a music. It is, like Pan's pipes in "An Origin" (C 79–80), an instrument. With such ends in view, the centrality of measure to the late poem "The Emptying" is evident: Finding the Measure extends even to the instrumentality of losing grip, being emptied out, hollowed into a purely conductive force, a vessel.

The vessel, chalice or grail has also been central to the work all along. I'll refrain from enumerating its periodicity, ending the scale of this particular measure of Kelly's work with citations of its signature as a pure empty circle. In the Tarot designs attributed to Mantegna,

> there is an angel
> on the card
> called Primum Mobile.
>
> She carries a circle
> a perfectly empty
> sphere.
> An utter circle.
> It is emptiness
> holy silence
> in which we ourselves are meant
> by voice that moves true in us,
> voice of which we are the only words.   (FDB 134)

> a perfect circle
> empty,
> a girl lifts it

>   to her back
>   & bears it
>   all her life
>   negative space for me to enclose
>   ... I refer
>   back to his text,
>   we have sunk
>   beneath a Nature
>   natured
>   by our un-nature
>   to suppose,
>   to suppose
>   it is empty,
>   empty,
>   Mantegna
>   will copy this image,
>   girl angel
>   with ball
>   on back
>   perfect gap
>   our vacuum
>   artifice of breath!
>   No space
>   too small   (MP 152–154)

What this poem, "The World," lights on in the end is the realization that "the light / breaks, / the vessel does not break":

>   What is a world?
>   a vessel
>   "pierced, not broken"
>   by the light   (MP 160)

The experience of being a body in motion, constantly experiencing growth and decay, being subject to measures that in turn must be measured, is oracular. The true nature of the vessel is the alchemical work, and "every orifice is a sybil's cave" (S 74).

9 · A BOOK OF BIRD'S EYE OVERVIEWS

TAKING HEART

The Loom is a book of the heart, which is to say an alchemical book, a recitation of the colors in search of the passionate resolution of the heart's motions in a "very bright red" flowering. "Learn the colors" is the injunction in "An Alchemical Journal" (AM 68). "To marry the colors, in interchange" in *The Loom* (320). "For the sake of the colors" (L 386) the "ordinary day / becomes Kabbalah" (L 264), Finding the Measure like the Irish stonemason fitting his prick to the artifact,

>   in orient
>   an erection
>   to compensate
>   for what goes down.
>   The colors of it,
>   carefully graded.
>   The oven
>   rests.   (L 264–265)

In the alchemic ovens all the colors are resolved toward red. *The Loom* begins with a glimpse of a crab "very bright red" and ends with some fallen petals near a well, also "very bright red." En route we encounter figs, "very sweet, the violent / surprising inner red" of that ancient female fruit (L 84); "a tantric / vivid leaf (L 92); "the necessary Rose" of course (L 96); the sacramental glass of wine with its "color / called ruby" (L 243) and "the ruby cat" (L 265); the flesh itself "its own fever, / 'scarlet' to know / & blushing to care, / rubescent, / swollen & red" (L 361); "the cock of his mind / locked / in his red garden" (L 369); all of this moving toward articulation by means of "Red, the color of / the tip of his tongue" (L 374) in preparation for the detachment of the death's head, the skull removed from the living body and given an altar to speak from:

>   It began to talk
>   & comment on the colors,
>   the black, the white,
>   the yellow, &
>   how they were not enough,
>   good enough in their time
>   but gone now...

> It spoke to me
> & when it did
> blood began to spread
> over its white dome.   (L 414)

The heart is the sacred vessel through all this, but the narrative passages in *The Loom* give the image not only a twist, but a wringing out. There is a scorching passion in play throughout, with a particularly vivid section called "Pain: Dream of the Burnt Heart." Readers long familiar with Kelly's work find this section an astonishing récit of his past preoccupations. Its proximity in *The Loom* to the "Theory of Narrative" section suggests that the medieval embellishment of the qualities and quantities of pain here amounts to a program of lyric ecstasy. The storytellers in the narrative theory section continue their tales on pain of death if they stop, and there is a suggestion in "Pain" that the task of carrying on the story is always insurmountable, that to tell tales is deadly. For "We are silenced / by the way things are" (a refrain to be repeated later in *The Loom*). The section opens with the burden clearly on the bringer of any message: "Whoever comes to this city / bearing the news / is first to suffer..." (L 168) — remember also the title of one of Kelly's books is *Kill the Messenger Who Brings Bad News*. But the message is inexorably delivered, the punishment administered, the story told, the narrator subject to failures of energy, imagination, tact, confidence — a host of enemies abound at every turn of the plot.

The central movement of this section on pain has to do with a dream,

> ... the wild
> blackhaired young man
> she dreamt of,
> who jerked off
> into a fire
> inside the ovens
> deep in earth ...
> but the delight he learned
> had charred black
> a patch of his heart,
> grew larger or blacker

> with each return
> to the cavern ovens
> where he burnt his substance,
> exulting in each spurt. (L 170)

The pain and the ecstasy are a single sulphureous commingling. "Pain makes howl" (L 178). The animal nature, to be burdened with pain, is at the center of even the most striking poem ("Sun of the Center") in Kelly's first book, *Armed Descent*. There is the thorn in the tongue making the animal howl into articulate speech in "The Exchanges." And here in *The Loom*, the "charred heart passage" (L 175). The recitation of self-inflicted tortures in this section is astonishing, culminating in one of those marvelous lists that ease *The Loom* into manageable rhythms from time to time as the intensity threatens to swamp the poem.

The charred heart is a painful image, but it goes back a long way in Kelly's work. In the poem "Receiving" it is quite plainly the furor of a man absorbed with the alchemical colors, beating at the gate of the oven, the heart, to fulminate a full glow. "Anger is way // way to the heart"; "I would be angry with my heart":

> The purpose of anger
> is to squeeze the heart.
> Batter. Futuere. Beat. (AM 129)

In "The Hallway of Isis" section of *The Loom*:

> Batter. Futuere.
> Foutre. To strike
> repeatedly
> demanding
> entrance.
> To fuck
> To knock on the door. (L 255)

> ... The expression
> is an old one, where beating or beats or beat
> translates a word like Latin futuere,
> to batter, jab repeatedly, to fuck. (AM 186)

394

To seek an opening, a way in; to penetrate any opening is fucking, and any fucking opens the heart, the heart that is at the center of anything. "Only the eye has center, & all that can help us comes to the heart of the eye, fucks the eye & we conceive" (AM 166). In "Texts: 14" "place fucked me," and in "The Exchanges" the "vowels & consonants fuck each other into speech" (AM 8). The masochistic realism is, as indicated above, written into the etymologies of words: to seek pleasure is to be beaten by the pleasure, to take heart to beat the heart. "To fuck" is desirable, yet to undergo some suffering is to "get fucked."

"Taking pains" to be accurate in *The Loom* is the dream of the burnt heart, being painfully aware of "things as they are." The easy connotation of the heart as simple feeling is dispensed with at the start: "Heart to heart is dumb squish" (L 25). The heart that moves or impels the story is the heart of the circulation of images. The girl Helen is attractively busy "all day long / with the motions of her heart" (L 33), which unlocks the first resolve of the poem to be full of heart:

> My heart is hubris
> to go beyond
> the simple pump
> & move
> the currents of
> divine intellection
> through the cellular
> (we are taught to
> think of it) cosmos.
> The heart is the only hybrid
> then, not the child
> who varies the powers
> of his immediate
> sources, but the heart
> four-chambered
> (the elements)
> & double-rhythm,
> systole, diastole,
> each faithfully recorded
> light years away

> in the smallest
> capillary,
> current of the heart. (L 34–35)

The image of the Pharaoh Mycerinus and his wife that regulates this section of *The Loom* is then integrated in it the emblem of the heart, as they become the King and Queen of the alchemical bath that will, finally, dissolve the panels of the heart in "The Hallway of Isis" (L 270–271).

The convolutions of the folds of the heart are increased in their ritualistic dimension with the Herculean sacrifices of the bull to the astonishment of the rancher's family (L 141). The sacrificial dream in the poem "The Emptying" clarifies the transfigurative nature of wielding a knife on the heart:

> I dreamed I was an animal and this animal I tethered to the
> furthest tent-peg of my compound my domain
> came to accurate focus in its carnelian eye
> seeing which I slew the animal to myself in worship
> of that which I was in the act becoming by killing
> the become the fine eyes the smart hair of the mane
> assy swellness of the rump sanctified withers
> these I dismembered and when I tore tine heart
> my heart was torn out of me by waking
> into the shivery abstract morning it is till the world
> arching over live in the shape of the beloved
> sucking one more secret from the universal organ (SE 153)

The heart is a charnel house, a depository of pain and sacrifice and loss and self-laceration. This heart of sacrifice is the effective heart of self-management & regulation, mechanical when so utterly contained,

> …the simple mechanism, labor-saving
> device denominate: the Heart.
> That it pumpeth. And what it
> pumpeth, no man knoweth. (L 287)

In the "Episode on Mars" the fact that the heart pumps causes the poem to break out in a rash of confrontation and embarrassment, a failed encounter. All the encounters with women are instructive, but this visit to Mars seems nothing but pure loss. Yet the heart felt beating in the lady's breast under the lecherous hand is more than a pump, more than a mechanism, which suggests in fact that all the women of these encounters have been used as "labor-saving devices" to get at the heart. Here they begin to take exception to this abuse of the heart.

There is a basic confusion about the heart that spans the poem, a fine line along which all the narratives and all the meditations feel their way. This has to do with the heart as woman,

> woman inside, my soul,
> mi alma
> tantrically chingando
> mi corazon)
> (her many arms & legs
> wrapped round tight,
> disguised as
> coronary vessels... (L 190)

Or later:

> My soul, her many legs & arms
> wrapped around my heart, pumping,
> interchanging ecstasy, in & out,
> heart cock, sun cock, for a little while
> hold all the rhythms together. (L 204)

It is a single drive holding all the rhythms, in which the pursuit of women and the search for the heart are the same thing. It leads on the one hand to the abuses of the devil beating his wife, punishing the woman inside himself; and on the other hand it leads to those interior vaults where masculine identity is revealed in its feminine dimension, the coincidence of opposites in the alchemical sense.

"Inside every image / another is visible" (L 91). The urge to return to the same place over and over again is not obsessive at heart, it is rhythmic, organic, rhapsodic, a rending of veils. There is a poem in *Kill the Messenger*, "The Devotees," which condenses the entirety of *The Loom*'s quest for the heart into a page:

> Till in the domestic fire the Sultan saw
> his own heart sealed in light
>
> he did not believe the stone that crumbled
> or the crystalline sand it became.
>
> "Time should have no sway with me at all
> because I am a lover, & that process never ends,
>
> I can never reach finish so I last
> as the swiftest of the slow who hurry there."
>
> Was anybody listening? Did the sky care
> how many lovers or sleepers rolled below it?
>
> "We are the clouds of the mind. From us
> the weather of time takes its direction,
>
> bringing storms to town or ships to safe harbor.
> Why am I the only one who loves?"
>
> Then they split open the fire & showed light,
> slit the light open & showed his human heart.
>
> "You are right," they told him, "you alone
> from the beginning of the world, only You." (KM 189)

In a work as devoted as Kelly's is — to its own principles of composition and manners of attention — the mark of accomplishment lies always in such a poem as "The Devotees." Not for the fascination of it as a poem, as such, but for the way it pumps, the circulation it affords to the fluids that traverse many poems. When Kelly's devotions find a measure as accurate as the action under hand here, every line & phrase carries connotations of other poems. For the close reader, it is a harmony not of themes or stylistic devices, but of the heart. Reading "The Devotees" a reader can take to heart, in a gesture few other poets afford, the entire range of the man's work. The heart is the synthesis of its evocations: I read the poem and, depending on my own mood, my own sympathy, can be moved or roused, feel closely or throb vigorously with the images collected from other poems, as if "The Devotees" were a single view into a whole flowing bloodstream. "The Convections" arrives at the end, preceded by a field of enhancements, including *The Loom*, "Under the Flashing Mountain of Heavenly Iron" (C 73), "Sixteen Odes" (AM 209), and "Arnolfini's Wedding" (MP 119) among others.

"The heart," wrote Kelly in "Equinox 1972: The Surfaces of Spring" (MP 99), "that smallest beehive, surrounds / all the others." In the plasma of a life's work that a poem like *The Loom* plays not only a role in, but has a stake in the redemption of, all the isolated acts of attention, all the individual poems, "whatever he thought to bring to grind" compose a mountain, or an ocean, a vast geography held together by something that moves. And in the end, when the patterns come clear, it will likely be seen that Kelly's work is moved by a heart that is no small box pumping inside, but a taking up of something other and elsewhere that, brought into the heart, makes it beat. In "Of Valentine" (C 61), he writes "Today is to lose our hearts to / but not lose heart," and in the next piece, "The Heavenly Country," he still yearning to unlock the heart as in *The Loom*, confessing himself "a divided man who has trifled with visions of degradation and visions of exaltation without admitting either to the center of my heart" (C 63). Taking heart, that search for the heart's center continues.

WHATEVER HE THOUGHT TO BRING TO GRIND

Two comments on the work of Ken Irby which Kelly made in 1978 are relevant to his own: reading his fellow poet, he says, "makes me think there is no history but personal history." And further, "there is no link but consciousness, no history but notice" (Credences HI, 126–127). These comments illuminate the strength of much of his work, as well as revealing the awkwardness of the quasi-historical work *The Common Shore*, which blatantly confuses personal history with temporal historicity, hoping they'll be the same. Kelly's strength is in his sense of the individual person. "No history but notice" does mean personal history because only persons, as such, notice anything. The history of we and they — the formal history America has always arrogated to itself — is hardly Kelly's domain. His quests and questions always turn significantly on the axis you/me.

> The we that are I's
> are not wise,
>   the I that is me
> after twenty years
>   begins to be.
>   The etymon or what is true
> begins with you. (AM 186–187)

This passage is from "The Stream on the Other Side of the Mind," which balances on the distinction of I from you and the story that unfolds:

> All this while
> I was looking for you.
> That is the predictable
> name of my story.
> I look for you. (AM 188)

A year later, in *Kill the Messenger*, the stream on the other side of the mind is revisited:

> somewhere on the other side of identity
> where there is a population
> I need to reach and blend with you as you are
> to become
> any of the wonderful destinations of the heart (KM 31)

"Across to the Other Side: A Tenderness" is a section of *The Loom*. The You presumed to be on the other side seems to be first posited as such in "The World," where the configuration of the I is so elaborately spun that the resulting figure makes it clear that the self "was not an island / just / the other / side of the stream // just the other" (MP 142). And this other, in the anger and ardor marshalled by Mars in the poem "The Convections," is imprinted with the same unmistakable attributes, as

> ... the changeable
> did change
> and the dust
> blew away
> till I was left
>
> alone
> with the difference
> in mind
> and named it
> You. (C 110)

In all these instances there is a crossing in several senses: crossing a field or a boundary, being at cross purposes, having a cross to bear, being cross. The burden of the boundary is infectious, and rises in the mind to an entire new stratagem, which I & You are only convenient integers of. The island on the other side of the stream, and the stream on the other side of the mind, are coordinates of the mill of particulars:

> On the other side of because there ground a Mill.
>
> It was the Mill of Particulars
> because we heard the word. "When the word comes down, in that respect like the dew, what can we do but wear it?" (MP 96)

Or, to engage the role of the Muses in this place where the words come down like dew:

> What happens is that men
> make things up .
> Up is this down to which it comes
> when it comes down (AM 206)

9 · A BOOK OF BIRD'S EYE OVERVIEWS

The Miller of Particulars confronts those assembled at the door, his countenance impenetrable, not unlike Kafka's doorman: "'Point your words with care,' he said. 'I have been chosen by this apparatus to conduct the discharge of its energy. I have no responsibility to you or your imagined grains. This is the Mill, and I am the Miller of Particulars.'" The supplicants are of course baffled. The leader implores the Miller to appoint a time "'when we can approach the Mill with what we have, to get what we need,'" but nobody seems very clear on what they need, and all are capable of getting by on what they have, their own particulars.

Kelly wrote in 1966, "we are workers / of the particular" (FM 111). The story in "The Stream on the Other Side of the Mind" is "my story,"

> that is, the story
>   I tell to myself
> to account for this time, I mean this particular   (AM 182)

And even recently the particulars inhere, in "A Grammar":

> ... My mass
> is equivalent (he thought) to your desire.
> My spin is precessional and wakes your seasons[142]
> as the thought of you flies back every spring,
> host of absolute particulars, flock of you
> whirring down through and shadowing my mind.
> Your birds are then the only alphabet I read.   (SE 50)

> How to live
> under the shadow
> of the bird that picks me out   (KM 19)

This is the bird "that hovers / over the text... that hovers over the page / reading the world." The passage above, in which the bird "picks me out"

---

142. This line is as good a clue as any to the fact that Kelly's Mill has behind it the mythology of the equinoctial precessions, adumbrated in *Hamlet's Mill* by Giorgio de Santillana & Hertha von Dechend.

— the thought concludes, "picks me out / under the carpet." "Sweep the pattern of the carpet under the carpet / where the pattern can sink through / & become the floor" (KM 19). The carpet pattern on the floor is texture, is text, ground of the "new / dances for my single situation / till all that's left of me is text" (AM 216).

With the text as carpet in mind, we're quickly entering a whirlpool that sucks up particulars throughout Kelly's work. The signs, the seeds, are everywhere, visible because of the birds descending to pick them out. As foretold in *The Loom*, the work begins in the conviction of death, the conviction equally that the life stains the carpet, becomes the text.

> ... So when the killers
> come to kill
> you have a simple word to say
> known only by those about to die.
> The great secret
>   but you leave it to the singing birds to say. (MP 29)

> The sack that holds the sandman's sleep
> is stitched of many birds, feathers still on,
> beaks still on & they cry out,
>   source of the high-frequency terror
> our throats try to imitate
> at the gates of nightmare,
>   groan of ancient door
> we struggle to keep closed. (MP 25)

In the hallway of Isis in *The Loom* an approach is made over a carpet ("dont look at the carpet, / the weaving / has magic in it") while a cloud of distracting particulars ("particles / of which my name is formed, / pressures / from which I grow") assaults the supplicant who "stumbles / & scatters / a flock of partridges" on his way to the goddess:

> He's left his heart
> to enter the room.
> When he remembers that,
> he knows he has only

> one thing to say.
> He says it to her,
> quietly. I
> am what you mean. (L 271)

This is one of several ritual dissolutions in *The Loom*, culminating in the building of the temple where the oracle appears as the skull slipping out of the head to address it. "It began to talk / & comment on the colors" — the colors of the carpet, no doubt — and "Its voice / was also like birds" (L 414). The colors, like the birds' voices, are oracular sounds: "And colors are frequencies" Kelly has it in "Rain" (C 82),

> but the colors he is trying to talk about here
> are those perceptible
> all at once in a grey cool rainy midday,
> but individually knowable
> only one by one as the stations of the process passing
> outside the often overcast windows of the One Work. (C 82)

"Even always bright / colors lose a certain edge from frequency," Kelly reminds here, trying to keep clear what is subject to shadow and what is actually primary. In "A Sermon" in "A Book of Building" — a cycle of poems preceding & preparing for *The Loom*, by constructing verbal equivalents of the Eiffel Tower, "leaving holes in it for the birds to go through" (MP 67) — the intersection of stories and women is taken to be the source of any such carpet that would collect the body's strains into pattern:

> There are now too many stories here. I catch the links of arches or notches, keyholes & ghosts. Now women enter, as they always do, that poignant shadow. But not a shadow. Woman is a primary, neither emanation nor spectre. Blake's tradition confuses Woman with Mother, & blames her energies for the ceaseless weaving on the generative looms. It is in her place that the shuttle moves, but it is in her power to make the shuttle bear a weft of light through the warp of her own energetic nature, yielding no child but light. The womb also teaches Emptiness. (MP 73)

The particulars fall like grain to the ground for the birds, whose flight may be patterned but whose descent to catch the seed is random, a any thing 'made up' must be, coming down as it does to a "condition which is not conditioned":

>   I picked a rock up from the slope
> to illuminate my discourse, This is hard you suppose, &
> crushed it so that the falling grains exhibited
> the pattern of a swallow falling from my hand
> before they distributed themselves on the chaff of the
>   threshing floor
> I stood on to address them & showed no pattern at all. (C 74)

The latest visitation of the deadly women of *The Loom* is "Texts: 3! [Hymn to Phrygian Aphrodite]" (KM 146–147). There is a descent, carpet, and birds.

> Spin the red text.
> You will not wake from me
> nor the world from you, knot over knot
> tightened, hyparxis, the node of Now.
>
> ... So I was land, book. So open
> or closed the text reads on. Land
> calmed into her arrival, the birds
> hung motionless in the air, her doves my
> humdrum sparrows. Hung in the weaving,
> filigree, what's it called,
> the tissue of our consciousness
> shared or not parted, imparted.
>
> ... Later putting her clothes back on she
> looked further inland: Time
> was what they forced there from the ground,
> then seasons spill
> thick in the gunny-sacks
> of seed.

9 · A BOOK OF BIRD'S EYE OVERVIEWS

The harvesting of time is what *The Mill of Particulars* is all about. In *The Cruise of the Pnyx* it is imaged as a bridge — "the bridge / is human life, & the tolls paid are years" — which was once in the reign of Saturn of no diminishment to the passerby. That was the Golden Age, "when everything you ever learned / stood ripe for your use all the time & no seed fell / wasted" (CP 33). The Sphinx in "A Book of Building" teaches this redemption of the particulars:

> Her riddle is resolution.
>
> Connect,
> reenage
> in the detail of your whole life,
>
> you are to find the pattern, find you.   (MP 78)

And it begins to emerge from this that the You so sought and named is nothing other than me-become-text. The riddle of the Sphinx is bestowed by the queen on Ralegh, in the poem of that title in *The Mill of Particulars*,

> where in the evening fire I see the faces
> of all her lovers
> dancing with her, amiable, not too fast,
>
> & therein even her particularity
>
> merges in all
> lovers whatsoever
>
> in that glowing white hot place
> below the flame
> in the heart of the incandescent wood
> where all the images stand still.   (MP 28)

The Mill may not be what the crowd assembled before its gate thinks it is. They may be 'taken in' by the Miller, but not admitted to the Mill. Its apparent structure may be "true to the deep suppose" (KM 146), but "No suppose / is worth the guess it's squinted on" (AM 212).

> A lumbar password: Dance for me
> you do it so it's all wild middle
> grind your mill my meat. (AM 212)

A lumbar password. The crowd in front of the Mill, after the Miller has gone back inside, comfort themselves for his uncooperativeness by presuming the Mill is really theirs.

> ... it wasn't his, we thought and talked, it isn't his, it's ours, our own mill on our own ground, worked by our waters. These conclusions were a comfort, so we broke up and went to our own homes, confident that in time the Mill would declare itself clearly, its work and purpose and choice of grain. Meantime we'd grow what we always grew, to eat and make beer from and feed our animals and save some to grow more. And time would tell.

> And if time never did,
> who among us
> would ever notice or recall
> when that time began,
> or stand out some day
> before the mill
> to call the Miller out
> to answer for his bluff
> and grind at last
> whatever he thought
> to bring with him? (MP 96–97)

[*Credences* 3 (Spring 1984) 127–175]

ELIZABETH ROBINSON

THAT HOLLOW PLACE INSIDE THE WORLD JUST ONE WORD DOWN

For the poet whose oracle famously told us to "Write everything," and who has, also famously, gone on to do so (under what other circumstance could a reader peruse the individual titles she owns by a poet and find herself vaguely ashamed that she has only 30?), the erotic, forward-rush of language would seem to indicate a compelling and positive interest in the transcendent capabilities of language. That is, poetry, and specifically Kelly's poetic language, evinces an optimism and energy "that language is adequate to reach out." Transcendence constructs itself around the accretions of renewing curiosity; Kelly drives the poem forward onto the ever-shifting frontier of what can be known, perceived, recognized. I use the term *transcendent*, in the Kantian sense, as "that which goes beyond" (transcends) any possible knowledge on the part of a human being, "like a shapely sentence never running out" (*Spiritual Exercises*, "Architectures," 37), though Kelly has also described this anecdotally:

> All through that same life dawning there kept getting clearer and clearer a vision, too fancy a word, a sense, just a sense of what I was to do with my energies. And it had to do with the violation of boundaries, with a reaching out toward the totality of human feeling and knowing and wanting, turning that transgression into a structure of its own. (Morrow interview)

Kelly's orientation toward the irresolvable dilemma of such transcendence is such that he engages language as it casts its intentions and queries ever forward of itself, in the leap of faith that we take to be meaning, even if what we intend by "meaning" is something transient, mottled, continually mediated. This risk is characteristic of the generosity and ultimate optimism of his work. Kelly states in his interview with Brad Morrow, "Here the political hope and the spiritual hope of poetry become one. Language is aspiration."

Approaches to anything as problematic as the transcendent (however we may define it) are best carried out with stealth (and in fact are barely permissible in contemporary conversation about poetics, as we all well know by now). Therefore, let me suggest that Kelly has developed a repertoire of strategies for contending with the obstacles inherent in such a project as his is. Among them: erudition, prodigious energy, reverence, irreverence, lasciviousness, sensuality, commitment, humor, empathy, disobedience, attention, and sly inattentions. Perhaps the slyest, stealthiest, sneaking-up-upon strategy toward the imagined wholeness of the transcendent is Kelly's multiplicative, many voiced, multi-hued, infinitely worded and eventually deceptive engagement with the excessive.

At first blush, his appears as a kataphatic, endlessly naming, poetry. That is, by positively engaging with language's ability to create, Kelly gestures and reaches out to, if not the divine, a richly envisioned world of possibility, what he has called "the sheer power of language to achieve the instauration of a new world... Every poet should be Columbus" (Morrow interview). The invocational quality of Robert Kelly's poetry has always moved me, for to call to, and to name, is also to conjure. The endless conjurations that constitute Robert's body of work renew his vision, and ours, in the most fecund of ways. Even while acknowledging that "language is in permanent *détente*" (*Not this Island Music*, 16) the poet returns again and again to rhapsodically name his world and therefore fulfill its being:

> No logic (I went on, growing confident) but the logic of the Secret Alphabet, the hidden firmament behind the sky, the eternally proliferating sculpture of light and warmth and turbulence through which we move all our lives and never look at, never see. Stare into boiling water and see the endlessness of art, the changefulness of beauty. It is movement, it is all movement. It is nothing but movement observed and cherished, lovingly observed and understood. (*Lapis*, 40)

Poetry, so invoked, is a generative, mobile interaction, calling on the artifacts of the world in order to *make* that world; for the restless movement of our conversations "leave records in the world / These memoranda in fact comprise the world // Not *thought* into place *talked* into place" (*Lapis*, 209, italics mine). The formidable force and resource of the poet wrestles the world into being through language. Relatedly, I love and find pertinent this bit from Robert's interview with Morrow: You're raving a bit.

KELLY: Raving is permitted. So is drollness, acuity, measure, sarcasm, sentiment, hope. So is precise knowledge, the names of persons and cities. Dead languages & living women. So is hope.

INTERLOCUTOR: So your excess is an excess of aspiration, it sounds like. When it comes down to it, what really does it compel you to do?

KELLY: To say everything I can. I want to say everything that language can. What else is there to say?

Despite the exhaustiveness and inclusiveness of this saying, the "Secret Alphabet," the memoranda of the world, almost always belie themselves in the circuit of a Kelly poem. The boiling water that comprises the endlessness of art does tend to boil itself away: evaporated. Here, in the kataphatic chorus of his poetry, Kelly feints, steps aside, and opens a via negativa that is the truer heart of his work. (Though I'm really not qualified to comment on this, it seems relevant that Kelly would adopt nondeistic Buddhism in its most colorful and seemingly deistic version, Tibetan Buddhism.) One can see this straddling between kataphasis and apophasis in "A Continuity," where Kelly writes:

> The persistent manifestations of change
> under the gloss of lustrous seeming permanence
> is what the stream had to tell her. "I am a name
> that lingers while the things I am run by."
> So much was obvious. Run dry. Persistent
> enactment of what isn't even there to mean
> is what the telling told her, "I have told
> myself a story in a million voices
> and called it the world." (*Not this Island Music*, 49)

As so often in a Kelly poem, the ecstatic activity of voicing and naming turns sinuously into the paradox of an "enactment of what isn't even there to mean." Here is the apophatic movement that *necessarily* recurs across Kelly's poems, the unsaying that demonstrates mystery by "perform[ing] (rather than assert[ing]) referential openness."[143]

---

143. Michael Sells, *Mystical Languages of Unsaying* (University of Chicago Press, 1994) 8.

As much as Kelly is a poet who desires to experience everything in language, he continually undoes that everything in silence, retraction, and contradiction: "And then I get born and inherit my silence" (*Lapis,* 170).

Apophasis works in this way. The effort to name, to conjure that is the basis of kataphatic theology, inevitably results in limiting and circumscribing the transcendent. By contrast, apophasis strives for the referential openness of negative definition: "*Not* that." Even this process, however, immediately runs up against its own difficulties, as an extended quotation from Michael Sells will clarify:

> To say "X is beyond names," if true, entails that it cannot then be called by the name "X." In turn, the statement "it cannot then be called X" becomes suspect, since the "it," as a pronoun, substitutes for a name, but the transcendent is beyond all names. As I attempt to state the aporia of transcendence, I am caught in a linguistic regress. Each statement I make — positive or "negative" — reveals itself as in need of correction. The correcting statement must then itself be corrected, ad infinitum. The authentic subject of discourse slips continually back beyond each effort to name it or even to deny its nameability." (2)

Consider now a poem called "Advertisement," which I'll quote in its brief entirety, Kelly offers what could just as well be a paraphrase of Sells:

> There is a Biblical quality in poetry, an impassioned rush to revelation. But, just as in the actual Bible, each revelation is of just another mystery. The curtain is swept aside to expose something even more concealed than what had hidden it. Language can never cast itself off. Its satin becomes the skin, as you can tell when you look close, close, at the soft luster of your nearest hand. And blood too is veiled in light.   (*The Time of Voice*, 94)

Here we have an irresolvable quandary, one so luscious that none of us, it seems, can resist it, least of all Robert Kelly. How to resist the beguilements of language? How to use the tool of saying to properly unsay?

In this process, the linguistic regress of modification, correction, and alternate recognitions acquires lavish textures and an eros all its own. Striving toward the site where the transcendent and the immanent conjoin in what I'll provisionally call mystical union, the immanent is supercharged. The poet-creature cannot *know* this transcendence except through "an affirmation of radical immanence. That which is beyond is within. That which is other, is the non-other" (*Sells,* 207).

Kelly's poetry overflows at exactly this conjunction: "It is in language that desires are stored / our bodies take out, try on, use / to quench the moral thirst the pronouns sing" (*Lapis,* 212). And a mere two pages later he writes: "Everything tries to answer the question at once / This eagerness begets a material world // You know better than I how close we are // My name is the same as yours only the letters are different" (214). Tumbling sensuously in the bedclothes of the immanent and the transcendent, one is brought to a state akin to what Fanny Howe calls bewilderment. In the clutch of that pleasure, one finally shuts up and lets the silence in, at least for a moment. In that spare moment, one arrives at the dawning confidence that there will be other moments — intersections — maybe many of them, akin to this one.

What is most important here is that language ceases to be a thing, an object or subject and subverts itself into an event. In Kelly's rendering, the transcendent is not a mode of knowing, but a mode of being that becomes its own unfolding disontology, its own process:

> To know the truth of things is to be on a ladder,
> a ladder of matter, reaching broken
> rung by rung to the mezzanine of soul, from which
> far off the gasping guesser sees
> cloudlessly far in blue the hills of mind. (*The Time of Voice,* 162)

The poem as event and movement provides Kelly with the ability to create "A wedge in the nature of the world / or clock whose numbers change / frequenter than hands" (Quoting from what may be my favorite poem of Kelly's, "For Mary"). Seen this way, the linguistic regress of apophasis that originates in a sort of doubt — the doubt that the transcendent can be named adequately — is transformed into affirmation in Kelly's work, the desire to continue on, discovering new intersections and possibilities within language that might otherwise ossify and close down. See how elegantly he articulates this process:

it's also a *spiritual* necessity, because our habit patterns are best reflected in our usual syntactic orders and the kind of natural fluency great writers have. They become fresh or great through wonderful syntactic inattention that at some moment they suddenly pay attention to. This coming-to-attend makes the difference between a *Typee* and a *Moby-Dick*. It makes the difference between writing that keeps writing one deeper into the system, and writing that might liberate one from it. (Morrow interview)

Can we understand from this (or relate it to) Kelly's statement that, "My answer to the adequate is the excessive"? Excess is a startling apophatic strategy, but it keeps language aloft as engagement and not stasis; its returns and recognitions take us through "wonderful inattention" to that silent place we have not encountered before and thereon into moments of liberation. This puts me in mind of the radical Old Testament conception of devotion as so giving over one's self and estate to the Divine that the result is destruction. The liberation here is an act of faith indeed, but as Kelly has said, "Eventually most of my words will be gone. Each loss changes the artifact remaining. I'm more interested in the changes, the silences to come."

It is at this juncture, right at the generative, paradoxical wedge in the nature of the world that I would like to end. It is at this beguiling, perplexing moment words fit together and open space itself shows itself beyond our ken, or, alternately, language clatters to a stop in its reckless, ramshackle clatter, refusing to fit together its elements into naming and knowing: revelatory white noise. Either way, Kelly demonstrates us in transit within our words:

    and here we go
singing of it, that sacred absence
which is what I mostly know of God.
To love and to be sure, in that hollow
place inside the solid world
just one word down.

9 · A BOOK OF BIRD'S EYE OVERVIEWS

For Mary

A wedge in the nature of the world
or clock whose numbers change
frequenter than hands. It may be milk.
What I remembered of you was cloth
I think, my blurred sight
helping itself out by hands. I feel
you coming across countryside. Be.
Be and make me glad.
The old words come again
sure as the fountains of
remorse that is the core of poetry—
that no one has ever loved enough
or left enough, and here we go
singing of it, that sacred absence
which is what I mostly know of God.
To love and to be sure, in that hollow
place inside the solid world
just one word down. Whose tears
are prime salt, our looks by mercury.
Sulfur dreams. We are apart by alchemy,
clock milk, terrible peace.
I wake to you again
and it is always your birthday.

MARY CAPONEGRO

INCESSANTLY THE SUM

How does one begin to write about an œuvre so vast; how does one focus when every word in every work foregoes its autonomy as it is married to another and another and another to form a vast, reticulate cosmos? *In the beginning was the word*, quotes the poet, winking between the lines, and the originary status of logos is crucial, seminal, nearly literal for Kelly, because in his world, words are eternally generating themselves of thin air, and of this seeming randomness he creates lyric treatises. He can start with anything anywhere and make mysterious sense: perpetually wording and making it flesh. His is the word that can't stop making love to the world, caressing its variety, specificity, complexity, beauty, mystery. To breathe is to say is to write; his CO_2 is language, and his linguistic proliferation disseminates his inexhaustible imagination.

His voice is that of prophet, provocateur, magus, troubadour. Spirit is speech, grammar is grace. "Language is the only fable, and utters, utterly able," he professes in "Peter Quince Heard From Again" (*Spiritual Exercises*, 108) and so his words — not only able but agile, and infinitely malleable — form stories, novels, poems, essays, and he doesn't concern himself much with boundaries, this sentiment made explicit in the afterword of *A Transparent Tree*: "It has never struck me that there is an interesting difference between fiction and poetry" (195). Even within each genre, Kelly must explore / occupy every possible configuration; incessant, supple breath shapes itself in myriad ways: short lines that form sections of a single book-length poem in *The Loom*; a diminutive book-length poem with very long lines — indeed in some sense, one single line — in *Sentence*; a multitude of tiny stories collected over time, four volumes worth — volumes that also include novellas, such as *Cities*; then there is *The Scorpions*, closest to a mainstream novel, but due to its occult preoccupations embraced by sci-fi readers/critics; and finally, off the charts, is the huge 2000-page unpublished *Parsifal*, a mega-novel. The sum total is an inversion of one-size-fits-all; for this is an author who, in evincing what becomes almost a parody of versatility, uses every means available to achieve his goal, though that goal — I'll risk tautology to posit — is to engage in perpetual processing of world and mind, to engage in one vast protean project whose evanescence calls to mind the seven skandas Buddhist see as the illusory component of identity. Anyone who knows his work knows Kelly is no dilettante; he's just a dynamo who can't ignore an opportunity!

Meaning accrues through sheer force of forwardness, of continuousness. But the subject is never less than all-ness, being itself, the world and all therein. Though he enjoys the imposition of structures, he refuses to be enslaved to them. Constraint for him is a casual thing. He can shrug it off as easily as put it on; it's just one of many devices or conceits to play with, as whimsically as a smoker blows an elegant smoke-ring. Whether he dons a device, or merely riffs, the end result is that inexhaustible inventiveness that draws from vast bodies of knowledge to amass a vast body of work, one which more often than not locates its center metaphorically in the body of a lover. Erudition is thus only one of the elements in that CO_2 exhaled by our compulsive creator. Compulsive say-er. (When Kelly cries "say," it can be the conjectural, hypothetical gesture or also the imperative "You — say!" as demonstrated in the poem "Binding by Striking," which opens, "Say I come to you circles," and continues as a catalogue of saying (Under Words, 87). To say is, in any case, to be.

Kelly is a fabular anthropologist, creating from his immense erudition and eloquent speculation whole universes of staggering complexity and specificity. The whimsical is brought to the nth level in his hi-brow sci-fi. *Under words* lie other worlds, and fantasy thereof is linked with fantasy of the erotic breed — betraying a hunger to know the other in two senses: a need to imagine the other, as in a fabricated universe, an alterity, through speculative fiction, and a need for knowing that is sexually derived, driven: to imagine and embrace the contours of the other. Whereas the speaker of the poems is often deeply passionate, the narrating *he* of Kelly's fictions is more likely to be dispassionate. That protagonist or narrator is often a traveler, a rather analytical fellow, perceiving, absorbing, reporting — a Marco Polo with a commitment to the exotic. And both Borges and Calvino come to mind, though *Cities*, unlike that novel whose title includes the modifier, *Invisible*, doesn't make the historical figure explicit. The Far East of Kelly's dreamscape is another continent or another planet, and he too is interested in commerce, exchange, flora and fauna; but the travel is as often into the skin or psyche of an archetypal female presence, and the hugeness of desire coupled with empathy animates all his genre's words. The exotic is not the exclusive locus of Kelly's imagination. "Everything I care for happens all the time," he states in "Love Song I" (*The Mill of Particulars*, 51), so the extraordinary is continually reconstituted of the ordinary. He is a voyeur of the interior, as it were, because he wants to *be* as much as *see*, to merge more than manipulate. A conventional feminist reading of Kelly is unlikely to be a smooth one, as such adoration as he professes seems archaic; the appetitive pervades poem after poem, and one need not wander far within the imagery to find objectification. His indefatigable troubadour stance creates a speaker who cannot cease his rhetorical courting, caressing, obsessing, and making of woman a mythology. The Virgin Mary, Kali, the girl next door — he wants and needs them all, and gives them equal billing. Mythology in general is one tremendous stimulus in Kelly's work, all manner of myth, be it Judeo-Christian, Buddhist, Kabalistic, ancient; he has a fascination with taxonomies (astrology, Tarot, alchemy) of mystery, of mysticism in general. The syncretic sum is too complex to bear a conventional rubric: call it Kellyology. He is himself a visionary, and his vision would appear to encompass every species of flower fused with every manifestation of deity. Spiritual and sensual are also fused. Psyche is speech. Voyeurism becomes a trope for empathy, and sometimes he gives it a creepy surface but more often a benign one, its thrust not harming but honoring and being complete, because in Kelly's mythology the male is inadequate; the woman's rib would have made the man, not vice versa. And the woman is redemptive. He is not intending to imprison her in his lust or hypostasize her upon his pedestal but to declare his dependence on her. It is not she who is incomplete without his gaze, but he, insufficient without her grace. Parity it's not, but one must understand this lust to be for soul as well as flesh.

Not only Mary, but the Christ of conventional mythology presides as well: his suffering and compassion (in passages too numerous to cite); Kelly's entire œuvre is predicated upon incarnation, and through his work, he aspires to render the world more compassionate, even while his fictive anti-heroes are more often than not a chilly lot. Cool journalistic observers, they leave the poet's warmth and humanity at the door as they enter novel or story with swagger or detachment. They are characters, after all (much less close to Kelly than the speaker of his poems and tiny tales), and I'd venture, his most successful fictional creations, because they are more "fashioned" in this fictive sense. They calculate instead of ruminate or meditate, the latter characterizing the consciousness delineated in the smaller or fragmented fictional pieces. Concrete detail here is again parodic in its prolificacy — because it catapults us further toward the fantastic. One is in awe as well as charmed, as with Amos Tutuola's *Palm Wine Drunkard* and his "spurious specificity." We find these Kellyfellows face to face with fate and fortune and determinism and such — Borges' turf. The world in its least salient aspect is fodder for wonder in Kelly's mythos, and he makes us marvel, whether he be regarding a speck of sunlight or creating a country out of thin air — because regardless of the scale on which he works his magic, he performs it with authority. Saying literally here makes it so; hurl a word into the cosmos and witness it become material.

> I want a language
> that cannot negate itself!
> Where every *said*
> is permanent! (*Spiritual Exercises*, 141)

This grand rhetoric of desire is in effect what his body of work accomplishes; it is unstoppable and apodictic, it overwhelms with, to use a Nabokov phrase, volume and volubility, and keeps us perpetually mesmerized. It is protean and ingenious. You can't catch me, it says continuously, but that saying is itself perpetual breath. This is the Christology of Kelly's upbringing transmuted, word to flesh to word again. His illuminated intimacy with language is expressed in "A Thing Forgives Language":

> they think language is a convenience
> we know it's laundry
> language the stains that wash out of experience...
> language would be natural and continuous and behaviorful
> as the sky or ocean is
> as all the chances of
> ocean wave typhoon and sea serene
> are water, are just water
> so all the enterprise of language is just breath
> serene and elemental
> air of us (*The Time of Voice*, 69)

Indeed there is something oceanic about the Kelly œuvre; he himself an ocean of mentation, erudition, and imagining, an amniotic medium through which the natural world and the world of intellection and the other-worldly gracefully, effortlessly, ceaselessly flow into one another. His natural status as sage and magus dictates that just saying pretty wouldn't be enough if he weren't also fashioning his own theology. His ars poetica *is* his art, his poetry; it is in every line and its interstices. He's not didactic but he is inherently apodictic. The etiology of this condition is suggested in the poem, "Every Language is a Second Language."

A gull crashed into my language and I fell

Into speaking, but how else could I have answered
All those old people my mother aimed me at
And told me "Speak, say something, Bobby!"

For Something evidently had need of my accounting
I've been attending to it all my life
With my animal alphabet, my hunger
Trying to still itself with their words. (*The Time of Voice*, 35)

This honesty (autobiographically interpreted) accounts, to the reader, for Kelly's vast output, and the compulsiveness that overcorrects with such eloquent intelligence. The "animal" hunger is that appetitive function that can never be sated, never have experienced enough saying, seeing, wanting. "Who is left to name the pieces of the world?" asks the poet in "Amsterdam Window" (*The Time of Voice*, 34), after chastising philosophy for doing the very thing the prior poem elicited from him: "accounting." Kelly, content to digest all the philosophical systems civilization has produced, seems perfectly situated to critique methodology, discourage enslavement to system in general, or point out the limitations of the "purely" analytical. We should, instead, "attend," he tells us, and the pathos of his psuedo- or anti-pedantry is that he no doubt feels responsible for those hypothetical/metaphorical "pieces of the world." Whether they be designated *unaccounted for*, or *unattended to*, one can guarantee his instinct is to caress every shard and create it anew: Adam's task revisited, redemptive. As he asserts in the poem, "Celestial Linguistics,"

> Well, simply, we should start out
> Giving everything new names.
> Since you asked me. What we have
> is good enough, but may not
> be God enough ... *(The Time of Voice,* 126)

How does he accomplish his own brand of Poundian making new? He defamiliarizes, in accordance with the Russian formalist dictum, *make it strange*, and so the ordinary is ever being reconstituted into the extraordinary. Even when his fiction hovers in the realm of the domestic it has an otherworldly quality (e.g. a woman ironing falls into a void etc.), but often he takes the fabular route; as in "Wheres" (*A Transparent Tree*, 141–148), in which a profusion of concrete detail achieves the opposite of what conventional fiction offers: it ingrains an ireality rather than reinforcing the mimetic. Kelly is a conjurer of customs, rituals, commerce; he delights in anthropological transmutation. And whereas conventional fiction would have us know a self more deeply as the text progresses, the protean quality of Kelly's vision insists that the kaleidoscopic other is as stable as any self (just as in Buddhist thought, identity is deconstructed into seven skanda), and the practice of compassionate non-attachment seems analogous to what Kelly won't allow his readers to glom onto through his crafty characterization (though glom on is exactly what "The Guest" does to his host, making for a chilly, icky-yet-intriguing intimacy in which the voyeuristic impulse is transformed into a causal agent). In the "travel-lit," discovery is constant; revelation is disseminated democratically if you will, and he resists the conventional fiction's build toward epiphany (just as he resists an expectation that the enormous sincerity and compassion in the poetry will find its way to his protagonists, whose lusts and detached observations are not thus warmed). The huge, unpublished *Parsifal* is an exception; its complex agenda includes a more complex mimetic characterization — even within an irrealist and allegorical framework — that embraces vulnerability in the male and allows male desire to move beyond objectification of the female, who is herself fleshed out in ways beyond the fleshly.

"A Line of Sight" (*Doctor of Silence*, 89–101), an early work from 1974, might be the closest to domestic fiction, though it is hardly fiction — something like the personal essay perhaps, before it was fashionable, or a form which parodically interpolates footnotes into fiction, but here playing it closer to "straight." This is, in fact, Kelly, speaking straightforwardly of his own house, but of course, that wouldn't be sufficient for him: he situates it geographically, historically, and innovates by using footnotes to contextualize and thus extend the horizons of the domestic. Some other Kelly fictions bring to mind the early Lydia Davis fables or the *Tropisms* of Nathalie Sarraute from 1939. They range greatly and are informed by Kafka, Borges, and Cortazar. They are meditations, suggestions of story, but identities are often swallowed up in a wash of pronouns, the speakers only nominally "subject-centers." A name could just as easily be another name, I suppose, for Kelly, so why bother to get attached to one? — the only stable ones being those many to whom poems are regularly dedicated, showing that sometimes the motivation for poem or story is a being in the world. He would wish to liberate fiction from such constraints as identity. One might paraphrase the Kelly stance as follows: Words keep passing through my mouth, how can I claim a single one and call it self? This evanescence is articulated without compromising its elusiveness in the catechism section of the poem titled "Toward the Day of Liberation" — and how like the all-encompassing, negative-capability-inducing, contradictory Kelly to be pseudo-didactic and deconstructive simultaneously:

Language? To use language for the sake of communication is like using a forest of ancient trees to make paper towels and cardboard boxes from all those years the wind and crows danced in the up of its slow.

> A word is not to hear
> And not to say—
> what is a word?
>
> The Catechism begins:
> Who made you?
> Language made me
> Why did it make you ...
>
> A word is the shadow of a body passing
> Whose body is that?
> The shadow's own. (*Not This Island Music*, 110)

He who is a scholar and subscriber to so many gods, holds one, the logos, supreme. Thus he comes full circle, for who made him he makes, and remakes, daily.

In his "Russian Tales" (*Cat Scratch Fever*, 49–72) morphemes burst into story: charming fairy tales, whose playful nod to linguistic/grammatical structures makes for sheer delight. Once again, language, and here linguistic *organization*, generates story, but not through strict procedural mechanisms. That's how it is for Kelly: he does not write systematically — though one might say, religiously! — and can range loosely since his brain contains a plethora of paradigms. Both enamored and suspicious of systems, in his voraciousness he consumes them whole. He alternates ingeniously between third person and second person narrative, creating in the former, endearing figures who inhabit a magical realm as white as *The Scorpion*'s is black, and in the latter, offering playful instructional narratives, that would seem to be the province of the fortune-teller. The catechistic gravity of "Toward a Day of Liberation" recedes. He casts his incantatory spell, but tongue-in-cheek, and by the time we get to XXXII, "An Old Couple Who Live Toward the End of the Alphabet," we surrender to the masterful improvisatory riff that builds sound into sense even as it suggests an irresistible lyrical nonsense. (Its effortless momentum suggests *Sentence*, to which we have yet to get!) In the afterword of *A Transparent Tree*, he tells us that a story's ending reveals the writer rather than ends the story. And this seems borne out in almost all the small pieces; they resist closure of any traditional sort.

As to personæ, he also plays the voyeur in much milder forms than those already discussed, in his persona poems, for example. He does explore family history, and history in general; he dons masks, he probes myth, but his huge mythological preoccupations are not, in other than a formal sense, masks. Unlike other poets who might hide behind them to avoid confronting real emotions, or the messier realms of self-ness, Kelly, in his poetry, traverses deep emotion without squeamishness, but his autobiographical impulses / gestures are never merely personal. For him, the personal is always part of a larger network that encompasses as well the linguistic, the cultural, the mythological, the historical, the philosophical. The 70's confessional gesture in poetry is transformed into something so much larger through his unparalleled erudition, passion, and imagination. He reconstitutes *how it is* as dream.

And we can also turn that idea inside out. He who knows etymology so thoroughly can authoritatively say (as in the epilogue of *Underwords*), "words are narratives intact in themselves." He is fully aware as he uses this or that word, of the evolutionary chain that brought it to its current state, and yet, as he says, a spiritual etymology is of interest to him; there is not only historical derivation but a more subjective one as well, & we're not talking *langue* vs. *parole* here, but something anti-scientific (or extra-scientific), almost a magical property, that Kelly, who just as he does not distinguish between genres, does not distinguish between the 'hokey' systems (homeopathy, astrology, alchemy) and the sanctioned systems (science, history); he uses these tools indiscriminately, one might say, democratically.

Everything connects to something else for Kelly, he can't really stop himself, or end a story, for breath must issue until death, continuous, during waking, during sleep. In the prose-poem, "The Nature of Metaphor," he playfully posits a hypothetical causal chain of misinterpretation, signals of threat that are passed on, like dominoes, and come full circle, with a gendered component: man fearing chaos, woman fearing man, boy fearing maternal fear etc. — not quite slapstick. The imagery is, as always, arresting. And Kelly is a master at peering under gestures as well as under words. We flee from each other and make of our interpretations alienation? But so often, he uncovers the opposite; the chain is of attraction of communion of connection. In either case, he brings all such tendencies to the mythic level. And as always, form and language itself lead the way, enact the proposition. Take *Sentence*, the lengthy poem first published as a square-shaped *Station Hill* chapbook, then included in *Spiritual Exercises*. By my reckoning, its objective might be formulated thus: to say the word a single sentence and let there be song! He fashions a thought which in turn absorbs everything in its path, the sheer linguistic exuberance of which propels it forward, as it embraces many elements, themes, reprises, tropes, what-have-you.

> ...where even the fashions of language disclose
> a mode of infinite analysis infinitely ready
> to do the will of what will it is that savvies
> the system we speak before we know its sense (*Spiritual Exercises*, 93)

Sentence's form truly is organic form. The stanzaic regularity available to the eye disguises its unique music, which, like an aerialist's death-defying, protracted acrobatics, defies gravity in the form of never needing to land, i.e. break the line, suspending itself majestically. (It does, however, find epiphany in exploration of divinity, and thus achieves a species of apotheosis.) The utter rigor of its stanzaic composition, against the anarchic freedom of its only-incidentally-causal confluence, makes for the music of a mythic mentation. The reflection's lyrical drive is as inexorable as narrative drive, but it seems determined to elude to the exact degree that it engages. In Part I, for example, the enjambment occurring between the last word of one stanza and the first of the next might be only vaguely logical, while in Part II, consistently "coherent," then drop away again in Part III. This is a poem that speaks in tongues; it traverses so many worlds of thought and feeling, floating and grounded at once, in its inscrutable ongoingness. It concerns itself with language, love, lust, nature, myth, the cosmos entire (writ both large and small). Here again Kelly sits at his linguistic loom weaving language from nursery rhymes and folksongs with complicated discursive propositions, and the language becomes its own motor with the momentum that is uniquely his. It is, again, organic, it is oceanic.

The topics are simple, elemental ones: light water earth stars weather sun wind, yet each as invoked shimmers with an immanence, with visionary fervor: a mythic ethos. The word joins word, they make chains, form aggregates, and often as not incline themselves in causal direction, but that might be just another option, another form of linguistic tropism; because if a reader stands back and receives them with appropriate negative capability, they can also shimmer in exalted anarchic splendor — not to the explicitly, polemically deconstructive objective of LANGUAGE POETRY, but in the service of a more musical, sensuous order that comprises an exalted, ineluctable riffing of the gods. Here we see, in action, the visionary as medium. There are so many rich strands of meaning; a line or thought is constantly undergoing conversion to a new thought or thing and thus interruption is transposed to continuity in that inimitable Kellyian fashion. Ultimately there is no irrelevant matter, as the poem achieves a zero degree of separation between any thing and any other thing. Flotsam and jetsam conspire benignly to form constellations.

Try to parse the poem & you'll end up stumped, but surrender to it, ride it as the oceanic wave it seeks to be, and the whole world is exhilaratingly made new. The radiant energy of a star or the sun is then at one with, for example, sexual dynamism, linguistic legerdemain. "Prise the metaphor right off the wall," he says in one line, and in a sense, that is what this sheer force of language does: an uncanny movement, self-propelled, never forced or strained, though the reader may, in trying to interpret, strain, and one could accuse Kelly of whimsy, but such intelligent erudite whimsy is on another plane altogether. Intuition leading intellect. The mention of a pair of socks leads effortlessly elsewhere, coalescing into theoretical, philosophical commentary that will, as well, eventually lead elsewhere, in the "infinite web" — "this camarilla of discourse that never stops."

> that nothing in this world is contrary
> and every star the sum of all! The taste of yeasts
> persuasion by which we are fermented
> in the illegible fullness of the dictionary
> spell incessantly the sum of all. (*Spiritual Exercises*, 95)

Sentence, in its inimitable inscrutable way "spells out" the Kelly project. For all the stories, poems, fables, novels, novellas, essays have that common enterprise. They are committed through his vastly prolific lifetime to "spell incessantly the sum of all."

THREADS 22: ROBERT SAYS

I'm fascinated by rain, it's my favorite weather, I love rain [...] and I keep thinking about the way people are with rain: the sky opens, a lot of water falls out of the sky and very shapely and pretty and focused and it doesn't last usually very long, and people scream and carry on as if God were angry at them, and in fact often create a god like Jupiter or Pluvius, who is angry, whereas what would happen if you stood in the rain for a long time is that you get wet, eventually you dry, you might even feel the wonderful sensation of coldness or, I mean the way last week we had terrible heat and the rain came and each day it came and relieved us. In fact it was raining when you talked with me on the phone, you were getting it and I was to get it a few minutes later. [...]

[It] hadn't started here yet, but I could hear the thunder over the phone as well as the thunder in the sky. But I think the way we react to rain is not unlike the way we react to art. We're somehow afraid of it without quite knowing why, it doesn't actually do *anything to us, it just gets us wet, and wetness has a way of taking care of itself and drying. [...] [T]hey are afraid it will do something to them, whereas all it will do is give them an experience. It's not an experience like violence or certain kinds of sexuality that leave a tremendous* effect *afterwards, it's an experience that you're left with. So the challenge of a piece of writing like mine, I think, shouldn't be the challenge of understanding it* as you go along, *but the challenge of reading it and then letting it rest in the mind. Because I keep thinking of natural examples, I mean if you look out a window and see a tree moving in the breeze, I'm seeing that now — if I tried to* understand *that,*

I would lose much of my contact with the tree and with the wind, I'd try to work out the physics of the wind, and eventually I might want to do that and become a critic of the wind or a critic of the tree, but in the meantime it's so much more gratifying to look at it quietly, *to experience it deeply and quietly, and then let it see what happens later on in yourself. You've had the experience I'm sure of meeting someone not making a big impression on you, and yet that night in your dream or the next morning when you wake up, that's the person you think about. You hardly noticed him when you met him [...] and that's what I think writing should be, you read it and say, Oh, so what, and then a day later or a month later, a year later, somebody come in your mind,* it has processed itself inside you.

in conversation with
Bonnie Langston (1994)

10.
A BOOK OF SPECIFICS

THOMAS MEYER

the origin, far side of a lake
is always shadow

THE MIDDLE VOICE

Now listen!

Gertrude Stein:

Can't you see that when the language was new — as it was with Chaucer and Homer — the poet could use the name of a thing and the thing was really there? He could say "O moon," "O sea," "O love" and the moon and the sea and love were really there. And can't you see that after hundreds of years had gone by and thousands of poems had been written, he could call on those words and find that they were just wornout literary words? The excitingness of pure being had withdrawn from them; they were just rather stale literary words. Now the poet has to work in the excitingness of pure being; he has to get back that intensity into the language. We all know that it's hard to write poetry in a late age; and we know that you have to put some strangeness, something unexpected, into the structure of the sentence in order to bring back vitality to the noun. Now it's not enough to be bizarre; the strangeness in the sentence structure has to come from the poetic gift, too. That's why it's doubly hard to be a poet in a late age. Now you all have seen hundreds of poems about roses and you know in your bones the rose is not there. All those songs that sopranos sing as encores about "I have a garden; oh what a garden!" Now I don't want to put too much emphasis on that line, because it's just one line in a longer poem. But I notice that you all know it; you make fun of it, but you know it. Now listen! I'm no fool. I know that in daily life we don't go around saying "is a... is a... is a..." Yes, I'm no fool; but I think that in that line the rose is red for the first time in English poetry for a hundred years.

Now listen:

Robert Kelly: Weeks

                    Let it be pleased
of origins,
    fat
of the shade's branch, be
root where it may.

In that stanza the shade's branch is fat for the first time ever in English.

Trobar Clus:

The opacity of the poem, its being in shade

Statement (1968):

the line, the hypersyntactic, the silence, to disturb the normal

deadening flow, the line, life / line

Map of Annandale:

(Sometimes I've had little sense of the matter.

I'm trying to provide you with a glyph

to recognize my movements by...

Something of that *glyph* is perhaps what I'm after.

100 useful things; not an enchiridion, nor a digest, nor commonplace book or even a list. More like notes or tabletalk.

A personal archeology. A florilegium. Some little project akin to Walter Benjamin's arcades?

Piths & gists. What "spoke to my condition" as George Fox might've said — or Martin Buber.

Sort of "an anthology of influence," which may in fact be no more than "the invention of influence."

THE MIDDLE VOICE

Speaking from a condition neither active nor passive but somewhere in between. Something like a field of possibilities where intention arises through observation.

The transubstantiation of attention and experience.

The poet as an instrument of the poem.

Finding the Measure:

> Finding the Measure is finding the
> specific music of the hour,
>   the synchronous
> consequence of the motion of the whole world.

FLESH: DREAM: BOOK:

The title *Flesh Dream Book* identifies the three great sources of human information: the flesh of sensory experience, dream & vision, & the holy book of tradition & learning, shared thru time. Perhaps at least it sets the priorities straight: *Flesh: Dream: Book.*

Lectiones:

lectio, a gathering, a reading aloud. Reading aloud the texts provided, going over the books of the law: coming or coming back to the *matter,* the information.

St Augustine:

Tolle Lege — Take Read

In order to understand anything in this world we must learn how to read it, which doesn't mean it will always be read the same way on subsequent occasions or even during the present one. That these variant readings can be concurrent comes as no surprise...

Robert Kelly's work asks us to take it up and read just as he takes up this world and reads it to us...

Take. To grasp, grip, seize, lay hold of, to touch with the fingers.

Read. The sense of considering or explaining ordinary writing expressed as speech.

To read is to be counseled, hence ready.

Walt Whitman: Democratic Vistas

... the process of reading is not a half-sleep, but, in the highest sense, an exercise, a gymnast's struggle; that the reader is to do something for himself, must be on the alert, must himself or herself construct indeed the poem, argument, history, metaphysical essay — the text furnishing the hints, the clue, the start or framework.

Reverie:

A play of engagement with the natural world, not in the sense of idle daydream, but the specifically French sense Rousseau gives it, or later Gaston Bachelard: an alert, mindful, yet spontaneous style of thought in which ideas follow their bent without resistance or constraint. Unlike scientific & deliberative thought, reverie is not governed by a particular purpose or ground plan — to establish a hypothesis, say, or achieve some goal. In its sensitivity to the "reverberations" of things reverie is a way we open up the world to ourselves & enter the space of elsewhere. Through its supple responsiveness, reverie nurtures a knack for connections, for a unity of the world in which — to the mindful observer — each thing is invested by its several relations to everything else.

Negative Capability:

that is, when man is capable of being in uncertainties, Mysteries, doubts without any irritable reaching after fact & reason...

Not the "**objective correlative.**"

Buddhist tourist. Hindu red neck:

The Making of Americans [Gertrude Stein's monumental novel] gives the impression of someone learning how to drive (as from the passenger seat...) Periodically there are smooth stretches, but these are interrupted by bumps, lurches, wild wrenchings of the wheel, and sudden brakings: all the while the driver can be heard muttering reminders and encouragements to herself, imprecations, and cries of alarm.
— Richard Brigman, in *Gertrude Stein in Pieces*

The next to the bottom line of the **I Ching**'s hexagram 26 reads:

A car. Taken away are two pieces of wood which hold the axle on both sides underneath. [*Drop all plans. Let the moment reveal the direction to move toward.*]

When that line changes we get hexagram 22.

Unlimited Resources changes to **Refinement**

It is perhaps amusing to note the etymology in Sanskrit of the words sukha (pleasure, comfort, bliss) and *duḥkha* (misery, unhappiness, pain). The ancient Aryans who brought the Sanskrit language to India were a nomadic, horse- and cattle-breeding people who traveled in horse- or ox-drawn vehicles. *Su* and *dus* are prefixes indicating good or bad. The word *kha*, in later Sanskrit meaning "sky," "ether," or "space," was originally the word for "hole," particularly an axle hole of one of the Aryan's vehicles. Thus sukha meant, originally, "having a good axle hole," while duhkha meant "having a poor axle hole," leading to discomfort.

Edmund Keeley (Jonathan Williams at Princeton):

When I was at a diner party at Princeton in New Jersey there were a great many of the big *vedettes* of that august literary scene. This was with Jonathan Williams whom I first met in Robert Kelly's drawing room. And I mentioned, or referred to what I thought was an axiom of Ezra Pound's, that the state of poetry translation at any given period in any given language will provide you with the mean that language's poetic accomplishment.

Keeley didn't recognize, but was intrigued by that idea. I thought I'd been told this by Robert Kelly during one of the first classes I ever had with him. Later I found that Robert Kelly had never heard this proposition.

Parataxis:

I want to share with you Jonathan Williams' last words. He was in the hospital (which by the way he hallucinated all that time as being Princeton University) having just survived a complete body sepsis and the doctors wanted him to sit up for a small while. They asked me to talk him through the maneuver, a couple nurses and aids had him upright on the edge of the bed and now they wanted him to stand, take a couple steps then sit in a chair. I said to him: "Jonathan, it's easy. You just put one foot in front of another …" And he turned to me and said: "Tom, this is no time for Chinese philosophy!"

Was Heisst Denken:

While I promote the previous as Jonathan Williams' last words, the final thing in fact he said to me was: "What do you think, Tom?"

Blaise Pascal:

All men's miseries derive from not being able to sit in a quiet room alone.

Mammon:

Doing anything for any other reason than doing it.

Openness:

The reciprocity of attention and experience. Their consubstantiation.

Attention:

Older than the body. Closer than the mind. Always with you. The simplest form of awareness.

W H Auden:

The cat has one creed: "To thyself be enough!"

Several years ago Jonathan Williams and I were taking our cat to stay with friends in Vermont before we went off to England for several months and we stopped to spend a few days in Annandale with Robert Kelly. He had a meeting that afternoon we arrived, and we were early so we went out to the site now of the Fisher Center and I was standing in front of Robbins House when it struck me: place. Place was the key, get yourself to the right place & the rest takes care of itself. People, events, karma, dharma… Bard was that place for me.

There is a vast ocean and on its surface floats a wooden ring and on the bottom of this ocean lives a turtle. Every thousand years this turtle rises to the surface. Now the chances of that turtle's head coming up through the center of that wooden ring are the same as my going to Bard and meeting Robert Kelly. For which I remain ever grateful.

DAVID LEVI STRAUSS

20 OR 30 THINGS I'VE LEARNED FROM READING ROBERT KELLY

> I had to be myself 15 years ago, 10 years ago, a torrid week ago, at the beginning of this sentence: but these are all lost states, & I am forced to view them & learn them as Herodotus learned the palaia of things, by report, by impression, by a veiled word here or there let fall by someone who presumes upon himself & me *to say he knew me*.[144]

I knew Kelly first in the early 1980s in San Francisco, when he came into Robert Duncan's Poetics Program, where I was studying. I had been reading Kelly for some time by then & getting a great deal from this reading, but what?

"It is difficult to get the News from poems"... especially when you won't stop writing them!

Some people say writing, and especially reading, and *especially reading poetry*, is useless, a waste of time. My father used to say this when he caught me reading: "Why don't you get up off your ass and *do* something?" he'd say.

Now the world has caught up with my father, and the world says that reading and especially reading poetry is no longer needed, but we needless few continue, and will, till it's all gone. The truth is, we do it for the pleasure, but out of fellow perversity, I want to offer a short defense, to my father, I suppose.

So, in defense, here are "20 or 30 Things I've Learned from Reading Robert Kelly." You will all recognize this title as the kind you give to someone before you have any idea what you're actually going to talk about, as an umbrella underneath which you can fit almost anything. My other choice for a title was "With Weasels and the Moon," but that is for another day, far, far away. ["To my friends when I am eighty-five / and my night comes" in *Under Words* [(1983) 126.] But in going back

---

144. "Identity Preference Temple-Complex," *In Time* (1971) 7.

and rereading all of Kelly, from the beginning to the present, poetry and prose, over the last months [really?], I did get to something, that I'll only have time to point to here. First, a couple of particulars.

A long time ago, I learned that poets today have to be "hidden, disguised as schoolmasters & divines, poetry tolerated as masturbation is tolerated, laws against it too hard to enforce."[145]

And very recently I learned that "Peeing gently really lets you hear them thinking... Releasing sphincters releases everything... We think by coming, we tell by uttering, we utter by outing, we out by letting go." That's from *The Logic of the World* (2010) 21.

Always the body, an erotics of language, *Flesh: Dream: Book*. "Difference is what we came into this Vale of Tears hot to have, hot to feel, peel, prong, prod, tingle, mingle, shove it in." ("I'm a Libra, I can't decide. I want *everything*.")[146]

But "It isn't all about sex and squirrels."[147]

The address to the Reader, the singular Reader (me, you) is often startlingly direct: "My dear, my favorite person, for you all my life is work and all my work is play and you can read me or look away ... You are my father & my lover & my child, and I am nothing without you" [*Not This Island Music*, 9].

Well then. Charming, sometimes ingratiating, often risking dissolution.

"A deep breath then. Poets out in the open? The shadowy aimlessness of the poet's motive the driving force of everything that moves? Which is close to the real burden of our responsibility" [*In Time*, 3].

As Duncan always said, "Responsibility is the ability to respond." To everything, always. My Kelly, understandably, is all mixed up with my Duncan, especially the Duncan of the 1980s, as we get in Kelly's "Burnt Offerings":

I have stood at the right hand of the sacrificer
stirring red cloth tatters into rice
red beans barley spelt

---

145. *In Time* (1971) 2.

146. Interview by Mark Thwaite in *Ready Steady Book*, online.

147. *Not This Island Music*, 38.

> sweet drops, the colors, till
> mixed with cooking oil
> it turned to fire in the fire.
> He chanted
>   hurrying
> things
>   from this condition to that,
> a wonder,
>   <u>Song is all sending</u>.[148]

And this, from "The Rainmakers":

> Poetry tries 'to bring all its experience into natural
>   grace'
> says Duncan, and keeps the numbers
> current,
>   the swells of speech
> whose ordered passion
> compels the restless lust of mind
> into the presiding metaphor of dance
> which here knows itself
> as particulate movements
> studied in noticeful economy,
> physicist at cloud chamber
> charming the incidents
> to hold some place in natural speech
> (trying to be natural!)
> as if it really were a world we speak.[149]

In rereading Kelly, I begin to draw a map ("to begin the preliminaries of geography / know where things are" [*Armed Descent*, 39]) and on this map, Duncan, I think, is there pretty much at the beginning, in that

---

148. "Burnt Offerings," *Not This Island Music* (1987) 20.
149. "The Rainmakers," *Not This Island Music* (1987) 32–33.

"Armed Descent into the world around us," in that "struggle to restore some aspect of the world's reality: to redeem man 'from the deadly innocence of not knowing where and what things are.'"

Duncan is there, in "The Alchemist":

> the origin, far side of a lake
> is always shadow [150]

But Kelly begins with an image, a deep image, of

HOW IT FELL

> and came down running
> on her feet and in her broad skirt
>   visual and strong:[151]

Visual and strong. Strong enough to be recalled vividly, 45 years later, as if no time had passed, in a story called "The Skirt," in Robert's latest collection of fictions, *The Logic of the World*.

It is an image of an unknown girl, glimpsed for a few seconds from the window of a northbound Eighth Avenue bus, "on the sidewalk, in front of a store, a girl, on the pavement, minding her young brothers & sisters, and flirting with other kids." She was the Queen of Eighth Avenue, wearing a skirt of "snug, smooth cocoa-colored gabardine." And she was free. "She was the freedom of the body, a terrifying sensual freedom because I could see, <u>anybody</u> could see, there was <u>nothing</u> she wanted to be but *free*." [152]

So that's where it all started. I had never understood what "Deep Image" meant until I read that, last year, and saw the girl in the cocoa-colored gabardine skirt, in my mind's eye. And then I knew what Kelly was talking about.

---

150. "The Alchemist," *The Alchemist to Mercury*, ed. by Jed Rasula (1981) 1.
151. *Armed Descent* (1961) 7.
152. *The Logic of the World* (2010) 135.

Duncan knew right away. In *The H.D. Book,* Book 2. Nights and Days, Ch. 3, from 1961 (the year of *Armed Descent*), he quotes Kelly to say: "Transformation aims at the continuum of all perceptions... Percepts are from dreams or from waking, rise from the unconscious or from the retina of the awakened eye. Poetry, like dream reality, is the juncture of the experienced with the never experienced. Poetry, like waking reality, is the fulfillment of the imagined and the unimagined." Then: "Poetry is not the art of relating word to word, but the ACT of relating word to percept, percept to percept, image to image until the continuum is achieved." And: "The progression of images constitutes the fundamental rhythm of the poem."[153]

The H.D. Book, that secret book that we all carried around in bits and tatters, finally published this year, 50 years after it was written, and 23 years after Duncan's death. During the time of the Poetics Program, 1980–85, Duncan often talked about wanting to write "the work of old age." He said Olson hadn't done it. But then Duncan was gone. Now we have Kelly, thank gods.

---

153. Robert Duncan, *The H.D. Book,* ed. and with an introduction by Michael Boughn and Victor Coleman (2011) 294.

MICHAEL IVES

1.

TWO MOMENTS FROM
"EAST OF THE SUN, WEST OF THE RK"

> *DISCLAIMER*: The author will concede that the values delineated in and arguments drawn from the following propositions represent only one among a multitude of possible readings of the texts in question.

1.

An RK (α) of texts is situated between a person, Robert Kelly, and a hypothetical reader.

Between "the way things are" (β) and "an imagined way" a textual RK has been inserted.

An archive of acknowledgements, of permissions and intimacies of every variety, occupies, in the form of an RK, the gap *between*.

Just as the letters, RK, stand between the name Robert Kelly and a blank space (as the name "Robert Kelly" stands between a putative organism, Robert Kelly, and other representatives of his species) so do the poems, perspectives, lores, temperatures, and colors of the RK itself colonize the hiatus *between*.

It could be said that the RK detects, approaches, and then metabolizes several varieties of "haitus *between*," among these the distance between two people, the space between silence and language, between a *now* and a *then*, the vacant areas between the words of existing texts, between meaning and void.

In abhorrence of vacuums the RK, a web of acknowledgements and permissions between two terms, would spin into legible flesh the distance *between*, would invade the emptiness of assumption, pour through and fill the inanity of heritable "positions" with a lively attention.

A Cusanian universe with center in all places, circumference in none, this RK (γ), which betrays no single strategy of articulation, but will embrace any and all methods to arrive at an uncommon *textual* intimacy, to get close, to draw near — to a reader, to the words themselves, to *the drawing near* itself.

To characterize, then, this RK: a thematics of *being with*, a narrowing of distances, the occupation of a hiatus *between*, verbal encroachment along all imaginable axes toward a ubiquitous center of acknowledgement.

Homologies pullulate throughout the RK and radiate outward from it, thematic redundancies, lusts for meaning (δ) interpose themselves *between* two terms, and words aspire to a haptic presence. Knowledge attains to the immediacy of touch in the RK (ε).

While the outer dimensions of the RK may undergo constant change — expansion as new material is added, contraction as disparate texts of common import fold into each other or pass out of print — within these apparent mutabilities a force endures. That is, though ostensibly comprised of discrete units — poems, stories, novels, etc. — a wish, nonetheless, arises to capture the entirety of this textual holograph; one is inevitably smitten with an intimation that the whole of the RK is homologous with the whole into which it has been inserted.

Not only to endorse but also to teach a posture, an attitude (in the sense of a considered disposition) that would open the reading animal to comprehensions it had previously neglected or surrendered to another (imagined) authority; to accomplish this not only by imperative but also by example; to return daily to the source or learn to stand in the heavy sea of mortal vicissitude; to provide a primary gymnastics, a *gymnopaideia* or naked learning: with such intentions does the RK vibrate.

For the reading animal deep in the interior climates of itself (or otherwise between an "inner" and an "outer") an attitude, as of a satellite dish, throwing verbal sightlines out across the crater and circumjacent debris ring left after the explosion into selfhood. Εδιζησαμην εμεωυτον (I went in search of myself) — thus Heraclitus, another strong attitudinizer, though hardly with an eye to the small advantages in "keeping up." (ζ)

α: after the Greek, *archê*: "beginning," "first cause," "origin"; also, derivatively, "supreme power,"
"dominion," "empire."

β: "Archive" as derived from archê: a public record, from the Latin *archivum*, likewise derived from the Greek archeion, a public building, residence of the magistrates.

(A)

γ: We are silenced by the way things are. (*The Loom*, 14)

    language is revenge / against the natural /condition / of which we are the lovely victims (*G of D*, 94)

δ: plexuses of a neurology / whose central brain is everywhere / nowhere (*CS*, 134)

    the center suspended / everywhere, where I can build my house / at the junction of itself
    with itself (*Weeks*, 134)

ε: Am I godlike because I love exactly? There is no lust like the lust for meaning. (*A to M*, 74)

ζ: Touch things, / touch them kindly / not gently ... touch them / till they're touched / & you can tell.
    I have been trying to touch you all my life / and all you ever are is my life. (*T of V*, 41)

η: Style is death. Finding the Measure is finding / a freedom from that death, a way out, a movement / forward. (*F the M, "prefix"*)

A: M. Foucault, in describing the "historical a priori" or "archive," comes very close to an approximation
    of the RK, or at least to its "fit" in the world: "... this a priori does not elude historicity: it does not
    constitute, above events, and in an unmoving heaven, an atemporal structure; it is defined as the group
    of rules that characterize a discursive practice: but these rules are not imposed from the outside on the
    elements that they relate together; they are caught up in the very things that they connect... It is the
    general system of the formation and transformation of statements" (*Archeology of Knowledge*, 127).

2. *christic section*

The RK does not contain a divine presence in any traditional sense, nor properly can the divine contain such a "thing" as the RK, however marbled it is with an awareness for which we have no better description than "sacred." Then too whole panoplies of gods striate regions of the RK. It is the pietistic distinction between sacred and profane realms, the gulf between the orders, that the RK (like the "great chain of being" of old) will instinctively fill with its precious kudzu of *parole*, with the effect of simultaneously secularizing the divine while divining the origins and motives of the secular. (α)

Therefore a christ may function in the RK as yet another Metaxu figure for whom, further, the question of attitude carries consequences of immense gravity. Thus the relevance of the christic for the RK, not only as a bridge to the mother of god, matrix of the "all" (β), but the exemplar of such an attitude as would compel one to respond to circumstances with as fully cultivated an attention as possible, as if one's life quite literally hung in the balance. By repeated christic plungings into the farthest extremities of meaning: thus does the RK enlarge itself from within, by insisting that all the time between the two occasions for which rite is especially reserved should be lived with an attentiveness commensurate in intensity with ritual observance. The RK insists that we never leave the temple but, just as when we place the broken, superannuated body of the beloved in a flesh-eating box — sarcophagus — and this into the flesh-consuming ground to offer it by slow decay to the quickening of the whole (γ) we must eat the broken, superannuated god with like fervor, that we may be reunited with our own vestigial quickening, that we may reanimate, BE, the god from whom we dissociated in our youth, our own and our species'.

Perichoresis (περιχωρησις): John of Damascus chose the word to describe that reciprocal inherence of divine and human natures in the person of Christ. It derives from *perichorein*, to go around, rotate, to come in succession. (δ) How better than by this rotary activity of interpenetration to capture the work of a Metaxu? One may go so far as to venture that were it cogent to speak of a stable center in the RK, it would be occupied by such a turbine of renewal, a mill for the ecstatic and perpetual particularization of things, meanings, relationships (ε) — which particularization (paradoxically at first glance) would emerge from a Bergsonian *devenir réel* as the given expression of a ceaseless and elementary flowing. Note Bergson's best exegete, William James, on the, as he describes it, "pooled and mutual" nature of the elementary datum of experience:

> Not only the absolute is its own other, but the simplest bits of immediate experience are their own others, if that hegelian phrase be once for all allowed. The concrete pulses of experience appear pent in by no such definite limits as our conceptual substitutes for them are confined by. They run into one another continuously and seem to interpenetrate. What in them is relation and what is matter is hard to discern. (ζ)

The RK answers this difficulty of discernment in the form of a poetic practice, a daily devotion that, rather than impugn the accuracy of language (a quixotic accusation in the end) stakes all faith and fortune in it as the *available* (let alone exalted) (η) means; in confronting experience with this radical instrumentality (a kind of experiential homeopathy) the RK, more than any other poetic testament, embodies the fluxional characteristics of the world in which it has arisen, and the more, becomes indiscernable from that world. (θ) This is language sacrificing its merely denotative function and entering the stream of objects it once thought only to signify. "Everything must have a title not / naming is not understanding — (*SE,* 100)": again, the enjambment here suggests that the work of recording (living) is never finished; the "not" at the end of the first line would appear to negate the foregoing assertion. Only upon taking up once again where one left off the previous day will the sense return, and only within the dispensation of the writing act. Several varieties, then, of *perichoresis* determine movement and direction within the RK, those of self and other, and of language and world chief among them. And if to "live" language to this degree, if to tell incessantly begins to erode the distinction between telling and living, all the better, since only an incomplete, an inadequate logos stops at any *given* notion of telling and living, of self and world. As a heritable source structure on, over, and through which the mind might work nourishingly ceaseless elaborations of metaphor (another *perichoresis*: of the given and its elaboration) we owe the received lexicon and syntax only as much honor as it returns by allowing us our insurrections and transfigurations within its bounds (and, epiphenomenally, all those parti-colored — centrisms of recent yore). Not Christ himself but the activity of which he is but one particular embodiment: a mitochondrial christ, whose work — this heat of exchanges (ι) that powers the "movement toward" of intentional consciousness (κ) — comes to an end only with a closing of all distances, with an intimacy unto interpenetration of opposing terms (λ) with an end of time itself (μ).

α: The Gods / broken into the pieces that are us. (*K the M*, 167)
   God me. (*Loom*, 221)

β: Let me pass through you and change my mind. (*The Loom*, Bk. 17)

   Credo in unam deam, Matrem / omnipotentem, creatricem / of all things sensible & unconscious, maker
   of heaven & heaven in earth. (*K the M*, 141)

   Be... The God. (*The Loom*, 183)

γ: Obedient / to the earth / we are shoveled / therein. (*CS*, 50)

δ: The equivalent Latin phrase, *Communicatio idiomatum*, a communication of idioms, is more illustrative
   perhaps.

ϵ: On the other side of because / there ground a mill. (*M of P*, 96) "On the other side of because"
   inasmuch as, since this mill provides for the possibility to ask "why," it must be apart from the "why,"
   effecting, like gravity, "action at a distance."

ζ: we are mapped as each other, / we are maps of each other (*G of D*, 92)

   What is hard / is always beginning and comes to an end no more / than the pattern on the scarlet Bokhara
   carpet does / though it meets its ornamental border and resumes / all the alternative directions its mystery
   is heir to / thing after thing. (*UW*, 108)

η: for syntax frees / and meaning / is ownership / and this art / is for those with nothing to say / and trust
    only them / incandescent unowners of a transpiring text / This House of Prayer For All People
    (*F of UC*, 45)

ALC IXH XAN: als ich kann : as I can — Jan Van Eyck's motto (see notes to "*The World*," MP)

θ: but there is something more / (nothing more than mind) (*T of V*, 87)

ι: the diet of self • consuming himself & stone / both of which we shall call Jesus / perches, outside / of
    time maybe, not / of rhythm (*A to M*, 21)

o flower / of emanation / language we learn with our fingers / deep in the ground, / language of hunger,
    syallables of pure animal vowel / since that continues, that / endures) / & sings through all form (*ibid.*)

κ: My darlings consciousness never dies / It always goes somewhere else and this else is our business
    Darlings our business is always this other/ Reaching (*UW*, 152)

λ: "The animal is in the world like water in water." (Bataille, *Theory of Religion*, 24)

μ: I want *now* to turn into *then* in such a subtle way it feels like now all the time. (*RA*, 102)

* * *

N.B. 1
We have in the schismatic era of christological controversy, during which the early church was repeatedly riven over disagreements as to the composition of the god-man, a clamorous rehearsal of sorts for the metapoetics of the RK. One of its most vivid set of changes on the *ars poetica* (and perhaps the most succinct statement of its kind) delineates a trinitarian

natura naturans, the interior relations of which could provide an abstract for the entire, and likely always controversial, RKic purpose (A) — controversial for its unmuted confidence in the wisdom both of unconscious motivation and the autonomous Brownian movement of language beyond the power of our "epistemologies" to domesticate (B).

Though plagued by political duplicities that contributed as much to the formation of doctrine as the mystery of the incarnation itself, still, the christological era proved to be the most fertile and exciting period in the history of the church as a publicly deliberative body (Γ) exactly because of several interlocking and/or concentric dramas of mutual permeation: aside from cross-pollinating heresy and cult, and the oftentimes violent politico-religious compromises of the great synodic councils, various demographic ingressions (D) and the consequent interfusion of cultures, the Mosaic and Classical especially, conduced to a levantine technology of spirit that drew as much from the Greek over-sophistication of eristic as from, in Gibbon's words, the Jew's "inflexible zeal." The coercion into intelligibility of the most unreasonable mysteries, whether the mystery of the trinity or the mystery of writing (both participate in a supreme *perichoresis* of finite and infinite, in the case of language, the infinity of meanings that arise from a finite resource of words and grammars): perhaps it is the destiny of such preoccupations to search for a person, a city (E) a time, uniquely disposed (Z) to entertain them with that rarest of combinations: brilliance and perseverance. Thus, the cosmopolitan RK recapitulates the Alexandria of Philo and Clement.

A: The organism / of the macrocosm, the organism of language, / the organism of I combine in ceaseless
    naturing / to propagate a fourth / the poem, / from their trinity (*F the M*, prefix)

B: since language like the rest of us
    always talks about itself

    with humility we partake its chorale
    map our functions onto its

10 · A BOOK OF SPECIFICS

and see the gauzy clamyses of Muses
sway on the uphill flank before us

big mountain of what we think it means
the sweet palaver we think communicates (*F of UC,* 84)

Her words are chance misprisions: / other morphemes would say her oomph as well. (*SE,* 115)

Writing... To make it say more than you know. / The patience to know that what it is saying is more important, / always, than what you want to say. (*T of V,* 188)

Γ: not till the nature of the godman is decided / does the evening news make sense (*SE,* 149)

Δ: Rome was purified and redeemed specifically by the influx of Jew & Syrian and African and
    Egyptian, by their bodies, wise loins, and memories of a wider measure brought back to the
    sharpness of focus Latium had lost. I have predicted a like novation for New York, that will bring it
    to the fully functional and unparalleled fruitfulness of the City balanced *between* sea and land,
    between New world and Old. (*IT,* 6) (italics added)

E: when all the singing / leaps through a thousand / mouths of what a / man actually is / a city! / I will not
    say only one gate. / **because I am in place** / axis of heaven and morning star / upright complexity. / The music passes through. / The self is other: "the festival begins" (*A to M,* 130)

Z: I point out two kinds of city: the cosmically-oriented city, laid out to be the type of the heavenly (i.e., the
    kosmos itself) the city that serves as focus for all the natural forces (Athens, Alexandria, Byzantium,
    Peking
    &

the other sort of city, that serves as refuge from the natural order, and strives to deny it as extensively as
it can. (Republican Rome...) (*IT,* 5)

* * *

N.B. 2
One could understand the Christian repetition compulsion of perpetual schism as the church's failure to accept the terms of its textual foundations, terms that the RK not only accepts but exalts, flaunts even. We read in *The Loom* (246, and *passim*) "But every error / is the meaning / of the text." The statement might not be as outrageous as it appears. Bear in mind how many of the great ecclesiastical conflicts erupted out of tiny textual interpolations (cf. *Mt Blanc*) the *homo ousion* vs. *homoi ousion* ("of the same substance" with the Father vs. "of like substance") and *filoque* controversies most especially. Under "Techniques of Enstasy" (*IT,* 55) we find this parenthetical: "(after all our schisms / startling revelations concerning the *Filioque*)." The force of this passing note may have less to do with the procession of the Holy Spirit than with a larger dilemma concerning the sovereignty of intention. Do we guide language or do its combinatorial vagaries guide us? In the end, who leads? The RK comes out decidely on the side of language:

> *We* dance oblique, the jut of our serentiy / into the unfailing measures of her Chance / till our drift becomes the only certainty. (*SE,* 117)

2.

Two pages of a Robert Kelly poem annotated by Michael Ives & used as teaching material. Ives wrote to the editors:

> Attached you'll find an old copy of "Thread 31" that I dug out of a box this morning, and which I brought in to my extraordinary Materials and Techniques of Poetry crew. They were overwhelmed by the scale of the thing, and by the economy of presentation — the mobility of the syntax, how it brought one way in close and threw one out into vast distances. They were fascinated by the possibility that stillness (equipoise) could allow one to see into time — that the expense of sight could be redeemed, that "Eternity is in love with the productions of time" — we spent quite a while thinking about that. We graphed the rise and fall of relative tensions and resolutions (vertical axis = intensity / horizontal axis = time) and considered the physiological miracle of the eye, esp. thanks to lines 38–45 …

They were floored by the poem, in other words.

> What means of thanks can one possess, can one offer, that such a thing exists in this world? I can barely contain the feeling its beauty elicits.

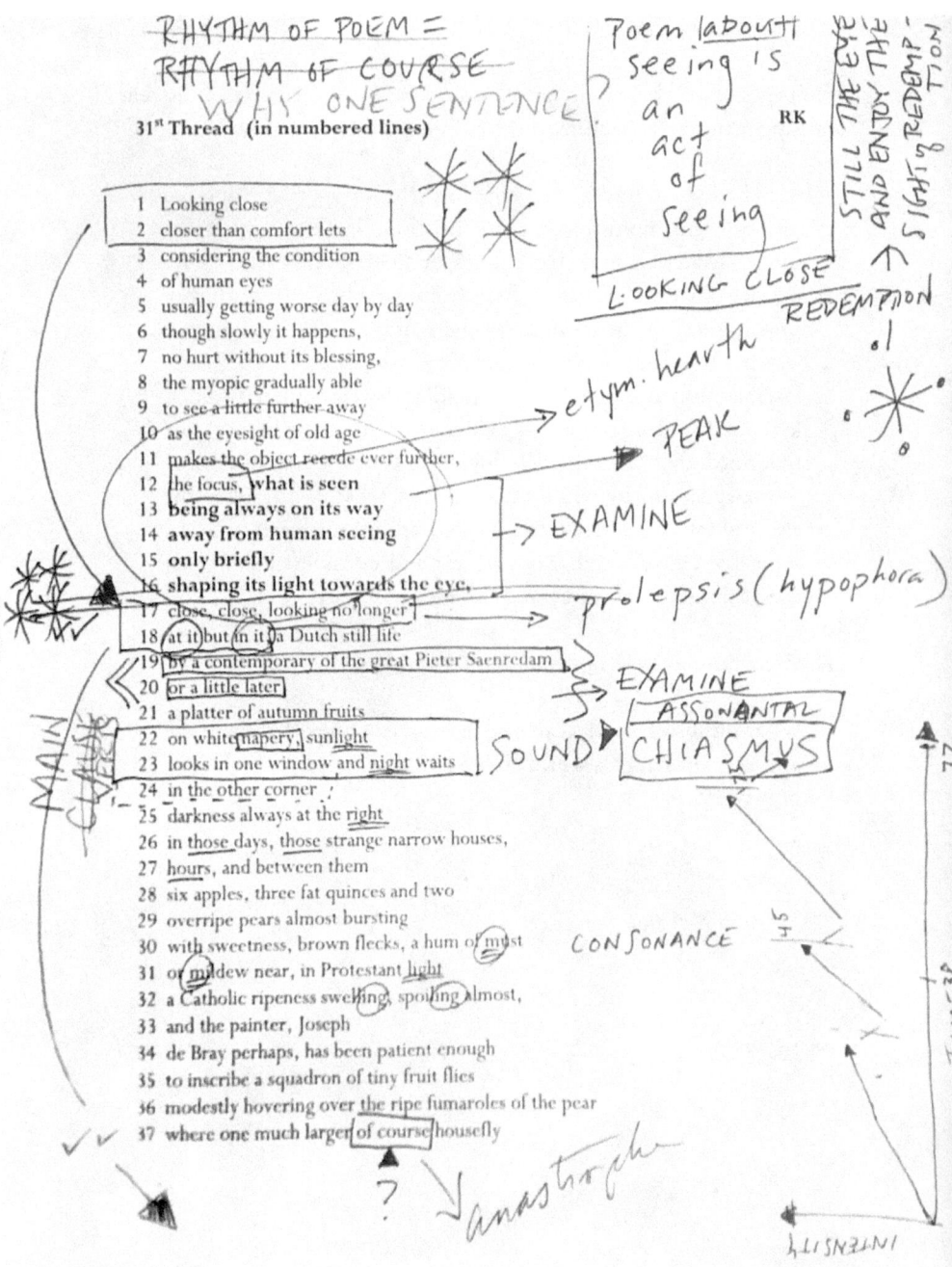

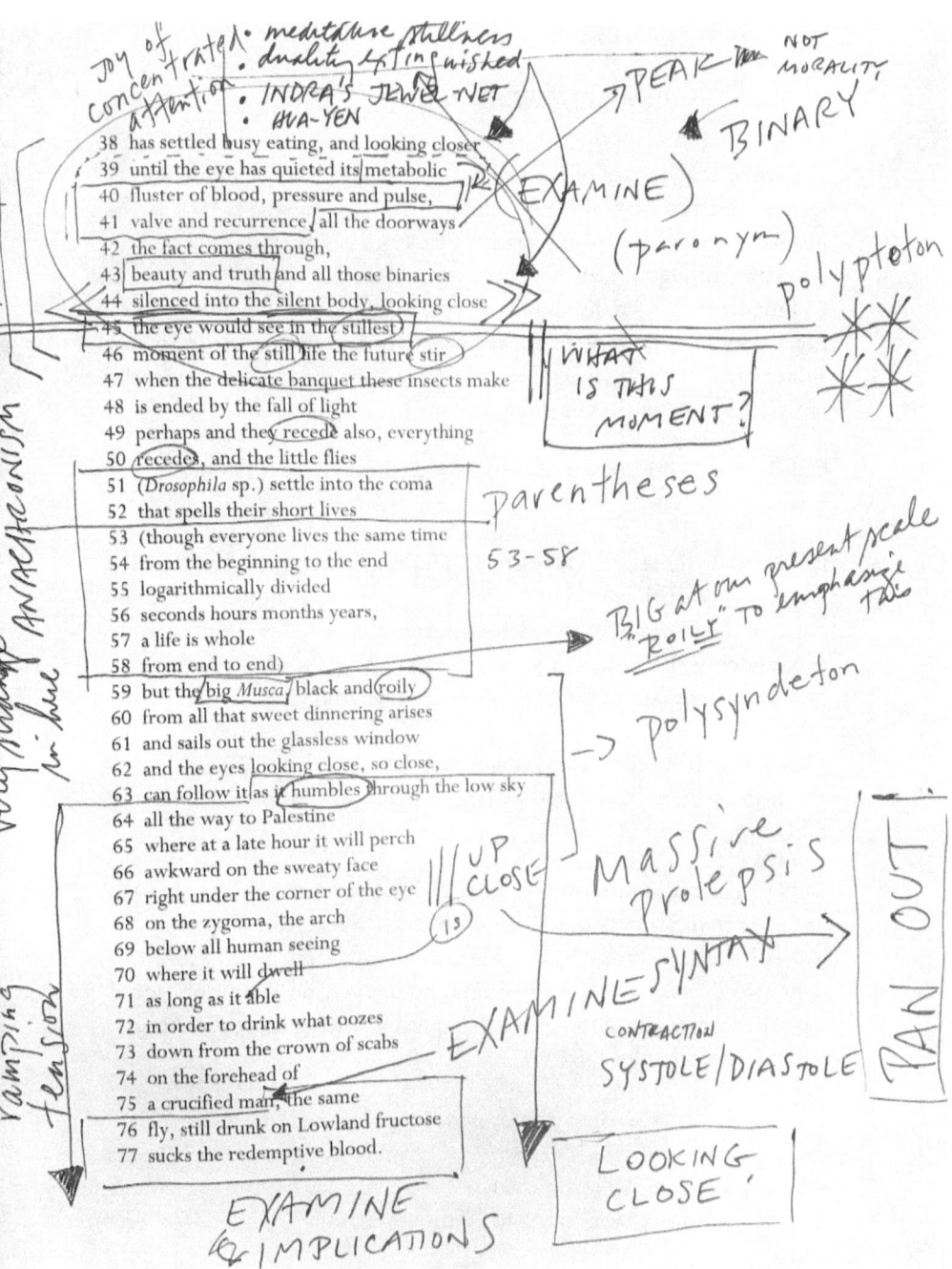

JOEL NEWBERGER

ROBERT KELLY'S CONSISTENCY

The scope & diversity of Robert Kelly's writings has been announced; so, too, the dexterity of his imagination and the hunger, as well as the intimate intelligence, of his song. What I must remark is Robert's consistency. Throughout all his transformations, his consistency, not as technique or as learning, but in the act of standing by words, a word. Metamorphoses in mind & music have never altered this fidelity, which subtends all the simpering *epoi*, the flirty and ranging arias, even the newest sinuous, endless, melodious sequences of *The Island Cycle*.

Consistency. All I want to note is how dutifully Robert has performed this office.

In "Some Preliminaries," an essay on Charles Olson, 1998, Kelly writes: "(remember that the angel with whom Jacob wrestles all night until the rising of the Dawn is, in the Hebrew text, *ish*, a man)." A simple gesture, a reminder — that a word is another word — but it arouses us to wonder, of what, exactly, are we being reminded? When did we know this?

Man or angel? A few months ago, Robert asked me what, in fact, I knew about *ish*, why it's translated as "angel," who was Jacob wrestling with till Dawn.

Though I'd read and striven with the Hebrew, I had no idea that the "angel" of tradition was the "man" of the text. What astonishes, however, is that Robert has stood by this old unassuming Semitic word for more than two decades, with no doctrine, no answer, no definition, minding the word, tending to it, gently inquiring, letting it speak, letting it remind us of what we might be.

Consistency. If we parse it part by part, I suppose it means: *to stand with one's other, to stand with one's brother or sister. To stand by Gabriel.* Words, shadows, angels. Kelly's whole œuvre is characterized by such encounters and recognitions, the crises. As in "Wintereve," from *Kill the Messenger* (1979):

> I am too afraid
> that I am really here, that this shadow on the snow
> is my own weltering eternal shadow...

Or from *The Loom* (1975) §36:

> When I opened my eyes
> I found to my
> satisfaction
> that my skull
> had slipped out of my head
> & sat on the altartop,
> looking at me.

For Kelly, the shadow, the other, is a word that has fallen to earth. See "Still Life: Origin of the Alphabet," in *Lapis* (2005):

> hello, these birds *leave* their shadows on the ground
> behind them when they fly away. Kabbalah
> is the art of wondering where the birds are now.

But that is somewhat beyond my eyes. Again, what concerns me is Robert's enduring fidelity to words.

To *ish*. I find, and rejoice in finding, this word palpated by poem after poem over the years. In *Opening the Seals* (2016) Robert asks, "Who man Jacob?" And answers: "a man who was the same." An answer which pertains to the meaning of the Latin word for the human, as he has it in "Dakota," from *The Mill of Particulars* (1973):

> homoio-, homo-,
> similar or same,
> we couldn't get straight

The controversy of the relation of the Son and the Father — of similar, or same, substance? — is the mystery of our nature, whether it be the indeterminacy of the human's place in the hierarchy of created beings, or the weird uncertainty of the individual's relation to species. Again, from *Opening the Seals*:

> Get out of my womb, backwards boy,
>   go fight with angels (ish, a man)

As in the Olson essay, it's a reminder, or the instauration, of a word; it is a sacred equivocation that initiates poetry.

But also a *bona fide* teaching. If Kelly is words' amicus, the custodian of their life, we ought to be able to see them quickening in the songs of friends and readers. Thus Billie Chernicoff, one of the poets closest to him in the past decade, has given us these tremendous lines:

> Ishim, angels
> of the lowest order,
> snow in flames or men inflamed.

Thus Kelly, in *Seaspel* (2019), a "mosaic," his newest book:

> Oak. Eke. Ache. Ash. Ish.

Here, as in Chernicoff's lines, Robert recalls that, in Hebrew, *ish*, "man," and *esh*, "fire," have the same consonants. The sounds, as he listens to them, summarize the human: a tree of Druidic vision that grows, suffers, burns to ash, and becomes an angel.

Look back at *The Loom* (1975). In how many of its sections is the hero or his shadow wounded, like Jacob, in the leg? §21:

>   worked
> some damage on his knee

§23:

> Leg not broken
> I think

These can be found quickly. There are others. Or in *Opening the Seals* again, Jacob section:

> I am lame.

If there must be a statement of the principle that guides these consistent attentions, it is in *The Loom*, §12:

> a man must become
> exactly other than himself.
> To do the Other.
> And break the story open again
> that the spiritual Seed
> be not forever locked
> in the material form: our oldest
> prayer. Sun, take this
> weight off my bones, these
> bones off my Name
> & let my Name
> speak in the world
> out loud alone.

Is this another revelation of Hebrew, where *shemesh* (sun) and *shem* (name) are hardly distinguishable from *sham* (that other place over there)? Despite all of Kelly's fluencies, and the years, it is apparently as a stranger or sojourner that he hears and speaks these permanent words: *ish*, man, homo-, and elsewhere, *aggelos*, angel, messenger. Consistency. But whose? Sometimes I have heard him say he is haunted by this word, worried by that word — do *they* stand by him?

So many of them, so many faithful words. To mind come "day," "achorai" (the backparts God offers Moses), "Orpheus," "fate" (as *fatum*), "scheide," "davar" (Hebrew: *word, thing, deed*) — a few of the words that Kelly has stood by, a few of the words for which Kelly's poetry has performed the beneficence of keeping them open, saving them from us, or for us. "Achorai," for example, has been, in the past year, the occasion for Robert to evolve a humane and sensuous anthropology of the other; but it appears, also, on the back cover of *Kali Yuga* (1970) in this statement:

> Poetry begins with the KADOSH KADOSH KADOSH of the angels. It begins with the thighs & hips of random women (wch also are achoraim, the backparts of God wch only we can see & live ...

I have dwelled on *ish* so long only because the angel is the word standing at the tent door, wanting to be written, or waylaying the poet along the ordinary road. As it is written: "If thou wilt, follow me." Or: "Get thee out of thy land." Or: "Lazarus, come forth."

The angel is the word that "comes to mind," but it makes us aware, as Kelly has written of *ish*, that "it means some other sort of thing or being as well." The word is that other thing, which confers on us its own angelic difference. It "break[s] the story open again / that the spiritual Seed / be not forever locked / in the material form…"

All the preceding comments lead me beyond Kelly's consistency, as I think of the ardent questioning that goes forth in all his poetry. Questions in faith, not in skepticism, in devotion, in praise, as Moses de Leon once named — named! — the visible heavens *What?* and the invisible heavens *Who?* Think of all of Robert's questions. Who am I? Who are you? It is not his way to assert the identity of "man" and "angel," but to suggest that the human may not be other than angelic, according to the mysterious indeterminations of *ish*. The word's truth; our equations be gone. A few months ago, he wrote: "*Ish*, 'a man' — but does that word (like Latin *homo*) mean woman just as much?" What does *ish* mean? I hear him say. What are we shadows of? who are you? what is behind us? where do we go at night? what grapples with us, ambushes us, twists us into speech? what do our words know?

CHARLOTTE MANDELL

THIS ISLAND MUSIC

> from a sea sleep I come
> and misty elegant ocean liners
> alive with adulteries not mine
> and small sneak thieves
> till bored with dreams I chose
> new light over old industries,
> the deep red brick of factories,
> the mills of Providence and woke.
> —"Dawn," *Not This Island Music*

I first met Robert when I was a student in his Twentieth-Century Poetry class — it was 1988, and I was a sophomore at Bard. In that class, Robert introduced me to many of the writers and poems I would translate later on: Apollinaire's *Zone*; Blaise Cendrars' *Easter in New York*; Saint-Jean Perse; Mallarmé. In the first class I attended, he somehow got to talking about 1950s New York Trotskyites, and Max Shachtman, and so naturally I went up to him afterwards and told him my father had been a Shachtmanite. No one I knew had ever heard of the Worker's Party, or Max Shachtman, or 1950s New York Trotskyites. Robert has a way of reading people's minds and talking about things one thinks are unknown to anyone but oneself — he did that just the other day with a nurse who had jumped into a frozen lake to save her dog. Somehow he knew about the episode without her telling him, and praised her for her selflessness.

Not This Island Music was the first book by Robert I ever read, and it made a deep impression on me as a 19-year-old. I felt it was speaking to me personally, especially the poems having to do with islands, since I had grown up on a tiny island in the Atlantic called Cuttyhunk. There is something at once intimate and familiar about Robert's poems that speaks to me in a way other poetry doesn't — the closest anyone else had come up to that point was William Carlos Williams, whose *Selected Poems* was a treasured part of my library.

Dear Ariadne,

the womb is full. Black tufts of autumn corn sag under the weight of their damp silk. It springs up as my foot settles, down in, everywhere, grassy mud. Womb happening hour, speak my baby for me,

I mean my body,

this piece of farmer, meek silo lofted, sleek money, hum, drum, valve of the day sluiced clean, hum of sun in the corn stob, hum of wind in stubble, sum of yearnings, touch,

touch!

Christ hears you from the dead, valve of Easter, lich gate of the tomb, broken barrier, bound over boundary, steep deciding, comes,

comes to town.

Do you hear all the things I am trying not to say?

Never is a sumptuous music, isn't it, more like Bruckner than Brahms,

bring me a glass of water, pour it in my lap.

Ariadne (1991)

Ariadne was written in 1990, when I was living in Seattle, after graduating from Bard. Robert had been my adviser for my senior project, which was a book of translations by the contemporary French poet Jean-Paul Auxeméry. *Ariadne* was, and is, the most beautiful love poem I had ever read. At that point Robert hadn't yet been to Cuttyhunk, but I had written him letters from there, and he seemed to know exactly what it was like in the poem. I love the lyrical, visionary, exalted tone of *Ariadne* — it reads as if it had been written very quickly, but purposefully — like certain sacred Tibetan texts called 'terma,' hidden treasures.

10 · A BOOK OF SPECIFICS

I think *Ariadne* marks the beginning of our shared life together, even though we didn't actually 'get together' until Robert visited me in Seattle, and we visited Victoria Island in Vancouver together. I lived in Seattle and Paris for a while before coming to my senses and moving in with Robert for good.

I.
The hand on my desk is my hand the everlasting
gentleman whose universe means you sometimes you
mean him and all the comfortable Hudson of named things
flows through the mind, in search of you now
for it is you who make things glitter, you
from whom the evening takes its violet
declivities that make me follow
down into the reflecting gloom.
Lend me your splendor, you whose secret
is no more than listening, yet such listening,
such a house of sheer acoustics rendered
palpable and marble and warm arms and wine
whose excess is the source of human thought.
All logic starts in drunkenness. It is the leery caution
of a mind at sea, posting by winds it alone
can apprehend toward a fancied seacoast
suddenly aground in what it thinks makes "sense."
It is a tribute to our madness that we made
so many streets, and cars to serve them.
We taught ourselves to drive strange cars,
over arcane bi-focals peered at life,
the life of waters we guess is running in their clothes.
The sound we make is only half our own.

Mont Blanc (1994)

Mont Blanc is a monumental work, and one that deserves more attention: in it, Robert somehow manages to include every word in Shelley's original "Mont Blanc: Lines Written in the Vale of Chamouni," while creating a poem entirely his own, a poem that is pure RK. Shelley's original poem is lovely but dated, written "in the still cave of the witch Poesy"; the Romantic hero contemplates the vastness of the mountain, and of the universe — "the everlasting universe of things" — while firmly positing himself as Poet. Robert's poem transcends the self of the Romantic Poet and investigates the actual universe of things: "The problem with most of me nowadays / is not sure where I end and it begins —." The world outside — the Dranse, the mountains, the "one grocery," the reblochon full of maggots — is more important than the one perceiving it. Every thing has its place in this poem, and somehow all the things fit together beautifully, and convincingly, and powerfully. It is a breathtaking poem in its ability to work with what is given and create something at once greater than the 'original' and greater than itself.

Mont Blanc was written while we were staying with my parents in the village of St. Jean d'Aulps, in the Haute-Savoie, in the summer of 1993. Robert and I would stay there several more times over the years; there was something in the bracing mountain air, and in the sound of the rushing Dranse river at night, that was good for the mind, and the soul. The deep ravine of the Dranse, meandering all the way from Thonon-les-Bains by Lac Leman to Morzine, was breathtakingly beautiful, and unlike any other landscape I have seen. I think it lends itself to creativity in the same way that Cuttyhunk Island does, for Robert.

FROM THE DIARY OF PARACELSUS

Waxed over sea the sun
is a bee — the light is wax
someone eats the honey
I need a pseudonym
to say what's on my mind

the sun is God's monocle
the poet said, slipping
on a wet plum stone
in market dawn

forty years before I was born
the sun was also shining
amazing things
knew how to be
before me and to do

one thing leads to another
that is the great rule the E at Delphi
the vav at Jericho to die
and not let it matter to be born
in no one's way the light decides

Saint-Terre, or The White Stone (2006)

Sainte-Terre, like *Mont Blanc*, is a tiny book, but equally monumental in scope. I think of it as the beginning of Robert's *Island Cycle*, which includes *Fire Exit, Uncertainties, The Hexagon, Heart Thread,* and *Calls*. All were written on/from Cuttyhunk Island, my childhood home in Massachusetts. I think the seeds of each of those books can be found in *Sainte-Terre*: "I need a pseudonym / to say what's on my mind." In the Island Cycle, we see a great mind becoming even greater through the Dharma: a surpassing-of-self to reach something beyond Self, beyond identity, something that is inherent in the sea. "To die / and not let it matter to be born / in no one's way the light decides." This is the alchemy of the Dharmakaya at work, turning one thing not into another but into something that is still itself but greater than itself, *chö nyi*, the essence of reality, the 'ordinary mind' which is anything but ordinary. I think Robert's work is phenomenal in its ability to go beyond itself, to study one thing leading to another until the truth of "the everlasting universe of things" is found, and revealed. I know of no other writer who is so selflessly true to the Word, and to where the Word can lead.

I have learned so many things from Robert over the years: how to pay attention; how to listen; the importance of gratitude and reverence; the pettiness of one's own emotions, and the ability to let go of them and forgive the world for all its shortcomings. My own translations have grown and flourished thanks to Robert's editing acumen and constant encouragement. There is a generosity in Robert that I have found in only a few other people in my life, & that generosity is apparent in his work: he gives all of himself, & more, with passion and conviction. There is a word, *energeia,* which means the quality of extreme vividness, radiance, or present-ness, derived from the Greek ἔργον (*ergon*) meaning "work." I think all of Robert's work derives from this energeia, which is boundless and endless, like the rays of the sun; like the sun, it replenishes both self and other, and creates more energy and work. "Write everything," Robert said, and he has, and he is.

THREADS 23: ROBERT SAYS

When I was a little boy, my father used to say, 'Running water purifies itself in a hundred feet.' It may still be true. I've never found anyone to say 'yes' or 'no' about it. But the image of water healing itself, clarifying itself just by being water, by running over the rocks and rills and all that. I've been thinking about that lately, because of what has happened to our language, to our nation, and in much of the world [...]. Language has always been in danger, & it purifies itself, I think, by speaking, by speaking, by going on, writing and saying. I think there are some poets who feel they shouldn't say anything anymore, that silence is the best cure for the debasement of language in our politics, in our merchandising, and all the rest of that. I don't think that. The more we talk, the more words purify themselves.

(Reading at Bard College, November 2018)

I'm not pretending, I'm just trying
to be honest as sunshine this minute
filtering through haze.
Who said that? Anybody who says I
really means somebody else,
and don't you forget it, hypocrite lecteur.
Can't you see how much work,
sheer noise and chattering it takes
to build a silent temple for you,
for you to walk in
and just feel, see, better than you do outside?

*

Call it Connecticut and be done with it,
a hundred miles away across the water
snug in America, with schools and rivers.

And be glad it's far enough away
that we have whales and seals and town meetings
and all that romantic stuff
where once a naked tribesman stood
and knew his world intimate, complete.

*

Half Samson now, all strength gone
but still can see, a little, now
it's time to build that temple up again.
Not Dagon this time but the sea
he sprang from, the sea. The mind.

*

Now the rain dove
has caught up.
The lyric democracy
out there begins.
Yesterday you swam
beneath a fish-crow.
No seals around.
This is a postcard.
The picture is pretty.
Who sent it? You can't
make out the writing.

*

Am I being obvious? Yes.
Does it matter? Yes.
Should I be more or less?

I hid myself in being right,
now I hide in clarity.
And still no one ever comes.

Seaspel (2019)

11.
A BOOK OF INTERROGATIONS

INTERVIEW WITH DAVID OSSMAN
FOR *THE SULLEN ART*

Kelly is the co-editor of *Trobar* and Trobar Books and the author of *Armed Descent,* published by Hawk's Well Press in 1961. Since then, his poetry has found print in many magazines, including *Origin,* which devoted most of its fifth issue to "The Exchanges" and other poems. He is presently a literature instructor at Bard College, up the Hudson from his Brooklyn birthplace.

DAVID OSSMAN: First of all, what is the relationship of the "Image" to *Trobar*?

ROBERT KELLY: With our first issue, we wanted poetry that qualified by being alive in one sense or another. We, in our own work and in our critical attention, grew more & more involved with the poetry of images.

Let me say this about the Image; if you want to divide all the ways of going into the poem, all the quanta and quotients of poetry, I think the division of powers that Ezra Pound made long ago, into three, is the best. His division was: *logos,* or word — word-magic, word-development, the development of meaning; *melos,* the musical gift, the musical development — singing, really — sound; and third, *phanos,* literally, "brightness," phanopoeia equalling, for Pound, "throwing the image onto the mind." This is the intellectual and emotional tone of the poem.

Now, if poetry deals with word, word is its ground — you might call word the mystical hypostasis of all poetry, of all literary art. At the same time, music (*melos*) is the space-time of poetry — its line, extent, duration. These two approaches to poetry, or these two behaviors of poetry, have been well analyzed and well discussed for a number of years — I should say about 2500 years at least. The third, *phanos,* the image, has gotten rather slighting attention. In the 30s & 40s, we heard a lot about "metaphor," largely, I suppose because Pound was talking about metaphor in the 10s & 20s; but we've also heard a little about image.

The image poetry that I'm talking about is not what Pound nowadays means when he speaks of the poetry *des Amy-gistes*. When I speak of Image Poetry, I'm speaking both of a way of looking at all poetry, and also, in our own time, of a particular stance of the poet as regards his material; that stand generates a kind of poetry not necessarily dominated by the images, but in which it is the rhythm of images which form the dominant movement of the poem. I'm not trying to say that all great poetry is essentially Image Poetry. I will say that all great poetry generates its images, both the Final Emergent Image of the work of art (Pound calls the *Commedia* a single image) and more so, the image as prime generated material of the poem — the primal image — which can be expressed as it normally is — in the word — but can also be expressed, can cohere in, sound.

Now this all seems rather remote from *Trobar,* but what I've been saying records part of the sharpening process that went on in my mind and in the minds of my friends and associates. This sharpening of focus led us to try to make *Trobar* a vehicle for Image Poetry. I certainly don't say that that's the only place it can be found, or the only place it will be found, because the poetry of image is coming more and more to life in America. For confirmation, don't look to any tendentious little magazine whatever, but to the work itself of more and more poets. I think the revival of interest in poets like Lorca and Neruda — they're becoming almost "standard" poets now — is based very largely on the enormous dark sentiment of Lorca, that darkness that "surrounds" us in *things,* and on Neruda's celebrations and love of the things of the earth. In their work, image becomes the motive force of the poem: their voice is in the images, as much as in the music.

If they play, they play on some ground. Really, this revival had to come, this awakening to the fullness of poetry, after the dry wit and tricks of words that marred so much of the poetry of the 50s. This is a partisan statement, but the worst thing you can say about a poem, any poem, is that it's dull.

DO: Do you think that a poetry concerned with the Image is likely to be a surrealist kind of poetry?

RK: I think probably the first stage an individual poet would go through in trying to let image emerge in his work would be a surrealist one. I really don't believe that surrealism and the Poetry of Image necessarily constitute more than a companionate marriage. Surrealism has its own technique at the heart — I think it is a technique — and I feel, rightly or wrongly, that the Poetry of Images (stress on Poetry: it's not a technique) is essentially a mode of Vision. Vision is something of enormous importance in talking about poetry — we very rarely talk about it, perhaps because it's so indefinable. (Pound, for instance, leaves it out altogether in the *ABC of Reading*: that book is so good because it keeps to the discrete: you can't teach the other.) The use of images constitutes a part of the poet's Vision. It has nothing to do with technique. You can simulate a surrealist poem but you cannot simulate, in a true sense, an Image Poem. This is no real criticism of surrealism — it has its own concerns. But if it can be extrapolated and a technique formed on the basis of it, it's not what we're talking about. Image is a vehicle for Vision. Vision discovers. What some consider Blake's fancies are explorations of the real world, discoveries through perception. Remember what Stevens said: Surrealism invents, it cannot discover.

DO: In your recent issue, you publish poems by Creeley, Duncan, and Snyder. How does their work in *Trobar* differ from their work to be found in other magazines featuring them and the "New American Poetry?"

RK: I don't believe it differs at all. I want to bring up again that I don't think that Image Poetry is the only kind of poetry. The poetry we publish, God knows, the poetry we write, is new and it is American; the important thing is that it gets written, that it stands.

I think Duncan is one of the greatest poets writing today in English. I think, as various people, notably Creeley, have said of him, that his work is enormously rich in technical solutions as well as in movement and meaning. I would think very little of a magazine that isolated itself from a poet such as Duncan merely because

Duncan operates on all levels of poetic meaning. His "Venice" poem, his greatest work I've encountered, is very strongly built on the flow of Image, as well as upon space and measure.

With Creeley, there's a different consideration. Creeley, too, is an exceedingly fine poet I think, if I can say so without anything at all except humble admiration of the man and his work — a man who's writing poetry of a beauty that I thought, a few years ago, impossible in this day and age — of an excellence I still think incredible. Again, for the magazine, similar reasons apply. Snyder is most relevant as far as the Poetry of Images is concerned. This most recent book of Snyder's, *Myths and Texts,* is in my mind one of the strongest books published by an American since the *Pisan Cantos,* let's say. And it is, by my definition, Image Poetry. That's a tremendously important book, not just as an accomplishment & a measure, but as a direction.

DO: The origin of a paper you have written, called "Notes on the Poetry of Images,"[154] was in seeing Eisenstein films and relating the Image in poetry to filmic montage. Do you still see Image Poetry in these terms?

RK: Since then I've thought about something that might be a difference, might not be a difference. The film starts out with a *known*

---

154. The paper referred to was privately circulated. A later version was published as "Notes on the Poetry of Deep Image," *Trobar* 2 (1961). Before the printed version came out, the author benefitted from a number of comments and criticisms generously and relevantly supplied by many people, especially Robert Duncan, Robert Creeley, Gary Snyder, Denise Levertov (whose critique was published in *The Floating Bear* № 11) and Charles Olson, whose brief comment: "not imageS but IMAGE," was fundamental. Most of these comments took exception to the terms of the paper or their development: the names given above are in no way responsible for the printed version, which, it should be noted, paid much less attention to the film. (R.K., 1962)

EDITOR'S NOTE: My own comments on Kelly's paper, which do pay considerable attention to the film, were also published in *The Floating Bear* № 13. [Cf. pp. 19–21 of this volume.]

reality: the reality the camera faces — and when you're building up film montage with the sequences and the strips and the cuts and finally the frame itself, I think that you are in a different position altogether from the poet employing images. Different only because, while you don't know what the outcome is going to be, you at least know what you have to start out with. The poet doesn't. There is a Mystery in poetry, and I really mean this with a capital M, a darkness, an atmosphere in which the author composes the Images before he really knows what those Images amount to. Now, if you take one of the famous Eisenstein frames — a long line of troops seen far in the distance across a snowy field — whatever this Image may amount to in later development, it is something in itself. It is white and black and grey and the very thin line of soldiers and the whole horizontal motion — and the motion in depth. You can take it out and print it in a book, look at it and know what you're seeing. It is a thing. The poetic Image is not a thing. It is process and a discovered identity. It discovers its being in its function.

I think there's that difference, and this is really why I bring in the question of rhythm. Image is the rhythm of poetry. I've said this over and over again in my paper, and I must say now, and give full credit, that this is a formulation that is not originally mine, though I've made use of it fully. Nicolas Calas, the surrealist writer and art critic, offers as a dictum (I really don't know in what context, since I've seen it only quoted) just this statement: "The combination of images constitutes the rhythm of the poem." Rather than talk of laws of combinations, I just want to say that the Image itself, in its development, constitutes the fundamental, basic rhythm of the poem, which all other rhythms — sound rhythms, stress rhythms and so forth — must subserve.

Now here again I think you come back to the film, with its interspersal of one shot with another and (I don't know what Eisenstein calls it) the visual similarity, if not identity, of two successive images of different subjects — their formal, structural nature being the same. The intertranslatability of all things is fundamental to all poetry: it is perhaps more obvious in Image Poetry, and perhaps there there's a tie-in with the film. If it does tie up with film montage, it does so not so much from the point of view of the individual frame, as from the rhythmic point of view of what is done with the frame. The processes may be analogous; the modular units are different.

DO: Is there any one experience, more than another, that prompts you to write a poem?

RK: It's something that I do. I don't know how to stop writing them. I don't know what the impetus is — or, I guess, we can all say in one theoretical way or another what the impetus is and we all know in one real way or another what the impetus is, but can we verbalize them? Have any people succeeded in verbalizing that impetus? The conformation of necessities in the unconscious, the conformation of shapes and structures that demand expression — I think it is that, or sometimes the song — the sound of music of some kind.

David Ossman, *The Sullen Art* (1963)

GEORGE QUASHA & CHARLES STEIN

TA'WIL OR HOW TO READ:
A FIVE-WAY INTERACTIVE VIEW
OF ROBERT KELLY

I. How to Read

Out of some 20 hours of recorded conversation with Robert Kelly (Annandale-on-Hudson, December 27–28, 1973) we have cut our way down and through to what feels like a one-issue dialogue. "Interview" barely conveys the peculiar quality of our interactions and circumambulations around the question of "how to read." Maybe the fancier term "interactive view" — or else, as we do think of it, "dialogical criticism" — is truer to our intentions. We're always anxious to find alternatives to the kind of criticism that whips out its carpenter's rule to measure a flash of lightning. So, we set ourselves a task, and on this occasion we were especially interested in drawing Kelly out on the question of how to read his own work — a work that not a few readers have experienced difficulty in reading. This practical problem suggests a larger issue with broad implications for poetics: the growing emphasis on "process," particularly in longer poems, seems to leave many readers without a handle on the event. In a sense the handles have been removed, and the reader is left to find alternative methods of holding on. Or instead of holding on she must now "hang in"...

The sort of "dialogical criticism" (DiaLogos) attempted here may only be possible where there is some genuinely shared ground among the participants. In that sense it's anything but "evaluative." The task of evaluation, whatever its future, must await certain kinds of understanding basic to new poetry in the present. We went to Kelly to talk about what we already knew he would be interested in discussing, and we went frankly out of the conviction that these issues are important. The focal issue we proposed was *ta'wil*, an Arabic term that Henry Corbin, the French philosopher / historian of Sufism, defines as "the exegesis that leads the soul back to its truth." Charles Olson got on to this notion in the '60s by reading Corbin's *Avicenna and the Visionary Recital*,[155] and he speaks of it in his Beloit Lecture, published as *Poetry and Truth*.[156] The availability of this notion to poetics seems to us one of the most significant developments of the past decade. In retrospect it seems the inevitable connection resulting from the double emphasis on the "visionary" and the "processual" that has been central to much of our poetry from Blake and Whitman to Pound, Williams, Olson, Duncan et al.

In the simplest sense *ta'wil* (discussed at length below) is a specific "how to read" that regards events in language as signifying or "signaling" events in consciousness. Admittedly this is tricky business. We have heard so much and said so much about the awakening and "expansion" of consciousness that the term itself begins to lose its edge, i.e., slip back into the linguistic unconscious of easy conceptualization. (Similarly it is now difficult outside of specialized contexts to use the term "Imagination" with the cutting force of a Coleridge or Blake. The trouble now is that people seem to feel the need to be either for or against alteration of consciousness or imagination. Clichés create holes in the sayable.) Yet the fact is that the *process* of reading referred to by either an exegete like Corbin or a poet like Olson involves a good deal more than the usual literary hunt for meanings — or for that matter the several familiar varieties of æsthetic pleasure. It involves a kind of attention and a degree of participation that produce an alteration of the very ground of what we can know through language.

This is not the place to argue the fine points of such a claim, but having said this much we might as well risk a further distinction. Kelly is one of those poets — Olson, Duncan, Mac Low, and Cage are others — who have composed in such a way as to make their work in some sense intentionally "difficult" (at least with respect to conventions of interpretation). That is, the act of reading their work at all requires some sort of special orientation to the methods and assumptions employed. An initiatory struggle is required. Now there is an established view justifying the difficulty of a poem like *The Wasteland*; it says that a poem is authentically difficult when that difficulty is an "objective correlative"

---

155. Engl. tr. Willard Trask (1960. Fre. ed. 1954).
156. Ed. G. Butterick (1971) 63.

of the complex experience *represented*. The assumption is that the poem represents something outside itself (outside its language) the poem is an artifact constructed in such a way that the experience represented may be recognized by any reader equipped to enter the discourse situation. Against this view is the notion of the poem as process — a primary activity of the mind or "creative imagination" that is ontologically and noetically unique, measured by itself, and ultimately referential to nothing outside its own embodiment. Any difficulty (any so-called "obscurity") arises from the *activity of composition* — that is, its own poetic process and the projective *faculty* affirmed by the poem's existence.

Now that some poets and intellectuals are once more getting interested in the "spiritual," the "mystical," and the "visionary," there are new energies afoot as well as new opportunities for muddle. So we will hear a lot about how much Duncan is "influenced" by Hermeticism, Cage by Zen Buddhism, Olson by Jung, Kelly by Alchemy, etc. And, while important perspectives will no doubt be established, the actual event might well get lost. And that event is the evolution of consciousness as a *poetic fact* — as deed, something done in, to, and by the language. The poem is not referential to any tradition; if anything, it is the other way around: any tradition that may be said to be "alive" is referential to the *activity* of knowing it. In the case of poetry, what we have are texts and events (the latter for what may not be on the page) and what we *do* with them is to read and hear. And in that activity itself lies the *further knowing*. The point of proposing a "foreign" notion like a *ta'wil* is to experimentally alter the "grid" of our perception. It is also to help recognize how much we need to re-order the frame of our understanding in order to know the event at hand.

During our talk with Kelly we tried to get him to speak about the new poetics emerging, say, in the year 1950. After all, that was the year of "Projective Verse," Concrete Poetry, etc. But Kelly insisted that "the interesting date would not be the first time that something was written, but the first time that somebody is able, say, to read Basil Valentine or Paracelsus as a *processual* document, rather than as a guide to operations with crucibles, and that date is probably after 1950 ... The issue that I'm at is when we were able to read ... and I think that our history will have to concern itself less with when a thing gets written than when a thing gets read, because I think those are the moments of achievement in our consciousness."

We [GQ & CS] had been talking for a couple of years about the right strategy in writing a "How to Read" book appropriate to the '70s, but it had not occurred to us to plot the history of consciousness in terms of how to *read* specific texts. Kelly argued that "someone who had read and perceived 'Projective Verse' and some other essays, 'The Gate and the Center' for instance, would be in a position to read anew. It strikes me that Pound had called it *The ABC of Reading* and before that *How to Read* [...] [but] that critics have supposed him really to be saying 'how to write' [...]. If there is any art or future in criticism, such that the work we're immediately concerned with can ever get read, or the thing that makes your book *America a Prophecy*[157] possible, will be a new method of reading, not a new method of writing."

It may be that the criticism truest to our needs will be the sort that simply plots new developments in poetic thought and practice — keeps us alert. A quarter of a century later Olson's "Projective Verse" can be read for what it was — a new mode of descriptive, not prescriptive, activity. It describes (without saying so) how he read late Shakespeare or *The Pisan Cantos*, what furrows that reading had cut in the mind, and what seeds were planted and had already begun to sprout. The fact that Olson (or Pound) *seemed* to be saying "This is what we *must do*" tells us something about the grammar of our critical thinking: we know no intermediate moods, no "middle voice" or "jussive subjunctive," no subtleties of the "evolving possible" impelling itself into action. No way to gauge the precise urge. A recent piece of self-descriptive criticism, Robert Creeley's "The Creative" (*Sparrow #6*) opens new ranges of the "intermediate mood" by embodying the processual truth of "Olson's sense, that art is the only twin that life has — it 'means nothing,' it doesn't have a point." "Twin" does not mean "representation" in the usual sense, but something like "co-presentation." Importantly Creeley also cites Corbin — the more recent *Creative Imagination in the Sufism of Ibn 'Arabi* — particularly to invoke the Arabic term "*himma*" as the "heart" of his own sense of "the creative." We reproduce it here for the light it sheds on the discussion that follows:

---

157. George Quasha & Jerome Rothenberg (eds), *America a Prophecy* (1973).

This power of the heart is what is especially designated by the Arabic word *himma*, a word whose content is perhaps best suggested by the Greek word *enthymesis*, which signifies the act of meditating, conceiving, imagining, projecting, ardently desiring — in other words, of having (something) present in the *thymos*, which is vital force, soul, heart, intention, thought, desire [...]. The force of an *intention* so powerful as to project and realize ("essentiate") a being external to the being who conceives the intention, corresponds perfectly to the character of the mysterious power that Ibn 'Arabi designates as *himma* [...]. Thanks to his representational faculty [...] every man creates in his Active Imagination things having existence only in this faculty. This is the general rule. But by his *himma* the gnostic *creates* something which exists outside the seat of this faculty [...]. In the first case, as it is exercised by most men, its function is representational; it produces images which are merely part of the conjoined Imagination [...], inseparable from the subject. But even here, pure representation does not, *eo ipso*, mean "illusion," these images really "exist," illusion occurs when we misunderstand their mode of being. In the case of the gnostic [...], the Active Imagination serves the *himma* which, by its concentration, is capable of *creating* objects, of producing changes in the outside world [...]. When in contemplating an image, an icon, others recognize and perceive as a divine image the vision beheld by the artist who created the image, it is because of the spiritual creativity, the *himma* which the artist put into his work. Here we have a compelling term of comparison, by which to measure the decadence of our dreams and of our arts [...].

II. Ta'wil: "The Exegesis that leads the soul back to its truth"

Helen Kelly: Well, I'd like to hear everybody's working understanding of *ta'wil*.

George Quasha: I don't think any of us has very original ideas about it, because basically we all get it from the same place, Corbin's *Avicenna and the Visionary Recital*. The first definition stamped on the mind is "the exegesis that leads the soul back to its truth," and the number of interpretations that you can have of that are presumably infinite. It depends on what you're doing with it. The classical instance for us is the Corbin book itself, or the second book, *Creative Imagination in the Sufism of the Ibn 'Arabi*,[158] where he not only defines *ta'wil* but performs it himself. What's always fun to watch is the way Corbin, writing as scholar, manages to get away with doing what the poet himself does, the *ta'wil* itself — an exegetical process performed in scholarly footnotes, while clarifying an exegesis of an obscure Persian commentary on Avicenna's Recitals. So the process is a discourse, usually on a specific sacred text, in which the inner meaning of that text unfolds within the very modality of the writing and thinking. *Ta'wil* is finding the secret of the text, getting to its root principle and meaning, by proceeding in such a way that the reader discovers it within his own mind. So poet and reader are united. In Corbin's case the bridge is scholarly rather than sacramental, since he is giving us the picture of Avicenna and Ibn 'Arabi, poets of the 11th and 13th centuries, who are unusual in literature in that they give us models for reading their texts. And Corbin is giving us a discursive model for reading the earlier models — i.e., he performs the critical task in the same spirit that the poet performs the poetic task, "making it new." I've had several conversations with medievalists where I tried to learn why they ignore Corbin's work or the Arabic and Persian exegetical texts; they simply know nothing of this. And it's a shame because the "how to read" models in European medieval literature are extremely scarce, and we can learn so much from the Arabic refinements of reading.

Robert Kelly: You do get some touch of it here and there, as in the *Gesta Romanorum*, the morals appended to the story, which is a *kind* of reflexivity. And that's quite early. And then later John of the Cross will do exactly that, *how* this poem is to be read.

Charles Stein: But that seems already to bear the presence of the Arab thing.

GQ: So *ta'wil* is also "how to read," a way of getting at texts, and the value of the early models is to get us started. Literary criticism is concerned

---

158. Op. cit., Ralph Manheim (1969. Fre. ed., 1958).

to articulate the various genuine ways of reading a text, and it can speak of the *Canterbury Tales* as allegory and as a text influenced by Dante or whatever. But there is always a *something else* that is harder to get at. And *ta'wil* involves a something else that seems profoundly mysterious because a *process* of knowing that is far subtler than allegorical interpretations or studies of influence. And the key point is that it's different every time it's done.

Susan Quasha: It has to be specific to the text.

RK: And that's how it's different, say, from the Christian-European medieval notion of the four levels of interpretation, the literal, allegorical, anagogical, and moral levels of reading a text; any text at all can be read in those four totally different ways, necessarily living only in the text. And that theory is so general and customary that Dante can assume it as a thing everybody knows. But *ta'wil*, as I understand from the Sufi books that we've been reading, implies a knowledge of when to go from one of those levels to another. We're not now reading it on a literal and now on an anagogical level; but anagogy is what they're really about in the first instance, how the soul appears in the world and retreats from it, which the Christians see always in the image of Jesus. The story of Jesus is the story of the individual soul reaching transcendence.

HK: Does the *ta'wil* of a text differ from reader to reader or is there a way of saying that this *is* the *ta'wil* of a specific text?

GQ: I think the answer to that has to be that there can be no single, authoritative way of reading, because there is no final authority. The authority that one has in speaking derives from the activity of *ta'wil* on a given text, but there are different events in which that imagination is called into action.

CS: The Sufi idea is that there is a particular function of the Imagination through which God "creates" Himself, in that the exercise of *ta'wil* is at once *your* act and *God's* act. God creates an Image of Himself by having an Imaginative function in man think about, read about, imagine, see God. So that it's not a question of there being variant performances of *ta'wil* on a given text, but there are different events in which that Imagination is called into action.

HK: So my question is in fact inapplicable to *ta'wil*.

RK: Well, in fact the Arabs have trouble with that.

GQ: Yes, that's the conflict between mainstream Islamic orthodoxy and the Sufi "heresy" or challenge to any authority outside the individual mind.

HK: So it's between each reader and God and the text.

RK: No, not so much between each reader and God, but between each reader and text. That the reader's perception of God, which is the only real knowledge we have of God, rises from that Imaginative, that noetic act, which is different from the physical act of imagining the things pictured in the narration. So that Ibn 'Arabi was in a lot of trouble for publishing poems that were taken as erotic poems, but when he published an interpretation of them [*Tarjuman al-Ashwak — The Dragoman of Desires*], a *ta'wil*, an exegesis, the authorities were set at rest — i.e., couldn't *act* against him because that text which produces exegesis is an authentic text. And if the text doesn't produce exegesis, it's soon forgotten.

III. Recital

CS: We thought that most of the things we were concerned to hear you comment upon could be brought up in relation to *Loom* 44.[159]

RK: But that would be something more available to you as reader than to me writing it, because you know there's this unspeakable way where I have to put that away from me, having written it. I don't mean in any fancy way, but I mean just that I have to stop thinking about it, or not think about it.

CS: But there are many things in that poem you think about, well, all the time: the whole question of "altars," death, the *place* of the making — i.e. where the making is taking place, where the builder is building.

---

159. In our dialogue the poem is designated as §44, as it had been published in *Caterpillar* #18 (April 1972) and reprinted in *Vort* #5, but in *The Loom* (1975) it would become §36 [Building of the Temple], 401–415, the final poem in the book.

RK: To work with one of those *Loom* sections, particularly that one, would interest me because it has that other aspect of *ta'wil* in it — *Récit*, or whatever the Arabs call that, you know, the Recitals. I can't think of *The Loom* in a better way than that; because when I want to find a type of *The Loom* somewhere, I find myself thinking about Avicenna in that Corbin book, and the stuff that's like it elsewhere in the world — the endless and / or beautiful stories that spill themselves out of uncertain meaning — I mean the clear absence of final moral focus in the *Récit* reminds me very much of the same thing in *The Loom*. It is not the building of a *temple*, but of an *altar*, and that altar's very ambiguous, and the whole relationship between myself and the skull is very curious. I mean I take the *Récit* to be that kind of fable that cannot be paraphrased, and thus all the *Récits* of Alchemy, which are, I suppose, as close to it as the West generally has — like the Thabritius and Beya stories, the people who go under the sea to teach the undersea people how to conjugate, or *The Chymical Wedding*.[160] These are stories that must be read and the reading of them is itself the "operation."

GQ: That seems to me the fundamental concept, which we return to in our notion of "process," and that's really what we mean by "process," though it doesn't sound like it.

RK: The non-paraphraseable.

---

160. "Thabritius and Beya" = "Sulphur" (Thabritius, Gabricus, Kybric, etc. from Arabic *kibrit*) and "The White One" (Beya, Beja, Beua, etc. from Arabic *al-baida*) = Alchemical "synthesis of opposites [...] often represented as a brother-and-sister incest, which version undoubtedly goes back to the 'Visio Arislei' [...] where the cohabitation of Thabritius and Beya, the children of the *Rex marinus*, is described." See Jung, *Psychology & Alchemy* (1968m) 153n. and 327 (pars. 434ff.). *The Chymical Wedding*, also called *The Hermetic Romance of Christian Rosenkreutz*, by Johann Valentin Andreae, was published in German in 1616 and in English in 1690 (tr. Exechiel Foxcroft). Perhaps the most important Alchemical work of the 17th Century, and a cornerstone of the Rosicrucian movement, its sheer literary power and certain historical importance have been strangely ignored until recently. Full text, with extensive commentary by Rudolf Steiner, in *A Christian Rosenkreutz Anthology*, ed. Paul M. Allen (1968). See also Frances A. Yates' important study, *The Rosicrucian Enlightenment* (1972).

GQ: Yes. We get it explicitly stated for the first time in Western poetics in Blake. I think it's present long before that, obviously, but I think we get it stated when Blake tells us that to go through *Jerusalem*, the poem, is to enter the New Jerusalem, the place [in the mind], and that the function of the poem is "to rouze the faculties to act" — that idea of the literal function of the poetic process, and the unmistakable nature of the presence of a process which cannot be paraphrased by anyone — the almost pathetic efforts of brilliant critics afterwards to do that very thing; to paraphrase it, to make a dictionary out of it, or an Aristotelian scheme out of it, or whatever.

RK: I've talked before about why poems are hard and have to be hard and have to get harder; that if they're not hard they're no good, and about how "poem" replaces "religion," I mean as its enemy — that it represents the development of the growth of our consciousness that we can transcend the religion that purports sacramentally or magically to perform an act for us, and instead forces us to the point of performing it for ourselves, transmutatively. I mean the only value of any church ever has been to preserve texts — the only good thing the Vatican ever did was to preserve the Gospels of Mark and John. It preserved two useful texts. What can one say about a religion that loses its text? I mean Mohammed, with his fantastic respect for just that — the "People of the Book" — the original Muslim pilgrimage wars of conversion were not supposed to touch Jews and Christians because they had a book. When you say 'book" it sounds superstitious. If you say "text," "*le texte*," then suddenly it appears as if they really did understand [...]. I mean from what of the *Koran* one looks at. Have you read much in that [...] strange book?

IV. The Poem as Ta'wil *of its own First Line*

CS: In thinking about the poem as "*ta'wil* of its own first line" [RK] I am reminded of something I think you mention in "Thor's Thrush"[161] or something written around that time, to the effect that you would "take each object as it comes and say what comes to mind." That seems an actual practice which you have applied in many different situations.

---

161. Written in 1962 and reprinted in *Twenty Poems* (1967).

RK: Yes.

CS: So that by the time you come to mention matchbook covers in "A Book of Building,"[162] you are already playing with that practice. The note sounds as though it's not true; it sounds like some kind of Nabokovian play; as though one didn't have to take it as actual information about the poems.

RK: [*With tone of slightly weary desperation*] Oh my.

CS: But it sounds funny: these poems that seem to be about all these different things are really about matchbook covers...

RK: But it's true! [*Laughter*]

CS: But anyone who didn't know your practice wouldn't think the statement true. Knowing your practice makes it perfectly true.

RK: There was a much longer note at one time — I don't know how much of it finally got into the book — about how, from the earliest days, my concern was to enlarge & dignify or realize anything that came into my hand — the more trivial the better, for the occasion. Since that's what I understood by the "Incarnation" and all the rest of it.

CS: Well, something of that got in.

GQ: It called to my mind that a good title for a study of that aspect of your work would be "The High Art of Making Mountains out of Molehills."

162. In *The Mill of Particulars* (1973). "A Book of Buildings" is a complex cluster of short pieces — some 16 in number, 25 pages in length — to which the following note refers: "American matchbook covers propose instruction. Helen found some she thought would provoke me, and so they did: blue-greyish badly drawn vistas of famous buildings, with a little letterpress on the back, telling about them. Big Ben. Arc de Triomphe. Eiffel Tower. Leaning Tower. Sphinx. There was a Taj Mahal too, but it came to nothing. I thought as I wrote these things: all my life I've felt such trivial things, such degraded images, as obligations. Hence the theme of all my life crept in, ineluctably caught up with Bruce Baillie's movie to Ella's song. To amend these things. Amende your selues, writes Myles Coverdale, to translate Jesus' call to metanoia" (163).

RK: Yes, why thanky, yes yes [*low laughter*]. Well, I think that's the name of our *whole* art. That's that marvelous picture from Michael Maier, of people looking for the Stone. They're walking along a river and the Stone is everywhere, in the air, floating past them, all this great cubical, nicely finished Stone. The Stone is everywhere and therefore by definition trivial, as anything found at the intersection of the three dimensions *would* be trivial.

CS: But take the example [in the notes], "American matchbook covers propose instruction" or "There was a Taj Mahal too, but it came to nothing." That doesn't sound like it's true, it sounds like a marvelous remark. It becomes more marvelous when you know that it is true but...

RK: Yes, certainly, I'm very fond of Nabokov... [*laughter*].

GQ: Life imitating art.

RK: Yes. I'll *show* you the matchbooks [*laughter*]. At one point I wanted to print them with the poems, but I decided against it finally. To let it find its own way in the world without reminding people of sources, because of my notion that one doesn't really have to articulate sources that are part of or even close to the final product. And there are lots of other sources not mentioned in the notes, but the ones I felt most especially responsible toward — like the van Eyck stuff George put into my hands, or Gerrit [Lansing]'s line that became the starting point of the "In Mahler's Sleep" poem. I didn't know where that line had come from then. Gerrit said, "Ah I see you've..." and I said "Oh." Stealing. Unconscious thoughts. But you were going to say about that?

CS: Actually this was to tie in with the question of *when* we learned how to read. At what point that became clear to you as a method, a practice to become engaged with. That seems to be a practice, and to understand that fact is to understand something about what it would involve to become engaged with a poem of yours.

RK: Helen used to complain of me that if she gave me a gold Cadillac and someone passing by handed me an old leaf, that I would write about the leaf and not about the Cadillac. And I would explain I suppose in this cartoon that the one needed something and the other didn't. That the business of poetry is to in some sense make *more*. That's what *mythos* is about, mythology is making more. So there are two kinds of sources: one is the matchbook that comes into hand and has some loathsome picture, a distorted or trivial picture of a famous building, that somehow has to be rescued from its apparency — in almost a Pataphysical, and thus Nabokovian, way. You have to rescue the thing from the trivial world in which it finds itself. How did a nice Taj Mahal like you get *into* a place like this...

SQ: This may be too simple, but in your description of the sacred as extraordinary...

RK: How to discover its extraordinariness again. But the other kind of source, and the one I would most normally be concerned with, is the first line. And when I say that the poem is a *ta'wil* of the first line, I mean very specifically that a line comes, a statement comes, carrying its own measure with it, its own length, its own etc. And then I have to find *what* that means, by finding in it the energy to go to the next lines and in that the energy to go forward. Now in *The Loom* that specifically becomes, for the most obvious time in my work, the Recital. The Recital emerges. The narrative develops. And I think *ta'wil* without Recital is impossible in a way; even if the Recital does not take narrative forms, it could take strictly imagistic forms. In a way I could point more exemplarily to a Duncan poem, "A Poem Beginning with a Line by Pindar"[163] — which seems to me always his best poem, the classic poem... because he proceeds [*laughter*] as I proceed.

GQ: That poem in particular, the variation of movements from section to section, the number of different voices and concerns that are allowed to come in — all out of a single line — seems preposterous to critics of poetry. The general feeling seems to be that Duncan blows it in the second section...

RK: The Eisenhower stuff?

GQ: Yes, and the "damerging a nuv. A nerb."

RK: The stroke.

---

163. Robert Duncan, *The Opening of the Field* (1960) 62.

GQ: Right, strokes apparently aren't the high matter of poetry like Goya's Cupid and Psyche in the lyricism of the first section.

CS: But can't they see that on the simple level of its content and strictly on organicist principles it's an illustration of what it's talking about?

GQ: Well, here we're up against the critic's presumption that he can tell what parts of reality are trivial and what not. The presumption that the poet is ever in danger of crossing the line into the unintelligible...

RK: At any rate I find that poem so pleasing and satisfying because it is one of the places where that mode of procedure most conspicuously happens — and you can point people to it and say that's where it's also happening. But that commitment to the first line, and the Recital that can be generated [...]. *The Loom*, § 44, which you refer to, seems to me interesting because the first few lines of that have no demonstrable relationship whatever, not even covert, to the Recital that follows from it. And yet it all lies there, in that beginning.

GQ: It seems to me we have to regard the first line as simply "The leaf," and that calls to mind the clearest example of the poem as a *ta'wil* of its own first line, namely *Paradise Lost*: "Of Man's First Disobedience, and the *Fruit*." There we get "the Fruit" hanging out over the end of the first line suggesting the various kinds of fruit we can think of, perhaps as many as ten, of which four are important, and of which the last is the poem itself, the redemptive process. To dangle the fruit out there is to insure the fact of the poem's happening. The opportunity of the poem as the life of the man and of the mind. And your "leaf" seems curiously like that fruit, though in this case the verb and syntax are different — "The leaf / I lent you" — and you play on that. And, it may anticipate our *ta'wil*, it seems that the poem grows out of the leaf or fruit and winds back around to it in the end, the desert "crashed into flower."

RK: Well, it's something that doesn't ask anything of *me*, except to write it or drive it or use it or whatever. Because I *do* sense reality as task. I mean I understand the perceptual world as a task, having to do with a nonperceptual or noetic world, and that it's our business or my specific business, and anybody else who wants to play that game [*laughter*], to apprehend and move from the perceptual into the intelligible, where only the thing has its truest meaning. And therefore I find myself so hostile to the Williams' *poetic*, while not being hostile to his work, which does precisely what anybody else does — rescues the Wheelbarrow from its wheelbarrowness.

GQ: Well, that brings me back to the "aphasia" point in Duncan's poem, the way the poetics develops in relation to an implied physiology of speech, rather than a preconceived notion of proper poetic matter. When Williams was writing the triadic poems, as Kenner points out I think in *The Pound Era*, he used the step-down device of indenting lines in threes in order to make it easy to follow the line-by-line progression. His physical disability before the typewriter created the specific task of getting somewhere, down the page, and awakened in him some very fundamental process — the real power of those late poems [...] based on a poetic utility rather than the simplistic "classical" poetic implied by Williams' sense of threes. It was a task defined by something as basic as getting across the page and back to the margin.

RK: A la Larry Eigner.

GQ: Right, though Larry Eigner just gives up the margin and the space of the poem is free-floating, or contoured by the ratio between physical disability and energy of speech / mechanical execution.

CS: His condition is different from Williams'.

RK: Unbounded.

GQ: Duncan speaks of Eigner as the first to relinquish the left margin, and particularly in *Passages* he gets that permission from Eigner.

CS: Though in Duncan it always looks like the shore is just over the horizon.

RK: I got my permission from Mallarmé, actually, how to move from the left margin.

GQ: But it's not totally free in Mallarmé, there's a musical / notational progression, down and across the page and from page to page, that is more rhetorical.

RK: It's hard to say. I mean in *Un coup de dés* it's not clear to me whether there are several margins or no margin. In my early long poem, called "Spiritum" [later published as "The Exchanges" in *Origin*, 1962] I first experimented with shifting or multiple margins (4 in that poem, 4 worlds of creation). Later, the ordinary left-hand margin avails as the base-line or "tenor," to which all pitch transformations (signaled in my work by indentation and "dropped" lines) return as norm, at the start of a "new line." The use of margin as notation or musical reference precludes the use of indentation for intellectual "organization of parts."

SQ: Olson said, "What make us write / slanted across the page / curve of mind."

RK: A luscious saying.

V. Ta'wil of The Loom, *44 [36]*

RK: Well, I keep sitting and kind of basking in the image of the poem as a *ta'wil* of its first line. In a way I bask in the light of the first line. Because that *is* the Aleph — which is not a word, doesn't *mean* anything, because if you hear it at all you hear it as [*gestures a silence, indicating the Hebrew silent letter*]. If you happen to be listening very closely you might hear it, i.e., it might be meaningful. But then it enraptures us somehow with its meaning, as it begins to spin. So the poem is... I think of the text as *tex-tile, tec-tum* [*Lat. = shelter, roof; related to conceal*], that this is the initial impulse from which the texture begins to weave, the clavicles begin to develop, the organism begins to assume its structure. In this *Loom* 44 where it seemed to happen was that phrase "The leaf / I lent you" — where "leaf" and "lent" were clearly sound-relations,

> The leaf
> I lent you,
>   where is that now,
> you who were so bold
> as to put cities behind you?

was someone speaking to *me*. "What have you done with this matchbook you've been given." I mean was the force of it as I heard it [...]. "The leaf / I lent you" — and then the question asked itself more clearly, "you who were so bold / as to put cities behind you?" — that made "you" clearly into "*me*," because I think of myself as having explicitly chosen not to live in cities [...].

> Only a loan at best
> the light reclaims our eyes.

GQ: "The leaf / I lent you" reclaims its sound relations in "Only a loan at best, / the light reclaims [...]" and it seems that it almost threatens to take off there but you don't let it.

RK: No, and force it into "Re-possession." The black man and his Cadillac, on "The credit / of our movement." But "Re-possession" is itself immediately revalidated by "The credit" — money and lending.

CS: The music of the whole poem isn't yet established and there's a feeling of tuning up, plucking the instruments that are going to be playing.

RK: Which I love, I love that in work. But then I suddenly realized in a conscious way that what was being asked as the price of the leaf was my life, that the "death" is what this had to be about: "A death / for Robert, to elicit life." And that made me think of what next happens, the image of those Renaissance or 17th-century paintings of the literary types, painted with their hands on the skull of the desk, the ape, in a portrait of Rochester like that, portraits of other people.

GQ: A Hamlet situation.

RK: Though later than *Hamlet*. The book open before the skull and the monkey and the appurtenances of their life, and that death's head looking out. And that picture becomes the only image I could form of what "Robert" and "death" might be about, as Donne prefigures his own death and has himself painted in shroud. And that etching occurs in "Death's Duel" I think first; it certainly turns up in all the Donne volumes — you know that incredibly frightening picture with sunken cheeks and closed eyes with shroud. And you know the image of Donne [...]. But that projected the painting of me: I was sitting here, which in turn [...] from the ape as accompaniment

> Ape
> over my head, blank stare
> of a creature-world
> that does not imagine death.

And it went no further than to look up and think about the "cholla" — you know what the cholla looked like, the dried cholla; the skeleton of the cactus is a beautiful column of arabesque tracery, very hard and firm — that Ted [Enslin] had left in our house after his visit. And it looks like a caduceus, it looks as though the snakes themselves are frozen into one, as if the track of all their curves or curls had been substantialized.

> Snake
> with seven mouths. To hold
> the water of our lights in,
> to redeem our eyes.

Again the "Re-possession / credit" thing. Then the "Lace ruff collar" just seen from that picture. "South is my destruction." And that line came with the same kind of autonomy as "The leaf / I lent you" came. And that proposed a focus then, the same voice as "The leaf / I lent you." "South is my destruction," but now the "my" was in "*my*" voice, but the poem had already allowed *me* to have that voice sound through *me*.

CS: It comes out of the *where*...

RK: "Where is that now" — yes.

CS: "Where have I seen the like?"

RK: Well, that's your whole Vivaxis thing,[164] the South as destruction. That's always been the direction of terror for me. I mean that simple observation. Hence I could recognize it as my own voice saying it, though it *is* a jump from what had come before. And if Chuck is right in saying that it comes from the "where" in the previous line — "Where have I seen the like" — I didn't know that, certainly it wasn't like answering that question.

---

164. "Vivaxis" is the name given to "the geographical point where a permanent magnetic alignment was introduced into the atomic structure of our bones [...] at the approximate time of our birth [...] characteristic of the earth's magnetism of that particular geographical point": Frances Nixon, *Born to be Magnetic*, Vol. I (1971) 13.

CS: No, it seems to be one of those places where the syntactical space is operating on a non-semantic or non-discursive level, or extra-discursive level. It's that concrete syntactical space.

GQ: You said that this South distinction came as the first line came...

RK: Yes but it came autonomously in the poem.

CS: Anyway you're certainly moving all of this around "A death for Robert, to elicit life." It's like all springing, it's like there are seeds within the seeds — each shoot is capable of being a new seed. The density of the thing is the way in which any point of it can become in a sense this first line.

RK: What's interesting is the way in which the Recital comes — in terms of what you're saying — a Recital chooses *one* seed to grow from, and all the other seeds do not. Now I could be left in a kind of typical lyrical impasse with all of the seeds and wanting to tend all of them and have them *all* grow and rush from flowerpot to flowerpot, as indeed I have done in lots of poems and in the way, say, Duncan always does, thus letting *no* seed go untended, until it all comes up in an odd, approximative kind of garden. But what happens constantly in *The Loom* — well, not constantly, but lots of times — is that the Recital begins, and the Recital which seems to be developing only *one* seed turns out by the time it's finished (and I look back at it) to have developed *all* the seeds. And it's *all* there. And I stand in awe of that narrative process. Because that's really the first time that I came to *know* about the spontaneity of narrative. I mean of course certain kinds of narrative *do* tell themselves — fantasies or dreams or whatnot — but to have the power expressing itself right in the moment of one's conscious, most alert activity, where I'm thinking about vowels and it's thinking about what's going to *happen*, seems to me so extraordinary. And if you were ever to look at earlier drafts of these poems, I think where you'd see revisions you'd see places where I had *tried* to pause to water a local seed, or tried to arrest the process because I had a sense of *procedure* that I could all of a sudden use — and then I would later have had the sense to cut all of that stuff out. But the Recital then comes to redeem all of its own beginnings — well, not redeem them but to clarify all of its own beginnings.

CS: Well, it's not a garden, it is that furrow.

RK: Yes, *sulca*.

CS: And the fact that the furrow is *there* makes the garden tending unnecessary.

RK: Yes, and it does have that comfort to *write* in it.

CS: Well, I've read now the *Loom* poems that have been in *Caterpillar*, plus the "Lady Isabella and the Mind's Geography" (§ 4) that will be in the *Active Anthology*[165] and the feeling of them all is that they proceed — though you read them vertically — there is a horizontal movement too, which is the cross-feeding process that seems to be happening. The poems seem to lie next to each other, and could be read across…

RK: Certainly that's the way I'd love to publish it one day, in 47 columns, like the Assyrian Ashurbanipal tablets, where the words are going over the pictures, and certainly I've loved columns *forever*. And I suppose the longest of them is short enough that it could be a column on a wall somewhere. So you don't fancy that just for yourself, I feel that always running sideways. The ones that have been printed in *Caterpillar* and the "Lady Isabella" and then many others that aren't printed are largely narrative ones. And there are sections that aren't narrative at all, where the Recital *never* begins and where it seems to me much duller, always, and I wouldn't tend to send it out. And yet those are the places which are the notes of the textual developments…

CS: Uncompleted strands in the fabric where *your* reference lies…

RK: Well, but there they get rewoven in another way. And those sections are in a way more interesting still, because they're as flat in linguistic procedure as most of the narrative sections *seem* to be — actually as you know they're *not* really all that flat, but they play at being flat — but if once you step down to the level of observing them phonemically or even rhythmically, they do, I think, acquire a character — but a character you could easily miss, and perhaps are supposed to miss, as you read along.

---

165. George Quasha (ed.), *An Active Anthology* (1974).

CS: I thought at various points of Enslin, not so much in *Forms* as in *Synthesis*.

RK: Yes, I talk in several places of how this very much *came out* of *Synthesis*, out of seeing how *boring* he was able to be in that poem, and how boredom seemed a conquest — the next thing I had to fight about, to allow myself to be utterly boring, even to me, for the sake of what could come out of that boredom.

CS: That's another interesting historical question; that seems very much to be what's happening in the arts, the discovery in the last few years — very much a live question.

RK: But you see I want to *create* a boredom, not simply tolerate it by virtue of repetition or some other boring process. I want a process that *isn't* boring, that *is* process, but that is *allowed* to be boring as it goes along, in the same way that *wood* is or a tree in November is, as compared to the same tree in January.

CS: I'm not saying really that there's a single event...

RK: No, no, there *is* a single event, but it's the event and its spectre again, and the spectre is far more conspicuous than the event, like what may be between the columns of a John Giorno poem, where I sometimes feel great excitement, something very, very authentic normally just sifts away and drains out of the holes in his *method* as much as anything else. I mean he *has* a method, and like any other method there might be some extraordinary stuff there. But the programmatics of boredom don't interest me. I guess Wagner is the first to dare boredom, to dare the implications of it without making it programmatic?

CS: I was thinking about it in terms of those Greek festivals where you'd sit for days and watch play after play.

RK: How many of those *did* you watch, do you remember?

CS: No, I don't, but the image of it has always been that you sit in a contest of forty playwrights or something and it all takes place before sundown on Friday.

RK: They may have clipped along in Noh play fashion with a lot of very fast chanting.

GQ: Well that's the other side of it that entered into Yeats' thinking and Pound's thinking — that sense of time that must have helped a lot with *The Cantos*, to have that image of an unfolding reality. And Pound returns in the late *Cantos* again to the image of the Noh plays and their characters, taken now *over* Odysseus with which *The Cantos* began; but as they begin to open out Pound thinks back to the Noh plays as containing the deeper sense of time — particularly in *The Pisan Cantos* and *Thrones*.

CS: And that in fact you need all those "dull" middle Cantos...

RK: You *do*.

CS: In order to make the poignancy of the recurrence...

GQ: People who object to those tend to be the people who don't take *The Cantos* as a whole.

CS: Reading on down now through the "furrow" to "the work / starts in the conviction of death":

> The shape of my death
> like a furrow like a Helen like a
> firebreak a warp in the mountains...

where it's like you're pushing over that recapitulation, going over all the things, reseeding, to get by very fast, and permit, instead of getting rid of, permit it to move on, so that the actual feeling of your working with it is sitting there...

RK: Yes, well, that's I suppose literally like a *stretto* in a fugue where everything enters, but very quickly, and in a fragmented way... [*reads*]:

> *L'aura...*
> settling down to a long story
> she reads in me.

I had no idea then what that story would be, except I did have a sense that it was about a skull. I knew that a skull would figure in it.

GQ: Though you already *had* the skull earlier...

RK: Yes, but that skull which appears in the varnished painting later becomes the thing that talks to me on the altar, becomes a *real* skull.

GQ: And in "*L'aura*" you're thinking of?

RK: The air, *l'aura*, and Laura as girl's name, and Petrarch's of course, but mostly Arnaut Daniel's. And that air which bears influence, since by Renaissance theory the influence of the stars were carried to us by the air, by *l'aura*, and hence "malaria," the bad air, could cause us contagion and disease.

That landscape where we were living in Altadena, California, the San Gabriels, was so extraordinary, to have those huge mountains right over head, and recognize them as so unstable, they're utterly like gravel pits ready to crumble down at any moment.

> Sweat it out. Which
> direction has the music in?

It was *my* question now to the feminine being who was interrogating me, or whose interrogation started this.

> North was always
> where I wanted.

As simple as that, and again something I knew of myself.

> Set out the oracle
> eye turned to the blind inside
> hoping.

And then "hoping" becomes "hopping" [*laughs*]

> The hopping
> frog-like people come
> waving their reminders —
> a pain in the ass...

GQ: Where do *they* come from?

RK: "Hoping."

GQ: You mean right out of the activity of hoping.

RK: Hoping is just that [*makes frog-like sounds, imitating frog-hops*], eager leaps.

> a pain in the ass
> but their fingers are lucky.

Their fingers up the ass, or their fingers to the ground, that allow them to spring.

> count them, they flicker
> & communicate
> what they learned
> under the mountain.

GQ: *Under* the mountain — is that like "She it is Queen Under the Hill" in Duncan's poem?

CS: "I was speaking, he said of American poetry, / or was it the other way round, / the way under the hill?"

GQ: Gerrit Lansing.

RK: "Under the hill" is the 19th century, or is it earlier, euphemism for going to the land of the fairies... to go under the hill. But that's what I had in mind here. It isn't a hill anymore, it's a mountain — so much greater the elf that will lie under it.

GQ: At one point you said that the sequence of poems to come after *The Loom* was to be called *The Mountain*.

RK: So I thought.

GQ: What has become of those poems?

RK: The ones that had been achieved entered *The Loom*. You know, I have the lowest of all respect for one's plans — literary plans or intentions. And the very fact that I knew that there was going to be another section meant that there *wasn't* going to be another, wasn't going to be another sequence. That was too programmed and I couldn't live with my own intention, because knowing that had baffled it. *The Loom* had to go on to its proper end, i.e., where it stopped.

If I were to be in a position of someone saying to a critic, "Look at this," I suppose what I'd call attention to is the way that each thing solicits the thing that follows it and summons it into existence — not necessarily directly — so that the "broad plain" is what is under the mountain in a literal meaning of the phrase — an obvious way of looking at it, there's the mountain, there's the plain.

> A broad plain
> not easy to see, drifts
> of mist on it...

again true enough to the circumstance of writing.

> but the movements
> aren't all in the air,
> something on the ground
> has its own directions,
> connections, does
> not approach me.
> Wrap the stole around me,
> pick up the cup.

And somehow that came, I suppose, from the sense of picture, the sense of priest putting the stole on, with which the Catholic or Protestant minister begins his sacred task.

CS: There's also something in the whole poem as it develops, which is very grounded — an image that has been with me since the first time that I read it, is that image of your feet walking the ground, knowing where to step...

RK: That comes out here, doesn't it — knowing the way, letting the contact with ground...

> Three times
> I walked around it,
> the place I knew it was,
> until my feet
> got the feel of the
> shape of it.

CS: The connection of that with death — that the work starts "in the conviction of death" seems to me to have to do with that feel of the ground. That the conviction is what gives one feel of the ground. I don't mean that in simply the sense of "grave," but that literally that apprehension is what gives the edge to awareness, that makes it possible to hold to the ground, that makes it possible not to be in the air in the next moment.

RK: P. Adams [Sitney] tells me that "human" comes from "humanus" comes from "Humus" comes from the "ground," the people "who walk on the ground." And the Greeks of course call people "the ones who die," the *brotoi*, which is the same as "mortos."

GQ: Which is *Adamah*.

RK: Ground, Earth, yes. But I don't believe *that* — I think the Latins were smarter than the Jews on that, I don't think men *came* from the ground, they came *to* the ground, and that ugly second chapter of Genesis...

GQ: Or maybe that the ground came from *them*...

RK: That would be all right, but that ugly second chapter where man is made from the ground, that's what's set us wrong ever since. Set right after the *true* story...

GQ: Doesn't Suarès quarrel with that meaning anyway in *The Cipher of Genesis?*[166]

RK: Here he takes "Adam" as "Aleph" plus "blood" or what happens to you if you fuck around with women, I think is really what he's after,

---

166. Carlo Suarès, *The Cipher of Genesis: The Original Code of the Qabala as Applied to the Scriptures* (Berkeley: Shambala, 1970; New York: Bantam, 1973).

that the spiritual "Aleph" is corrupted by the menstrual blood and flows into animal, becomes "Ruach." Aleph lodges itself in the "Ruach" rather than the "Neshamah." He doesn't say that explicitly but I suppose [...]. That book is itself one that has to be read cabalistically, don't you think. I mean he talks very blithely as if he were saying the whole story, but then you have to drop blithely a level down. Doesn't he seem to talk about the Aleph lodged in the wrong one of its human faculties?

GQ: You like that book?

RK: Yes, very much. It's a different take, a different kind of discourse about Kabbalah, than one is familiar with from the dreary pieties from the Jews and Christians who have unusually written about it; I suppose mostly Christians have written about it, and Hermeticists. Could you tell me why you thought *Loom* § 44 would be an interesting one to talk about *ta'wil* in respect to?

GQ: Well, there was the sense of altars. And there was the fact that you seem in the poem to be literally circumambulating the Ka'abah — and that's what I'd hope we get to when we come to the "three times" refrain (if we proceed in this line-by-line fashion). The other thing is that the poem seems to me a *visualization*, and I'd hoped to draw out of you some statement about your take on "Deep Image," which we presented in *America a Prophecy* in your emphasis on the connection with "Projective Verse." That hook-up you make there seems to flower in the idea of Image as *process*, Image as spiritual exercise or visualization in, say, the Tantric sense. And § 44, like many of the others, seems to have that quality of image-making.

SQ: Also the question of *ta'wil* as the poem's exegesis of its own first line, "The leaf."

CS: For me it was the depth you reach — that image of the building of the altar that takes place when the narrative goes under, is so *prepared* and so profoundly created, it strikes me very deeply. Because it is that act of the maker, not now stated in some reverential fashion of the maker, but dramatically presented, and presented in a way which creates a multiple context for what that event actually is, and leaves it in the problematical nature that is essential to the depth that is being recalled.

RK: Here I must in honesty admit a speaker of a dream, or not quite a dream but a hypnagogic condition, which for many years I lived in, not every night but many nights, from I guess the time of my early 20s or something like that. And that was I was building a wall of a cathedral, in just the way it's described there, picking up blocks — lifting them and raising them to build an apsidial arch, or rather, the wall of the apse. And never in those dreams did it rise higher than my waist or chest — I don't know whether I never *could* get it higher, but it never did grow higher. Because it's a large task to drag these — *lift*, not drag — these great blocks of rock, which were dressed by someone unknown, or not by me, and were just found already dressed — bring them and place them. So for years that hypnagogic image remained there as a rather sacred thing. I may have told a few people about it but I certainly haven't talked much about it. So that was lying in wait all this while. And as I got to the place in this poem where the building of the temple is *proclaimed*, in capital letters, almost as the title of what follows, I realized that I would finally have to disclose that in a direct way, live through that, enact that in the poem — and I did so. But that allowed me to find the altar. Because all those years I had built the wall, surrounding the place where the altar had to be, and then finally here was somehow able to assemble the altar as well. So it seemed like a realization of the meaning of that act, which, as a dream or hypnagogic condition bore always on the laborious nature of my life — you know, constantly writing, constantly making things and composing at a time when young men were not supposed to be doing that but whatever it was I was supposed to be doing. But the simple laboriousness with which I perceived my life, as this endless block-building, seemed now to be the same as my death, a death from which a life could be elicited, if finally that altar could be built, in the place *so* long prepared for the altar. And so it happened here. And that dream has not been with me since.

GQ: Since the writing of the poem...

RK: Since writing this.

CS: The poem has the feel of being that crucial an event...

RK: It's interesting that it would have that for other people, it certainly did for me.

11 · A BOOK OF INTERROGATIONS

CS: That's what it does, it seems to be — If I had to guess, I would have guessed it exactly as you say. I've never heard you talk about that dream, but the meaning of the dream in terms of your self-apprehension is clear. And that this represented a stage or an absolute rite of passage — and that it was the rite of passage, you could *feel* that.

RK: And the night before this was written another dream came, which is also in here. That is, I dreamt that I was lying in the rain, and the rain came and came and came and changed my face, as I slept; as the rain poured down on me my face changed. And that was as much as the dream gave me, and that turned into the — I think the same thing occurs here, the face is transformed by rain, something is washed away.

There's another section of *The Loom*, not published, where I or somebody in my voice falls into a pit, in the rain, where he lies for seven days before he's able to learn that he can tunnel through the mud as well as try to climb it; by becoming closer to it he can get out of it, in some way and in some odd country. And the theme of altars is established early on in the poem, long before any of this was happening, where there's a lot of chit-chat about Protestants and altars and the importance of altars and that what we really need is a table to sit around. The altar is a sadly abstracted image of what men really *need*, humans really need, namely a table to sit down and talk to one another around. And that goes off into Olson and me playing with his table in the kitchen, a few reminiscences, and doesn't really come *back* to tables. Except that table becomes *text*, the thing between us, which allows us to relate and deal. I think a lot of it gets into this section. But what specifically pleased me when you chose to talk about this was that it *is* Recital. And like any real Recital is not paraphraseable. Its source can obviously be pointed out, even as Corbin can say the image of the pearl comes from this gnostic fable, the image of traveler comes from that gnostic fable. The actual terms of the Recital are non-paraphraseable, but still exegitible, somehow.

But this gets painfully close to the problem where process becomes procedure. Or where, in talking about one's process, one could seem to be talking about a procedure, that would be transferable as a method, to somebody else.

GQ: And here we're back to the thing we were talking about before, of a performance that cannot be repeated. One time forms, one time events. Do you want to go on with this same sort of process?

RK: Well, I've said the unknowable things, the things as to its source that could not be *known* — they could be intuited as Chuck does intuit them — but I think anybody is as able as I to see the connections, perhaps better able than I.

CS: There's one other theme that moves through it, and that is the question of "the lights":

> But now I hastened
> over this unlikely plain
> lit by the glow
> that forced itself
> out of my heart,
> a consort of pains
> lighting up
> wheels of my body,
> *rotae*, the turns
> that gave off light
> inside me —
> that was the strangeness
> in running,
> that I was source
> of the only light
> & source of the running too.
> I could do as well
> to stand still. I did
> & the lights went out.
> Wherever the valley
> was coming from it
> wasn't from me.

Though the source of the "lights" seems to be yourself, you propose, why should I do anything, but that then the lights go out and you have to get back into doing it in order that the source that's behind it will in fact in-form it. This seems to be a resolution or statement of both sides of a concern which at various points you are at pains to express either side of: either to express the interest of the silence, the emptiness, the receptiveness, or the abhorrence of the emptiness. And in this case you seem to get it straight.

RK: Yes. Very much so. Getting it straight. It seemed like one of the purest fairy-tale parts of that Recital — just the observation that when you stop doing it the light goes out. Whatever that is. To locate, not the source, there, but the condition in one's own activity.

CS:

> *John of the Oak was here:*
> these words, as letters,
>
> hang in the air
> over the mercurial eye
>
> that maybe saw & always
> answered as if it did.
>
> The words pretend
> to be painted on the wall.
>
> John. Everything pretends
> to be just the place where we find it.
>
> We find it sighing, we kiss it
> singing, we call it Real
>
> & measure with our newfangled minds
> the distance from that glistering Real
>
> to those heavenly twins our eyes,
> & call that *the world*. That is,
>
> the place where John was
> when he wrote or said, *John was here.*
>
> *
>
> Now John is somewhere different...
>
>   ("Arnolfini's Wedding" (1972))[167]

---

167. Published in *The Mill of Particulars*, op. cit., 119; also *Red Crow II*, ed. Thorpe Feidt (Gloucester, Mass., 1973).

In a sense, *Loom* § 44 is a demonstration of that place, of that difference. What happens when the whole thing turns inside out at the end of the poem? It opens on that space in which the altar is being built.

RK: Certainly. And that would be the first thing you'd see in it, or that I'd see in it. It is one continuous landscape and not, I think, discontinuous from this, I mean, anymore than the inside of a hat is discontinuous from the outside of a hat. I think the room does turn inside out. I've seen rooms do that, you've been in rooms that turn inside out.

GQ: Of course — we have that convex mirror in our house — it seems a literal property of the convex mirror, which we're dealing with after all in the Arnolfini Wedding situation, how a room seen in a convex mirror "invaginate[s] voluptuously" was I think the phrase that came to mind in "Somapoetics 11: The Metazodiac."[168]

CS: Gerrit's living room on Washington Street had a trick of doing that all the time —

RK: Washington Street — the house with the white curtains?

CS: It was on a hill so that at any moment if you would become aware of what was outside of those curtains you would feel yourself continuous with it.

SQ: There was a recurring dream of mine as a child, my mother walking in the bedroom door, the distance growing growing and the whole place — inside becoming outside — I can still find the place in my head that has that image.

RK: It's hard to feel that now though. I've tried to feel that in bed at night, the first time when I was a child when I suddenly knew that I was in an immense place and at the far far end of it there were dinosaurs — in no way threatening, I liked dinosaurs quite a lot — but they weren't there either as zoo or as threats but there, where they lived. And my sense of the sudden vastness was frightening — the size was frightening — that what I thought was a room was in fact all there was and that all there was

---

168. George Quasha, *Somapoetics* (Book One) (1973) 103.

was an immensity incomparably greater than the feeble sky a few thousand feet above us whatever those layers of color are that we see as a color. But I think the continuousness of all the spaces is important for me and that all those works open into the same place, not into different places, so that perhaps ultimately all my poems have to be turned inside out to find that single region that they refer to.

Vort #5 (1974)

CLAYTON ESHLEMAN

20 QUESTIONS FOR ROBERT KELLY

Clayton Eshleman: How would you characterize the primary innovative events in the American poetry of the 1960s? How have such events developed or vanished over the past 30 years?

Robert Kelly: The poem is the shaping of time, it is shaping by language (words plus silence plus intonation) our experience of time. So the poem is a score, a language *mise-en-page* for the reader as performer. The reader as performer. A peak shared by unlikely mountaineers: O'Hara, Blackburn, Mac Low — all demanded an alert performing of the page from the reader, otherwise nothing would make *sense*. That score idea has diminished in recent years — you need it for O'Hara, but not for Ashbery. You need it for Blackburn, but not for Creeley, who has a different sense of compelling music. Or maybe just a simpler music, more simply scored.

But innovation is such a slippery word, a promo word, shiny easy packaging kind of word. Every time two words rub up against each other in a proposition, or in a public space (which is always what language is) where propositions arise, imply, kiss, depart, then that's new. Innovation is what we do all the time. So I would say, in terms of your question, that the innovative events of the (late 50s and) 60s, those individual sudden awarenesses of what could be done — like Mac Low's *The Pronouns*, Olson's *Maximus*, Spicer's whole work, utterly lyric yet utterly remote from sentimentality, Duncan's "Pindar" and the prose-rhythmed *Structure of Rime*, Blackburn's *Journals*, Creeley's miraculous breath alone as music, his suspensions, Ashbery's gorgeous lyrical disconnects, Berrigan's sonnets, Lansing's symphonic essays cloaked in poem raiment — all that is still with us. Look at Mackey's miraculous polyphonic Gassir workings. Nothing has been lost, as impetus. The only thing that strikes me as having vanished is the page itself — the page as the stage on which the poem acts. That tradition, stemming from Mallarmé and Apollinaire, climaxing in Pound and Olson, has drifted out of sight now — partly I'm sure from the technology of web "pages" — the page now is of infinite length, so there is no longer a rectangle (golden or otherwise) within which our words disport themselves. Now it's the endless going down —

as if Kerouac's teletype roll were the defining trope for all computer poetry & internet poetic presence. The words run toward us frontally — there's not much lateral thrust in contemporary work. And the oral delivery of poetry has literally no space for the lateral gesture, it's all on-going-through-time, therefore linear — in a way that written poetics had escaped half a century ago. Much contemporary practice — on screen or podium — is essentially retro, restoring (or confining) poetry to the linearity and literalness in time of ancient spoken poetry. That is a real achievement, a presentness & gift. But there's also the loss of something we used to know and practice not so long ago: the sideways maneuver, the quick shunt from the margin that carried us *out of time*.

CE: In a recent interview, thinking of the future and what you might hope for poetry in it, you wrote: "Perhaps poets will reach toward a kind of star-like, radiating continuity, something that makes the poem in front of you continuous with all your experience." Could you open up that statement and concretize it with some examples?

RK: If I can just get the reader to keep reading past the end of the line, edge of the page, her eye will presently engage with the world. Then a new line begins again, summoning him back to the book. In this shuttling forth and back the weaving of that continuity will occur. "Continuity" in Sanskrit is *tantra*, a word that also means "loom," and "weaving on the loom." The star-like radiating (I had forgotten this phrase, and thank you for reminding me) means to me that the poem has to be, or be read as, an event in the space of the world. No æsthetic isolation — no more than a cathedral is isolated from the marketplace in which it stands, the beggars on the steps, the weary tourists taking photos. The poem has to be like that, accessible from within life, and at the same time offering a way out. Through the portal of the cathedral, you enter sacred space. Where another kind of tourism takes its pilgrim course. You ask for examples, and I'm answering with architecture. Sorry. I have the poets reaching toward that continuity — more a stance for them, a way of gesturing as men and women toward the men and women who read them. I'm not talking about performance here, or performance space — that can get lost in the abyss of Entertainment or Education. I'm talking about an attitude in the language & gesture and urgency of the poem or text itself, one that invites the reader to work with it, dance it, might even be with it, interact, bringing the reader's expectations of form and story to a text that proposes to deny them both in aid of some more intense transaction, a more pungent giving. The poet needs to leave space for the reader to enter. "I am the Door," said Jesus, the great poet who instructs us in John's Gospel. The poem must be the door. Examples? Dickinson. Olson. Ashbery. Language civil in its permission to engage.

CE: You once wrote, in 1973, that "short poems don't teach a poet how to live." I wonder if you still believe that today. If so, how do you understand your statement relative to the poetry of Bashō, Cid Corman, and Robert Creeley?

RK: Bashō did not look to poetry to learn how to live. For better or worse, he had the fierce light of the Buddha's teachings to help him with that. Creeley did not write short poems, in my sense of "short" — and to my mind Creeley was richest, best, when he gave himself the time to go onward. Time to go onward. Poetry doesn't in general teach how to live, does it? Doesn't it rather speak, out of living, a word that only living knows, but only the poem can speak? Poetry reveals, tells, even shows. But only life teaches how to live. Poetry listens.

CE: Please comment on the following words:

craft

RK: Once I called craft "perfected attention," and somehow that phrase caught on a while, long enough to be quoted. I think it's true enough as stated; I could gloss it: listen. Listen all the time. Listen especially to the spaces between words, the friction that rubs there, word against word, sound eliciting sound — from such attentions, propositions speak, images arise, truth happens. That is the truth: truth happens. As we speak. What the poet has to do is constantly look away from the poet's own intentions, own meaning, and focus intently, intently, on what's going on with the words in front. The words that alone can speak what you really mean.

bonobos

RK: I don't know much about these simians and their postulated linguistic gestures. In fact, I have trouble with all the apes and monkeys. I want to look away. I am Darwinian enough to see them, like ourselves, as products of evolution. But I am sad when I look at them, because they seem to be descended *from us*, from humans; they have continued evolving in directions I find comprehensible but immensely sad. They are my lost children. Of course they'll retain some linguistic enterprise (as we retain coccyges and appendices) — vestiges of what they were. I think we should look away in modesty and pudor from the simians, and leave them to the sensuous journey, so different from our own, on which they have perhaps willingly embarked. We can't help them except by carefully refraining from harming them by hunting, imprisonment, vivisection. Vivisection of any creature is hellish — of a simian it's a blasphemy.

Atlantis

RK: Well, I've had a lot to say about this in many places, most recently, and most explicitly in a long review of Peter Lamborn Wilson's book on Atlantis (Shivastan Press) which I think is the best and briefest of all books on that subject. I have only one contribution to the idea or practice of Atlantis — it is this. Consider how so much of the ancient scriptural and mythological material that has come our way over the past few thousand years often has to be understood in rather a special sense — typically, backwards or upside down from the "plain" meaning. (I have been working secretly for years on a Project Achorei that reads Genesis and Exodus that way — hint: Cain means strong, Abel means vain, empty. Hint: we are born from women's bodies — when Genesis shows the opposite, it is teaching us how to read the rest of sacred history.) Back to Atlantis. I know how to find Atlantis, the real Atlantis. Follow this thought experiment: the sea level changed. But the sea did not rise, it sank. Atlantis did not sink invisibly below the waves. It rose invisibly to be part of the land — it is hidden in plain sight to this day. Now find that hill on which the seven terraces of its citadel once rose.

Bugs Bunny

RK: His is the voice of my childhood as much as any other — Bugs's sassy sagacity, decency, and teasingness, struck me as plausible armor in a Fudd world, full of softy dopes with guns. Here he was, impossibly long ears, in and out of every hole. But those tiresome carrots. I ask you, did you ever try to eat a carrot? No wonder they call them *crudités* in the Old Country.

closet

RK: Ah, my closet. I love the word, the thing, the environment. I'm very, very claustrophobic — so in all my life, *par example*, I've only twice ventured into a cave, and the last one was a pretty modest cave indeed. But in the closet: fear turns into desire, as Dante says. The closet, stuffed with tender garments and floored with weird obstacles — boots, vacuum cleaners (maybe even your old Kirby) boxes of ornaments — what a place this is to experience the fear, and inside the fear find oneself, the only breathing entity (you hope) inside the closet, alone. What a place of discovery! And the only thing to discover there is yourself — body and soul, time sense, space sense, trusting the hands to touch and know, trusting the nose. Total darkness. For a kid living in a crowded small apartment, the closet was heavenly silence and solitude. The smallest, tightest place became a glorious and innocent Mohave of silence. (This is the paradox, I come to know now, that is the heart of poetry. The smallest is the largest: a poem is a topological solid whose interior is larger than its exterior.) (As an aside, I'd refer here to the collaborative work I've done with the German poet Birgit Kempker, exploring the trope of the closet (*Ein Kollabor*) and shame (*Scham / Shame*).)

CE: Around 1980, I believe, you lost a lot of weight, some 200 pounds as I recall. What effects has this regenerational act had on your life and work? I recall that you once wrote that doctors had told you that you would not reach your 35th birthday. Your weight loss at 45 must have been a tremendous second life confirmation.

RK: The real affirmation was passing 35 — and right after my 36th birthday — as you well know, we were together in Los Angeles, you in Sherman Oaks and me in Altadena — I began *The Loom*, the longest single stretch of poetry I've ever done. And it was with a "Look, we have come through!" (DHL) attitude that I began it. I felt freer than I had ever felt in my life. I was in the clearing now, and all my time was free.

Then, as you say, losing all that weight in 1979–1980. That was affirmation too. Suddenly, the greatest thing (something most people will never experience) suddenly I was invisible. That is, I looked like anybody else. Talk about freedom! All my life I had been cynosure, collected every stare and many a rude remark. Now there I was, mid-40s, healthy, and indistinguishable half a block away from any other tall white male. I could walk down a street all to myself, and people passed with the celestial civility of inattention! It was wonderful. I still enjoy it. Even thirty years later I still expect to see those eyes swivel toward me. And they don't. And if they do, it's because someone knows me.

CE: One of your salient self-commands is "write everything," which has appeared in *Finding the Measure*, *The Loom*, and *Kill the Messenger*. How are we readers to understand such an admonition? What role does it play in the size of your body of work?

RK: Write everything. It came to me that way, the way certain words or sentences do, coming from on high, or from down low, it's not up to me to decide about that, just to listen. Listen and think it through. You call it "self-command," a phrase with a whole other range of meaning, but I can accept it here — certainly a command to myself, but I'm not sure if it was, is, a command from myself. Doesn't matter. To me, the command (and that's what it does amount to) to write everything meant this: when something comes to mind, deal with it. When a word or phrase comes into mind or mouth, deal with it. Deal with it = write it down. Inscribe it, and work with it. Work with the words that are, as Olson said, before us, there, on the paper, under hand. With the same fidelity that Jackson Mac Low addressed the results of his chanceful procedures and strategies, I try to address *the words that begin*. So what comes to mind becomes the matrix, casual, random to whatever degree the neuronal processes of a human are random, the matrix from which poems come. Another thing that "write everything" means is something trivially like Keats' great articulation of Negative Capability, in this case, meaning never to resist the words under hand if they say, or seem to be saying, something "I" don't like or don't believe or don't want. "I" have no business in that stage of the poem. If the poem is ever going to be greater than the poet's self-awareness. If the poem is ever going to be *itself*.

Incidentally, write everything doesn't mean write *anything*. So I don't think my obedience to that stern command has much to do with the size of the body of my work.

What it does influence, though, is the variegation of my work, all the kinds of writing that come to me to want to be done. Let me tell you an anecdote. In a London pub once, standing around with some English poets, a man just introduced to me, said: "Aha, so you're the Kelly who defeated Eric Mottram!" I asked what on earth he meant, I loved Eric, no way I'd fight with him, let alone defeat him. "No, no," the man said, "Eric wanted to write a study of you and your work, but you do too many things, write too many kinds of thing, and he felt baffled and over-challenged." That did not make me feel happier. But it's something that comes from my obedience to the Write Everything command — this past summer, I suddenly found myself writing a play, obedient to a title that spoke into my head: *Oedipus After Colonus*. And so it had to be written, and I had nothing but the title to go on.

CE: In your poem on one of Messiaen's symphonies, *Turangalila Meditation*, you write:

> The fat space of the cathedral chants her dark
> litanies, the cool grey stone light of the Lady Chapel
> lets me sit down. There is rest here. The traffic
> is not far. I hear it
> through the ideal blue of the ogival windows,
> glass stained color of consciousness, love her,
> everywhere I have gone was for her sake

In other poems in *Kill the Messenger*, you wrote: "Love means to find / your original religion," and "Eros was my master." Here we have a cluster of vectors: love, religion, and Eros. The "her" in the cathedral appears to be the Virgin Mary (in contrast to a living woman). Tell me about the role women play in your poetry.

RK: Novalis says somewhere: My Beloved is shorthand for the Universe. Something like that. Never, never the Virgin Mary *in contrast to* "a living woman." The blue robed Madonna in the window is a picture, "ill-silenced by the [glass] itself," of a living woman. The woman to whom such constant (do you find it tiresome? some do, maybe I do too, from time to time, but who am I? My views are not the point.) references gesture is the woman who stands before me. To whom it wants in me to speak. That's all. There's no definition I could give of woman, or prescription for how or what she is or should be. Every woman is different. And there is no essential woman, any more than an essential man. Dozens of genders and thousands of sexes, but only one you. Everything I have spoken was for her sake, this "you" to whom I speak. The living woman. You (as Whitman, no woman in mind, surely, wrote) you who are holding me now in your hands.

CE: The title — *Kill the Messenger* — puzzles me. According to the book's title page, the full title appears to be: "Kill the messenger / who brings bad news — / the world is only / description." How do you intend this title to be read? Didn't Bruno bring bad news?

RK: And those who thought that the news Bruno brought was bad news, they up and killed him for bringing it. But for us, he brought very good news indeed: we can change the sky, can change the stars that preside over our birth — the way Robert Duncan used to say that you can't pick your parents but you can pick your grandparents — as he chose Baudelaire and Brahms to be his.

My point in choosing that title was not so much the killing as the *only*: "the world is only description." The world we describe (to ourselves, to other people, and obviously to posterity) is the only world there is. The world (to amplify Wittgenstein) is whatever has been asserted to be the case. How we describe the world conditions utterly how we live in it. And how we live in our minds and souls and hearts as we do go on living in the described world — Rilke's "interpreted world."

CE: In your marvelous 1993 poem, "Man Sleeping," you write:

> No one will relinquish money, a revolution
> is shattering mirrors only,
> doesn't change the endless empire of Light,
> every blood-slimed sliver of the glass still reflects
> the intolerable injustice of this one-life universe.

One might conclude from such a statement that you do not believe we can change the way things are. And it is also true that you have written: "We are silenced by the way things are." But as I understand your body of work, its primary drive is to change the way things are. Are poets locked into an impossible situation in this regard?

RK: The situation is possible. An effective outcome is unlikely. But we must work for it. Changing the base — Stalin denied that linguistic (poetic) change could affect the working mind of society. I think it can. The marxisant poets of the 80s (Language poets, etc.) soldiered on, fueled by that great hope. I don't know any poets nowadays who still evince much in the way of hope (other than for venal entitlements of job and fame). But hope is still one of the "theological virtues" — the three virtues (*strengths*) by which we speak God into the world. Faith, Hope, Love. Yes, my body of work is driven by that hope, to change the way things are, to open onto an otherness from which our own true instinct toward kindness and love might welcome a nurturing breath from a harmless world. I am a child trying to talk my way out of punishment. I am trying to talk the killer out of killing us. I am trying to beguile the monarch into listening to my stupid poem instead of killing anybody at all. A one-life universe is unjust, is terrible. We must live again. The poem must give us the will to want to, the gumption to get around to life.

CE: Michael McClure wrote (in the early 1970s) that "It is conceivable that the most colossal example of vanity that can be found in history is held by the peoples of contemporary North America." How does this statement reverberate, or not, to you today?

I recall in this context lines from a poem in your 1998 book, *The Time of Voice*: "o my country / how I long to love you, / be love-worthy, be factual, / be a face / of liberty / and let love in..." What would have to happen for you to be able to love the United States now?

RK: America. How can I answer. I love the skin and rock and skies, and the people of us, our ways, our folkish madness. I do not love our masters. I do not love the word democracy as it is used to hide from us the fearful (in both senses) oligarchs who rule us. I don't think it has much to do with the United States. It is the world, or the world now. We are complicit in a vast nightmare of enslavement, indifference, control. SONY/BMG hurts the world as much as Monsanto does — mind-control by mass music, lifestyle compulsion through image-manipulation (Entertainment is the largest single industry in America, and sculpts the world more than the Pentagon has managed to do). I do not like war, and think it is always evil. We have lived for more than a century with that evil. Even the Civil War was evil — our bloodiest war yet, and some other way had to be found. And the War in Iraq is the vilest evil we have yet contrived. We sink, we sink lower — and I say we only to the extent that we tolerate (and god forgive some of us, actually endorse) the vileness of our masters. We know not what we do. If some states seceded, some states whose populations abstained from war and mass imprisonment of minorities, then those states could be the Re-United States of righteousness, and those I could love. But for the moment, I can only love America. Which was before our politics. And will be after. America in eternity. You know it too. Every honest word is an act of contrition. Every word is a pledge of allegiance.

CE: When we read Zukofsky's translation of Catullus, are we reading Catullus? Or Zukofsky? Or something else? What do you consider to be the value of homeophonic translations?

RK: Answering the last part first: the value of all procedures and constraints used by the poet. Procedures and constraints are powerful tools, but they are tools to build the house we have in mind — especially the house we have in mind but don't know it, or don't know it's there, or how it's shaped. I mean that homoeophonic translation (or any other strategy of compelling words to appear where none, or others, were before) is finally of greatness and power when it succeeds in shaking something out of the poet's head, shocking the poet into seeing what was never there: letting her shout out with full conviction what she didn't know, a second before, that she meant at all. And now she'll stake her life on it, because that is what one does, in fact, in the poem, throw a handful of grit into the machinery of eternity and change, hopelessly change, the pattern of the real. Any poem does this, and the more it changes and defies and renews and challenges the reader's expectation, his habit of attention, the better the poem does its work. When I hear Celan or Hölderlin *as* English, I am hearing that most wondrous music, a song nobody sang. So, to answer: neither Catullus nor Zukofsky. No One's Song we hear, like Celan's famous No One's Rose. But it's Zukofsky's ears we bless, his "lute" for letting us hear.

CE: Here are a few names for you to respond to:

Miles Davis

RK: Damn braces, bless relaxes, said Blake. Davis relaxes, I guess, irritates me. Too smooth, too crossover, too popular, too smoky, too clean. I feel I ought to say something, at least, given your question, to bring jazz in. Not that I know much about it. Fats Waller when I was a child, Parker when I was half-grown, a one-night stand with John Birks Gillespie in San Francisco, Don Cherry on Tenth Street, Ornette all the time. But that's not a life with jazz — it's moments of vivid interruption during my Mahler life, Bellini life, Biber life, Strauss life, Bach life.

Richard Pryor

RK: Blank. I really don't know him. Sorry. I gather he's a comedian, from seeing ads. Never saw him in a movie or on TV. You maybe are just teasing me with this reference, since I think you know how notorious I am for not being fond of narrative film, but for loving "experimental" films. As far as I'm concerned, and I know I'm eccentric here, there really is in film a place for story, but only when it makes its way to the viewer by eye (Atom Egoyan, say, or Tarkovsky, or the supreme Sokurov) rather than by dialogue (Truffaut, Cassavetes) or narration. Think of the way Pasolini, who is a powerful writer and poet, nevertheless does it all in film *by eye*. What a great being he was. Right up there with Brakhage and Bergman. Anyhow, my heroes of comedy are the purely visual: Keaton, Tati, Lloyd, Chaplin.

James Baldwin

RK: You're the second person to ask me about him today. With his quiet, tenebrous anxieties so elegantly summoned, aired — he's the one who taught, told, most of us, the white audience, what we needed to know, so little wanted to know. About race, yes, but not just race but all the shades and infamies and tendernesses of human difference. And he did so with a beauty of style, a *parlando* eloquence, unstoppable flow, that made us listen. Made me listen. Thanks for reminding me of him.

Gaudí

RK: Greatest underappreciated sculptor of our time, maybe the truest one. Instead of sculpting objects (Moore, Lipchitz) or environment / atmospheres (Smithson, Serra) he sculpted vast invisible art works that stand solid in the sky as buildings. We call it architecture, and smile, and walk in and out. But he gestures in the sky (Sagrada Familia) or on the ground (Parc Güell) and the gestures last. He's wonderful. He made the angels smile.

11 · A BOOK OF INTERROGATIONS

Joan Mitchell

RK: That grand era of art, the body gesture lifting to the sky, intercepted, "ill-silenced" by the canvas itself. She was I suppose the last of them, the painters who threw themselves into the marks, the body's gestures make on surfaces, the self as fresco, sudden, vivid. In my mind, she inherits a little of the excitement I felt around Kline and de Kooning in The Old Days, that the mark can be enough, the gesture can hold space intact, the gesture can be the mark, and the mark can be read. I haven't followed her work particularly, which I suppose means something. It pleases me to look at it, but it has not yet drawn me to build a house in the mind around her way of work.

CE: How do you understand "improvisation" in poetry?

RK: All poetry is improvisation. It is listening to the voice in the head (no bets on where that voice resides, or where it is coming from, or what "from" could possibly mean) listening: to the first thing that comes to mind. Then following up on that, riffing on that, sometimes with a formal intention, sometimes (better) just the intention toward form.

So-called jazz-poetry misses the point. Poetry is there already — doing it "with" music or "to" music just hides either the real poetry or the inept imagination of the performer. Poetry is the other side of music. And in any case, poetry is doing what jazz is doing, but with greater freedom — no chart, no time signature, no dance floor packed with rowdies. It is improvisation at its purest. Something out of nothing.

CE: Write me a poem here called "Moments with Shostakovich"

RK: Here is the poem, I wrote it as soon as I read the question — so it's the first question answered of all these. Thanks (as they say) for asking!

MOMENTS WITH SHOSTAKOVICH

for C.E.

I am fourteen it is New York
he is walking toward me, his sallow
face his glasses the two goons beside him
keeping him in line, the world's

greatest composer (Strauss has died)
walking me towards me,
I stand in awe but try not to look
impressed, I am a kid, as a kid
I am always performing for myself
just like the poet I would become
or am I, I am I am a poet Williams
said was he speaking for me then
there with the Waldorf-Astoria
then the classiest joint in America
hovering over D. D. Shostakovich
walking towards fat little Robertus
Jacobus whose heart filled immensely
with the authenticity of this
unbelievable occasion, me with him
on this very street in my own town
forever I am real! this is now! this is
the real thing the real world, I am in it
at last, here he comes the man
whose music lives in my head
we share space, I belong to the world!
By now they had passed, maybe
he was smoking, I probably was,
maybe he caught my adoring eye
maybe he saw it was all too full
of self-importance to see him,
too busy with I-am-with-Shosty
to actually be with him, there,
on the grey street, a frail unhappy
looking man between his two
apathetically vigilant bodyguards
and they too might like him have
looked at me then looked away.

Actually, a few months ago I wrote a number of pieces "listening through" some of the Shostakovich preludes and fugues. That was part of a big cycle of compositions, working also through Biber sonatas, Bax orchestral works, and most of the Mozart piano concertos. At the moment, I am working on a text "listening through" Franck's Prelude, Chorale and Fugue as performed by Robin Freund-Epstein, towards a live enactment with her of music and text next spring. But I'm very happy that you made me write a new Shostakovich poem, one that, as you see, breaks into the stifled air of my childhood, to reclaim a memory that's important to me. A child, even a child, is in the world.

CE: Christopher Wagstaff has written: "Robert Kelly shares the view that in poetry something of permanent and ultimate importance to man is revealed." If you agree with Wagstaff, tell us something about the revelation of permanent and ultimate importance in poetry.

RK: I do share that view (but with whom am I said to share it?). I think it is in language that the importance (permanent is a hard word, ultimate harder, but important, yes, has import for us, big import) and poetry — which I keep defining as the shaping of time by language alone — pre-eminently allows language to do its work, work from its depths, which are our own depths, caverns to which we have — as you have shown us vividly in your poetry as well as in *Juniper Fuse* — access only, or perhaps most fully, in language: the linguistic consequences of what happens to us in the abyss, what we come out spouting and sometimes get to write down. It happens down there. So we have to write it *down*. (Prepositions, aren't they the purest words?)

CE: You have often mentioned the word "lust" in your poetry, especially in *The Loom*. You have written that it is more important than truth, that there is a purity in it, that you yourself are lust, that your lust is faithless, that it monopolizes, and that "What I have made / I made from lust / for eternal conditions, / open systems." How does lust operate in poetry?

RK: Once I wrote something like this: "Fear / and lust / Trust / nothing else." I mean simply we know it when we feel lust, we know it when we feel fear. These feelings are guides. I by no means intend to endorse either as operators in a situation. No, they are criteria from which we can decide our actions. We blunder fearfully when we *deny that we feel* lust, or deny that we feel fear. I'm not saying (I'm not Blake) indulge the lust, indulge the fear — do as you will with them, and it is right and good sometimes to turn away, and sometimes not — but know that they're there, working in you. So lust is something that turns us towards the world. That is wonderful. What is terrible about lust is that what it focuses on becomes the Figure, and all the rest of the poor world just the Ground. This gestalt effect of lust is the danger — while seeming to grant more ("I want, I want!") it confers always less and less. The more you grasp, the more you let fall away. So I speak of trusting those feelings as signposts — not as destinations.

CE: In his 1990 book, *Words With Power*, Northrop Frye writes: "Blake was, so far as I knew and still know, the first person in the modern world to see the events of his day in their mythical and imaginative context. He realized that the old mythical universe, in its ideological form as a rationalizing of traditional authority, was dead, and that it was time for a new emphasis in mythology that would accommodate the revolutionary movements he saw rising all around him."

In responding to this statement, I wonder if you would keep in mind another of Wagstaff's perceptive comments on your work: "Unlike many contemporary poets, Kelly views mythology as something which arises up out of the human mind and hence as something quite different from poetry. Because mythology presents a certain world-view or picture, it cannot embody the basic forms of experience in as immediate a way as poetry can. As Martin Heidegger points out, poetry exposes one to 'divine lightnings' rather than to world-views."

RK: I really don't know what Chris means when he says that mythology is quite different from poetry. It is only different in the sense that the fruit is different from the tree, yet they can both be called "apple," yes? This one is a very important question — let me try to do something with it. What comes to mind: *mythos* and *logos* started out as two words in Greek, each meaning roughly the same: "something spoken — a word or words together making up a story or an argument." Over time, the *mythos* word (I think Pindar may be the first to use it this way) drifts away and takes on the restricted meaning of "story — not necessarily factual," while *logos* tends to be restricted to "statement of fact." The former eventually gives us myth, the latter logic. But look at: *mythos / logos* and what you really get is "story / telling." That's what mythology is — there is no myth except what is told. All the gods we know arise from telling — whether the telling of poets or the telling of "prophets." And Frye certainly is right about Blake, if we understand him to mean (leaving aside the tendentious remark about revolutions "all around" — there was only one) that Blake was the first poet willing to let myth arise out of his own telling, the first one who allowed a full-blown mythology to be told 'in his own words.' But thank God not the last: what else are *The Cantos, Maximus, Paterson, The Changing Light at Sandover*, but myths of our day, of our telling. And in them our gods move, swift and enigmatic and confusing as ever — no clear sign ever from Zeus, the Greeks said, and our gods are no more explicit. And no less energetic in the workshops of the heart and mind. If Heidegger's lightning flashes are indeed divine, they light up — moment by moment, flash by flash — the only world there is. As poems do, in their own moments. Their flashes. Which are, alas, seldom as long lasting as the whole poem might be. The flash shows the god. The *duende*, we used to call it back in the 50s, stealing Lorca's thunder to make our own lightning with.

CE: In *The Time of Voice*, one poem is titled "Every Language is a Second Language."

Does one write poetry to break out of second language into first language? Is the language shamans tell us they hear, and converse with animals in, a first language?

RK: No, shaman talk and beast talk are second language too. First language is what happens to our skin and eyes and mind in the world, the hurt of happen. The touch of hand. The wind. We can name all those things later, but when they happen, they are first language talking to us, and we speak that language by moving, touching, tasting. I mean the movement from perception into language is far greater in its abstraction, its *terror*, than the movement from English to Japanese or Tibetan. My title, its idea, is to keep people firmly aware of how remote *all* language is from the healing joyous horror of primary sensation.

CE: At one time you wrote: "Dreams are dragon-snorts, / worth little." At another: "dream is translation from dreamless sleep into waking." What is your position on dreams at this time?

RK: There have been periods (I'm in one now) when I dream obsessively, oppressively, and wake relieved by morning light. Other times I go months without dreaming (i.e., to soothe the science brethren, without remembering a single dream). In those times, I feel nostalgic about dreams, and come all over Breton-like about the magistry of the dream state, and its wisdom. Right now, I dread the dream because it imposes on the awakened dreamer the responsibility of taking notice — interpreting, maybe, or reporting it to spouse or friend or counselor, or just writing it down, or just carrying the heavy thing through the day, stubbing against odd corners of dream remnants that show up through the day. The converse of Freud's famous phrase (*Tagesreste*) is also true: the day is a remnant left over from dream.

I also have felt for years that in addition to all the other ways dreams have been received or understood (messages from the gods, from the collective unconscious, from the personal unconscious, scraps of the day, somatic impressions symbolized as narration — cold feet dream of snow) there remains for us to explore the possibility that dream is an authentic *language*: that is, like any natural language, a social event, that we dream in a community. I infer that we owe it to that community to report our dreams; our dreams are for the other, are the words our nights speak to the community. Dreams are the News of the Night, and need to come to us every morning. I have some other notes on this in my old book of essays, *In Time*, and some more, along with other people's responses, and community dream experiments, in Lynn Behrendt's interesting and ongoing *Annandale Dream Gazette* online.

CE: In "On Discourse" (1973) you posed the following question: "What is the other side of *this* place?" At that time, you did not respond to this question. Would you do so now?

RK: You have given the answer. The other side of this place is now. Now has been waiting for us all along. Are we ready for now yet? Maybe I should ask you.

4 September 2007

THREADS 24: ROBERT SAYS

Interlocutor: Forgive the skeptical tone now, but when I hear you say Language, it sounds a little like the name of a religion, or a proposition. Is this common noun after all enough of an answer? William Carlos Williams keeps saying, "The language, the language!" in Paterson, but doesn't say much about it. Are you using it that way, sort of a divine name to intone?

Kelly: No, I mean it in a more or less economical, anthropological, or human sense. Language is the ocean in which humans swim. It is the relationship between us, whether close or far, and it is the air we breathe that keeps the living in touch with the dead. Nothing is lost. It is the ground we move on, the contour map by which even our desires are inflected, shaped, expressed. Sea, air, land: Language is all. By experimental operations conducted in language — i.e., poems — we have some hope of operating on the world that language makes by describing. Here the political hope & the spiritual hope of poetry become one. Language is aspiration.

Interlocutor: It still sounds mystical to me. Or are you just excited?

Kelly: Mae West asked, "Is that a pistol in your pocket, or are ya jus' glad to see me?" Both are true, always. We are armed, and we are horny. The whole — there is no point, no merit, no sense, in trying to achieve less than the whole.

Interlocutor: Is that your famous WRITE EVERYTHING! oracle?

Kelly: Yes, the only oracle worth attending to. But notice that Write Everything! is not the same as, is in fact the strict opposite of, Write Anything! Write Everything means: Devote yourself steadily to language to express the whole.

Interlocutor: What is the whole? It sounds Platonic, as you say it.

Kelly: I'll use it as an adjective, then, not as a noun. The whole capacity of human perception, the whole faculty of human expression, the whole infinity of human aspiration. As simply as I can say it: to deny no aspect of human enterprise. To violate all the decorums that tell me things like: "Only the real." "Only the imagined." "Art is spirit." "Art is flesh." To make room for the spiritual bluster of Tolstoy and the intellectual sinuosity of Baudelaire both, to silence des Esseintes again with even more numerous senses, to welcome Whitman's orgasmic whispers under the broad nonsense of his proclamations, to free Pound from the need of naming any enemies other than human greed, to recall the keen skepticism of Blake and the credulity of Newton the alchemist.

Interlocutor: You're raving a bit.

Kelly: Raving is permitted. So is drollness, acuity, measure, sarcasm, sentiment, hope. So is precise knowledge, the names of persons and cities. Dead languages and living women. So is hope.

Interlocutor: So your excess is an excess of aspiration, it sounds like. When it comes down to it, what really does it compel you to do?

Kelly: To say everything I can. I want to say everything that language can. What else is there to say?

"Self-interview," *Conjunctions* (1989)

12.
A BOOK OF RECENT WRITINGS

BARBARA ROETHER

THE ISLAND CYCLE:
FIRE EXIT, UNCERTAINTIES, THE HEXAGON, HEART THREAD, CALLS

Robert Kelly's newest work *Calls* marks the completion of a major undertaking: a decade long series of five book length poems he calls The Island Cycle (named for being written during summers on the Island of Cuttyhunk). Beginning with *Fire Exit* in 2009, followed by *The Uncertainties, The Hexagon, Heart Thread*, and concluding with *Calls*, these books trace a master poet's decade-long journey along the deepest rivers of language.

Kelly listens to the world with a virtuoso ear, and what he hears is the music of everything:

> as we near them
> each thing speaks its own
> dialect of thought
>
> the manyness of them
> at work in us
> signs from afar
>
> [from *Calls* #1]

In this work the poet hears, for us, the signs of language unfolding from its sources — all types of utterance, all longings, all meanings nascent and known, are part of this song. It is poetry that retains the skin of the sacred sources from which language arises. While Kelly records faithfully what the world sings; he never for a moment forgets the reader who is with him. He coaxes us to listen too, and in the midst of the roaring torrent of language, he is bending toward us, whispering the translation into our ears. He is forever intimate, and his work is supremely alive.

Kelly's erudition has long been legend among students and readers, and much of his earlier work was more explicitly engaged with a range of overtly esoteric themes: the Kabbalah, alchemy, the grail, Orphic myths, Ariadne, etc. It was a poetry dense with blooms of reference, etymologies, imaginary cities, and forgotten elixirs. Beginning in the early 1980s, Kelly began an ongoing practice in Tibetan Buddhism that has subtly shaped his work since. Where scholarship once formed the content of much of his work, his focus is increasingly on the exploration of perception itself. His poetry is now more likely concerned with what is happening to a man on a beach in the wind, than with a historic text. His book *Flowers of Unceasing Coincidence* (1988) began to explore that juncture, and in some senses is a precursor to the current works.

In considering the role of the Island Cycle in the poet's work as a whole, an apt analogy might be Kurosawa's *Dreams*, the film in which the great Japanese director revisits the original sources and images of his work. As viewers we realize that the sources, the essential dream images, were always the best part of the movie, the subconscious energy that flows through the work. And though *Dreams* lies outside of the historic sagas of Kurosawa's career, it is somehow the very essence of his vision. As a divergence from previous directions and as a distillation of all that came before, The Island Cycle forms a similarly distinct œuvre in Kelly's long career.

It is a remarkably prolific career, not simply in the number of books published (over 50) but in decades of honing and perfecting the craft. It seems that by working in poetry longer and more consistently than most everyone else (he is 82 now) Kelly has moved further into its interior. Mapping this territory, tirelessly examining the geology of language — where it folds and where it shifts, how it creates the world and yet is apart from it — is the motive that joins these books. They are in essence about what it means to be an artist in continuous interaction with language:

> Bravery, slavery words are always trying to tell
> us something we don't want to know
> but language purifies itself in speaking
>
> as my father told me rivers do in running
> leaving all silt behind, a deposit of evidence
> from which only poetry and revelation grow. [*Calls* #35]

Each of the five books in the cycle has a different formal structure, and each structure is designed to allow the poet to examine one or another aspect of poetic language more clearly. There is a symphonic quality to their progression, though Kelly has stated "No narrative is delivered or implied; as with any actual cycle, the reader can begin anywhere."

Fire Exit has 132 sections of varying length, written entirely in three-line stanzas. The three-line form is dynamic, often naming, then commenting, then changing its patterns, each somehow igniting what came before. There is an incantatory quality to lines: "Oh god the things we clearly dearly know/ And never tell, every single one of us" [#103].

The next long poem in the cycle, *Uncertainties*, consists of 125 sections written in two-line stanzas. Kelly writes his intention was "to solicit the dissolving of certainties, in between the inbreath and the outbreath, where nothing is fixed, and freedom begins." One can hear the rhythm of in and out in lines like these:

> Now that I lost the line the man whispered
> by the cellar door I must go down
>
> down there are papers from a former life
> everything written down slays the one who writes it   [#115]

The sometimes-static quality of the two-line stanza makes *Uncertainties* slightly less immersive than the other volumes; Kelly's natural lyrical flow is perhaps overly compressed in order to fit into the couplet. Fortunately in the next volume he chose more over less: *The Hexagon* contains 640 verses of six-line stanzas. In the introduction, Kelly writes: "These stanzas are meant to borrow some of the properties of a cube... who can know what goes on inside the cube, and what the inner faces might look like, or what they might behold." He goes on to outline that each side of the cube (each verse) must be made of complete lines of poetry, and lists six things that can make a line complete. To paraphrase, it can make a statement, offer material for thought, propagate and abort syntactical sequences, haunt the mind, start a story rolling, or be taken as a command. This list also forms a useful note to much of Kelly's work. In "Hexagon #578" he writes:

> Now you know who you've been listening to
> Wizard in a shriner's fez wet from the infidel sea.
> All smoke and no mirrors mirrors are hard.

I baffled them by sticking to the truth.
I kissed your shoulder and heard a whistle blow.
Our little business part of a vast unseen event.

The syntactic switch in the third line to "all smoke and no mirrors" is typical of the way Kelly uses syntax to undercut our expectations, and the poem questions each image even as they appear. A wizard who tells the truth? Are we as readers the "them" he baffled, or is that the rest of the world? Is the whistle on a ship? Does he have to leave now? Kelly evokes worlds with just a few lines; their juxtapositions become vibrant, living events.

The grace Kelly shows in moving between one perception and another foregrounds the universal humanity of this work. The poets world (like ours) is full of longing and questions, which he constantly moves toward, like a surfer choosing waves. This sense of motion in the language, letting go of one direction to take up another, roots us in the living world. Kelly never becomes lost in abstraction. He knows better than to think an idea to death — he knows he'll find another.

The Hexagon's cubed form is followed by *Heart Thread*, which consists of 325 twelve-line poems. The 12 lines are of varying length, and could be called sonnets, or not, depending on how they are read; some certainly have overtones of being love poems. Kelly subtitles *Heart Thread* "a fugue" and offers this gloss: "Body Speech Mind what else have we, the heart is the thread that links them together that runs through all voices and variations of our fugue."

The Buddhist connection is explicit in *Heart Thread*, the book's title borrowed from the Heart Sutra (thread being a literal translation of the Sanskrit word, sutra) which famously states that "Form is emptiness; emptiness is form. Emptiness is not other than form; form also is not other than emptiness." The parallel grammatical structures, as well as the conceptual unity of opposites, at work in the Heart Sutra can be heard often in Kelly's work: "language is in us, we are in language," is a kind of meme that reoccurs, or a shore at which we keep arriving at. These lines from #244 suggest as much: "give me the word that flees its thing / let me go to the country music goes to when it fades away / let me live on the ashes of what someone sang."

In this sense, "the word that flees its thing" is a form around emptiness, a reference to the nature of the inquiry itself. How can one ever comment on language, except with more language? How can one speak, without thinking of the listener as a separate person, the one who is spoken to? To use language implies our separateness, yet Kelly wants reader and writer to be as one. The sections in *Heart Thread* grow increasingly clear and urgent about this spiritual quandary:

> Perception of the other is the first mistake
> till then Mind is peace and luminous
> once it senses other all the stuff begins
> the offerings and the arsenal the blood and fear
> until the only cure for me is to be you
> make the glad of the other my whole work
> then mind will be mine
> full of its own serene excitements
> beyond the dark and light
> try it if you don't believe me
> do enough for the other and nothing for me
> let the ocean show the quick way home. [#222]

Calls, the final volume in the cycle, returns to the three-line stanza, and in 236 sections concludes the series with a crescendo of intensity. *Calls* may be the most moving part of the cycle as whole; it is deeply self-revelatory, because the poet returns as a subject to consider the shape of his own life here — and his presence allows him to refer more consistently to us, his readers, urging us to look at what he is looking at and urging us to listen. This is the work of a poet purifying himself through making poetry, and it is a moving performance. In *Calls*, the work more clearly takes on the character of a spiritual exercise, and even of a sung spiritual in the sense of call and response. *Calls* gets to the primary nature of language, i.e. each of us calling out to the other. Kelly never gives up on the public purpose of poetry, he is calling us with all his might.

In both breadth (the cycle contains over 1000 poems) and passion, The Island Cycle's closest precursor is Whitman's *Leaves of Grass*. Indeed, Kelly shows himself here to be the twenty-first century's natural inheritor of the project Whitman set out upon. It is as if he is extending

Whitman's transcendental sense of human relationships into a transcendentalism of language, revealing not how "every atom belonging to me as good belongs to you" but how every word belonging to us all, those who use the language, links us all, and is linked to all others. Like *Leaves of Grass*, The Island Cycle is a poetry of inclusion. Kelly's project is not to sing first of the people, their occupations, or their open road, but to sing, finally, of the song itself. His work is a celebration of the democracy of words, longings, images, questions, birds, all the varieties of saying "we hear" — all are given an equal hearing, as they enter the realm of the poet's awareness.

Kelly, like Whitman, was born on Long Island; both writers spent their early careers in New York City. Both have had an outsider relationship with the mainstream literary establishment while remaining vital to other poets. Both connect poetry to aspects of spiritual inquiry. Kelly too hints at this connection:

> Thank you dear Walter, island brother
> voices fewer, deeper,
> still trying to burrow through
>
> the awful silences of human speech
> where every word says Love me or I die
> and take you with me
>
> a word, a lone assassin.
> a redeemer.
> open the bloody window   [*Calls* # 80]

It is sometimes easy to think that the sheer quantity of Kelly's writing obscures the quality. If among the thousands of lines we find some repetition or a tired phrase, the wonder is how rarely. We simply are not used to so much good poetry being available in one place. It can't be that good if it's that plentiful, we think — but it is. Language, as Kelly knows, is free for the taking.

Like Whitman in his time, whose fleshy dreamscapes appalled the public sense of propriety, Kelly's constant output creates a body of work that conflicts with our current ideas of creative production and ownership. What if instead of the hard wrought (or hard fought) poem of revelation, the poem as record, or poem as object, we were only interested in one poem, which was a continuous one that we all share? What if there is an endless amount of what we need? Scarcity may increase value in goods, but the world is in need of Kelly's bounty.

JORDAN REYNOLDS

THE PLACE OF LOVE:
SAY WHAT WE DO TO EACH OTHER GOES ON

1.

It would be a disservice to Robert Kelly's virtuosity to label him as a certain *kind* of poet who writes a certain *kind* of poem. Instead, it is instructive to investigate his work as *kindred* to his contemporaries. Of the kind of poetry he writes, Kelly finds good company with a poet of similarly enormous stature, Charles Olson. Inside of Olson's breath, on the space of his reaching pages, the *place* of the poem is investigated, resolved, questioned. The poem and the poet are moored by the body and the breath to the very moment of the poem just as a shadow is moored to the ground. Olson's poems are found "among stones," as in his great work, "The Kingfishers," but he also uncovers his honey within the place of his body:

> I have this sense,
> that I am one
> with my skin
>
>   Plus this—plus this:
> that forever the geography
> which leans in
> on me I compell
> backwards I compell Gloucester
> to yield, to
> change
>
>   Polis
> is this
>   "Maximus to Gloucester, Letter 27 (withheld)"

The Oxford English Dictionary traces the word *place* back to 12th-Century Old English, where the meaning was often difficult to pinpoint, being used to signify town squares and fortified outposts as well as a private residence. The term coexists publically *and* privately, both interior (in the sense of a room-as-place) and exterior (the place of the field, open, exposed). Olson's *polis* (the perfect city-state of his body *and* of Gloucester) is kindred to that sense of place that Kelly identifies with in his quietly important poem, "Wintereve":

> There is nothing but this purple landscape
> fell down on us from the hump-backed moon
>
> at the middle of a month, a mouth
> under a mountain.
>
> Wives yearn with eyes & mice & crows
> across this river topped with blades of ice
>
> too thin to walk on, too slow, too slow.
> There is an hysterical logic of winter nights
>
> quiet women afraid of their porches,
> their spruces blue in moonlight. I too am afraid
>
> that I am really here, that this shadow on the snow
> is my own weltering eternal shadow
>
> that the birds fly past with ice in their beaks
> & this place is my place. *Kill the Messenger* (1979)

If this poem is addressed to any*thing*, it is addressed to Olson's "Songs of Maximus," song 2:

>   where
>   shall we go from here, what can we do
>   when even the public conveyences
> sing?
>
>   how can we go anywhere,
> even cross-town
>   how get out of anywhere (the bodies
> all buried
> in shallow graves?

The fear in "Wintereve" arises from a fear of being stuck in place, unable to cross the razor-thin ice blades, the women afraid, even, "of their porches." Kelly interrogates place, the terror of the given outside, there being "nothing but this purple landscape," and nowhere to go. The yield and change of Gloucester that Olson insists upon in "Letter 27" is in this poem mimicked by the very words of place as they morph in stanza two from "month," to "mouth," to "mountain" (from the abstract, to the personal, to the public/exterior). In Kelly's poem this shifting is not fast enough (like the ice: "too slow, too slow") and/or does not allow a "forwarding," as Olson calls it in "I, Maximus of Gloucester, to You." Still, Kelly's poem is received directly from place, "There is nothing" but it, after all, at the beginning of the poem.

For Kelly the *fact* of his "eternal shadow," of his really being there in his place, forever generates the anxiety of the poem. It is the possession of this private space, of his own realization that he is one skin, that permits Kelly's projection onto the wives who "yearn with eyes" for what is outer (beyond the frozen blue exterior that they have at their disposal). Again, Olson's company provides a foil for Kelly's issue, in his poem "The Distances": "Love knows no distance, no place / is that far away." For Olson, the realization of a possessed and personal space is the ultimate freedom and the culmination of a spiritual as well as a physical geography.

The resolution of Kelly's anxieties of rootedness can be found in his poem "Binding by Striking," where it becomes clear that it is a proliferation of spaces that suits him, where he can make the shifts, quick, between "month, mouth, and mountain," and through those shifts in his physiological and geographical landscapes, arrive at a place where he can compel the assumed strictures of geography, as Olson finds himself doing in "Letter 27." Here is the poem entire:

> Say I come to you by circles. Say the line
> that carries my name keeps me
> from knowing you as a car knows a garage.
> Say I am a wine you know better than to drink.
> Say I, seeing the pale skin inside your upper arms,
> become a better animal and become water.
> Say this water doesn't pull but when you fall
> takes you altogether in. Say you are in.

Say we sit on some steps together, or a wall.
Say something falls. I come to you then confused by lime,
sand, long hair holding the mortar together.
Say we stand a long time and one of us falls and one
catches, one catches and one lets go and it's night already.
We are still together. Say I am oily and you're dry.
Say a straight path and a twisted gate. Say something
not easy to say. Say the self-renewing knot of flesh
they call the rose blocks at times the future prong.
Say we belong to each other. Say the same thing
that holds us holds us apart. Say we struggle
to get in and stay in and not ever leave. Say for a change
you are out and I am in and I have trees too
your path gets lost in. Say you have numbers I can count
and numbers that leave me out. Say we change
but say we are always being held to the same.

Not to say little of same. Not to say one is more than some
or some less worth than every. Not to say every.
Not to say your pale skin is paler than this or this wall higher.
We rise where we fall. Not to say the word that draws us
doesnt some way let us in. Not to say in is the only.
We are held where we call. We know something and are held
to what we know. We fall through the wall. Not to say
there is only one garden or one car. Not to say one
when we mean "a road" and not to say going when we mean "home."
Not to say time when we mean space. Not to say stone
when a wind blows through the place where we've fallen.

Say you come to me by line. Say the circle you understand
has more light than a bone and more air than a tower. Say
the broad leaf of burdock plays two pieces of music:
bug-holes and leaf-shadow. Say a skin is like that and that
what we have consumed gives us light and what is gone
is the constellation that guides us. Say you have come
and will come. Say the language is dry and the wall is low.
Say a word gets over the wall. Say we are in. Say my skin
draws you. Say what we do with each other goes on.

> Say a voice that you hear. Say that we know ourselves
> chiefly in many. The Oil of Others is the light-giving flame.
> Say we are the same. Say we come to it simply again.
>
> *Under Words* (1983)

It is "the line that carries [his] name" that keeps Kelly from knowing his beloved; instead, Kelly comes to the beloved "by circles," by the infinitely complete, with centers all around. His instruction here is taken directly from Emerson in his great essay, "Circles": the "incessant movement and progression which all things partake could never become sensible to us but by contrast to some principle of fixture or stability in the soul. Whilst the eternal generation of circles proceeds, the eternal generator abides." And, elsewhere in that same essay: "The only sin is limitation."

The power of the anaphoric "say" in this poem allows Kelly literally to assume everything. His beloved *is* all, already in the first stanza: "Say you are in." And it is by comparisons of the nature of fixity and the nature of an infinite generosity that Kelly can come to assume knowledge of both himself and the beloved by the end of the poem: "Say we change / but say we are always being held to the same." Here is Emerson's "contrast to some principle of fixture or stability in the soul." Kelly is already wine, an animal, a circle, and skin at the beginning of the poem, and his release of a vocabulary of stricture and fixity releases him into the infinite unity of his soul-self, what is Olson's personal and spiritual geography, by the end of the piece:

> Not to say in is the only.
> We are held where we call. We know something and are held
> to what we know. We fall through the wall. Not to say
> there is only one garden or one car. Not to say one
> when we mean "a road" and not to say going when we mean "home."
> Not to say time when we mean space. Not to say stone
> when a wind blows through the place where we've fallen.

Kelly's compellation of the vocabulary of being tethered ("Not to say in is the only") is essential for the poem to culminate in a space where lover and beloved are free to be everything ("Say that we know ourselves / chiefly in many") as well as *one* thing ("Say we are the same").

Susan Howe, who must also be entered into the conversation here, quotes Felix Guattarri and & Deleuze in the beginning of her poem "Thorow" as stating that:

> The proper name (*nom propre*) does not designate an individual: it is on the contrary when the individual opens up to the multiplicities pervading him or her, at the outcome of the most severe operations of depersonalization, the he or she acquires his or her true proper name. The proper name is the instantaneous apprehension of a multiplicity.
>
> Singularities (1990)

So, Kelly names every thing one *and* many. The lover and beloved become the names of each thing: in, out, path, rose, and flesh. And after such a radical transformation of the norm (and of the name) living everywhere and nowhere becomes the easiest option, and proliferates in itself: "Say we come to it simply again." And again, and again, and again, the reader assumes.

Through these assumptions, Kelly's "Binding by Striking" eventually moves *beyond* language in a way that creates a phenomenology all its own.

> We are still together. Say I am oily and you're dry.
> Say a straight path and a twisted gate. Say something
> not easy to say.

The recognitions of the strictures inherent within language provide Kelly with the tools for him to begin to dismantle it. "Say a skin is like that and that / what we have consumed gives us light and what is gone / is the constellation that guides us." The constellation of a language that *means* is replaced, by Kelly, by the ever-present and infinitely proliferating generosity of a language that *is;* a language that permits a "forwarding": "Say what we do to each other goes on and on."

The privacy of the language generated by Kelly in "Binding by Striking," is, to *call* it a thing, a language of love. Michelangelo's admission of an inexplicable love in the beginning lines of his sonnet XXVIII is perhaps the best primer for discussing a love poetry that exists outside the conventions of a language of love: "What gives my love its life is not my heart, / The love by which I love you has no heart" (tr. by J. A.

Symonds, quoted in Pater). Like Michelangelo, Kelly's love poem must function outside of cliché and signified meaning, and does so through both accumulation of *things* (again, Susan Howe's "Thorow" is instructive: "Must see and not see / Must not see nothing / Burrow and so burrow / Measuring mastering") and velocity: something like the explanation Olson gives of Melville in *Call Me Ishmael*: "He had to be wild or he was nothing in particular. He had to go fast, like an American, or was all torpor" (13).

And it is his affinity for velocity and his unflagging recognition (he knows it *over* again; *new*) of the phenomenological that aligns Kelly with two of the American tradition's greatest love poets: James Schuyler and Frank O'Hara. In the love poems of all three of these poets, there is a tension between the language used to describe a *known* world, and the more private language of intimacy used between lovers and loved friends, that participates in combination with phenomenology and velocity to create a *new* space where love is born new *each time*, is original (in that it creates new space, departs from the true center and moves out).

It is the intimate connections between these concepts (of the familiar and the most private) that generates the expressions of these poets' love, and the creation of original frontiers, literally charged, within the spaces of their real lives:

> Then I say, yes,
> and the world lights up like the hot star they say it used to be
> or may become,
> burnt by the sun.
> It's still glowing!
> That's not my sleeve, that's my heart.
>
> Schuyler, "Having My Say-So," *Other Flowers* (2011)

The transformative powers of Schuyler's loving, in this poem, are activated by his saying "yes," and the consequences of his actions turn the clichéd into the real: his heart becomes his sleeve and vice versa. A similar consequence occurs in Frank O'Hara's poem "Aubade," written to "Jimmy Schuyler" in New York, 1952.

A million stars are dreaming out
the murderous whims of the apples.
Sinking like celestas in the dawn
already growing faint, beyond temples

whose silent throbbing dictates
a green life to my waking heart. Bids
the bones decorate this shore
become the pearl of loved eyelids'

sunlight, withdrawn until unseen
at night, when like the cat's hand,
the sea, they warmly flutter near
upon the belly of the sable sand.

A meaning of my life volleys
thus into the sky to rest, breathes
upon those vessels by the sea,
to be wrought in the frothing waves.

There is so much making in these lines, and all because of vision: the transformation of bones into the "pearl of loved eyelids' // sunlight." The velocity of O'Hara's enjambment weaves the fabric of his mournful love poem into an entirely new landscape, here, as in Schuyler's poem, with green life dictated to a heart (i.e. a new heart made). And it is the transformative properties of this "green life" given to O'Hara's heart that reverberate into new makings of the world surround: "A meaning of my life volleys / thus into the sky to rest" after such velocity up to this point, whereby respiration is enough to make the newborn vessels that arise from the "frothing waves" at the poem's end.

So, the *act* of loving and *saying it* are the qualifications by which O'Hara's and Schuyler's love poems intimate language. The conflation of the everyday "yes" of Schuyler and the entirely new "murderous whims of apples" seen by O'Hara bring each writer to an intimate space, newly made. In his poem "The Alchemist," Robert Kelly discusses love within these terms (from *Red Actions* 1995). In the end notes to the poem, he called it "the first full poem" he had written, because of its "cross[ing] some line that made me me." Kelly begins the poem at "the origin" and later, in the third stanza proclaims "man, the / origin." By beginning his poem with an origin, Kelly again orients his writing within the space of Olson's description of Melville as "an original, aboriginal. A beginner" (*Call Me Ishmael*, 13). The poem begins at the only beginning and stays there. From that origin, Kelly's alchemist makes a new world (as do Schuyler and O'Hara) through a specific physics of being *in* the world:

> The alchemist
> (twenty years over the alembic)
> his left hand fisted, snotrag on cheekbone,
> who shall weep
>   and wake up in the morning
> selling flowers in the veins of his arm
> crying down the street jonquils jonquils
> the needle stuck in his brain
> inventing true north

The making of "true north" in this poem, is the posturing that Kelly arrives at which allows him, later in the poem, to inhabit an entirely intimate space where "the leaf is subjected only to the patterns of its own green veins / which out of all patterns only will feed it when I am dark." This arrival, as in Schuyler's and O'Hara's pieces, is achieved via a collision between the public and the private (in this poem, the public space of "the street" where the alchemist yells "jonquils jonquils" and the private space of his lab "twenty years over the alembic"). The encroachment of the "I" opens the private space and leads Kelly's poem into a discussion of the physics of the alchemist's vision: "brown blood wreathing the heart muscles // he holds to his eye" and eventually the discovery that holds the entire resonance of the poem's tensions: "NAME IS LOVE." The climax of the poem is as much a conflation of the word name with the word love as it is a conflation with the concept of body and vision. Susan Howe discusses this same profundity in "Thorow," realizing that her "whole being is vision." Kelly's admitted working with, what he calls (again, in the notes) the "chilly love duet between Calaf and Turandot in Puccini's opera" is, of course, a given in the original piece of music, but the recontextualization of the moment by Kelly must be examined in the space of the love poem in which it finds its situation, and by way of the velocities of mixture that combine vision and body and a tradition of giving name with a tradition of loving exactly, intimately, singularly and infinitely.

Directly following the admission of "NAME IS LOVE," is the connection of the poet's vision to a world *made* new on account of the fact of his love, and a space made real by "movements somewhere in time / since our own eyes are not still." For Kelly, the combination of a velocity of sight and a world new-made culminate within the body, which, at the end of this poem, is found "in a cloak chewed into rags by its symbols // a body, / under it, / whose name is love & which only of all light love can eat." As in "Binding by Striking," "The Alchemist" resolves in a language that becomes everything: both body and vision, a language that is most intimate because it is distilled in the alembic of experience where the deepest symbol and meaning of any *thing* is the thing *itself*. The act of loving transforms the world *into* the new thing called love. Within this new-made cosmology, the singular prerequisite for a thing made is that it be a thing loved.

2.

In his most recent books of poetry, *Fire Exit* (*FE*) and *Uncertainties* (*UC*) Kelly continues to work within the framework outlined above, but moves his attention inward, from the "thing" of the outside world, to the ambiguous "I" of the lyric tradition ("what does the inside look like/ of anything I mean" (*FE* 219)). This rinsing of identity leaves Kelly in a space where he can enter the purity of the void (where the possibility of activity is ever-present, and infinite). "Of course it's a love story everything is / if we can get out of the way long enough" (*FE* 57)

In *Fire Exit*, Kelly admits to the phenomenology outlined in part one of this essay: "thank God for the thinginess of things... //...I call this thanking my theology" (64). If his theology is a meditation on the singularity of objects in the vacuum of space, then Kelly's prayers are directed inwards, where he is left wrangling with the problems of place, and the reality of existence (i.e. what it means to be an "I"). The speaker in both books is constantly at odds with fixity, but the voice always tumbles into a new void, a space where "the trachea of earth [can] ease open / to breathe that gold light in / it knows to work within the relentless interior" (*FE* 11). Through the meandering two- and three-line stanzas, Kelly realizes that the "outstretched body is the borderline itself" between an insulated soul, and an interconnected presence (*UC* 11). So, what to do but erase the body, erase the self and begin again:

> A name is a baffle of identity no names
> to measure up against no names
>
> because a name is just more politics
> I was never born I am not with you I am just here (*UC* 16)

and in *Fire Exit*:

> all the words clear, meaningless
> but no names, just like now
>
> build a whole life that way
> with no names, a ship
> to get away from your life

This task, as might be obvious, is not an easy one. These latest poems teem with activity, labor, and exhaustion (an echo, again, of Olson's "forwarding")*:*

> "as in between the go" (*FE* 13)
>
> "Nostalgic for agency" (*FE* 30)
>
> "Forget the target / the arrow itself /
> is the instruction" (*FE* 111)
>
> "going/is all you're good at, so go //
> so you go forward" (*FE* 218)
>
> "I am waiting on a door / a kind of food" (*UC* 53)

"Knowing is so much less than going" (*UC* 58)

"Whether it exists or not is hardly the question / the reverence of our mind set towards it is" (*UC* 78)

Activity, in these poems, is rooted in saying; *tout dire*, as the epigraph to *Uncertainties* posits. The poems constantly argue for the shedding of knowledge and meaning to get to the purer heart of the matter, the language: "it isn't about knowing at all it's about saying // a poem is a Ouija board without the wood/it shows you where you want to go" (*FE* 118–119). The task seems (if possible) to say language until it is no longer language, until the saying becomes a "song of gibberish" (*FE* 225), and the "I" a "self without a land" (*FE* 212). This divesture is the first step into an infinite void, where the "I" can disappear into a purer presence of activity, sight, and rebirth:

> trembling with intensity of namelessness do nothing
>
> called it feeling and let it lap you
> till the edge of feeling was the edge of seeing and you saw (*UC* 35)

The culmination of the body without language, and without name is a position at the fulcrum of what it means to be, an ultimate uncertainty that leads always and only to infinite possibility, which Kelly finds synonymous with love: "nothing sustains us like uncertainty/this thing I would rather call love" (*UC* 142).

If the ultimate boundary of the self is the body, then Kelly also recognizes the boundaries implicit in acknowledging place, admitting "people forget where they're coming from and where they're bound" (*UC* 100). In his most recent work, Kelly explores the contradictions inherent between place and presence, and seems to argue steadfastly for the freedom inherent in a pure presence (unbound by the body and by place) which signals an evolution in thought and practice from his more kindred associations with Olson earlier in his career. "There is a way out hidden in each thing," and these poems not only find it, but walk through to the other side (*UC* 123).

Once the restrictions of place are lifted, possibility expands infinitely into "a million other worlds // you'll get around to living in / just close your eyes" (*FE* 109–110). The freedom from the strictures of place, also frees the body from time, allowing presence to take place on a phenomenological scale (immeasurable and indefinable):

> just be young with me in magic doubt
> touching for good luck
> the witchcraft trees of every passing woods
>
> and genuflect before the moment only
> only the instant is beautiful (*FE* 129)

The pure possibility in these instants stacks up to form a shapeless existence with no beginning or end, as with Ashbery's "acres of just now" in *Flowchart* (209). Being in these instants is the pinnacle of what it means to be alive, the possibility that "anyone can be coming from anywhere to love anyone" (*UC* 117).

For all of the labor and anxiety inherent in the tasks outlined in Kelly's most recent poems, the underlying current is still love, and an enjoyment of life; "that is the journey / to get there living" (*FE* 70). The relaxation into the paradise of pure presence is everywhere in these poems, what Kelly calls the "heaven that is here now, thingly and will-free" (*FE* 104).

It is interesting that these poems leave the reader in a void, where so much of Kelly's other work relies on a referent, a thing to be loved, but Kelly seems most interested, now, with that moment when "something is about to begin to begin" (*FE* 117). The in-between, in these poems, is the ideal because of the potential kinetic energy found there:

> I want the other side of water
> just the momentary whims of wind
>
> that spill a thought from one glass to another
> till the alchemist sets down her tumblers
>
> content with how well mixed the seeds are again
> fire with water water with fire. (*UC* 19)

The cyclical nature of the void of the in-between generates phenomena endlessly, like a perpetual motion machine. From this formless chamber, pure being becomes possible immediately, always, and endlessly for "an old old people almost born," as Kelly calls us (*UC* 48). The brim of this reality presents a "cusp of an understanding [that] never comes" (*FE* 26) because it is not understanding that brings love, but an acknowledgement of existence. "Nobody knows what the sea's saying either/because it speaks so beautifully//all form and no information" (*FE* 143). Kelly turns back to the language of love to articulate the poet's connection to this void, in part by describing "the ailment of the thoughtful,/the need to touch and not desire" (*FE* 154) and again relies on the uncertainty of situations above all else:

> I lick the rock
>
> in love with where it's been
> and it can't tell, what we love best
> are our guesses (*FE* 157–158)

Birth, death, and re-birth tumble through the voids in Kelly's poems to shed light on the constant novelty of the world we wander through, and his own struggle to find the right language to describe his position creates frenetic energy, alive in the void of his own hesitancy and charged with the desire he holds sacred. After a life in poetry, Kelly humbly admits to what might be the ultimate truth, to "just be unsure // uncertainty is all" (*UC* 3).

GEORGE QUASHA

UNCERTAINTIES: ROBERT KELLY, *TA'WIL*, AND THE POETS OF SINGULARITY

I.

> "...this unique reading, each time the first reading and each time the only reading..."
>
> — Maurice Blanchot[169]

As a species humans love firsts. Firsts are to die for. We shape mind, mood, body, and wallet in order to get there first or be rewarded in top position. Best poem, bestseller, first lover... With notable exceptions: *last* to die is usually number one on our lists; and in a different register: last *noticed*, best *spy*, best *con*, best *loan shark*, number one predation you can *bank* on... And words? "First thought, best thought"? Well, it depends. We mainly pursue firsts that are *not yet present* but instead are distant, hard to get, lofty, beyond reach. When *first* means *present* it's problematic. "This is the first moment of your new life" makes for anxiety, because it's instantly untrue and instinctively we know that living firstness is challenging — in fact, it's next to impossible to sustain for more than a special moment. A true paradox of the poetic may be that it both *presents* a language reality in immediate firstness and *extends* that lingual immediacy over time, so that intense temporality may become indistinguishable from *a*temporality or some form of hyper-temporality. Gertrude Stein brought heightened awareness to this paradoxical poetic reality in her theory and practice of *the continuous present*. Ezra Pound enlarged historical access in the present with ideas like "all ages are contemporaneous in the mind." Robert Kelly variously exploits these and a number of other angles of *entry to time in a timeless present*, which he accomplishes *parapoetically*; that is, ever renovating his own poetics by prioritizing certain resources of language and consciousness only possible

---

169. "Reading," tr. Lydia Davis, in *The Station Hill Blanchot Reader: Fiction & Literary Essays*, ed. George Quasha with Charles Stein (1999) taken from *The Gaze of Orpheus and Other Literary Essays*, tr. Lydia Davis, ed. P. Adams Sitney (1981).

in a *poetics of singularity* — of *firsts* available in the [absolute present]. I bracket those words as anything truly parapoetic implies bracketed status, as *uncertainties*.

In 1973 Charles Stein and I initiated our long-contemplated project in dialogical criticism (DiaLogos) as poet-centered exercise in "how to read" difficult work, focusing on issues important to a given poet whose work was in some sense hard to read.[170] For our engagement with Robert Kelly that year the dialogue had a single focus that we already knew he shared with us: *ta'wil,* the historically significant exegetical practice among medieval Sufis like Avicenna and Ibn 'Arabi as presented by the great French scholar of Islam, Henry Corbin, celebrated by Charles Olson, Robert Duncan, and Robert Creeley, among others.[171] We discussed the meaning of *ta'wil* — famously defined by Corbin as "the exegesis that leads the soul back to its truth" — as a unique event, a particular reading of a given text, rather than a procedural approach to conventional or dogmatically sanctioned understanding. Kelly emphasized the connection of *ta'wil* with "Recital" (*Récit*) as developed in Corbin's *Avicenna and the Visionary Recital,*[172] which dealt with a species of narrative and there-

---

170. A few years later, 1976, I wrote about the ideas behind this project in an extended piece, "DiaLogos: Between the Written and the Oral in Contemporary Poetry," *New Literary History* (Vol. VIII, № 3, 1976–1977) reprinted, minus the last section, in *Symposium of the Whole: A Range of Discourse Toward an Ethnopoetics,* eds Jerome Rothenberg & Diane Rothenberg (1983) online at: http://www.quasha.com/writing-2/on-poetry-poetics/dialogos/dialogos-between-the-written-and-the-oral.

171. "*Ta'wil* or How to Read: A Five-Way Interactive View of Robert Kelly," *Vort* #5 (Summer 1974) 108–134; online at: http://www.quasha.com/writing-2/on-poetry-poetics/dialogos/tawil-or-how-to-read. Others drawing upon Corbin include Gerrit Lansing, Kenneth Irby, & Theodore Enslin. [A slightly revised version of this piece is included here, pp. 476–508.]

172. Engl. tr. Willard Trask (New York: Pantheon Books, 1960; French edition, 1954). This is the book that had been important to Olson, whereas Duncan, Creeley, & Kelly later also address *Creative Imagination in the Sufism of Ibn 'Arabi,* Engl. tr. Ralph Manheim (Princeton Univ. Press, 1969. French edition, 1958; this later translation was not available to Olson, who died in 1970).

fore was appropriate to the text we elected to discuss in the dialogue: a section of the long poem *The Loom* from 1972.[173] Kelly comments:

> To work with one of those *Loom* sections, particularly that one [then #44, later changed to #36 in *The Loom*], would interest me because it has that other aspect of *ta'wil* in it — *Récit*, or whatever the Arabs call that, you know, the Recitals. I can't think of *The Loom* in a better way than that; because when I want to find a type of *The Loom* somewhere, I find myself thinking about Avicenna in that Corbin book, and the stuff that's like it elsewhere in the world — the endless and/or beautiful stories that spill themselves out of uncertain meaning — I mean the clear absence of final moral focus in the *récit* reminds me very much of the same thing in *The Loom*. It is not the building of a *Temple*, but of an *Altar*, and that altar's very ambiguous, and the whole relationship between myself and the skull is very curious. I mean I take the *récit* to be that kind of fable that cannot be paraphrased, and thus all the *récits* of Alchemy, which are, I suppose, as close to it as the West generally has — like the Thabritius and Beya stories, the people who go under the sea to teach the undersea people how to conjugate, or *The Chymical Wedding*. These are stories that must be read and the reading of them is itself the [alchemical] "operation." (*Vort*, 114)

Uncertain meaning. The kind of fable that cannot be paraphrased. The récits of alchemy. The reading is itself the operation. These four interrelated notions, articulated in a single clarifying statement in the course of the conversation, point to important ongoing concerns in Kelly's work and to what I'm calling a *poetics of singularity*. *Uncertain meaning*: uncertainty is the matrix of the kind of *récit* that drives Kelly's visionary and unparaphraseable tale such that we find in much of *The Loom* — a rather

---

173. In our dialogue, the text is designated as "Section 44," as it had been published in *Caterpillar* #18 (April 1972) and reprinted in *Vort* #5, but in the book *The Loom* (1975) it would become §36 [Building of the Temple], 401–415, the final poem in the book.

dreamlike, non-ordinary personal process that seems performative of a ritual action of profound, initiatic, and transformative consequence, and yet does not map onto any identifiable religious or traditionary dogma or procedure. It suggests a sort of unnamable genre that is said to fit the notion of *récit*; but what is a *récit*?

A story born of uncertain meaning, in Kelly's indication, implies that there is, and can be, no encompassing ideology that gives the story authority. The story therefore cannot be known in advance of its performative narrative action, at least not as it will now be known. The previously unknown and now unfolding story *acquires* a special kind of *author*ity through the event of *author*ship, through the telling, the recital, the action of its own coming into being as writing. This is what makes it a *visionary* recital: it appears only inside the telling, inseparable from an individual's own necessity in performing its action, and without it that individual would not complete an aspect of self-realization — realization such that is not otherwise achievable than by the poem itself. It cannot be characterized by an abstraction referencing previous actions or authorized by literary, mythic, religious, or psychological precedent, because any such precedent would miss its singular necessity, its poetic ontology unknowable outside the action of its telling.[174] It's important here to resist recounting or summarizing the action of §36 of *The Loom*, for according to the principle of *ta'wil* as described by Kelly, paraphrase of the narrative action impedes the real event by absorbing it in abstraction. And, to be sure, a reader of our dialogue "*Ta'wil* or How to Read" (1973) would optimally read the poem for the occasion; the purpose was to make vivid the full presence of *récit*, both as a text and as a *ta'wil*-like reading (the poet's, ours, a new reader's) in order to evoke the further unfolding of a *core principle*: a poetics of singularity.

To create a kind of meta-context for this principle I would point to two key notions. First, Charles Olson's insistence on a statement he sometimes treated rhetorically as a secret: *That which exists through itself*

---

174. It may be unnecessary to point out that this is not a discussion of literary merit, æsthetic quality, or critical judgment as such, which is a relative matter of largely cultural-context evaluation and ſpecial consensus.

is what is called meaning.[175] The statement is a slightly modified phrase taken from the Taoist alchemical text discussed by Jung, as translated by Wilhelm/Baynes, *The Secret of the Golden Flower* ("That which exists through itself is Meaning (Tao)") but the important shift was in taking the phrase from a context with extensive commentary and setting it in a context of poetics where, stripped of all reference, it points to the self-nature of performative language action. Here language is not functioning primarily as reference or communication but as a manifestation of being with a particular intensity of focus. I'm not interested here in the question of influence, although Kelly of course has known Olson in depth from very early; perhaps we could shift the emphasis from influence to a context or field of *transmission* of a certain possibility: *the poetic as performative of singular action inseparable from how being itself means.* When Kelly takes *récit* from the context of extensive commentary in Corbin and lets it indicate his own uncertainty-narration, he performs an action parallel to Olson's transposition of a classic Taoist phrase to a radical redirection of poetry toward a *further nature.*[176] The sense of the poetic as having such a profound and evolutionary role in human consciousness amounts to a poetic paradigm that puts the poetic act on a plane with Taoist and Sufi *text,* the purpose of which was to guide a reader's mind on a productive path of self-awareness *outside* dominant cultural, religious, or literary tendencies. Exactly what constitutes such a path and any given outcome inevitably remains uncertain.

Another meta-contextual frame to help us with *récit* is Blanchot's very special usage, which Kelly would not have been familiar with in 1973. Blanchot used the term to distinguish certain works, in fact most of his prose fiction, from the traditional story (*histoire, conte*) and novel (*roman*) and he characterized a *récit* as "not the narration of an event, but that event itself, the approach to that event, the place where that event is made to happen — an event which is yet to come and through

---

175. See Olson's *Causal Mythology* (Writing 16) (1969).

176. Olson's poignant phrase "further nature" occurs in the "Proem" in "MAXIMUS, FROM DOGTOWN—I" in *Maximus Poems IV, V, VI* (1968) and in *The Maximus Poems*, ed. George Butterick (1983).

whose power of attraction the tale [*récit*] can hope to come into being, too."[177] Blanchot calls it "the secret law of the tale" which relates it to the unknowing we are discussing in terms of uncertainty as "a movement towards a point, a point which is not only not known, obscure, foreign, but such that apart from this movement it does not seem to have any sort of real prior existence, and yet it is so imperious that the tale derives its power of attraction only from this point, so that it cannot even 'begin' before reaching it — and yet only the tale and the unpredictable movement of the tale create the space where the point becomes real, powerful, & alluring."

That Olson and Blanchot invoke *secret* in presenting their radical core notions may acknowledge the difficulty of grasping their subtle force. I place them beside Corbin in the service of understanding something fundamental to Kelly's poetics and to show a basic uncertainty in the relation of their ideas to context: poetic, philosophically critical, &, in a rather special sense, esoteric. That is, everything depends on how we read, for the context itself is in the process of being revisioned.

In the same *ta'wil* dialogue, we say in the introductory statement:

> During our talk with Kelly we tried to get him to speak about the new poetics emerging, say, in the year 1950. After all, that was the year of "Projective Verse," Concrete Poetry, etc. But Kelly insisted that "the interesting date would not be the first time that something was written, but the first time that somebody is able, say, to read Basil Valentine or Paracelsus as a *processual* document, rather than as a guide to operations with crucibles, and that date is probably after 1950... The issue that I'm at is *when we were able to read*... and I think that our history will have to concern itself less with when a thing gets written than when a thing gets read, because I think those are the moments of achievement in our consciousness." We [GQ & CS] had been talking for a couple of years about the right strategy in writing a "How to Read" book appropriate to the '70s, but it had not occurred to us to plot the history of consciousness in terms of how

---

177. "The Song of the Sirens," tr. Lydia Davis, op. cit.

to *read* specific texts. Kelly argued that "someone who had read and perceived 'Projective Verse' and some other [of Olson's] essays, 'The Gate and the Center' for instance, would be in a position to read anew. It strikes me that Pound had called it *The ABC of Reading* & before that *How to Read...* [but] that critics have supposed him really to be saying 'how to write'... If there is any art or future in criticism, such that the work we're immediately concerned with can ever get read, or the thing that makes your book *America a Prophecy* [GQ co-editor with Jerome Rothenberg; 1973] possible, will be a new method of reading, not a new method of writing."

I remember Robert Duncan speaking about how he and Olson created a poetry that had to be read at the level of its poetics. I took this to mean that, while poetry clearly can be read in many ways and have very different functions for different readers (often context specific) they insisted on a *level* of reading that is inseparable from the kind of thinking in language — the *language-living*—that generates the poem. What is at stake is not only "change" from the perspective of literary history, or formal innovation, but what Olson insisted on calling "a stance toward reality," an orientation toward what is taken to be otherwise (without, that is, the action of the poem) an unknown dimension of reality. That dimension is reflected and engaged as a language reality, a *linguality*. Our access to it is by reading in a way that meets the poem at its own level of action, and for Kelly (1973) that way of meeting the *récit* of *The Loom* is named *processual*. One does not so much circle the poem mentally to appreciate its perfections and tease out its stylistic devices as *undergo* its narrative process, including circumambulating its interior constructions, a perhaps proto-ritualistic but unsanctioned action, engaging its continuous present as one's *own*.

A reading of this process as *ta'wil* may have psychological and indeed variously cultural force, but the emphasis is on where and how it leads one to a further access to unlived reality that is now, and only now as a result of the narrative process, one's own. It's an initiatic event in the sense that, having crossed a *readerly* threshold, by virtue of an engageable poetics, one is now *of* the poem, no longer who one was, but a further oneself. This does not mean that one becomes the "self" of the particular poet (as perhaps one does in an empathic reading of a very personal poem) but one enters a self-otherness in a sense equivalent to that which the poet entered by way of the *récit*. And this is not a matter of interpreting the particular poem as such, or assigning an interpretation or meaning to the poem, although of course the process may include meanings of all kinds, but of awakening a zone of continuing resonance which the *récit* imparts, an event of transmission of possibility. It can be associated with any number of related textual realities but it does not *belong* to a separately defined context (religious, literary, psychological, etc.). Its ontological status remains open, that is, uncertain.

Reading as *ta'wil*, in the non-traditional way emphasized by Kelly in relation to *The Loom*, yet nevertheless related to the way Corbin tracks the practice in Avicenna's "Recitals," which was attractive to so many poets, foregrounds the importance of being in step with the compositional principle of a given text. The "how to read" is tied in with the way of writing and in a sense conveys a permission of *reading as further writing* intrinsic to a poetics of singularity: a readerly event that is also *writerly* far more than literarily interpretative. To the extent that reading processually is initiatic to a reorientation within personal vision, a reader takes on the compositional possibilities opened by the text. And this gives special importance to any auto-exegetical commentary offered by the poet directly, which in fact was the theory behind our exercises in dialogical criticism. Consider Kelly's remarks about the way of working in *The Loom*:

> What's interesting is the way in which the Recital comes... A Recital chooses *one* seed to grow from, and all the other seeds do not. Now I could be left in a kind of typical lyrical impasse with all of the seeds and wanting to tend all of them and have them *all* grow and rush from flowerpot to flowerpot, as indeed I have done in lots of poems and in the way, say, Duncan always does, thus letting *no* seed go untended, until it all comes up in an odd, approximative kind of garden. But what happens constantly in *The Loom* — well, not constantly, but lots of times — is that the Recital begins, and the Recital which seems to be developing only *one* seed turns out by the time it's finished (and I look back at it) to have developed *all* the seeds. And it's *all* there.

And I stand in awe of that narrative process. Because that's really the first time that I came to *know* about the spontaneity of narrative. I mean of course certain kinds of narrative *do* tell themselves — fantasies or dreams or whatnot — but to have the power expressing itself right in the moment of one's conscious, most alert activity, where I'm thinking about vowels & it's thinking about what's going to *happen*, seems to me so extraordinary...

Spontaneity of narrative. Narratives tell themselves. The power expressing itself right in the moment of one's conscious, most alert activity. What the poet is indicating here, if we allow our understanding to align with his sense of compositional event, is the way in which *récit* — the telling that occurs on its own and without authorization or premeditation — has the same *firstness* for the poet that it has for the poem's reader. Poet and reader have a similar ontological status as recipients of a telling. There is a sort of *self-similarity*, if we relate it to the concept of fractal, a principle of processual scale-invariance between reading and writing process. I also relate this inevitably initiatic reciprocity to a notion of *mirroring by alterity* by which we discover ourselves in otherness, the otherness of the self.

The statement of the text is "objective," not with respect to a world truth or outside status report or interpretability according to any sort of standard of correctness, but by a *shared and willing uncertainty that is an openness to what is ready to be told. Objective* as an object one agrees to hold in common — an object mirrored and self-mirroring. The "message" is the *state of receptivity itself,* the realization that telling is what happens when we declare ourselves receivers, listeners, readers. The *ta'wil* is the intentional participation in what is active on its own, what in Greek grammar (a mood lost in modern languages) is designated as *middle voice* (neither active nor passive) and is the voice in which, traditionally, the epic poem begins, the poet's declaring oneself to be in the state of request for the song. (Obviously the conventional "Sing, Muse" doesn't capture the mood.) The art of subtle receptivity is an evolutionary process, and accordingly it's a practice that is refined over time. It may even be *the* state of what is increasingly recognized as *conscious evolution*. At any rate it indicates a way of being with unfolding narration that applies equally to *poet* writing who is also reading the self-telling and *reader* who is also within a writing unfolding process. It is an event that is always happening the first time ever. And first-time things are by nature profoundly uncertain.

II.

In our 1973 dialogue with Kelly we bring up his having spoken of the process of the poem as "*ta'wil* of its own first line." This striking notion extends the way he was speaking, as cited above, about the Recital telling itself. It implies that the initial gesture unfolds as a reading out of its own "seed," and it can do this because, it seems, the *whole* is coinherent with the *part*. First gesture, first line, first word, first sound—they are of the same nature, the substance of the telling, corresponding to a level of intensified awareness that opens to an unknown event. It is not a matter of development, as conventionally a plot develops a story or a book develops a theme. Unfolding is different from development. A Visionary Recital, the *récit,* is a process of appearance, of something contained in the nature of a thing that *is,* now coming into appearance. It may show up somewhat the way recalling the dream instructs the conscious mind in what it hasn't yet seen in itself. But the unfolding telling is happening without the mind going unconscious in order to be receptive to what it can't ordinarily bring up or let come forth, and in fact it is happening in the state of greatest alertness. This in itself is a non-ordinary state in an ordinary waking context, which context, however, is subtly reoriented by the event — a disturbance of the ordinary that calls for the extraordinary act designated by *ta'wil*. On this model *ta'wil* implies that non-ordinary text can be journeyed through, initiatically and transformatively, in what looks like ordinary reading, a literary act, but which, in the nature of text with consequential poetics, effects a reorientation of reading itself as a singular and incomparable event.

Jumping ahead to a text written nearly four decades after *The Loom* and which bears the name of our recurrent theme, *Uncertainties* (2011), we seem initially to be looking at an opposing poetics. *Uncertainties* appears to be a non-narrative series of 125 numbered and untitled poems of irregular length, which are discontinuous and non-unified in theme and detail. The single regularity is what stands in for a formal principle: it is written in two-line stanzas in which each line is more or less self-contained. Preceding the main text, in the place of a dedication or part title, is an expression of the core desire of the book:

tout dire

Perhaps the great aspiration of being incarnate as poet: *to say it all*. Next page, still preceding the main text, a short preludial poem declares:

Speak language

the way thunder does,
all the words at once

what lingers
turns slowly into meaning

meaning is not what you think
meaning is what stays

The book opens with a double valence, a twist of the grammatical axis: It speaks, first, to itself, in the presumption of a kind of intimacy: Speak in *language* the way thunder does in *all sound together* (beyond a mission of controlled or consensual human discourse). At the same time it *addresses* language, sounding an approximation of the middle-voice mood of epic, an invocation to language itself as if the muse has gone inside the physical mouth, and conjures speech with a trans-comprehensible noise of wild nature (like the thunderclap of *Finnegans Wake*) to say all with all words at once, cultivating faith in meaning as residue of a slow process of transmutation within apparent chaos. Implicit is the view of language as self-organizing matrix, a field of intelligence, to which access is by permission gained in a state of release, trust in surrender to the telling. The species of lingual intimacy is both personal and impersonal, embedded in what is.

The main text of the book is that slow process. It begins with an unexpected connection to *récit* now in the absence of story on the grand scale:

1.

Tell it just enough to begin
then the form takes over and tells

12 · A BOOK ON RECENT WRITINGS

The will of the poet to inhabit the state of the poem is only a spark to jumpstart a self-generating process. The "form" that assumes the power of speech is, on one level, little more than a limit of irregularity, a neutral container with no assigned value, no privileged nobility of formal or aesthetic accomplishment, barely a source of legality as governor, and yet an opportunity for measure within variability of the self-accounting voice.

The speaking text — half-forgetting the name Robert Kelly in this call to language itself, yet language as intimately inhabited — is aspiring to the condition of *all-speaking*, occupying a sort of midpoint between Adam of the Garden and the Tower of Babel. This is not language as abstract system (linguistics) but as bodymind membrane, liminal, that is, to the autonomous magical power of a sovereign human creator and a common social property uncontrollable in its infinite variability. It's as if poetry is a zone in which "two truths" — body & mind, person & world, this & an *other* dimension, ordinary & non-ordinary language — are in play/at play, and meaning is the residue of any complete action thereof. And an activity of the midpoint, middle voice, limen: the speaking that occurs in the surrender of message-control, letting go of the core habit of a dominator culture built on certainty.

What does it mean to call a book *Uncertainties*? Needless to say it's uncertain, but not in the sense of a poet confused, indecisive, tentative, or indefinite. Also not in the sense of literary ambiguity, however many types you can count; not, that is, poetry as rhetoric. We might consider it as indicating a willingness to be as uncertain as things are, and not necessarily in a negative sense; it's not a lament or any personalized mood of receptivity re: the problematic of unpredictability. On this plane of meaning, the personal response, it might better be seen as an alignment with the world on its own terms; to be in step with what is never fully in step until *you* are. Poem as specific alignment in process, so to speak. The poem inside the moment happening, then, is a medium for exposing what is otherwise invisible, the maneuver of bodymind to maintain a certain upright balance amidst perceived attractions and torrents of the day. One name for this perceptual process is *proprioception,* "self-knowing," applied, with some license, to verbal events, as a sort of lingual register of how a being knows and maintains itself in spacetime. Yet it's not strictly personal; in fact it's interactive with the world, something happening between. And this self-identifying lingual interdependence in a processually unfolding "world" could be called *eco*-proprioception.

One of the Uncertainties (cap to acknowledge unique qualities) is the status of identity. It's rather hard to allow a poet with the name Robert Kelly the space of "open identity" which requires momentarily forgetting that he's the author of many dozens of published books; that is, to read him as he writes himself free from who he already is. But this is notoriously difficult where identity is considered cumulative, which is why poetry — especially a poetry where the poetics values uncertainty — verges on the impossible in the sense of its most radical possibility: to come upon singularity. The mind tired out by the school of hard knocks, literature as the crowning achievement of a culture of comparative assessment, and the pursuit of identity status can barely resist evaluating according to the abstraction du jour (Modern, post-Modern, etc.) and trying to make out the stripes of the home team. It's only human. The will to be first. Identity as triumphant certainty.

What, then, is the way into the Uncertainty poem as it is to itself?

28.

Meshes mean me the voices
family matters murder the ear

I am deaf from sheer neglect
the snow perishes hence is beautiful

men ask women for the time of night
men don't know women are the sun herself

it's all about hiding and being found
all the rest of culture is a battered rose

we are stronger than war we can give it a name
to have seen with own eyes Danube's Iron Gate

leaving the sea behind came to this brown hill
the opposite of everything

he took the long-stemmed rose and pounded it on the table
spread its petals and found food he gave to a child

> we are nourished by mysteries alone
> calm this morning like a book you read before.

One way to track a work is to look for its very own poetics. Where there is no discernible tradition-based prosody, procedure, concept, or theoretical dogma, we might allow a given textual process a *parapoetic permission* by which it defines its "rules" as a singular dynamic. I've been calling it here, ad hoc and sui generis, an Uncertainty poem, written it seems in flexible units: numbered sections made up of a variable number of two-line stanzas in distinct (more or less separate but linked) lines, wherein, so to speak, the deuces are wild. They *contain*, but somewhat like corkless bottles as stopovers for genii in passage.

The poem does not progress; it lives along. The journey home is uncertain, perhaps in the sense of the Taoist classic: *The land that is nowhere, that is the true home.* Speaking from where it is, it can say: Today poetry doesn't quite know what it is. And so it feels its own "true," its ways of being true to its moment, with no room for apologies. How long it takes to reach a fecund not-knowing and offer no resistance to sudden awareness, that's how long the poem is *in every line*. And every line is a site of possibility only available as singularity.

The mind can't help trying to say something true. Nothing wrong with that, unless it *believes in what it says*. We become fundamentalists of our own constructions. Perhaps poetry is what saves us from ourselves, from our continuous surrender to the siren of our own voice claiming to tell the truth. The will of the poem to continue, to keep coming back, to leave behind the already said—a rescue mission from a part of the mind that knows better. But this too is uncertain.

2.

> Smart ones would tell you too much
> be a mirror until you break
>
> be a tumbler till you fall
> fill or drown, just be unsure

uncertainty is all and your appeal
the way your eyes so steady are clear

while your fingertips are roving
through the frantic jungle of what you really mean...

The present is the greatest uncertainty — the precarious edge over the abyss below. "Form" here is not a wall of protection against unintelligibility or an aggressive instrument of reform, analysis, satire (social, psychological, political...) which presumes intellectual certainty and a standard of correctness (inheritance of 18th century "Age of Enlightenment" values) but a sort of valve for release of the unknown "through the frantic jungle of what you really mean." Its social/political function is to clear linguality of false occupation and the coercive discourse of control. In this view the distracting, dubiously intentioned, controlling duplicity of public discourse, limiting freedom of mind and being, exploits an absence of actual complexity and subtle polyvalence of language. Discursive health requires the self-true multiplicity that speaking bears when we allow it to show itself. A moment of true speech contains more than we know how to hear, but the poem hears more.

The embrace of multiplicity shows it to be far more than a rhetorical strategy or proliferation of effects. It's a discipline of the mouth obedient to the *more* that mind can say. The art of poetic *aporia* — the intrinsically unresolvable because replete with variable yet irreducible mental directives — is a reality challenge, a state of presence within complexity, and its access is rooted in acknowledged doubt and uncertainty. In the realization of the Uncertainty poem it's a call, not to resolve or explain, but to stand within the oscillations of possible meaning until mind knows a sudden and necessary *sense of the present moment*. Meaning as a residue of the process of engagement does not detract from the intensity of self-aware presence.

In a parallel to the contribution of Corbin to the poetics of *récit*, another scholar of Islam and a range of medieval ontological hermeneutics, Michael A. Sells brings traditionary perspective to a poetics of apophasis that goes beyond rhetorical denial, often associated with so-called "negative theology." He shows a tendency in mystical writing (Plotinus,

Eriugena, Ibn 'Arabi, Porete, and Eckhart) where saying the unsayable is worked through apophasis as saying/unsaying ("speaking away"). "Genuine *aporia*," he states, "instead of leading to silence, leads to a new mode of discourse."[178] I'm interested in how such an approach can help us see wherein a poetics of singularity is connected to a profound problematic of language-thinking, with a range of historical antecedents outside what is usually considered literary history, and how it has led to many practices of saying/unsaying and what I call *further saying*.

Further saying in this sense is more than avant-garde innovation and experimentalism, but it can be that too; I think, for instance, that Alfred Jarry's 'Pataphysics, the "science of imaginal solutions," understood as a poetics of singularity, has broad implications that go beyond any particular exploitation of them (such as OuLiPo). One could read aspects of Kelly's *Uncertainties* as at once in an alignment with the 'Pataphysical & with a tradition of apophasis, and both as modalities of dealing with the always newly unsayable requiring further language invention in step with mind-opening initiation. They lead to new ways of reading in which passage through the text is "the operation," the alchemical working that alters both the possibilities of reading and consciousness itself — "be a mirror until you break // be a tumbler till you fall / fill or drown, just be unsure…" Uncertainty could be viewed as something like a Nigredo stage within the alchemy of reading, and its recognition can help discover a power of the *mind-degradable* within discourse. Such a power makes our need for positive assertion, the kataphatic or "bringing down" the elusive real into speaking, a constructive possibility of the moment which, by virtue of sustained transformative intensity, is reabsorbed into the open processual.

Blake gave us permission to escape the "mind-forg'd manacles" of belief while remaining *poetically* respectful of our acts of faith and attachment: *Every thing possible to be believ'd is an image of the truth*. Truth in poetry is viewed as a multiplicitous play of images, indeed a species of *play*, not a hierarchy of more or less valid truth claims. Perhaps in the Uncertainty poem we are at the threshold of a Blakean *ta'wil*: Any possible

---

178. *Mystical Languages of Unsaying* (1994) 2.

reading in poetic process is an *imaging* of meaning as a poem's truth. Reading is itself the alchemical operation *and* its ludic enhancements.[179]

37.

To rise without compunction
into a day without a word

all travel tunnels through my thought
stay home glad sunlight dim in amber

licking shadows of travelers off the wall
Atlantis rises in our houses (...)

One's life stand as Atlantis the always-disappearing continent, the Atlantean condition of our islanded living, the day empty of language calling us out, all times contemporaneously tunneling through the mind, poem pulling into disjunctive time where thinking enters into a continuous present.... *Zero point poetics* — the return to unknowing — is the state required for singularity, wherein we do not accumulate meaning but "rise" to its possibility "without compunction." By reinstating us to zero as instantaneous *still point*, line-by-line the poem teaches *emptiness (shunyata)* as the openness of reality, its intrinsic capacity to be lived without preconditioning, the possibility of speaking *between* ourselves and the world/others. Here the poem instructs — restructures — how being emerges into the new by way of a new linguality.

If there were a persistent rhetoric behind the lines it would be something like a *charm* — a quasi-intelligible language act performative as magical operation, a reordering of syllables to tempt the tongue into sovereign behavior driven by a will to change. However, the intention — the aim of the charm — remains sub-intelligible and polyvalent.

---

179. Peter Lamborn Wilson refers to "serious joke" as "alchemical term," applicable to art, in "Magi-ism," *Alchemy & Inquiry: Phillip Taaffe, Fred Tomaselli, Terry Winters* (exhibition catalog: Wave Hill: April 3–June 19, 2011, Bronx, New York). The likely source is from 1611: Michael Maier, *Jocus Severus, A Serious Joke*, tr. Darius Klein (2010).

57.

Day of quarrel no man tiger knife knife
spill an island off your chest and spit

Micro-narratives with instant *récit* force open out as fleeting *ta'wil*, meaning on the fly. Story unfolds in the instant, turns upon a split-second axis, and moves on to a new grip through renewed traction. If there is mimesis in complexity it is revelation as *aporia*, nature as *linguality* in its mode of operation. The spin, genetic shifting as axial force in the releasement of a constantly moving center, regenerates discursive energy. Mind asserting and apophatically taking back or cutting off leaves a residue of poetic meaning with traces in the reading mind. It wakes in what it finds and lets go.

The two-line stanza (as distinct from couplet) according to the poet, sets up "experiments in duration, in complex syntax and melodic demands."[180] The sense of continuity derives not particularly from content as such but from how the "melody of the first line necessitates the melody of the next. Shape shaping shape." Melody here functions as "*ta'wil* of the first line," that is, the principle of unfolding in which a thing realizes its further nature in the way it goes on, staying in step with itself freshly responsive, as opposed to getting ahead of itself by following prescription. He acknowledges constraint at the level of a line's desire to be itself: "each line wants to be semantically intact"; "yet it also must link syntactically or narratively with the line that follows" — sovereignty subjected to inevitable variability. And stanzas stand "in relation" with those before and after, but that relationship is quite open — a neighborhood where most anything can happen, and does.

54.

Follow your own femoral artery long enough
you'll find yourself in the body of another person

---

180. Robert Kelly's comments on the poetics of *Uncertainties* are recorded on the book cover.

this sometimes called love was called by the ancients the Red Thread
stitches life together with itself you wake in the mountains

the girl brings you small gentian flowers you go on sleeping
she says Spring is here and you dream Old Persian verbs...

"Hypersyntax, where phrases link with what comes before or after, or plausibly stand alone" are "strategies in 'mental strife'" — attractors of a state of *mental warfare* which Blake opposes to *corporeal warfare*. Robert Kelly wishes the poem in its mind-degradable axiality to "solicit the dissolving of certainties — in between the inbreath and the outbreath, where nothing is fixed, and freedom begins."

All lines are first lines, and lines are *ta'wil* of themselves — self-accounting, self-regulating like Blake's bird that never soars too high if he soars with his own wings — a surge of language in autopoiesis of a single line. Or, in two-line stanzas, co-self-organizing in mutual pairing in a field of such co-piloted flight patterns.

Poems as Uncertainties declare an order in process, the track of their moving forward, the actual order of composition, not programmed or symbolic order and yet not arbitrary; a self-organizing, its own necessity wherein poems in fact can be read in any order without disrupting the overall sense of the work. That is its spacetime reality: go anywhere, know anything, in your actual *own time*. The public signs are non-paranoid: *If you see something, write something*. It's a poetics that continuously points back to the singularity of readerly configuration. Reader furthers the reading which is writing. Poem as eco-proprioceptive matrix of world reconfiguration. And it's a world without censorship, beyond dogma, without arbitrary control, where taboo cannot get a foothold, and desire is never made less than what it is—desire. And all our secret personal fundamentalisms dissolve into breath.

Barrytown, New York
May 2014 / revised
January 2019

BILLIE CHERNICOFF

ON ROBERT KELLY'S *SEASPEL* (2019)

How does he do it, I've wondered of every one of Robert Kelly's books, and I still have no answer. You can't parse miracles, only witness them.

A mosaic *formed by shells of perception,* the poet says about *Seaspel,* the latest in a series of book length poems he has written, one each year over a summer month, on the island of Cuttyhunk, off the coast of Massachusetts.

> *...fragments of all sorts of shell. Clam, oyster, scallop, side by side——their origins do not matter, only shape and color——not the source, only the found fact.*

The stanzas of *Seaspel* are various, some as small as two or three trim lines, none bigger than the palm of your hand——none you can't hold and turn and admire in its singularity, and hold in mind even as it yields to the whole and rounds out a shoulder, conjures foam from a wave. Birds appear. The weather changes. From broken pieces, a world takes shape, and a story.

Two figures emerge. They walk and converse, stop and rest. They are the teacher and the student, the physician and his assistant, Christ and John the Baptizer, or Christ and John the Evangelist, author of Revelation. They are the truth & its witness. They are Lama Norlha, *sustainer, friend,* and John, his beloved disciple.

> They drove into town
> to see a sick friend.
> Can't heal, might help
> John said. The other was silent,
> unless a smile somehow
> creates a small soft turbulence in the air,
> who knows, some might hear.

Many other things happen——*tambourine, sea poppy, bell in the channel, pencils, salt, bottle of milk.*

Things come to mind.
There is no reason.
That is the reason.

The two companions come & go in the mist. You can't always see them. After a while you see them in everything.
East and West also keep company here, and understand each other perfectly. Christ, the Buddha——both teach kindness, mostly, and, like poetry, silence.

Swans look like they know——
do you think they do
John had asked, and he
had just smiled.
Hours later, out of context,
out of silence, no smile,
he suddenly said
We all do.

Seaspel is a love story——ἀγάπη, agapē, the true Christian love that Buddha taught——and it may be the most tender of Kelly's books. There are passages that both break and heal the heart, that open the heart & walk right in.

John never learned to fish
though he had many fisher friends.
They told him it was simple——
with hook and fly (angling)
or with a big soft net
scouring the inhabitants of the sea.
Lake. Stream. But he
could not bring himself to try it.
What if they died?
What if someone cried?

Seaspel, gospel, God spell, a new testament, a new listening. Here are the joyful, sorrowful, glorious, luminous mysteries, reported with profound simplicity by a poet who is the master of his instrument. I've read the book twice, and both times wished for it never to end. And it doesn't.

Learn all you can / before he seems to go away.

Kelly is devoted to the things that happen, and to the words they happen in——words, those broken shells and truest colors. Fragments wash up on the shore and offer themselves, the sun rises, a teacher comes along——this is grace, and if a poet is as wakeful and willing as this one, revelation.

> John barely glimpsed
> what all that was supposed to mean
> so he asked him and he said,
> Dear friend, Everything is right here.

KUSH · CLOUD HOUSE

NAME DREAMS RITUAL

for Robert Kelly

Dream R Unfolding **inner college**, the eternity campus; Benjamin steps out of the whirlwind with Heinrich & Hannah.

Dream O Moonlit road the owl's tornada marries Cruger's Isle.

Dream B Come in Paul Blackburn, the Ur text of CITIES made whole, recognitions retrieve their premises and seven poems wander back in with more fuel for the soul.

Dream E Fireflies in the palace ruins of the heart.

Dream R Evening prayers, Rimbaud's Caravan lays down rugs made of African lexicons.

Dream T Three hearth stones celestial eye Cloudy Place the mind inscribes Orion's Turtle.

Dream K Luminous Globe Dark Rune A Door.

Dream E Whaleback bones and boundary stones, beauty with all strings attached, twelve eight six, I swear ten times and remain silent.

Dream L Lute what is! That is the Loot you say.

Dream L Water lily water lily canoe Stingray Maize Jaguar, paddle across the manuscript of the night.

Dream Y Take up the Earth. Take down the Sky.

RK summon the World Tree
                      Living Rune
Simultaneous in All Fields of Bard
Where the inner maize dances forever
Stand on the Head of This
                      Earth
Hold the ecliptic between your arms
Make a right angle with your feet
Assume the posture of the Milky Way
Bring It All Back Home

EDITORS

PIERRE JORIS most recently published *Arabia (not so) Deserta* (Essays, Spuyten Duyvil Press, 2019), Adonis & Pierre Joris, *Conversations in the Pyrenees* (CMP 2018); *The Book of U* (poems), *The Agony of I. B.* (a play), *An American Suite* (early poems), *Barzakh: Poems 2000–2012,* & the translations *Breathturn into Timestead: The Collected Later Poetry of Paul Celan,* and *Microliths: Posthumous Prose* by Paul Celan is forthcoming from Contra Mundum Press (2020).

PETER COCKELBERGH is editor of *Pierre Joris — Cartographies of the In-Between* (2011) and translator of, among others, *Portrait de l'artiste en masochiste* by Boris Groys (2012). He also edited with Pierre Joris the companion volume to the present book: *A Voice Full of Cities: The Collected Essays of Robert Kelly* (2014). He lives in Lille (France), and teaches at the Da Vinci High School in Sint-Niklaas (Belgium) — much to the alarm of his poor students.

JOEL NEWBERGER's most recent book is *Hexateuch* (Lunar Chandelier). Before that, *A Caw* (Oread). Poems and essays also published in *The Doris, Mint Julep, Dispatches.* He is currently at work on a sequence of new psalms. He lives and writes in Manhattan.

CONTRIBUTORS

PAUL BLACKBURN was born on November 24, 1926, in St. Albans, Vermont. He spent his youth in Vermont, New Hampshire, South Carolina, and New York City. He attended NYU and the University of Wisconsin. He received a Fulbright Grant in 1954 and spent two years at the University of Toulouse in southern France and then in Spain until 1957, when he returned to New York City. Blackburn was the author of more than 10 books of poems, including *The Cities* and *The Journals*. He translated El Mio Cid, Cortazar, Paz, Picasso, and the entire canon of Provençal lyric poetry. For the last years of his life, he taught at SUNY, Cortland.

STAN BRAKHAGE was one of the foremost American avant-garde filmmakers. From 1952 till his death in 2003, he made nearly 400 films, ranging in length from a few seconds to several hours. Among his best known film works are *Dog Star Man*, *The Act of Seeing with One's Own Eyes*, and the hand-painted *Dante Quartet*. His many books on film include *Metaphors on Vision* (republished in 2018 in a new edition by Light Industry and Anthology Film Archives), *Film Biographies*, *Brakhage Scrapbook: Collected Writings, 1964–1980*, *Film at Wit's End*, and *Telling Time*.

MARY CAPONEGRO is an experimental fiction writer who works in short story, novella, and collage form. Her books include *Tales from the Next Village*, *The Star Café*, *Five Doubts*, *The Complexities of Intimacy*, and *All Fall Down*, as well as *Materia Prima e Altri Racconti*, published by Leconte in Italy. Among her honors is the Rome Prize in Literature. Her fiction and non-fiction have been anthologized in *You've Got to Read This*, *The Anchor Book of New American Fiction*, *The Italian-American Reader*, *A Convergence of Birds*, *The Review of Contemporary Fiction*, *Not a Rose*, and *The Brown Reader*. A multilingual collection of essays on her work, *La Squisita Interruzione: Saggi, Note e Appunti sulla prosa lirica di Mary Caponegro/The Exquisite Interruption: Essays, Notes and Fragments on the Lyrical Prose of Mary Caponegro* was recently published by Campanotto Editore (Zeta Quaderno) in Italy. She holds the Richard B. Fisher Family Chair in Writing and Literature at Bard College.

BILLIE CHERNICOFF is the author of three books of poetry — *The Red Dress*, *Waters Of*, and most recently, *Bronze*, and several chapbooks published at Metambesen.org and dispatchespoetrywars.com. She is a co-editor of *The Doris*, a magazine of new writing and translation. She lives in Catskill, New York, not far from Bard College, where she studied with Robert Kelly, whom she still considers her teacher.

ROBERT CREELEY published more than 60 books of poetry, prose, essays, & interviews in the United States & abroad, including *If I Were Writing This*, *Selected Poems 1945–1990*, *The Collected Poems of Robert Creeley, 1945–1975*, and *The Island*. His many honors include the Lannan Lifetime Achievement Award, the Frost Medal, the Shelley Memorial Award, and the Bollingen Prize in Poetry. He taught poetry and poetics for nearly three decades at SUNY, Buffalo.

GUY DAVENPORT was born in South Carolina and lived for more than forty years in Lexington, Kentucky, where he died in 2005. The author of more than 20 books, including *Geography of the Imagination*, *Eclogues*, and *The Death of Picasso*. Davenport was also a noted translator of ancient Greek poetry and philosophy. He was Distinguished Professor at the University of Kentucky, and a MacArthur Fellow in 1990.

THEODORE ENSLIN was born in 1925 near Philadelphia, and grew up there. He studied musical composition with Nadia Boulanger in Cambridge during the war years and moved to Cape Cod in 1946. He wrote and raised cranberries there until going to Maine in 1960. He was the author of *Synthesis*, *Ranger*, *Then and Now: Selected Poems 1943–1993*, and many other books.

CLAYTON ESHLEMAN has published roughly 100 books and chapbooks of original poetry, translations, and nonfiction writings, and edited 70 issues of magazines and journals, including *Caterpillar* and *Sulfur*. His writings have appeared in over 500 literary magazines and his books & writings have been translated into a number of languages.

STEVEN FAMA enjoys reading poetry, and hopes you do too.

ALLEN FISHER is a poet, artist and art historian. His long sequence of poetry, *Gravity as a consequence of shape* (1983–2007), is now available in a single volume & the books of *PLACE* (1971–1981), are available from Reality Street Editions, UK. A book of essays, *Imperfect Fit: Æsthetics, Facture & Perception* was published in 2016 by University of Alabama Press. His last one-person exhibition was in Hereford, UK in 2013.

Born in Bowie, Texas, KENNETH LEE IRBY (1936–2015) grew up in Fort Scott, Kansas, and attended and received degrees from Harvard University, the University of California, Berkeley, and the University of Kansas. From 1960–1962, he served in the Army in Nevada, Hawaii, Albuquerque, and Johnson Island, where, from the deck of an aircraft carrier, he witnessed the detonation of a nuclear weapon. He managed a tailor shop in San Francisco in the late '60s, taught in the early '70s at Tufts University, and received a Fulbright Grant to Denmark in 1973, where he taught as visiting professor in the English Institute of Copenhagen University. He was associate professor of English at the University of Kansas. Irby was the author of many books of poetry, including *The Intent On: Collected Poems, 1962–2006*.

Poet, editor, and critic, GERRIT LANSING (1928–2018) was born in Albany, New York, raised in northern Ohio, but lived most of his life in Gloucester, Massachusetts. In the early 1960s, he edited *SET*, an influential journal devoted to what he called "the poetic exploration of the swarming possibilities occult and/or unused in American life." Lansing's life's work — titled *The Heavenly Tree Grows Downward* (1966; 1977) and then *Heavenly Tree, Soluble Forest* (1995), and finally *Heavenly Tree, Northern Earth* — was a single book he revised and republished in four editions. *A February Sheaf*, a volume of selected poetry and prose, was published by Pressed Wafer in 2003.

DENISE LEVERTOV (1923–1997) was a British-born American poet. She wrote and published 20 books of poetry, criticism, and translations. She also edited several anthologies. Among her many awards and honors, she received the Shelley Memorial Award, the Robert Frost Medal, the Lenore Marshall Prize, the Lannan Award, a grant from the National Institute of Arts and Letters, and a Guggenheim Fellowship.

DAVID LEVI STRAUSS is the author of *Co-illusion: Dispatches from the End of Communication* (MIT, 2020), *Words Not Spent Today Buy Smaller Images Tomorrow* (Aperture, 2014), *From Head to Hand: Art and the Manual* (Oxford University Press, 2010), *Between the Eyes,* with an introduction by John Berger (Aperture 2003, and in a new edition, 2012), and *Between Dog & Wolf: Essays on Art and Politics* (Autonomedia 1999, and a new edition with a prolegomena by Hakim Bey, 2010).

KIMBERLY LYONS is the author of books of poetry that include *Capella* (Oread Press, 2018) *Approximately Near* (Metambesendotorg, 2016), and *Calcinatio* (Faux Press, 2014). Her poetry may be found in various anthologies including *Quo Anima: Spirituality in Contemporary Women's Poetry* (University of Akron Press), and *Readings in Contemporary Poetry: An Anthology* (DIA Foundation (2017)). Kimberly Lyons has written about the work of Joe Ceravalo, Basil King, Bernadette Mayer and George Quasha for the journals Aufgabe, Dispatches from the Poetry Wars, Jacket 2, and Talisman. Lyons graduated from Bard College. She lives in Chicago and is the publisher of Lunar Chandelier Press.

CHARLOTTE MANDELL has translated over 40 books from the French, including works by Mathias Enard, Jean-Luc Nancy, Jonathan Littell, Marcel Proust, and Jean Genet. She has been happily married to Robert Kelly since June 1993; they live near Bard College in the Hudson Valley, where they curate Metambesen https://metambesen.org, a website that publishes free downloadable chapbooks. You can see some of her translations on her website: http://charlottemandell.com

THOMAS MEYER's latest book of poems is *Modern Love: Songs* (Verge Books).

CHRISTINA MILLETTI's novel *Choke Box: a Fem-Noir* won the Juniper Prize for Fiction and was released by University of Massachusetts Press in March 2019. Her fiction, articles, and reviews have appeared in many journals and anthologies, such as *Best New American Voices*, the *Iowa Review*, *The Master's Review*, *Denver Quarterly*, *The Cincinnati Review*, *Studies in the Novel*, *Zeta*, *American Letters & Commentary*, *The Brooklyn Rail,* and *The Buffalo News* (among other places). Her first book, *The Religious & Other Fictions* (a collection of stories) was published by Carnegie Mellon University Press. Her new collection, *Now You See Her*, began with the help of a residency from the Marble House Project. She is an Associate Professor of English at the University at Buffalo where she is the Executive Director of the Humanities Institute and co-curates the Exhibit X Fiction Series.

PETER MONACO writes and performs work that explores the intersections between experimental and investigative poetry, comics and visual culture, the Western Esoteric Tradition, and writing and "composition." He is a full-time lecturer in the Program in Writing and Critical Inquiry at the University at Albany, SUNY.

Poet JENNIFER MOXLEY's most recent collection is *Druthers* (Flood 2018). Her book *The Open Secret* (Flood 2014) won the 2015 William Carlos Williams Award, and was a finalist for the Kingsley Tufts Award. She is Professor of Poetry and Poetics at the University of Maine.

CHARLES OLSON (1910–1970) was the author of the *Maximus Poems* (1960, 1968, and 1975) and *The Archaeologist of Morning* (1970). His essays of the 1950s & '60s — above all, "Projective Verse" and *Proprioception* — remain influential statements of what he called "OPEN verse." He was the rector of Black Mountain College in its last years. At the time of his death, he lived in Gloucester, Massachusetts.

TAMAS PANITZ is a graduate of Bard College, currently living in Catskill, NY. He is the author of *Blue Sun* (Inpatient Press); *Uncreated Mirror* (LCC); *Upper Earth* (Oread Press); *Invisible Marches* (LCC); and several chapbooks at metambesen.org, including *Numbers*, a recent collaboration with the artist Louise Smith. He is a co-editor of *The Doris*, a magazine.

GEORGE QUASHA is a poet, artist, and musician, author of two dozen books, including four recent volumes of "preverbs" — *Verbal Paradise*, *Glossodelia Attract*, *The Daimon of the Moment*, and *Things Done for Themselves* — and, previously, *Somapoetics* (1973) and *Ainu Dreams* (with Chie Hasegawa [Hammons]) (1999); six books on art, including *Axial*

Stones: An Art of Precarious Balance, foreword Carter Ratcliff (2006), and *An Art of Limina: Gary Hill's Works and Writings* (with Charles Stein), foreword Lynne Cooke (2009). New from Spuyten Duyvil: *Poetry in Principle,* foreword Edward S. Casey (Dispatches Poetics) and *Not Even Rabbits Go Down This Hole (preverbs).* Video art (Guggenheim Fellowship, 2006) includes *art is/poetry is/music is (Speaking Portraits)* (www.art-is-international.org). Co-publisher with artist Susan Quasha of Station Hill Press (www.stationhill.com, www.quasha.com).

JED RASULA published RK's work in his poetry magazine *Wch Way* (1975–1983) and was on the editorial board of *Sulfur* (1983–2000). His books addressing contemporary poetry include *The American Poetry Wax Museum* (1996), *This Compost: Ecological Imperatives in American Poetry* (2002), *Syncopations: The Stress of Innovation in Contemporary American Poetry* (2004), and *Modernism and Poetic Inspiration* (2009).

JORDAN REYNOLDS has published poems, essays, and reviews in *Interim, The Offending Adam, zero ducats, The Agriculture Reader,* and elsewhere. He lives in Mill Valley, California.

ELIZABETH ROBINSON is the author of multiple collections of poetry, most recently *Rumor* (Parlor Press / Free Verse Editions). A new collection, *Vulnerability Index,* is forthcoming from Ahsahta Press in 2019. Robinson is the co-editor, with Jennifer Phelps, of *Quo Anima: Innovation & Spirituality In Contemporary Women's Poetry* (Akron University Press). Robinson has been a winner of the National Poetry Series and the Fence Modern Poets Prize and a recipient of grants from the Foundation for Contemporary Arts, the Poetry Fund, and the Brown Foundation/Museum of Fine Arts, Houston.

BARBARA ROETHER is a writer and teacher recently exiled from San Francisco to Asheville, where she coordinates the literary reading series Why There are Words. She is the author most recently of a poetry collection *Saraswati's Lament* (Wet Cement Press), the novel *This Earth You'll Come Back To* (McPherson & Company) and *The Middle Atlas* (Ocean Beach Books). She frequently reviews books, and writes of faraway places whenever she can, a travelogue of Japan, *The Used Machine,* is forthcoming. There is more information on her website BarbaraRoether.com.

JEROME ROTHENBERG is an internationally celebrated poet, translator, anthologist, and performer with over 90 books of poetry and 12 assemblages of traditional and avant-garde poetry such as *Technicians of the Sacred, Shaking the Pumpkin* (traditional American Indian poetry), *Exiled in the Word* (a.k.a. *A Big Jewish Book*), and, with Pierre Joris and Jeffrey Robinson, *Poems for the Millennium*, Vols 1–3. His most recent big books are *Eye of Witness: A Jerome Rothenberg Reader* (2013) and *Barbaric Vast & Wild: Outside & Subterranean Poetry from Origins to Present* (Vol. 5 of *Poems for the Millennium*, 2015). A new book of poems, *The President of Desolation*, was published in 2019 by Black Widow Press, and he is now working on an anthology of North and South American poetry, again "from origins to present."

ED SCHELB is the author of *The Traffic of Words: On the Early Poetry of Robert Kelly*. His most recent critical projects have focused on the relationship between poetry and painting, particularly in the work of John Yau and Mei-Mei Berssenbrugge. His recent poetry is inextricable from the rivers of northern Virginia where he lives.

For over 60 years, CAROLEE SCHNEEMANN made visionary work in painting, photography, performance, film, and video. The recent retrospective *Carolee Schneemann: Kinetic Painting* originated at Museum der Moderne Salzburg (Austria, 2015), then traveled to the Museum für Moderne Kunst Frankfurt am Main (Germany, 2017) and MoMA PS1 (New York, 2017). Her work has also been the subject of exhibitions at the Musée départemental d'art contemporain de Rochechouart (France), the Museo de Arte Contemporáneo de Castilla y León (Spain), and the Samuel Dorsky Museum of Art, State University of New York, New Paltz (New York). Her publications include *Parts of a Body House Book* (1972); *Cezanne, She Was a Great Painter* (1975); *More Than Meat Joy: Performance Works and Selected Writings* (1979; 1997); and *Imaging Her Erotics* (2001).

G.E. SCHWARTZ, the author of *Only Others Are, World, Thinking In Tongues, Murmurations...* and the forthcoming *Hear*, lives and writes from Upstate New York.

ALANA SIEGEL was born in Los Angeles in 1985. She graduated from Bard College in 2007, earning a B.A. in Language and Literature. Her first full-length book of poetry, *Archipelago*, was published by Station Hill in 2014. Her chapbooks include *The Occupations, Semata,* and *words from Ra Ra junction.*

RON SILLIMAN's *Five Poems I Did Not Write* was published by Happy Monks Press and *The L=A=N=G=U=A=G=E Letters: Selected 1970s Correspondence of Bruce Andrews, Charles Bernstein, and Ron Silliman* was published by the University of New Mexico Press, both in 2019. The University of New Mexico Press will also issue an expanded edition of *Legend* by Silliman, Bernstein, Andrews, Steve McCaffery, and the late Ray di Palma in 2020.

P. ADAMS SITNEY is Professor Emeritus of Visual Art at Princeton University where he formerly taught cinema history and "great books." He has written five books — most recently *The Cinema of Poetry* (Oxford University Press, 2015) — and edited six others including Maurice Blanchot's *The Gaze of Orpheus* and Stan Brakhage's *Metaphors on Vision.*

Born 1944 in New York City, CHARLES STEIN's work comprises a complexly integrated field of poems, prose reflections, translations, drawings, photographs, lectures, conversations, and performances. Web site: charlessteinpoet.com. Most recent books: *Black Light Casts White Shadows* (Lunar Chandelier); *Twelve Drawings (Station Hill); Views from Tornado Island* (Lunar Chandelier).

DIANE WAKOSKI, who was born in Southern California and educated at UC, Berkeley, lived and began her poetry career in New York City from 1960–1973. She has earned her living as a book store clerk, a junior high school teacher in Manhattan, a library story-teller, a Visiting Writer and, for 10 years on-the-road, by giving poetry readings on college campuses. Since 1975, she has been Poet in Residence at Michigan State University, where she continues to teach as a University Distinguished Professor. Her work has been published in more than 20 collections and many slim volumes of poetry since her first book, *Coins & Coffins*, was published by Hawk's Well Press in 1962. Her selected poems, *Emerald*

Ice, won the William Carlos Williams Prize from the Poetry Society of America in 1989. Her collection *Diamond Dog* was published by Anhinga Press in 2010. *Bay of Angels*, also from Anhinga Press, was released in October 2013.

NORMAN WEINSTEIN is a poet and critic focusing on imaginative investigations of poetic, musical, and architectural processes. His books include *No Wrong Notes* (prose poems), *Suite: Orchid Ska Blues* (book-length poem on the birth of Jamaican jazz), and *A Night in Tunisia: Imaginings of Africa in Jazz* (essays on Afrocentric musical themes). He lives with his wife Mary in Boise, Idaho, where they share weaving textiles as well as a daily life fabric.

JONATHAN WILLIAMS (1929–2008). His work of more than half a century was such that no one activity or identity takes primacy over any other—he was the seminal small press publisher of The Jargon Society; a poet of considerable stature; book designer; editor; photographer; legendary correspondent; literary, art, and photography critic and collector; early collector and proselytizer of visionary folk art; cultural anthropologist and Juvenalian critic; curmudgeon; happy gardener; resolute walker; and keen and adroit raconteur and gourmand. Copper Canyon Press published *Jubiliant Thicket: New and Selected Poems* in 2005.

JOHN YAU is the author of 17 books of poetry, four books of fiction, and two collections of criticism. His most recent book of poetry is *Bijoux in the Dark* (2018). Alongside these publications, he is the author of many monographs and has contributed to numerous museum catalogs. His publications on art include *Philip Taaffe* (2018), *Thomas Nozkowski* (2017), *Catherine Murphy* (2016), *Richard Artschwager: Into the Desert* (2015), *Joan Mitchell: Trees* (2014), *William Tillyer: Watercolours* (2010), *A Thing Among Things: The Art of Jasper Johns* (2009), *Wifredo Lam: Catalogue Raisonné of the Painted Work: 1961–1982* (2002), *Dazzling Water, Dazzling Light: Pat Steir Paintings* (2001), and *A. R. Penck* (1999). He has received awards and fellowships from the John Simon Guggenheim Memorial Foundation, National Endowment of the Arts, Academy of American Poets, New York Foundation of the Arts, and the Foundation for Contemporary Arts. He has been named a Chevalier in the Order of Arts and Letters by the French government, and the Distinguished Alumni Award from Brooklyn College (Class of 1978) and an honorary doctorate from the College of Creative Studies in Detroit. He is Professor of Critical Studies at Mason Gross School of the Arts (Rutgers University) and lives in New York.

ALSO BY ROBERT KELLY

Books of Poetry

Armed Descent. New York: Hawk's Well Press, 1961.
Her Body gainst Time. Mexico City: Ediciones El Corno Emplumado, 1963.
Round Dances. New York: Trobar Press, 1964.
Enstasy. Annandale: Matter, 1964.
Lunes/Sightings (with Jerome Rothenberg). New York: Hawk's Well Press, 1964.
Words in Service. New Haven: Robert Lamberton, 1966.
Weeks. Mexico City: Ediciones El Corno Emplumado, 1966.
Song XXIV. Cambridge: Pym-Randall Press, 1966.
Devotions. Annandale: Salitter, 1967.
Twenty Poems. Annandale: Matter Books, 1967.
Axon Dendron Tree. Annandale: Salitter, 1967.
Crooked Bridge Love Society. Annandale: Salitter, 1967.
A Joining: a Sequence for H.D. Los Angeles: Black Sparrow Press, 1967.
Alpha. Gambier, Ohio: The Pot Hanger Press, 1967.
Finding the Measure. CA: Black Sparrow Press, 1968.
Sonnets. CA: Black Sparrow Press, 1968.
Songs I–XXX. Cambridge: Pym-Randall Press, 1968.
The Common Shore (Books 1–5). CA: Black Sparrow Press, 1969.
A California Journal. London: Big Venus Books, 1969.
Kali Yuga. London: Jonathan Cape, 1970. A Cape Goliard Book.
Flesh Dream Book. CA: Black Sparrow Press, 1971.
Ralegh. CA: Black Sparrow Press, 1972.
The Pastorals. CA: Black Sparrow Press, 1972.
Reading Her Notes. Uniondale: privately printed at the Salisbury Press, 1972.
The Tears of Edmund Burke. Annandale, privately printed, 1973.
The Mill of Particulars. CA: Black Sparrow Press, 1973.
The Loom. CA: Black Sparrow Press, 1975.
Sixteen Odes. CA: Black Sparrow Press, 1976.
The Lady of. CA: Black Sparrow Press, 1977.
The Convections. Santa Barbara: Black Sparrow Press, 1977.
The Book of Persephone. New Paltz: Treacle Press, 1978.
Kill the Messenger. Santa Barbara: Black Sparrow Press, 1979.
Sentence. Barrytown: Station Hill Press, 1980.
Spiritual Exercises. Santa Barbara: Black Sparrow Press, 1981.

The Alchemist to Mercury: an alternate opus [Uncollected Poems 1960–1980. Edited by Jed Rasula] Berkeley: North Atlantic Books, 1981.
Mulberry Women [with drypoints by Matt Phillips] Berkeley: Hiersoux, Powers, Thomas, 1982.
Under Words. Santa Barbara: Black Sparrow Press, 1983.
Thor's Thrush. Oakland: The Coincidence Press, 1984.
Not This Island Music. Santa Rosa: Black Sparrow Press, 1987.
The Flowers of Unceasing Coincidence. Barrytown: Station Hill Press, 1988.
Oahu. Rhinebeck: St Lazaire Press, 1988.
Ariadne. Rhinebeck: St Lazaire Press, 1991.
Manifesto for the Next New York School. Buffalo: Leave Press, 1991.
A Strange Market (Poems 1985–1988). Santa Rosa: Black Sparrow Press, 1992.
Mont Blanc (a long poem inscribed within Shelley's). Ann Arbor: Otherwind Press, 1994.
Red Actions: Selected Poems 1960–1993. Santa Rosa: Black Sparrow Press, 1995.
The Time of Voice. Poems 1994–1996. Santa Rosa: Black Sparrow Press, 1998.
Runes. Ann Arbor: Otherwind Press, 1999.
The Garden of Distances (with Brigitte Mahlknecht). Vienna / Lana: Editions Procura, 1999.
Lapis. Boston: Black Sparrow/Godine, 2005.
Runic Workbook. Annandale-on-Hudson: Matter Books, 2005.
Threads. Lawrence: First Intensity, 2006.
Earish: Thirty Poems of Paul Celan. Annandale-on-Hudson: Matter Books, 2006.
May Day. Toronto: Parsifal Press, 2007.
Sainte-Terre, or The White Stone. Kathmandu: Shivastan Publishing, 2007.
Fire Exit. Boston: Black Widow Press, 2009.
Uncertainties. Barrytown: Station Hill, 2011.
Winter Music (poems written to photographs by Susan Quasha). Rhinebeck: T Space Editions, 2014.
The Color Mill (poems written to paintings by Nathlie Provosty). Brooklyn: Spuyten Duyvil, 2014.
Opening the Seals. Brooklyn: Autonomedia, 2016.
The Hexagon. Boston: Black Widow Press, 2016.
Heart Thread. Catskill: Lunar Chandelier Collective, 2016.
The Secret Name of Now. New York: Dr. Cicero Books, 2016.
Calls. Catskill: Lunar Chandelier Collective, 2018.
The Caprices. Catskill: Lunar Chandelier Collective, 2018.
Seaspel. Catskill: Lunar Chandelier Collective, 2019.
Reasons to Resist. Catskill: Lunar Chandelier Collective, 2019.

Fiction

The Scorpions. New York: Doubleday, 1967. London: Calder and Boyars, 1968. (2nd Ed., with a new afterword, Barrytown: Station Hill Press, 1986).
Cities. West Newbury, Massachusetts: Frontier Press, 1972.
A Line of Sight. CA: Black Sparrow Press, 1974.
Wheres. CA: Black Sparrow Press, 1978.
The Cruise of the Pnyx. Barrytown: Station Hill Press, 1979.
"Russian Tales" in *Likely Stories*, ed. Bruce McPherson. New Paltz, Treacle Press, 1981.
A Transparent Tree. Kingston: McPherson & Co., 1985.
Doctor of Silence. Kingston: McPherson & Co., 1988.
Cat Scratch Fever. Kingston: McPherson & Co., 1990.
Queen of Terrors. Kingston: McPherson & Co., 1994.
Shame/Scham (with Birgit Kempker). Kingston: McPherson & Co., 2005.
The Book from the Sky. Berkeley: North Atlantic Books, 2008.
The Logic of the World and Other Fictions. Kingston: McPherson & Co., 2010.
Ten New Fairy Tales. Kingston: McPherson & Co., 2019.

Other Books

In Time. West Newbury, Massachusetts: Frontier Press, 1972. [Essays & manifestoes]
A Controversy of Poets (with Paris Leary). New York: Doubleday Anchor, 1965. [Anthology]
Abziehbilder, Heimgeholt (with Jacques Roubaud and Schuldt). Graz and Vienn: Droschl, 1995.
Atlantis Manifesto (with Peter Lamborn Wilson). Kathmandu: Shivastan, 2009.
Oedipus After Colonus and Other Plays. New York: Dr. Cicero Books, 2013.
Certainties: The Maxims of Martin Traubenritter. Annandale-on-Hudson: Metambesen Books, 2016.

COLOPHON

A CITY FULL OF VOICES
was handset in InDesign CC.

The text is set in *Adobe Garamond Premiere*.

Book design & typesetting: Alessandro Segalini

Cover design: Carolee Schneeman & CMP

A CITY FULL OF VOICES
is published by Contra Mundum Press.

Contra Mundum Press New York · London · Melbourne

CONTRA MUNDUM PRESS

Dedicated to the value & the indispensable importance of the individual voice, to works that test the boundaries of thought & experience.

The primary aim of Contra Mundum is to publish translations of writers who in their use of form and style are *à rebours*, or who deviate significantly from more programmatic & spurious forms of experimentation. Such writing attests to the volatile nature of modernism. Our preference is for works that have not yet been translated into English, are out of print, or are poorly translated, for writers whose thinking & æsthetics are in opposition to timely or mainstream currents of thought, value systems, or moralities. We also reprint obscure and out-of-print works we consider significant but which have been forgotten, neglected, or overshadowed.

There are many works of fundamental significance to *Weltliteratur* (*& Weltkultur*) that still remain in relative oblivion, works that alter and disrupt standard circuits of thought — these warrant being encountered by the world at large. It is our aim to render them more visible.

For the complete list of forthcoming publications, please visit our website. To be added to our mailing list, send your name and email address to: info@contramundum.net

Contra Mundum Press
P.O. Box 1326
New York, NY 10276
USA

OTHER CONTRA MUNDUM PRESS TITLES

Gilgamesh
Ghérasim Luca, *Self-Shadowing Prey*
Rainer J. Hanshe, *The Abdication*
Walter Jackson Bate, *Negative Capability*
Miklós Szentkuthy, *Marginalia on Casanova*
Fernando Pessoa, *Philosophical Essays*
Elio Petri, *Writings on Cinema & Life*
Friedrich Nietzsche, *The Greek Music Drama*
Richard Foreman, *Plays with Films*
Louis-Auguste Blanqui, *Eternity by the Stars*
Miklós Szentkuthy, *Towards the One & Only Metaphor*
Josef Winkler, *When the Time Comes*
William Wordsworth, *Fragments*
Josef Winkler, *Natura Morta*
Fernando Pessoa, *The Transformation Book*
Emilio Villa, *The Selected Poetry of Emilio Villa*
Robert Kelly, *A Voice Full of Cities*
Pier Paolo Pasolini, *The Divine Mimesis*
Miklós Szentkuthy, *Prae, Vol. 1*
Federico Fellini, *Making a Film*
Robert Musil, *Thought Flights*
Sándor Tar, *Our Street*
Lorand Gaspar, *Earth Absolute*
Josef Winkler, *The Graveyard of Bitter Oranges*
Ferit Edgü, *Noone*
Jean-Jacques Rousseau, *Narcissus*
Ahmad Shamlu, *Born Upon the Dark Spear*
Jean-Luc Godard, *Phrases*
Otto Dix, *Letters, Vol. 1*
Maura Del Serra, *Ladder of Oaths*
Pierre Senges, *The Major Refutation*
Charles Baudelaire, *My Heart Laid Bare & Other Texts*
Joseph Kessel, *Army of Shadows*
Rainer J. Hanshe & Federico Gori, *Shattering the Muses*
Gérard Depardieu, *Innocent*
Claude Mouchard, *Entangled, Papers!, Notes*
Miklós Szentkuthy, *St. Orpheus Breviary, vol. II: Black Renaissance*
Adonis, *Conversations in the Pyrenees*
Charles Baudelaire, *Belgium Stripped Bare*
Robert Musil, *Unions*
Iceberg Slim, *Night Train to Sugar Hill*
Marquis de Sade, *Aline & Valcour*

SOME FORTHCOMING TITLES

Carmelo Bene, *I Appeared to the Madonna*
Miklós Szentkuthy, *Chapter on Love*

THE FUTURE OF KULCHUR
A PATRONAGE PROJECT

LEND CONTRA MUNDUM PRESS (CMP) YOUR SUPPORT

With bookstores and presses around the world struggling to survive, and many actually closing, we are forming this patronage project as a means for establishing a continuous & stable foundation to safeguard our longevity. Through this patronage project we would be able to remain free of having to rely upon government support &/or other official funding bodies, not to speak of their timelines & impositions. It would also free CMP from suffering the vagaries of the publishing industry, as well as the risk of submitting to commercial pressures in order to persist, thereby potentially compromising the integrity of our catalog.

CAN YOU SACRIFICE $10 A WEEK FOR KULCHUR?

For the equivalent of merely 2–3 coffees a week, you can help sustain CMP and contribute to the future of kulchur. To participate in our patronage program we are asking individuals to donate $500 per year, which amounts to $42/month, or $10/week. Larger donations are of course welcome and beneficial. All donations are tax-deductible through our fiscal sponsor Fractured Atlas. If preferred, donations can be made in two installments. We are seeking a minimum of 300 patrons per year and would like for them to commit to giving the above amount for a period of three years.

WHAT WE OFFER

Part tax-deductible donation, part exchange, for your contribution you will receive every CMP book published during the patronage period as well as 20 books from our back catalog. When possible, signed or limited editions of books will be offered as well.

WHAT WILL CMP DO WITH YOUR CONTRIBUTIONS?

Your contribution will help with basic general operating expenses, yearly production expenses (book printing, warehouse & catalog fees, etc.), advertising & outreach, and editorial, proofreading, translation, typography, design and copyright fees. Funds may also be used for participating in book fairs and staging events. Additionally, we hope to rebuild the *Hyperion* section of the website in order to modernize it.

From Pericles to Mæcenas & the Renaissance patrons, it is the magnanimity of such individuals that have helped the arts to flourish. Be a part of helping your kulchur flourish; be a part of history.

HOW

To lend your support & become a patron, please visit the subscription page of our website: contramundum.net/subscription

For any questions, write us at: info@contramundum.net

www.ingramcontent.com/pod-product-compliance
Lightning Source LLC
Chambersburg PA
CBHW022101290426
44112CB00008B/512